The
Great Business

The
Great Business

David J Tipton

Xulon Press

Xulon Press
555 Winderley Pl, Suite 225
Maitland, FL 32751
407.339.4217
www.xulonpress.com

Paperback ISBN-13: 978-1-66288-846-5
Ebook ISBN-13: 978-1-66288-847-2

To the B
Who has for fifty years
Walked this road of life with me.
Until I have become her, and she has become me.
And others looking on no difference see.

ACKNOWLEDGEMENTS

Sally who pulled on the same rope with me until we pulled this book across the finish line.

David, Katie, Tiffany, and Robert for their encouragement of this project and love for their father.

Patsy Tipton who prayed that these words would be a reality in me before a writing for others.

Paul Culp who came into the kitchen of my writing and helped me mop up the mess that had boiled over on my kitchen floor.

Art Nuernemberg who labored through the manuscript offering encouragement and much needed guidance.

The Bricklings, Dave Galler and Randy Martin, for their lifelong love, honest comments, advise and labors in prayer over this book.

Kit Lathrop for his listening ear and hours of conversation about this work.

CONTENTS

PREFACE

> *"Let not the wise boast of their wisdom or the strong boast of their strength or the rich boast of their riches, but let the one who boasts boast about this: that they have the understanding to know me." (Jer. 9:24)*

THIS PAST WEEK, one of my spiritual heroes and a true giant of the faith, J.I. Packer, went to be with the Lord. Hearing of his death I was reminded of the impact his book had on me in college in the early 70's as a young Christian. His classic book, *Knowing God*, shaped my ideas about the importance of knowing, praying to, and communing with the triune God: Father, Son, and Holy Spirit. It was the beginning of my understanding that Christianity was more than church attendance and service for God. It was a personal relationship with the living God that could be known and enjoyed. I would learn from reading Dr. Packer that this relationship with God was to be the priority in the Christians life and that service and work would flow out of my life when I was rightly related to Him. I have learned that nothing in this life or world can compare with the wonder of knowing God. God is no respecter of persons, therefore class, status, wealth, intellect or health give no special privilege in the eyes of God. All men stand on equal footing before God and all must come humbly through the same gate, the Lord Jesus Christ. So whether you are a billionaire or impoverished, the strongest man on earth or a paralyzed in wheel chair, in slavery, prison, or oppressed, you can know God and worship Him which is the great business of human life.

Packer's Book *Knowing God* is needed more today than it was in the early '70s when it was first published. Packer gives his purpose for writing the book in the foreword: "The conviction behind the book is that ignorance of God, ignorance both of his ways and of the practice of communion with him, lies at the root of much of the church's weakness today." If ignorance of God was behind the weakness of the church 50 years ago, how much truer that is today. Oh, for the church to return to the business of knowing God, of worshipping God, Packer's book is a good place to start.

Packer opens *Knowing God* with a quote from a Charles Spurgeon sermon preached in 1855: "It has been said by someone that the proper study of mankind is man. I will not oppose the idea, but I believe it is equally true that the proper study of God's elect is God; the proper study of a Christian is the Godhead. The highest science, the loftiest speculation, the mightiest philosophy, which can ever engage the attention of a child of God, is the name, the nature, the person, the work, the doings, and the existence of the great God whom he calls his father." There is no loftier thought a human being can think than that of his God. There is no greater person in power, in intellect, or in beauty than God Himself. You will find no greater love for you than that which you find in God's heart. The greatest and best of human experiences are to be found in God. You were made for God, and in finding God you will find what you were created for. The highest, most noble work a man can do is to make God his business. We are all called by God to share in His life and in His Kingdom. Your great business is not the job you do here on earth, not ministry, nor even some service to humankind. Your vocation, your great business, is to know and share in the life and love of God.

Isaac Ambrose says in his book *Looking unto Jesus*, "Surely there's too much expense in thy spirit upon vain, and transitory, and worldly things. Alas! Thou hast but a short time to live; and the strength of the mind is the most precious thing thou hast. Oh then let thy inmost thoughts and deep affections be acted and exercised on this subject. If God and Jesus, and all thy good, be included here, why should not thy whole soul be intent on this? Why shouldst thou spend it on the creature? Why should thou be so subject to carnal griefs and fears? Surely all these are fitter to be fixed on God in Christ, on Jesus in a covenant of grace." He's asking why ar we wasting our precious time thinking and worrying about vain and transitory things when we can be thinking about the greatest thing in existence, "God in Christ, and Jesus in a covenant of grace."

Torstein Hagan, CEO of a cruise line, speaking in one of his commercials says something very profound. "There is only one thing you don't have enough of, and that's time. Time is the only truly scarce commodity. When you come to that realization, I think it's very important to spend your time wisely. Most of us have no regrets about things we did, but I think we can have regrets about things we did not do. So, what one wants in life is experiences, and that's a way of filling the time one has." Time is your most precious commodity, and you don't know how much of it you have. When you spend your time gazing on the Lord you may find it is the most productive use of your time. And just here one might experience the person and pleasures of God; what experience could rival this? Don't regret not having spent time with our God.

Here is the treasure hidden in the field; here is the pearl of great price, a treasure that you can never lose and is worth giving everything you have to gain. Christian, have you made God in Christ your treasure, your chief end, your business? Have you set the goal of giving your all, of seeking with all your heart, that greatest thing a human being can discover, God? You will not come away with this Treasure by half measures. This treasure is reserved for those who will sell everything they have to buy it (Matt. 13:44–46). The Gerber baby food company used to have a slogan: "Babies are our business, our only business." Perhaps we should borrow that slogan and change it a little: "God is our business, our only business."

If J.I. Packer saw weakness in the Church 50 years ago, how much weaker is she today? Ignorance of God is an epidemic in the Church today, and because of that ignorance there is a power shortage in our lives, in our churches, and in the society around us. We have made the world our business, expending our spirit, strength, and life on transitory things and have lost our spiritual power. So what are we to do? Repent, and make God our main business. Paul in describing his life said, "For me to live is Christ, and to die is gain" (Philippians 1:21) He considered anything else as a loss compared to knowing Christ. "I want to know Christ and the fellowship of His suffering." (Phil. 3:10) Christian, is Christ your goal, is He your business, your all in all?

What to do? "Even now, declares the Lord, return to me with all your heart, with fasting and weeping and mourning" (Joel 2:14). "Desire Jesus, the great business, or the all in all, in a covenant of grace the most proper object of desire, especially to fallen man…Christ and none but Christ; give me Christ, or I die, I am undone, I am lost forever. But what is Christ, or Jesus, to the covenant of grace? I answer, he is the great business, he is the all in all" (Isaac Ambrose, *Looking Unto Jesus*). Jesus is the great business, God has made Him such, and God desires that you do so as well. What is your business? Can you cry, "For me to live is Christ!"?

Many of us have earthly jobs that are necessary to put food on the table and roofs over our heads. Too many of us have made earthly jobs, trades, ministries, or businesses our great business. These good things have supplanted the best thing: Jesus Himself. Our true business, our work, our craft, our trade, our ministry, and our art should be to seek after God with all our hearts, find Him, and know Him. Knowing God is the highest point, the greatest accomplishment in any person's life. The man who knows God is a success, no matter his education or financial status. Knowing God is transformational to the individual's life. Knowing God is something to boast about. "Let not the wise man boast of his wisdom or the strong man boast of the strength, or the rich man boast of his riches, but let him who boasts boast about this; that he understands and knows me" (Jer. 9:24).

By the grace of God, I am someone who has never been apart from the Church of Jesus Christ. From infancy my parents carried me to church, and I grew up in her. In my life I have lost count of churches I have been a member of. We moved often when I was a child; grades one through twelve I was in 12 different schools, and Sally and I have moved 30 times in our marriage. In all those moves through life we have been a member of some church. I remember the many times we would go forward as a family to join a new church and would receive the right hand of fellowship as the whole church came to shake our hands and welcome us. In this way we have seen this bride of Christ in many different places and over many years now. We have had the high honor to pastor in a couple of those churches. I have lived my whole life in the church and have never known a period of separation from her. I have seen her weaknesses and her strengths, I have seen her go through fads and hobby horses, I have seen her in growth and expansion, and I have seen her in decline. In this 70th year of my life I still love her and her people. I was once asked if I had any message for this church, what would it be. This book is that message, it is my love letter to her for all she has done for me and been to me.

The purpose of this writing is to encourage men and women to make God their great business, to give all you have in the search and discovery of this one thing, to learn of the depths of His love, and to know that love, to learn what it means to commune with God, to grow in the grace and knowledge of the Lord Jesus Christ. We want to learn what it means to make Christ our husband and to be intimate with Him. Have you given yourself to this task? Have you made seeking and getting to know Christ your great business? In Christ you will find Excellency that can be found nowhere and truths higher than any other you might know. In Christ you will find the height of man's happiness, illumination to walk in a dark world, a physician to heal, and a warrior to defend you, and One to comfort you like no other. You will find Him to be springs of water when thirsty, and manna when you are hungry. He is the Savior the way to God. This is eternal life, to know God and Jesus Christ whom he has sent.

Imagine that a courier comes to your door and hand-delivers a message to you from God. It says God will be at a certain location, at a certain time, and He requests your company and asks that you come alone. The messenger speaks God's words to you and then puts an engraved invitation into your hands. You look at the messenger with those unbelieving eyes and say, "God wants to meet with me?" He responds, "Yes, God wants to meet with you!" The messenger lets the message sink in and then asks, "What should I tell God? Will you meet with Him, or will you turn down His invitation?" Dear brothers and sisters, the courier is at your door. Listen: He is knocking. Listen: He is crying out, "Behold I stand at the door and knock. If anyone hears my voice and opens the door, I will come in and eat with him, and he with me" (Rev. 3:20). Christ is the courier from God with a divine message. He's at your door; will you let Him in? Will you sup with Him? Or will you let your earthly job, business, trade, ministry keep Him behind the door knocking? Would you suffer to go be with Him? Would you sell everything and invest in this great business? This book is about taking God up on His invitation, about opening the door to Christ, and making God in Christ your pearl of great price, your treasure, your ministry, your great business.

Introduction

OUR BUSINESS

 "And He said to them, 'Why did you seek Me? Did you not know that I must be about My Fathers business?'" (Luke 2:49)

Business / n. **1** a person's regular occupation, profession, or trade. / an activity that someone is engaged in. / a person's concern. / work that has to be done or matters that have to be attended to." Thus begins the definition of the word "business" in the *Oxford College Dictionary*.

IN 1972 PARAMOUNT Pictures made the motion picture *The Godfather*, based on Mario Puzo's bestselling novel by the same name. The story is about the Corleone crime family, part of the New York mafia. Francis Ford Coppola directed the film, which starred a who's who of actors—Marlon Brando, Al Pacino, James Caan, and Robert Duvall, to name a few. The movie is regarded as one of the greatest and most influential films ever made, selected for preservation in the US National Film Registry of the Library of Congress in 1990 and ranked by the American Film Institute as the second-greatest film in American cinema, behind *Citizen Kane*. For a time it was the highest-grossing film in history.

In *The Godfather*, Vito Corleone (Marlon Brando) has a legitimate business, but few people who've seen the movie can name it, for his real business, head of a crime family, is what the movie is all about. The sign over his business door reads Genco Pura Olive Oil an import business, but the real business going on behind closed doors is illegitimate. Many Christians are like Vito. They have a sign over the door of their hearts that reads, "God is my business," but the business going on inside is often illegitimate. If we are to love the Lord with all our heart, soul, and mind—make him our great business—how is it we find so much time to do business that has nothing to do with God? We find time for hobbies, entertainments, TV, social media, and the Internet, time for everything but God. How is it we can find time for all these things and friends but find little or no time for God? If I find no time for Jesus, can I really say He is my business?

When God gave his Law to Moses, the heart of it was the Ten Commandments. These laws were set down in order of importance. Jesus in Matthew 22 was asked which law was the most important. "An expert in the law, tested him with this question: 'Teacher, which is the greatest commandment in the Law?' Jesus replied: 'Love the Lord your God with all your heart and with all your soul and with all your mind.' And the second is like it: 'Love your neighbor as yourself.' All the Law and the Prophets hang on these two commandments'" (Matt. 22:35–40). Jesus is telling us what our main business is to be. He is to be our great business, our first business, and there are to be no other gods (business) before him. You were designed by God to make God your business. God designed man to be able to love Him and fellowship with Him as Adam in the Garden. When Adam fell into sin, man's main business and relationship with God was disrupted and broken. God has provided a way for us to keep this first and greatest command: by looking unto Jesus and growing in relationship with Him. God has designed you for Himself so that your main business in life is to be close to Him. Because we are designed that way, you will find your greatest fulfillment and reward in this life in doing the business you were designed to do. Growing in this relationship, this business, you will find you will be transformed into His image. No business you do on earth will be as rewarding or fulfilling as loving God and making him the first business of your life.

In answering the questions about Commandments, Jesus is saying that the greatest Commandment and therefore the greatest work a person can do is to love God. Love speaks of a relationship. When we think about the great business, I want you to think about your relationship with God, not about some business in which you earn money to live. I want you to think about living in a love relationship with God. How do you live in a love relationship with someone? The business of relationship is one of getting to know someone. It is having a relationship where love can be exchanged. It is the business of trusting someone and being trusted in return. It is the business of relating, communicating, and communing with another person. Do I love God, and am I in a relationship with him? Facebook has a place where you can declare you're in a relationship with someone. This declaration is often of the most important relationship in one's life. Along with this declaration of relationship, people will list their occupations. When we say we are in relationship with some person here on earth we know what that means; when we say we are in relationship with God many have no idea what that means, yet it should be your main business.

In this command to love God, Jesus is showing us how to find the greatest meaning in life. Man finds his meaning in relationship, more than in the physical work or business he builds here on earth. In relationship we find love, which is the great need of our hearts. Some try to fill that need for love with business that has nothing to do with their relationship to God or their fellow man. This ends in despair and emptiness, for no business or dollar bill will love you in return. We see business as something to do to earn money or make a living, but in the end the money will be of little importance and the loves of our lives will be most precious. I want you to see that our great business is to live in a love relationship with God.

Just before my father died, the family gathered to say their last goodbyes. I remember his hospital room being packed with his children and relatives. He motioned to me to come near and then pointed to everyone in the room and said, "This is worth more than all the money in the world." The relationships he had built with family and friends were the great treasure of his life, and that day he was being loved by those around him. My father had a trade, a business in which he worked to support his family, but his God and family were the main business of his life.

I have walked through life married to a precious person for almost 50 years now. Almost every day of that marriage, I have worked at some job. That business was always secondary to the relationship. The reason to get a job was so we could eat and live in a house and maintain our relationship to each another. No business has come between Sally and me, though we have known times of separation while I had to work away from home. The business of our relationship has always taken precedence over any earthly job or occupation. The job and occupation were done to support the relationship we have with each other. As we talk about the great business of life, I want you to think of it as being a relationship with God, as in marriage, while you may be supporting yourself with some earthly occupation or business. So often we are made to think that if I'm going to make God my business, I must surrender my earthly job and go into to some full-time work for the Gospel. Over half of the pastors in America are bi-vocational; they do some other work to help support their families. The Apostle Paul made tents at times to support himself while he walked with God, tended his churches, and wrote nearly half of the New Testament. God may or may not call you to leave your earthly job and business, but he will call you to making Him the first business of your life.

We have heard people say, "Michel Jordan was born to play basketball," or "Arnold Palmer was born to play golf." When we see someone exceptional at what they do, we say they were born to do that. This is not said about everyone who plays a sport, only about the greats. What if I were to tell you that you were born to do something? That, as a matter of fact you, were specifically designed by God for a certain business, and that that business is to be in relationship with Him? This is something that we all can be very good at, so good that someone might say they were born to do this. You and I were created by God for God. To make God our business is to find what we were created for, what we were specifically designed for, what God meant for us to do. It is to discover that God wants a relationship with us, one in which we can love him and be loved by him. Anything other than a meaningful relationship with God is a step down from the high purpose you were designed for.

Have you ever been asked, "What's your business?" or "What do you do for a living?" Our response to that question is usually what we do to earn money to provide for the necessities of life. What we do to earn that money is what we usually call our occupation, business, or trade. What should our business be? What is the primary purpose for which God created you? Your primary purpose may have little to do with the business or work you do to earn money in order to live in this world. What did God create you first to do and be? A plumber, a doctor, a preacher? Your business is to love God with all your heart. God created you first for Himself, to be His bride, to love Him and live with Him. He has called you into fellowship with His son Jesus Christ. This fellowship, this communion, this calling, this love is to be the goal of your life and your great business.

There are many Christians who say they were called by God to preach, be a missionary, teach, or work in some Christian ministry. Seeing this as their business and calling can pull them away from their true business of a love relationship with God. Many a Christian in full-time Christian work has found him- or herself in a place where they have lost their first love and had to repent of loving their ministry and go back and do the real business God first called them to of loving Him.

We should see our earthly business as a means to an end, that end being to love God with all our hearts. Why do you work? You work so you may provide for the necessities of life in order that you may have strength to love and worship God. I work so that I may live and have time to make God my priority. I work so that I may provide for my family and lead them into the family business of making God their great business. When the business of the world pushes God out of the picture altogether, God is no longer your business, your first love. Some will have to repent of worshipping the god of earthly business if they are to love God rightly.

When I was younger, I wanted to know what God's will was for my life. I would pray and ask, "What do you want me to do with my life, God?" What I was asking God for was who should I marry, what city should I live in, and what earthly occupation should I take up. What I really wanted to know was the future. I didn't want to wait for it and wanted to know what it was going to be, where it would happen, and with whom. I would learn that God's will for my life was God, and all the other things I thought were God's will were really secondary and less important than Him.

We put an emphasis on what I will call the geographical will of God: what earthly occupation I should take up, whom I should marry, where in the world should I live. These things will never be written in the Bible for us to find. There are no end of books on knowing God's will, and most of these focus on that geographical will. When we look to the Word of God to find His will for our lives, we find He wants to be that will. He wants us to know Him and love Him with all our hearts. He wants to pour out His love into our hearts. He wants us to come and trust Him with everything in this life. He wants us to grow in the grace and knowledge of the Lord Jesus Christ. Finding this geographical will can cast a shadow over God's will that you know Him and give Him first place in your life. We worry and spend our lives trying to find our place in this world, and this effort and worry often distract us from spending time with God, loving Him and being loved. We set our minds on knowing what earthly job or occupation God's will is, instead of resting in His revealed will to know and love Him. Thinking we are finding God's will for our lives, we take on businesses that crowd God out of our lives and become little gods we worship. If we just start doing the revealed will of God of knowing Him, loving Him, and seeking Him, the geographical will falls into place. And while we wait for answers of what job to do or whom we should marry or where we should live, we have communion with the living God. What could be better? When God does give us a career, spouse, or place to live, we will have our priorities in the right order and continue doing the great business as we walk into that career. Young person, if you're seeking God's will for your life, start with what you know: Love the Lord with all your heart soul and mind by finding a place to meet with Him daily and begin building a relationship with Him.

This God business will be the pinnacle of our lives. God designed us so His love alone would ultimately satisfy our hearts. He brings His love to our relationship and manifests that love to our hearts. Our business is loving and being loved by God, who alone knows best how to satisfy our hearts. Can a person really know God? Can I really have a loving relationship with Him? The answer is yes and amen, and it is your business. Add to this Jesus's injunction to seek first His Kingdom and His righteousness, and all these things will be added unto you. What are "all things"? They are what we wear, what we eat or drink, the necessities of life, that geographical will we spoke of. If I make God my business, loving Him with a full heart, seeking Him and His Kingdom first, my earthly occupation and provision will be taken care of by God. This has been my experience throughout my life.

The great reward of our God business is God Himself. Making God your business is the road to knowing God and loving Him. The loving is not one-way, not just us loving God, but Him loving us as well. "I have loved you with an everlasting love; I have drawn you with unfailing kindness" (Jer. 31:3). God's call is to a loving relationship with Himself, to love and be loved. This relationship is our main business, no matter what other trade we might have. The love with which God loves us is to be known and experienced. Paul writes, "Then you, being rooted and grounded in love, will have power, together with all the saints, to comprehend the length and width and height and depth of the love of Christ, and to know this love that surpasses knowledge" (Eph. 3:17–19). Many Christians know their earthly business as a calling, they know church doctrine; many know some order of worship; some have known a confirmation service, baptism, and church attendance, but even with all these things some Christians have never known and experienced God as a real person. Paul is praying that people will know and experience the love of God, a love that surpasses knowledge and is unexplainable. What joy will be ours as we enter a relationship with God where He pours out His love into our hearts by the Holy Spirit. This is the business you are called to.

I had some basic rules in my house that were said so many times, they were memorized by my children. When they would break one of these rules, I would start to quote the rule, and before I could finish, they would say, "I know, I know," and begin to repeat the rule with me. The problem wasn't that they didn't know it; the problem was they didn't do it. We have heard the first and greatest command so many times, we say to ourselves, "I know, I know: Love the Lord with all your heart, soul, and mind." Like my children, we go past it without obeying it, thinking that knowing is obeying. Have you set the first and greatest command as your life theme? Have you taken it up as your business? Your business is to know God and something of His love for you.

Countless Christians say, "Yes, yes, I know, I need to love God with all my heart" and then go about their lives with no intention of entering into or improving their relationship with God. If you would make God your business, you must learn the trade of entering into His presence and speaking with Him. Prayer—conversation with God—will be vital in your trade. You must know and love the Word of God, for this is God speaking to you. You must establish a place of meeting, an observatory where you might gaze upon Him. There will be tools in our toolbox that we use to accomplish this task. Each of the following chapters will add tools that we can use to build our relationship with God.

As Christians, we live in two worlds at the same time, the physical and the spiritual. Human beings are made up of both physical and spiritual dimensions. We have a physical body and a soul or spirit. The body is made for the physical world and the soul for the spiritual. We can see a man's body, but we cannot see his soul. We see the physical world but have trouble seeing the spiritual. We have business to do in both worlds. The physical world usually takes precedence because it is easier for us to see. This physical/spiritual division can cause us a great deal of confusion when we think about our business, occupation, or vocation. The question is, How do we live in both worlds? The great business for the Christian is learning how to live in the spiritual realm, how to seek first the Kingdom of Heaven. The great business is learning how to live with God, who is invisible. The sensual man will live by his senses, where what he sees with physical eyes becomes the real world to him. What a man sees with his physical eyes can become the foundation for what he believes. If he doesn't see God, it is easier for him to believe God doesn't exist. Some men believe only in what they can see and touch, and the physical world can overwhelm their spiritual senses. We must learn to see an invisible world and an invisible God; this is basic to our business.

In 1929 the Hungarian physicist Kálmán Tihanyi invented an infrared-sensitive electronic television camera for anti-aircraft defense in England. This was the beginning of technologies that enabled men to see in the dark. This technology has been improved to the point that our soldiers can have night-vision goggles attached to their helmets, allowing them to see and conduct missions in complete darkness. Seeing in the dark was thought impossible until this invention, and now it is part of every soldier's equipment. If we are going to be good soldiers for Christ, we must have the ability to see what is in the dark, in the spiritual realm. We must make it part of our business to learn to see with the eyes of the heart, God's spiritual night goggles.

Paul teaches us in II Corinthians 4:18, "So we fix our eyes not on what is seen, but on what is unseen, since what is seen is temporary, but what is unseen is eternal." There is a seen world, the world we see with our physical eyes and that we touch and taste. There is also an unseen world, the spiritual world of our Lord, of His Spirit and His Kingdom. We need visual help to see what for most is unseen. If I am to do the great business like the soldiers above, I must have goggles to see in the dark. If Paul is telling us to fix our eyes on the unseen, then we must be able to do so. Our business is to learn how to see and walk in this unseen world. In Ephesians 1:17–18, Paul says, "I keep asking that the God of our Lord Jesus Christ, the glorious Father, may give you the Spirit of wisdom and revelation, so that you may know him better. I pray that the eyes of your heart may be enlightened in order that you may know the hope to which he has called you, the riches of his glorious inheritance in his holy people." Here is what we need in order to see in the dark—the Spirit of wisdom and revelation and the opening of the eyes of our hearts. Our business is to see into this world that most can't or won't. Seeing the unseen, the invisible God, seems impossible for many, yet this is the business to which we have been called. God knows it is impossible for man without His help, so he has sent us a Comforter and Counselor who grants us revelation to see in the dark, to see Him, who is invisible. The ultimate purpose is "so that you may know Him better." The objective of Paul's prayer is that people would know God. He wants them to know the hope to which God has called us, the riches of His glorious inheritance, and His limitless power for us who believe. Hope, riches, inheritance, and power are things we think we can gain with our earthly physical jobs or occupation, yet there is no hope, riches, or power if they are just temporary. Our great business is not temporary but eternal, for it is knowing the eternal one who is our hope, riches, and power. It is being able to see God and gaze upon Him.

How does someone see what is invisible? How do we hear that which may be inaudible to someone else? We have seen that God will grant us a spirit of wisdom and revelation to know Him better. We must develop our relationship with the Holy Spirit that we might appropriate this revelation. "So I say, walk by the Spirit, and you will not gratify the desires of the flesh. For the flesh desires what is contrary to the Spirit, and the Spirit what is contrary to the flesh. They are in conflict (war) with each other, so that you do not do whatever you want" (Gal. 5:16). If the business you are seeking feeds the flesh, you will not know God; He will be foreign to you (Gal. 5:16–17). How do we learn to know and enjoy the love of an invisible person we are called to love with all our hearts? We walk with the Spirit; we walk in relationship with this person throughout our lives. As we grow in this relationship, He will teach us to see more of the glory of God and quench the fiery lust of the flesh. We have a vital relationship with Him as our great teacher; walking with the Spirit is synonymous with walking with God and Christ. This is what we are called to do: called to fix our eyes on the unseen, to listen for the still small voice that may be unheard by others. Those who are led by the Spirit of God are the sons of God.

How much time do we spend in physical exercise training our bodies? Many of us have some exercise program and go to a gym on a regular basis. Some even have personal trainers—all of this in order to train and shape our bodies, have better health and more strength and stamina, and maybe even live a little longer. In America, we are obsessed with our bodies; diet, physical fitness, exercise, sports equipment, and even workout clothes are all part of a multibillion-dollar industry. We think nothing of giving hours every week to exercise and training of our bodies, so why don't we think about training and exercising our spirits and souls in the same way?

As with other businesses, we have to serve an apprenticeship in the great business. Once we have answered Christ's call to come follow him, we must learn how to live in the spiritual realm by the Spirit. God apprentices us to the Holy Spirit, who becomes our instructor, our teacher, in the trade of the great business. His school is one we never graduate from. This is a course we never really finish. We are to walk with our instructor as Adam walked with God in the Garden. We will be trained by Him and His words; remember that the Bible was breathed out by the Holy Spirit, and the words on the pages of the Bible are His. Our training is first to have a vital relationship with our instructor by yielding our wills to His training, leading, and friendship. Our training is not just to learn techniques of how to live; the training (business) is developing a living, vital relationship with God. It is seeing the invisible, hearing the inaudible, and following the One whom others can't see or hear. If we do not enter into this course of training, we will end up trusting only ourselves, our flesh, and our earthly sight and hearing will drown out the true business of our lives. The things of heaven will grow strangely dim in the distracting light of this world.

The sensitivity to seeing and hearing in the invisible world comes when we sit down with the invisible God and act as if He is real. We come to Him and talk with Him as a man, face-to-face. We learn how to have a conversation with God in which we speak and we listen. We spend time alone with Him and learn who He is. We set aside time for Him and keep our appointments. Then, with the gift of His spirit of wisdom and revelation, God will begin to open the eyes of our hearts to see God and the wonders of His Kingdom. Is this your desire? Do you desire to see God? Can you say this is your business?

Man's normal inclination is to use his natural gifts and abilities to survive in this world. In Matthew 6, Jesus is discussing what all men worry about, what they see as the primary business of their lives, how to survive in this world. "Therefore I tell you, do not worry about your life, what you will eat or drink; or about your body, what you will wear. Is not life more than food, and the body more than clothes? Look at the birds of the air; they do not sow or reap or store away in barns, and yet your heavenly Father feeds them. Are you not more valuable than they? Can any one of you by worrying add a single hour to your life?… So do not worry, saying 'What shall we eat?' or 'What shall we drink?' or 'What shall we wear?' For pagan run after all these things, and your heavenly Father knows that you need them. But seek first his kingdom and his righteousness, and all these things will be given to you as well. Therefore do not worry about tomorrow, for tomorrow will worry about itself" (Matt. 6:25–34).

Jesus's answer to the survival question here on earth is to seek first His Kingdom and His righteousness. This is making God your great business. Then notice what he adds, "And all these things will be given to you as well." What will be given? What we eat, and drink and what we wear. The very things we think we must work for to live. This is backward from the way many of us think. This shatters the conventional thinking on how one is to provide for oneself in this world, and what one's business is to be. We think I must first work for the survival things in life and then work on my God business. When just the opposite is true. Resolving to make God the business of my life is solving the provision problem that often consumes a person's life. Jesus is saying we are not to seek first our survival or our provision; rather, we are to seek His Kingdom and make Him the great business of our lives. Jesus is making the startling statement that the way to live in this world, the way to provide for yourself and family, is not by seeking your kingdom first but to seek His first, and He will take care of providing for you. We don't trust God to supply what we need in this world to live. We trust Him for salvation and then live as if God helps those who help themselves. The priority becomes what I should do for a living, and then we run past the great business to the work of taking care of ourselves in this world. Jesus said if we worry about God's business, he'll worry about our business, making it his own. You are God's business, and He knows how to care for you better than you do. Is God your great business, or is some earthly business crowding God out of your life? What's your business?

I know from experience how tough it is to have to live in both worlds and yet make the spiritual one your business. For over 25 years as a pastor, I was bi-vocational. I worked as an ironworker to provide for my family while pastoring the flock of God. I know how tough it is to find time for the great business when you must leave the house at 5:30 a.m. in order to get to work. I know what it means to work ten- and twelve-hour days with two hours of commute and still make God the business of one's life. I know how difficult this is, and I know that there will be times of success and failure. One must choose what will be the priority, what not to give up, what to focus on. There must be time for looking at God that not even the busiest day will push aside. "Do not store up for yourselves treasures on earth, where moths and vermin destroy, and where thieves break in and steal. But store up for yourselves treasures in heaven, where moths and vermin do not destroy, and where thieves do not break in and steal. For where your treasure is, there will your heart be also" (Matt. 6:19–21). Jesus goes on to say you can't serve God and money. Do you want God to be your business, or money? This is the decision all Christians have to make: God or money?

Our world is saturated with materialism. There has never been a richer people living on the earth than we Americans today. We are tempted by a world that is obsessed with telling people how they might get rich. The Internet is overflowing with schemes for how to make money in real estate, crypto-currency, Internet retail, being an influencer, and a thousand other side hustles. There is no shortage of ideas and training to teach us how to make our way prosperously in this world. I have noticed that most of these don't start with seeking God and His Kingdom first. The devil is clever in the ways he gets us to fix our eyes on the seen instead of the unseen. He wraps the seen world in large houses on the water, in clothes that are covered with high-end brand names, in cars that cost hundreds of thousands of dollars; he wraps the seen world in the most beautiful packages, making them irresistible. There is no shortage of seminars and training videos on how to make some business in this world your great business—all of which is to get us to look away or set our hearts on that which is not God.

Making the decision to make God our business can cause us some worry. We ask ourselves, How will I live in this world if I don't worry about money? And then we conclude: "If don't make money the issue, I won't have any and will suffer because of it." Jesus knows that the devil wants to turn your attention to this issue of survival, which is a good thing, in order to get you to focus on a business that is not the best thing.

As Christians we have a vocation, a religious calling to make God the central business of our lives. "God is faithful, who has called you into fellowship with his son, Jesus Christ our Lord" (I Cor. 1:9). "He called you to this through our gospel that you might share in the glory of our Lord Jesus Christ" (I Thess. 2:14). When we answer God's calling, it is a calling to fellowship with His son, to share in his glory. What a trade, what a business, to have fellowship with the living God, to have the veil that covers our eyes to the spiritual world slowly removed. With our blinders off we will see a melding of the spiritual and physical world into one. We will see that our calling to fellowship with God comes with provision for our earthly needs. Our earthly occupation will flow out of our occupation with God. Here is the great test of faith for many believers: If I make God the great business of my life, can I really trust Christ to take care of me, or must I take over this responsibility?

Jesus said, "Do not work for food that perishes, but for food that endures to eternal life, which the son of man will give you" (John 6:27). Jesus is speaking of the situation all men find themselves in. Humans think to themselves, "I must work to earn money to live. If I don't work, I won't be able to live." When Jesus says, "Do not work for food that perishes," He is saying do not set as a priority the temporal things of this earth above that which is eternal. Jesus is not saying that a man or woman should not work, for as the Apostle Paul teaches us in the book of II Thessalonians, "If a man will not work, neither should he eat" (II Thess. 3:10). Jesus is saying that we must set as a priority working for the food that endures to eternal life. What is that food (business) that endures to eternal life? Dining on the bread of life (Jesus) as the Israelites dined on manna in the wilderness. The Israelites would gather that manna daily in order to live. Our business is to go out and gather daily the bread of heaven that we might live one more day by this divine food.

Jesus gives us this discourse to explain what he means by food that endures to eternal life. "It was not Moses who gave you the bread from heaven, (this was physical bread) but it was my Father who gives you the true bread from heaven. For the bread of God is he who comes down from heaven and gives life to the world" (John 6:32–33). Jesus is saying the bread from heaven that God gave to Moses was a type or symbol of the bread that God has now given to the world. Jesus answers the question, What is the food to work for and what is the food that endures to eternal life? by saying, "I am the bread of life. Whoever comes to me will never hunger, and whoever believes in me will never thirst" (John 6:35). Jesus, the bread of life, is the food that endures to eternal life. He is the food we should work for. He is the bread we are to work for and dine on. He is to be the great business of our lives. Have you ever thought to yourself, "I must have Jesus, or I will die"? If we make Christ and his Kingdom our primary business, we discover by so doing the best way to provide for ourselves. Whether a person earns much or little will have no effect on their ability to earn and dine on the bread that matters, the bread that is eternal, the bread that is Christ.

Hearing Jesus say these things, the people inquired, "What must we do to perform the works of God?" (John 6:28). They might have asked how can we do the great business, which is earning the bread the endures to eternal life. "The work of God is this: to believe in the one he has sent" (John 6:29). Our primary work is to believe in Jesus Christ, who is the bread of life, to believe He exists, to believe He is there and I can fellowship with Him, to believe He will speak to me as I speak to Him, to believe that I can receive some revelation of this one here and now. Our business is to make the great business (Jesus) our great business by believing in Him, loving Him, looking at Him, building a relationship with Him. This act of believing will include all these acts: knowing, considering, desiring, hoping, believing, loving, and the enjoyment of

Jesus. Our main business is to seek Jesus and His Kingdom first. Our business is to love Jesus more than anything else in the world. Just as our earthly life is sustained by the physical food we work for, our spiritual life, our real and eternal life, will be sustained and maintained by eating the bread that comes down from heaven. When we pray the Lord's Prayer asking for daily bread, how many of us see this as asking for Jesus the bread of heaven? Our occupation will be seeking with all our hearts this bread that endures to eternal life. Our occupation is to gather this bread daily as the Israelites did in the wilderness and then to dine on it. Our business is to go daily and gather enough manna for the day from the Scriptures to feed us and then do the same the next day. As we dine on this bread of heaven, the bread becomes me and I the bread. Do you know how to work for this bread? What skills are required in this occupation?

When we learn to dine on Christ, we shall truly live, and be able to say with the Apostle Paul, "For me to live is Christ" (Phil. 1:21). I make my living by finding and dining on Christ. Jesus closes this discourse by saying, "Just as the living father sent me and I live because of the father, so also the one who feeds on me will live because of me" (John 6:57). Have you made it your business to believe on the Lord Jesus Christ, to look unto Him, to dine on Him who is the bread of life and in the dining on that bread find abundant life? Have you learned to sip at the cup of His blood and taste its sweetness, to take of the bread of His life daily as it was given in the wilderness? Have you learned to taste and eat it and see that it is sweet? "O taste and see that the Lord is good: blessed is the man that trusteth in him" (Ps. 34:8).

Making Jesus the great business of our lives is the only way to be truly successful, happy, and fulfilled in this life. Things such as love, joy, peace, self-control, and the fruits of the Spirit come only from the person of Christ. Jesus fills what Augustine called the God-shaped void that lies in every man's heart. The goal of this writing is not so much to have a philosophical conversation on what it means to really live in this world, as it is to get us to think about how to make Jesus Christ the great business of our life. You can earn a great deal of money here on earth and never live, or you can have no money and live fully. Jesus said, "I came that you might have life and life abundantly" (John 10:10). True living can only be found in the person of Jesus Christ. So I ask you: Is Jesus your business?

For too many Christians, Jesus is a side hustle, something they do to add a little value to their lives. He is just a sideline or a hobby to be done when there is time left over from the chores of life. We are busy taking care of ourselves, our families, and even our churches. We think that by our works and labors we will gain what we require to live, to survive, to succeed in this world. Our Jesus business is often a charade that hides the illegitimate businesses of self-love, self-worship, and self-aggrandizement. Like Don Corleone, much of what we do for business is illegal and violates the law of God, which says, "Love the Lord with all your heart and soul and mind." Is Jesus your business, your only business?

For most people the self-life, and all it desires, determines our business. Turning away from self and its desires and turning to Christ, making Him and his desires the business of your life, can be difficult. Christianity means relinquishing one kind of business and taking on another, relinquishing one master and taking on another. The business and the master you must relinquish are yourself and your goals. The business and the master you take on is Christ. This transformation, this transfer from one business to another, is salvation. Making God our business is the first step of repentance and faith. He becomes the boss, He becomes the chairman, and we take on a new business plan, a new focus. Fallen man doesn't naturally trust God; we don't think He can provide what we need to live, so we try to do it. Fallen man goes about seeking the things he thinks he needs to get by in this life. When we put all our effort into surviving in this world, we may find we have ignored our real need for Christ. This may be why the story of the rich young ruler scares many Christians to death; they are busy in an illegitimate business and don't want to give it up. Trading the old business for the new one of Christ is part of what the Bible calls repentance. The sign over your heart might say, "God is my business," but what is the real business going on in your heart?

In Florence, Italy, you will find the Franciscan Church of Santa Croce, built in the late 14th and early 15th centuries. At the east end of the Basilica de Santa Croce are several chapels surrounding and including the high altar. In one of these chapels, Cappella Bardi, there are 28 scenes or frescos from the life of Saint Francis, attributed to the painter Giotto. One of those scenes in the series called the *Legend of St Francis* is titled *Renunciation of Worldly Goods*. The fresco has a clear division between two worlds: On one side stands Francis's father and his fellow merchants of Florence, representing the business of the world, and on the other side St. Francis, the bishop, and two friars, representing God's business. This fresco records the moment when Francis renounces his old business, the business of his earthly father, and chooses a new business, the great business, the business of his heavenly Father.

The painting depicts Francis's father accusing his son, before an episcopal tribune, of squandering his fortune, and wanting Francis to renounce any claim to that fortune, which Francis does. When Francis renounced his father's fortune, he took off his clothes and gave them back to his father, not wanting to take anything from his father's house. In the painting his father is holding Francis's cast-off garments. Francis is depicted wrapped in the bishop's cloak, which the bishop took off and put on Francis to cover his nakedness. Francis is reaching up toward the sky, and above him is the hand of God reaching down through the clouds as if to say, "Francis, come follow me." Francis would never practice his earthly business again. God may be bringing you to a point of decision like Francis, where you cast off the garments of an old life to pick up the livery and business of Christ. This is not loss; this is eternal gain; this is exchanging the rags of this world for the riches of God. "For what shall it profit a man to gain the whole world and lose his own soul? (Mark 8:36) Like Francis, every true believer will have a renunciation moment when he or she exchanges earthly love and business and for heavenly ones. Your renunciation may not be as dramatic as that of Francis of Assisi, but God by his Spirit will bring you to that place of decision where you will have to decide what the true business of your life will be. Have you renounced anything, have you changed your priorities, have you found a new love, a new business?

As a young man beginning to sense the call of God on my life, I saw that the answer to that call was to go into Christian ministry. The way to serve God I thought was in some full-time capacity like pastor, missionary evangelist, or Christian educator. Working in some Christian full-time job would be the way to demonstrate my full heart's commitment to God, I thought. I was mistaken in my thinking, for I thought the outward job (ministry) was the true business God calls one to. The business God calls us to is knowing and loving Him. The relationship is the first, second, and third thing. Those who are not abiding in Christ often become stumbling blocks when they get into ministry. Many have thought ministry is the great business and know little of Jesus being their great business. Just because a man's outward business is preaching doesn't mean his inward business is Christ. The reason for the loss of power in the Church today may be that our teachers are doing the wrong business. The great business is first a love relationship with a living person. It is finding and eating the bread of life. It is doing the works of God by believing in Jesus. If God adds a ministerial job to your life, amen, but that ministry is not your main occupation. Jesus is to be your first ministry. He will be your main occupation. The calling is to relationship, fellowship, and communion with Jesus Christ. Who do you love and serve, who do you want to adore, who do you want to follow? Nor does someone who has a secular job need to feel like a second-class citizen in the Church. If Christ is your business, you may be making tents and still be able to say, "For me to live is Christ" (Phil. 1:21). How many men and women who had ministry vocations ended up with moral failure because ministry was their business and not Christ?

For those who aren't in the full-time ministry, we use the terms "lay ministry" or "lay pastor" or just "layman," as if this position were something less than that of those who are in full-time ministry. Your ministry may not be large, but your great business—making Jesus the business of your life—may be. Much of our ministry to Christ may be unseen by others but is seen by God. Your ministry may be larger than you think. Many who have what the world would call large ministries may discover all too late that Jesus wasn't their business. "Many will say to me, 'Lord, Lord, did we not prophesy in your name, and cast out demons in your name, and do many mighty works in your name?' And then I will declare to them, 'I never knew you; depart from me, you evildoers'" (Matt. 7:21–23). Just because you have an outward ministry doesn't mean you have made Jesus the true business of your life.

Karl Vaters, writing on Church leadership in *Christianity Today*, says, "If I could only teach one vocational principle to young pastors it would probably be this: Learn how to pay the bills outside your pastoral salary. You will probably need it." He goes on to say, "A large percentage of pastors are bi-vocational. Always have been." Fewer than two-thirds of all churches have a full-time pastor. Vaters explains that bi-vocational ministry isn't rare, and it is becoming more common. Bi-vocational pastors are not half pastors. Through the centuries bi-vocational pastors have been more the rule than the exception. This demonstrates that we may have a job that God gives us to support ourselves financially, but it won't be the great business of our lives. The focus will be on my great business, my ministry to Christ. Mr. Vaters closes his article by saying that bi-vocationality is not something that needs to be fixed. Many pastors, church planters, and those in other types of ministries are also called teachers, realtors, small-business owners, even Uber drivers. Don't be disappointed by the size of your ministry; be disappointed if the real business and ministry of your life is not Christ.

In the mid to late 1980s, God began doing a new work in my heart. I had spent the prior 10 years trying to make professional football the business of my life. Toward the end of our football career, I began to look for other avenues of business whereby I could make a living for my family when our football career was over. At an alumni reunion at my alma mater, I talked with an old teammate who was working at the Chicago Board of Trade, and he said, "Come to Chicago. I would like to show you my business." After spending a couple of days with this friend, I decided to make trading commodities my business. While still playing football, I raised the capital I would need to get the business started. I studied everything I could get my hands on to learn as much as I could about this business. This business took my mind captive and consumed my life. It was what I thought about, worried about, even dreamed about. I found that the same passion and drive that I had applied to playing professional football, I was now applying to this new business. I found just as with football, the business was all-consuming, leaving little time for God's business.

During this time at the Board of Trade, God was doing new work in my heart. By the revelation of Himself he was increasing my appetite and passion for Jesus Christ. I was beginning to learn what intimacy with Christ was. One spring day, while walking from the train station to the Board of Trade building, I looked up between the buildings to see the beautiful blue sky that had been hidden by the long gray day of winter. When I looked up, I saw not only the blue sky but a 40-foot statue of the goddess Ceres that crowns the top of the Board of Trade building. Carved into the stone just beneath this statue are four hooded priests. I stood there, gazing at the scene for several moments, realizing for the first time that this was a temple, but not a temple to the living God. It was a temple to the material things of this world. It was as if God was saying to me, "David, this is not my temple. You are worshipping in the wrong temple, for this is Babylon!" In the next few weeks and months, God would be calling me away from this business, this temple, to the great business of knowing Christ.

This was a very difficult time in my life. I had spent a great deal of time and money setting up and developing this new business. I had settled into a new city, found a new house, and completely remodeled it. Now a call was coming from God to leave all and come follow him. I must admit I was both confused and afraid; the whole thing seemed illogical. The pressure continued to mount for several months till I realized this was what God wanted me to do. God wanted me to trust Him for the material things of this world, to make Him the business of my life. He wanted to teach me what He meant when He said seek first His Kingdom and all these things would be added unto me. His calling was to a school and a city I had never been to, to be taught by people we had never met. This would be my Francis of Assisi moment, when I stripped off the clothes of the old life and walked away naked, following Christ. He would lead us to places that were both fearful and uncomfortable. He wanted to teach me how to make Him who was the great business the true business of my life. I would learn that when I had the right business, all things were added unto me.

I moved to a new city and began a course of study learning a new business. The school that God chose for me emphasized developing a relationship with Jesus Christ, making Christ my great business. The training was in growing in the grace and knowledge of Jesus Christ. I wanted this business more than anything else. I didn't realize it at the time, but God was taking me out of one business to train me in a new one. God brought me to a quiet place where the distractions of normal life and business were removed, and I had only one thing to do and learn. In the quiet of those days, God was teaching me the trade of walking with God, of fellowshipping with my Lord. He brought me to a place where my workday was focused only on Jesus. For the first time in my life, Jesus was becoming my business.

After attending classes for many months I found myself in a bad financial situation. I can remember the day as if it were yesterday. I woke up and sat up in the bed, getting ready to go to class, when Sally sat up beside me, looked me in the eye, and said, "David, there's no food in the house. What will the children eat today?" The oatmeal was gone, the peanut butter was gone, the bread was gone, and all the old dried-up pasta was gone as well. I had no answer for my wife that morning. So I took that question to the Lord: "Lord, you said if I would seek Your Kingdom first, you would add all these things unto me. Lord, what shall my children eat today? Lord, you've called us here; will you not provide?" The food had run out because the money had run out; there was nothing in the bank. I had left behind our business, our means of making money, and gone forward to seek His Kingdom. My jug of oil had run out, and our sack of flour was empty, or so I thought.

I went to class that morning as usual, continuing to do what God had called me to do. After first period class, a friend came over and said, "David, I have something for you." With that she handed me an envelope. In it was an anonymous gift of money with which I could buy food for my children for the next few weeks. When that ran out, I found there were other anonymous gifts that came to make sure our cupboards were full, as well as the stomachs of our children. God was sending ravens with food in their mouths to feed us. God was making real for me the verse "Seek ye first Kingdom of God and all these things will be added unto you." He was teaching me that if I truly made him my business, He would take care of the rest. It was difficult to relinquish the control of my life and business into God's hands. God may not call you to relinquish your business, but He will call you to make Him the first business of your life.

Jesus was teaching me that my earthly business and my finances were of secondary importance to His Kingdom and His righteousness. He was showing me that regardless of my financial circumstances, my priority, my business, would never change. I was not to seek first my business or my ability to provide for my family; I was to seek Him and His business and trust Him for the rest. Whether you are rich or poor or somewhere in between, His command to us is to make Him and His Kingdom our primary business. God's command to seek first His Kingdom comes with a promise: If we seek His Kingdom first, the other things will be added unto us. And they were! I saw Jesus take care of things I couldn't. "So the one who feeds on me will live because of me" (John 6:57). My business was to learn how to make Him my business, to learn how to dine on Him and live. I found that Jesus was good to His word.

The training, education, and preparation for any business can take years of study and practice. Doctors have years of schooling before they ever touch a patient: undergraduate school, medical school, internship, fellowships, before they are finally on their own. Great artists will tell you that they continue to study and learn all their lives. They go and study with other great artists to learn technique, vision, and approach to work. Once they receive instruction, they apply it to their work, adding new dimensions to it. Through practice and continual learning, people become masters of their craft. Are you developing your skills in the business of knowing and loving God?

Masters of a craft would take on apprentices and teach them the craft they were doing. Today we have college professors teaching people business courses when they have never done any business themselves. You might call these fake teachers for they have never done what they are trying to teach others to do. It might be better to spend five minutes with Warren Buffet, someone you could call a real teacher, for he is doing real business everyday then two years with this kind of professor. When it comes to the great business, you must find a real teacher who has made God his or her business, one who knows God, who has made God the business of his or her life and spends time with Him every day. One who has become a master of the secret place, knowing God, will be more able to teach you how to become a master of the secret place making God your business. I'm afraid many of our teachers (pastors) are fake teachers. They are not teaching people how to make Jesus the great business because He is not their great business. Many teach the Word of God without making known the God of the Word and without making the God of the Word real to others. They may not be teaching you how to pray, for they don't pray. They are not teaching you to make Jesus your great business because He is not theirs. Someone who has spent time with God on the mountain, who knows how to fast and pray, will come back shining and will desire that you come and see the same God, and make Him the business of your life.

Trades have apprenticeship schools where the apprentice learns about the trade, its language, its tools, and how to use them. Once they have learned the basics of a trade, daily use can sharpen their skills into an art. It only takes a couple of years to learn the basics of a trade, but it takes at least 5 to 10 years to master the craft. If you want to be good at your business, you must give yourself to the work, spending hours of hard work and discipline at your craft. Why don't we think like this when it comes to the great business of knowing

God? Seeking God, getting to know Him, and growing in our love and intimacy with Him is the business He has called us to. Continual education, sacrifice, discipline, and hard work should be a part of that great business. We should sacrifice for the business of knowing God at least as much as we do for earthly business. The great business will be our greatest craft, but we must work at it daily, honing our skills. We should be looking for teachers who know God, asking them how we might know Him better and how to look upon Him. Why is it we don't think about training our minds and bodies and spirit to draw closer to Christ?

Great players in any sport will put in years of practice doing the same motion or action over and over, striving for perfection. They are still working on their skills even when they are the best in the game. A friend of mine told me that Benny Goodman had his first clarinet lesson at 10 and his union card at 13, but in his 70s he still practiced scales before breakfast every day. He had his fatal heart attack while practicing these scales. The greats at anything know there is no substitute for hard work. Many athletes have been playing their sport for more than 10 years before they even go to college, with thousands of hours of practice and study doing the same thing repeatedly. For some reason, when it comes to making God our business, we don't see it as something we can get better at. We don't see the great business as something we are going to have to work at or put endless hours of work into to accomplish our goal. We don't think about studying to learn more about Him or studying with the greats in the field of knowing God. We don't even know who these men or women are. We don't think about prayer as something we can practice and get better at. We don't even see a time commitment as being important to the success of our business of knowing God. But God says, "You will seek for me and find me when you seek for me with all your heart" (Jer. 29:13). Many Christians wonder why they don't know God when they only spend five minutes a day on making God their business, and most of that time is spent asking God for things they need or want. If you gave your employer five minutes of work out of an eight-hour day, how long you would last at that job?

If we are to make God our business, shouldn't God have the same effort granted a craftsmen give to his trade or a musician to their instrument, or an artist to their art? Isn't God worthy of 10,000 hours of your life? Have you spent 10,000 hours on your God business? If God is our business, then where are the hours spent on Him? Do we want to be a success in knowing God, and can that be done on five minutes a day? It will be difficult for those who haven't made God their business to help you do the same.

So how do we go about becoming a success at the great business? Perhaps we start by treating the great business like a business. In our regular jobs, we know we are going spend about 40 hours a week doing our business. We give priority to that time and put everything else aside. How many times have you said, "I'm sorry I can't make it; I have to go to work"? How many times have you said, "I'm sorry I can't make it; I have to go be with God"? My guess would be not many. If the great business is not a priority, it gets pushed into the corners of our lives, where it is often neglected and even extinguished. What would happen if the Church in America treated Jesus as its real business and made Him the priority of their time and effort?

You say, "I'm so busy with work, family, and church business, there is little time for God." If we are busy with ministry, it is easier for us to justify our absences from God. We don't really find or make time; there are 24 hours in every day for everyone. What we do is prioritize that time; we determine how we will spend it, and usually we prioritize it according to what we think is necessary or what we prefer or love to do. Until we see Jesus as necessary, or as a great love, it will be difficult to find any time for Him.

When you love yourself, it is never hard to find time for yourself. Hobbies, entertainments, people you love and who love you always find room in our lives. Those who love themselves will spend most of their time on themselves. According to Nielsen survey, the average American watches more than four hours of TV a day, and you can add to that another two hours a day for social media. Some people are spending so much time gaming, on social media, or watching television or other entertainments, they have lost their ability or desire to socialize with other people. We have time for TV, laptops, notebooks, and our phones, but some of us can't find time for God. We are not suggesting you throwing out the baby with the bath water—your regular job, TV, and social media—but if you have time for these things, shouldn't you be able to find time for the great business, time with God? The time we spend on social media and TV might reveal to us what we really love. Maybe what we really love is the world and the things of the world. Could we squeeze a few hours out of our social media and TV time to be with God?

The average American today has a better life than kings and queens did in the late 19th century. We are richer in America than any people in the world have ever been. We have more labor-saving and time-saving tools at hand that should free us to spend more time on our God business. What are we spending that free time on?

Many years ago now, I went to Rochester, Minnesota, to attend a L'Abri conference to hear Francis Schaeffer and C. Everett Koop speak on issues of the day. One of the speakers at the conference was Francis Schaeffer's daughter Deborah Middelmann. During her talk she told the story of group of Jewish students of Hebrew who had regular jobs and after work would go and study the Torah for four or five hours. It illustrates how people will find time to do what they love or what they are passionate about. I wonder if it would be possible for us to find five hours a day for God. Is Jesus really someone you love, someone you're passionate about? Can you find a few hours for Him?

Present-day Benedictine monks follow this daily schedule for the purpose of "seeking to glorify God and know Him." At 5:40 a.m. the day begins, proceeding to 6:00 a.m. vigils, followed by Lectio Divina at 6:45 and Lauds at 7:15. Breakfast is at 7:45, then work at 8:30. Eucharist starts at 11:45, followed by lunch at 12:25. Daily prayer is at 1:05, then back to work at 1:30. Vespers begins at 5:15, followed by Lectio Divina at 5:45. Supper begins at 6:15, followed by recreation at 6:45. At 7:15 there is Compline and then sleep. I share this not that you might embrace the Benedictine monastic life, but rather to demonstrate how someone who doesn't want to spend this time on TV can organize their day to spend it with God and still have a seven-and-a-half-hour workday. I can take on the great business and hold a job at the same time. How can we find six hours a day for social media and TV but not find an hour for God?

Saint Paul wrote to the Church in Thessalonica, "For you yourselves know how you ought to follow our example. We were not idle when we were with you, nor did we eat anyone's food without paying for it. On the contrary, we worked night and day, laboring and toiling so that we would not be a burden to any of you. We did this, not because we do not have the right to such help, but in order to make ourselves a model for you to follow. For even when we were with you, we gave you this rule: 'If a man will not work, he shall not eat'" (II Thess. 3:7–10). Paul had time to support himself making tents, do missionary work, teach and preach to the churches, write letters, pray, and then say, "For me to live is Christ" (Phil. 1:21). Here Paul is an example to us that we can still work a job for supporting ourselves and still make Christ our great business.

The great business is building a relationship with the living Christ. He speaks to and leads those who make Him the priority of their lives. Christianity is first, second, and third a relationship with this living God. You don't start this relationship and move on to something else. You live in this relationship, this union with the living God, and out of it will flow ministry. You will soon discover that your real ministry is serving and loving Jesus in the secret place. The pastor who doesn't have a vital relationship with Christ can do much in the flesh but won't be building the Kingdom of God. Some of the largest churches in America have the smell of flesh about them. Your first business is to know and love Jesus. This is done by living in union with Christ. Your business is to get to know God, to pursue Him daily. We should know His voice and His leading by the Spirit. We should know and love His Word and make Him and it the manna of our lives.

If Christ is your business, there must be communication within that business. Can you imagine trying to run some business where the employees never communicate with one another? For the Christian, the prayer life, communication with God, can be a thermometer, or measure, of how well the business is going. It can demonstrate how much we want to be with Him and involved in His business. If we are honest, we would have to say the prayer life of the Church is dying out, if not dead altogether. In many of the evangelical churches you are hard-pressed to find a prayer meeting. Is our lack of desire to talk with God an indication that we are involved in some business that isn't Him? If God is the priority, then we should be forsaking other things to make room for Him. If someone is not talking to God on an individual basis, they probably won't want to talk with Him corporately either. How far we are from Herrnhut and the Moravians' 24/7 prayer meeting that lasted over a hundred years. There are signs of hope with prayer vigils around the world. When God is the business, there will be prayer, in the individual and in the Church. There is still hope for America if people are crying out to God.

What is the return or pay for this business? Those who seek Him in secret, He will reward openly; those who seek Him will find Him. To make God our business is no small thing, for He is the creator and sustainer of all things; God spoke all we see into existence with only a word. He wove us together in our mother's womb, which means He specifically designed us according to the pattern of His heart and mind. He designed us for the purpose of knowing and loving Him. "For we are His workmanship, created in Christ Jesus for good works, which God prepared beforehand, that we should walk in them" (Eph. 2:10). These good works will fall into two categories: love God, and love your neighbor as yourself, though these are actually not two separate categories but one, for you can't love your neighbor without loving God first, and all love for your neighbor flows out of a loving relationship with God. God's great business is His glory, so in His love for humankind He shines the light of that glory into our hearts in the face of Christ Jesus. He makes His Son Jesus our great business, and as we look at His glory in Jesus's face, we are transformed into Jesus's image. Then shining with the light of His glory we go into the dark places of this world so others might see the light of His face as well.

Our business is to learn of the greatest wonder of all, God Himself. "Then the Lord came down in the cloud and stood there with him and proclaimed his name the Lord. And he passed in front of Moses, proclaiming, The Lord the Lord; the compassionate and gracious God, slow to anger, abounding in love and faithfulness, maintaining love to thousands, and forgiving wickedness, rebellion and sin" (Ex. 34:5–6). God was introducing Himself to Moses by giving him His name. He was telling Moses what he is like. He was showing him his perfections and awesome beauty. To see God is to see a beauty that transforms. To know Him is to experience the love He has for us. To invest your life in seeking Him is the most fulfilling and thrilling thing a human being can do. If you seek God, he will come and proclaim His name to you.

Bonaventure writes in *The Tree of Life*, "From this fountain flows the stream of the oil of gladness, which gladdens the city of God, and the powerful fiery torrent, the torrent I say of the pleasure of God, from which the guests at the heavenly banquet drink to joyful inebriation and sing without ceasing the hymns of jubilation." When Paul said not to be drunk with wine but be filled with the Holy Spirit, he was saying don't be drunk (controlled, influenced) with wine, but be inebriated (controlled and influenced) by the fullness of the Holy Spirit. "Drink to joyful inebriation and sing the hymns of jubilation." This is to be drunk on the love of God, the most intoxicating thing in the universe. To intoxicate can mean to excite or exhilarate, to thrill, elate, delight, captivate, enthrall, and more. We don't find much joy in God alone these days. We have forgotten how to enjoy this fountain of gladness by drinking the wine of the pleasures of God. We do not know what it means to be inebriated with the Spirit. Many Christians have never experienced the "fiery torrent of the pleasure of God." "What is the chief end of man? To glorify God and enjoy Him forever" (Westminster Confession of Faith, Larger Catechism). How have we missed enjoying this God, and what have we exchanged for the pleasures of God?

John says in one of his epistles, God is love. Paul prays for the Ephesians, "I pray that you, being rooted and established in love, may have power, together with all the saints, to grasp how wide and long and high and deep is the love of Christ, and to know this love that surpasses knowledge" (Eph. 3:17–19). Our business is to know and experience the love of God. "Dear friends, let us love one another, for love comes from God. Everyone who loves has been born of God and knows God. Whoever does not love does not know God because God is love" (I John 4:8). Part of our business is to know a love that is like no other, for it is higher, deeper, and broader than any other love. Your business is to draw near to God and let Him love you with the most powerful and satisfying love in existence. God is the source of infinite love, and He wants us to know that love—not after we die and go to Heaven but here and now. By the way, you are commanded to remain in that love.

The first step in the great business of knowing Christ is what we call the devotional life. This is the place of discovering God. It is like the altar built by Abraham to seek God and have conversation with God. It is the like the tabernacle where God would appear to the nation as a pillar of cloud by day and pillar of fire by night. It is like the temple where God's people could come and seek Him, where they could listen to the songs of Zion sung by the choirs. It is where they could offer gifts of devotion upon an altar to love their God in some small way. It is a spiritual location, a place to meet with the living God. Here is where we study the Word to know the God of the Word. Here is where we pray, talk to God, and listen in the stillness to hear from Him. Here is the place where we come into His presence and adore Him. This is where we learn to commune with God, to remain in His love, to become His friend and let Him be ours. Here is where we remain and bathe in the love of God. Here is where we will see the fire fall from heaven. Yet for many, Jesus is as dead as when he was taken off the cross and placed in the tomb.

What is the best job or business to have? The Apostle Paul had one the best answers I ever heard to the question, "What's your business?" Paul said, "For me to live is Christ and to die is gain" (Phil. 1:21). If we were to ask what's the greatest business, there would be lots of discussion and even arguments. What if there was a greatest business? Wouldn't you want to know what it is? What if everyone could do that business, and no one had to be excluded; wouldn't you want to know what it was? What if you could have a business where you would never lose the profits, never lose what you have gained even in death?

The answer should come immediately: "Jesus is the great business!" That answer is heard less today, as Church business and the great business are often in conflict. Often, we don't know the God we should know. "Do you not know? Have you not heard? The Lord is the everlasting God, the Creator or the ends of the earth. He will not grow tired or weary, and his understanding no one can fathom. He gives strength to the weary and increased the power of the weak. Even youths grow tired or weary, and young men stumble and fall; but those who hope in the Lord will renew their strength. They will soar on wings like eagles; they will run and not grow weary, they will walk and not be faint" (Isa. 40:28–31). God is saying, "Don't you know me? Haven't you heard of me?" What should we know about this God, and shouldn't it be our business to know this one? It is by learning who God is and seeing something of His glory that we are changed. This God is the one who pours out His love into our hearts by His Holy Spirit. The love of God is to be experienced and known; we are to be intoxicated by it. God's beauty is to be seen and enjoyed, the kind of beauty that inspires awe, takes our breath away, and changes us forever. No man is richer than when he knows this God; no man is more loved than when he remains in the love of God. The great business is Jesus, and when we make Him our great business, we will be doing the greatest business that we can.

One can only assume that when someone sets all their attention, strength, and effort on the things of this earth it is because they know nothing of the value and greatness of Jesus Christ. As the devotional life of the Church dies, the things of earth have become its great business, and Jesus is seen as less valuable, unique, and precious. When something loses its value, it is easy to toss it in a drawer and forget about it. When we see Jesus as unimportant, we slowly push Him out of our churches and individual lives, making room for the things we think are more valuable and more important. The death of the devotional life of the Church is evidence that much of the Church has set its love on something else.

What to do? "Even now, declares the Lord, return to me with all your heart, with fasting and weeping and mourning" (Joel 2:14). "Desire Jesus, the Great Business, or the all in all, in a covenant of grace the most proper object of desire, especially to fallen man…Christ and none but Christ; give me Christ, or I die, I am undone, I am lost forever. But what is Christ, or Jesus, to the covenant of grace? I answer, he is the great business, he is the all in all" (Isaac Ambrose, *Looking Unto Jesus*). God desires that Jesus become your great business. God wants you to be able to say, as Paul did, "For me to live is Christ!" Our business, our work, our craft, our trade, and our art is to seek after God with all our hearts and to know Him. Knowing this God is the highest point of human experience; it is the greatest accomplishment in any person's life. Finding God is the greatest adventure of life. Finding and knowing God is transformational to the individual. Finding and knowing God is something to boast about. "Let not the wise man boast of his wisdom or the strong man boast of the strength or the rich man boast of his riches, but let him who boasts boast about this; that he understands and knows me" (Jer. 9:24). Do you know this God, and is He your great business?

Chapter 1

GAZING

 "One thing I ask from the Lord, this only do I seek: that I may dwell in the house of the Lord all the days of my life, to gaze on the beauty of the Lord and to seek him in His temple." (Ps. 27:4)

A FRIEND AND mentor of mine posted this conversation on Facebook. I thought it very profound, so I asked him for permission to reproduce it here.

> JERRY: I recently had a texting conversation with a pastor of a large church who has had wide exposure to pastors and churches in many places. I asked him this question: "Do you think the average church member knows how to 'gaze' on the Lord? And does it?"
>
> PASTOR: Jerry, I'm certain the average church member doesn't know how to gaze on Him. In fact, it has never crossed their minds that they could. I'm still learning myself. Sometimes I

still feel like a rookie worshipper. [Notice he is tying gazing and worship together here; more about that in a later chapter.]

JERRY : Think of this: Moses, David, Daniel, Jesus, Peter, Paul, John, and so many others did not have a Bible and devotional books for a quiet time. All they had was the Lord Himself, alone and in stillness. And they got to know Him one-on-one. I wonder if "doing" devotions has become a hindrance.

PASTOR: And I believe that is a very significant insight. Some years ago, I was struck by the fact that the second-century Church did not have a complete New Testament as we have today, yet the Church flourished. But I had not applied that to the Apostolic generation. That's so encouraging and important. Yes, for me, doing devotions has kept me from coming to Him only. I am just learning at 56 what I wish I had understood at 17.

This conversation brings to light what our devotions should be but seldom are: gazing on Jesus. Gazing on Jesus is what transforms us into His image. If the focus of our devotions is not on Jesus, we may not see the power we need to be changed into His image.

The subject of devotions is a whole book by itself, maybe several volumes, which we don't want to rewrite here, but we should make some comments: Devotions are an area of frustration for many Christians as they fight a battle for faithfulness and consistency in this area. Why is this? First, many don't know why they have devotions. When one becomes a Christian, one is instructed in what to do to grow one's faith. One of the first instructions we receive is, "Read your Bible and pray." We begin reading and praying and find it boring and fatiguing. Then we feel bad because how could God's Word be boring and fatiguing? Yet we find ourselves falling asleep as we read it. The prayer life doesn't fare much better, as we end up saying a Protestant rosary, something we can say without thinking. Until we have answered the why of devotions, we are in for an uphill battle.

The first why of devotions is not to read so many chapters to learn how you're supposed to act as a Christian, or learn more doctrine, or memorize verses; it is not helping people by praying for them. The first why of devotions is to make Jesus the main focus in your devotions, the great business of your life. Devotions are an act of faith whereby we come into the presence of Jesus, and gaze on Him and then describing back to

Him what we see. This is worship. Allowing the light of His glory to shine on us is the transformational part of the Christian life. We behold (gaze), and in our gazing His glory shines on us. That glory shining on us changes us in ever-increasing measure into the image of Jesus Christ.

If our focus is just on Bible reading and prayer, then the amount we read or the amount of time we spend praying can quickly become the goal. How many of us have gotten a copy of *The One Year Bible* and never finished reading it in a year? The problem can be the goal itself. If reading so many pages is the goal, then when the reading is finished, you are satisfied; you have achieved your goal and are not looking for anything else. We want to get our duty done, our chore for the day, so we can get on to whatever we have to do for a living. We can treat prayer the same way, and our goal becomes praying through so many names, or countries, and when we have gotten through our list we are done for the day. This is why I think the pastor above said devotions can get in the way of gazing on Jesus.

Changing the focus of devotions from just Bible reading and prayer to gazing on Jesus is what the pastor above did. Instead of the goal being so many minutes of prayer and so many chapters read, it becomes what we see of Jesus from the Word. Gazing is discovering what the Bible has to reveal about Jesus. Why do we study the Word of God? To learn the rules of Christianity and keep them? No. "We study the Word of God that we might know the God of the Word" (Joseph Carroll). We're not seeking to be a Bible answer man; we're seeking Jesus. The first purpose of Bible reading is to see Jesus and then to meditate on His glory. When the glory of Jesus is revealed in Scripture, the heart is moved to worship and adore Him. Part of prayer then becomes describing the beauty and glory of Jesus back to Him in adoration and love. This is worship, this is prayer, this is gazing. We will talk more about worship in a later chapter.

Jesus teaches us the priority of worship in the Lord's Prayer, which opens with "Our Father which art in heaven, hallowed be thy name." Hallowing God's name is worship, and the order is no accident. The worship of God is the act of describing Him and His attributes, adding praise and thanks. As we worship God we are focused on Him and who He is, we are gazing on His attributes and glory. God wants His children to begin their devotions, their day, by gazing at Jesus and not at themselves, their problems, wants, and needs, to gaze upon what they have in Jesus and not at what they don't have in themselves. Many Christians have prayer lives that are so focused on themselves, they never raise their eyes high enough to gaze on Jesus.

If Jesus is the first person in the universe, then He is worthy of first place in our lives, first place in our thoughts, and first place in our prayer. "Wherefore God also hath highly exalted him and given him a name which is above every name: That at the name of Jesus every knee should bow, of things in heaven, and things in earth, and things under the earth; and that every tongue should confess that Jesus Christ is Lord, to the glory of God the Father" (Phil. 2:9–11). Gazing at, worship, and adoration of Jesus Christ should be the first goal of our devotions but so often isn't. Shouldn't Jesus have first mention in our prayers and devotions?

We read the Word, trusting God to reveal Jesus to us by the Spirit, for "Faith cometh by hearing and hearing by the word of God" (Rom. 10:17). This revelation of Jesus from the Word of God gives us reasons to worship Him. We use those reasons in our worship as we declare his wonder. Then as the individual worships Jesus, he or she is given more revelation. C.S. Lewis said, "It is in the act of worship that God reveals Himself to man." Worship then brings more revelation, which should bring more worship. Griffith Thomas said, "Worship and revelation are the foundation of everything." This should be the never-ending cycle for the Christian drawing nearer to Christ. Gazing, worship, revelation, transformation—and then it starts all over again. The more we gaze, the more we'll see (revelation); the more we see, the more we'll worship; the more we worship, the more revelation we will have; the more revelation we have, the more we'll be transformed into Jesus's image. This cycle of gazing, worship, revelation, and transformation will include communication and communion with the living Christ being revealed. I don't read the Bible as some empty duty for trying to absorb some wisdom or learn some principle of how to be a better Christian; I read the Bible to see Jesus and bathe in the light of His glory and commune with Him. This bathing in His glory is what washes me and transforms me into His image. This is gazing.

If it's true that average Christians don't know how to gaze on Jesus, then what are they gazing on in their devotions? The focus could be on having devotions. The pastor above said he thought his devotions had kept him from gazing only on Jesus. If your goal is reading so many chapters in the Bible and praying for so many minutes, Jesus may never be a thought in your head. Some might be focused on their failures, what they have done wrong, and asking for forgiveness and for power not to do it again. Some might seek to know more principles and commands of God so they can learn how to be perfect. Others might be focused on material needs, food, shelter, and a job to provide for those we love. What do you want to see? We should determine to look at Jesus and fix our gaze there.

Pastor, you might be focused on your church or ministry; no shortage of needs there. Pastor, will your focus and prayer on the needs, brokenness, and failures of your flock inspire, feed, and transform your soul? Even our intercession for others can distract us from gazing on the beauty of the Lord. We can end up like Martha, running around serving in intercession, and miss Jesus and what He has to say to us. When we turn our gaze away from Jesus in our devotions, we may be looking at something that will not help us or empower us to walk through our day. We may be looking at something that will only burden us more and leave us feeling helpless. We need to look at something that is empowering and transformative. We should be gazing at Christ.

I'm not saying that we shouldn't think and pray about the things I've just listed. The problem is when we make the things we are praying for the focus and never gaze on Jesus. Our prayer lives should first be focused on Christ in worship and praise and then led by the Holy Spirit giving time to pray for people, circumstances, and needs, "Praying in the Holy Spirit at all times" (Eph. 6:18). By the way, when you are praying in the Holy Spirit you will find He leads you into gazing upon and worshipping Jesus more, not less. "Howbeit when he, the Spirit of truth, is come, he will guide you into all truth: for he shall not speak of himself; but whatsoever he shall hear, *that* shall he speak: and he will shew you things to come. He shall glorify me: for he shall receive of mine, and shall shew *it* unto you " (John 16:13–14, KJV). This focus on Jesus will also be transformational, as we are changed by beholding (II Cor. 3:18).

Isaac Ambrose writes in *Looking Unto Jesus*, "Looking to Jesus is the cause of this (Transformation into the image of Christ); the sight of God will make us like to God, and the sight of Christ will make us like to Christ; for as a looking glass cannot be exposed to the sun, but it will shine like the same, so God receives none to contemplate His face, but He transforms them into His own likeness; and Christ hath none that dive into these depths of His glorious incarnation, but they carry along with them sweet impressions of an abiding and transforming nature. Come then, let us once more look on Jesus in His incarnation, that we may conform to Jesus in that respect." If your devotions don't bring you to a place where you are gazing on Jesus, they may not be transformative in your life. Ambrose is saying transformation in the Christian life comes by looking at Jesus. The sight of Christ will make us like Christ. This idea of looking (gazing) unto Jesus is the theme of this book and one we hope each chapter will expand on. Ask yourself the question, Are my devotions about Jesus, or are they all about me and my little world?

Paul teaches us in II Corinthians 3:18, "But we all, with open face beholding as in a glass the glory of the Lord, are changed into the same image from glory to glory, even as by the Spirit of the Lord." This goes beyond learning more Bible truth and praying over a list of requests. It is gazing on the Lord's face and beholding Him, and while we are beholding Him, we are transformed into His likeness. We have a whole chapter coming titled "Changed by Beholding" in which we consider what Paul is saying in this verse. I believe Paul is giving us a principle that many of us have missed: Change comes by beholding the Lord. ("Jerry, I'm certain the average church member doesn't know how to gaze on Him, in fact, it has never crossed their minds that they could.") We are called to learn what it means to gaze upon the beauty of the Lord.

My friend Jerry told me he learned this poem by Thomas Blake as a young man at a conference and would repeat it to himself almost every day as he began the day with the Lord.

> *Every morning, lean thine arms awhile*
> *Upon the windowsill of heaven,*
> *And gaze upon thy Lord.*
> *Then, with the vision in thy heart,*
> *Turn strong to meet thy day.*

Dr. Theodore F. Adams, pastor of First Baptist Church of Richmond from 1936 to 1968, heard this same poem at a vesper service while vacationing in Wisconsin in the early days of his ministry. He never forgot it and committed it to memory, loving it so much that he made cards with the poem on them and gave them to the members of his church. Later, during a renovation project at his church, stained-glass windows depicting events from the life of Christ were installed. Along with these Dr. Adams installed a stained-glass window depicting a believer in prayer, looking up to heaven, with the light and glory of God shining down on him. At the bottom of this window this poem is written out.

This gazing on the Lord is so important, but so few Christians know how to do it. If I could teach you one thing for your daily walk with Christ, it would be these words: "That you might gaze upon Christ daily and turn strong to meet thy day." My friend Jerry used to live in the Richmond area, so I asked him if he knew Pastor Adams. He had attended the church and sat under Pastor Adams's preaching but didn't know about the stained-glass window with the verse on it.

The Word of God, the Bible, is the window we rest our arms upon to gaze on our God. "We study the Word of God that we might know the God of the Word" (Joseph Carroll). The Bible is God's revelation of Himself and His plan for humankind. If Jesus is not the goal in our study of the Word, it is easy to become pharisaic and see only law in the Word. When the Bible becomes the goal, we can end up seeing only the law. Paul was a Pharisee of Pharisees and said that all that learning was as nothing compared to the surpassing greatness of knowing Christ Jesus, his Lord. Ask yourself the question: Today when I had my devotions, was I looking at Jesus or was I looking at the law? Was I looking at myself and my problems and needs? When I read the scriptures, did I see Jesus or just so many words on the page?

The Bible reveals Jesus, starting at Genesis 1:1—"In the beginning God," and ending with the last book of the Bible, Revelation. In the Old Testament, Jesus is revealed in types and shadows. He is then revealed in prophecies from both major and minor prophets. The New Testament is the revelation and fulfillment of all those types, shadows, and prophecies. It tells the story of the King coming to earth, His incarnation, life, ministry, sacrificial death, resurrection, and ascension into Heaven. The vision is no longer through types and shadows but by incarnation of God in the body of a man. All that God had promised in the Old Testament was fulfilled in the New Testament in Jesus Christ. In the New Testament we see what God looked like in coming to earth and living as a man. We see His work to redeem humankind and purchase for Himself a people. On a personal basis, you will see what Jesus has done for you. The more I studied and look at this revelation of Christ, the more I was being changed into the image of Christ. This change comes not so much by doing as but by looking.

At Bible school our Old Testament professor brought Jesus out of every book. Five days a week we sat in his class and worked through the whole Old Testament in a year. At first, I was shocked, because every morning I was learning about Jesus from the Old Testament. Growing up in the Church, I had been taught that the Old Testament contained the law and that the New Testament was revelation of Jesus. With this teacher, the Old Testament became a study about Jesus. I had never heard someone preaching and teaching Christ from the Old Testament as this man did. Every class was a measure of the oil of gladness being poured over my head as I saw and heard of the grace of God for me from the Scriptures that predated Christ's incarnation. I was resting my elbows on the windowsill of heaven and gazing on Jesus in my Old Testament class.

I know that to some who read this what I'm saying may sound foreign or hard to believe. The idea of just looking at Jesus sounds too good to be true, too easy to be Christianity. Where is the struggle with the rules and regulations of Christianity? Let me assure you trying to keep your eyes on Jesus and maintain this contact will be one of the hardest things you have ever done. It will also be opposed by the devil placing obstacles in your path to get you to stumble and fall away from this looking.

My own journey to this place of learning to gaze on Jesus came in phases, and almost by accident, as I read through J. Oswald Sanders's *The Incomparable Christ*, which had a powerful impact on my life even though I didn't know why at the time. I used the book for my morning devotions, going through a chapter a day until I finished the book, something I have done repeatedly over the years. The more I looked on Jesus through the pages of the book, the more change I saw in my life. I wasn't studying laws or principles on how to be a better Christian; I was just looking at the perfect Son of God. This transformation wasn't coming from some effort on my part to learn what a good Christian was and then trying to become one. I was simply looking at Jesus, and transformation was happening in my life. My goal had changed from trying to be a better Christian by looking at the rules and regulations to looking at Jesus. In the looking I was enjoying the greatest beauty that man can behold, and in the beholding, power was being released to change me. The incidental result of looking (gazing) at Jesus was transformation in my life without my realizing it.

My devotions were consumed with this gazing on Jesus instead of gazing on myself, my needs, or the needs of my Church and friends and missionaries. This gazing moved me to worship. The more I gazed on Christ, the more I was preoccupied with Him, the more power and transformation I was seeing in my Christian walk. It took me some time to realize that this was happening. For the first time in my life, my devotions weren't about me becoming a better Christian; they were all about Jesus. I hadn't put it all together yet, but I knew something new was happening in my spiritual life. I kept coming back to Sanders's book again and again and really didn't know why, but God did. God wanted to transform me into the image of His Son, and the way He did that was to get me to look at Jesus. If God is leading you through the Gospels to see Jesus, or he puts books about His Son in your path, know that He wants to do a transforming work in your life by getting you to look at His Son.

During this time of discovering how to gaze, the Spirit of God also led me to begin to worship Him through the book of Psalms. "One thing I have asked of the Lord, to dwell in the house of the Lord and to gaze on the beauty of the Lord all the days of my life" (Ps. 27:4). As with the early Church, here was my first hymnal. I would read the psalms out loud back to God, making them my own songs. I marked what I called the praise psalms and would sing them over and over to the Lord. God was leading me to make Christ the center of my devotions rather than centering them on myself or my needs. The worship of God turned my focus from me to Him.

As I worshipped Jesus Christ, I began to see that my life was changing. I wasn't trying to change; I was just trying to gaze on Jesus. The more I was gazing, the more I saw sanctification being worked out in my life without me thinking about the rules and regulations I was commanded to keep. I was seeing victory in the areas of my life where I had been defeated, not by working on those areas or by memorizing verses about a particular problem but simply by looking at Jesus. Many of these mornings were nothing but praise and worship of Christ, and I never got to my prayer list. At first, I felt badly about this because I didn't get to the work of prayer and intercession for other people. Then I began to see that God doesn't need me to change the world but that I need Him to change me by simply looking at Jesus.

As I was beginning to gaze upon the Lord, I discovered another book that would help me in my gazing, answer some of the questions I had about what was happening to me. It was a book titled *How to Worship Jesus Christ,* by Joseph Carroll. He taught me that the things I was learning about Jesus from scripture, from Oswald Sanders's book and others, I could turn into worship. Worship is speaking back to God, with praise and thanksgiving, the wonders He reveals to you about Himself. I came to see that my work to study the Scripture was to see Jesus, who was my great business and then to worship Him. I was learning that in the act of worship, God was revealing Himself to me. It was during these times of worship that I was experiencing Jesus's manifest presence. Jesus wants to spend time alone with His children and will come to them and sup with them. I began to see that it wasn't just gazing on Jesus in the Bible or in Heaven; it was gazing on someone who was present with me. God took me to the place where I was actually spending time with Jesus. This is the great business, gazing on Jesus in close intimate fellowship. Being with Jesus is the greatest thing that can happen to a human being. Growing in the grace and knowledge of this one is our great business.

When I began to worship Jesus Christ, everything changed for me in my Christian life. For most of my Christian life, I had been working on being a better Christian by obeying God's Word or applying the rules and principles I had learned from the Bible. My life had been a rollercoaster experience of winning and losing, mostly losing. Now, as I began to worship (gazing on) Jesus Christ, I was seeing power over sin in a way I never had before. I was seeing sanctification worked out in my life not so much by focusing on my effort to be righteous but by on focusing on the One who is my righteousness. The more I worshiped Him, the more power I was seeing manifested in my life. I was seeing positive transformation, not by looking at what transformation was needed but by looking at the Great Transformer. I was learning that transformation was the by-product of my gazing on Jesus instead of trying to be a better Christian.

I know there are some who will say we must confess our sins, repent, and turn away from them if we are to walk with God and know Him. Others will tell us that we must make Jesus the Lord of our lives as if this is work to be done that will allow us to climb the spiritual ladder. Others will remind us that Jesus said, "He who loves me will keep my commands" (John 14:15), that the way to victory is keeping the law of God. All of the above we would agree with andwould come under, "Continue to work out your salvation with fear and trembling." (Philippians 2:12) Notice what we are called to look at above: our sins and how many of them we confess, our repentance and whether we have repented enough, making Jesus Lord in every area of life until he is Lord of all. How much surrender can we do to achieve acceptance? Then there is the law, a never-ending set of rules that often reveals how helpless we are to keep them. We can look at all these things and miss looking at Jesus. The subjective focus is on self and sin can keep one from seeing the objective truth and transformation found only in Christ. Over all these things I write: "Look unto Jesus."

This looking unto Jesus and the worship of Jesus is what a personal relationship with Jesus Christ looks like. Here is a deep and respectful conversation with the King of kings, filled with worship, adoration, and thanks. Worship is the love language with which we speak to God. This is the door He knocks upon to come through and sup with us. This personal relationship with Jesus Christ is the missing element in many Christian lives. For many Christians, Jesus is as dead as he was that first day in the tomb; there is no life in their relationship with Christ. When John had his vision of Heaven we see those around the throne of Christ worshipping Him. The four Creatures with the four faces worship, and the Elders fall down and worship holding bowls of incense, which are the prayers of the saints. Then he sees angels worship, and then every creature in Heaven worship Jesus Christ. These are relating to the Jesus by and through their worship. These are having their relationship with Christ manifest in worship. Worship will be a vital part of our relationship with Jesus Christ, the means of relating to Him.

A.W. Tozer said, "Man was made to worship God. God gave to man a harp and said, 'Here above all the creatures that I have made and created I have given you the largest harp. I put more strings on your instrument and I have given you a wider range than I have given to any other creature. You can worship me in a manner that no other creature can.' And when he sinned, man took that instrument and threw it down in the mud and there it has lain for centuries, rusted, broken, and unstrung" (*Worship, The Missing Jewel of the*

Evangelical Church). The purpose of God sending His Son to die and rise and live and be at the right hand of God the Father was that He might restore to us the missing jewel, the jewel of worship, so that we might come back and learn to do again that which we were created to do in the first place: worship the Lord in the beauty of holiness and spend time in awesome wonder and adoration of God, feeling and expressing it, and letting it get into our labors and doing nothing except as an act of worship to the Almighty God through His Son Jesus Christ. A tragedy in the world today is that God has made man in His image and made him to worship Him, made him to play the harp of worship before the face of God, day and night, but man has failed God and dropped the harp. I had dropped my harp, but the Spirit of God led me back to the place where I had dropped it. Finding it, I picked it up again and began to play. This new paradigm was the missing element in my Christian life. I believe we see what sin we must repent of when we look at our devotions and see nothing but self, sin-tied, defeated, in poverty of power and in love with money. Praying for us has become something of self-glorification seeing only ourselves and the needs we have. I believe that repenting of our self-focus, and of our gods and coming to look at and worship God alone will be the first obedience.

By gazing on Jesus, we see wonders manifold; these wonders stir us to worship and adore Him, and in this worship and adoration He reveals even more of Himself to us. It becomes a self-perpetuating cycle. More gazing leads to more worship, which leads to more revelation, which leads to more transformation in our lives. This transformation we call sanctification. I learned that sanctification doesn't just come from obedience but from gazing, worship, and adoration as well. This will be hard for many to believe, for we have been taught all our lives that obeying the law will lead to sanctification. We have busied ourselves looking at these laws, memorizing them, and then trying to obey them, which has led many down a road to defeat. Our education system has taught us to say, "Just tell me how to live the Christian life, and I will do it." This has taken the focus from Christ and placed it on ourselves, and like Peter walking on the water, when we focus on ourselves and our circumstances we begin to sink. Worshipping Jesus is gazing on Jesus, and Jesus is the great business.

I grew up in churches being taught that transformation came from the effort of faith. You see what you are, you learn what you should be, you memorize the law, and then strive to fulfill it. If I wanted to be a better Christian, if I wanted to change, I was told, "Read your Bible and pray." So I did. I asked how can I live a pure life, and I was told to hide God's Word in my heart, so I did. I saw these as the steps to sanctification, but found they had little or no power to rescue me from sin. We have many devotional books and daily guides, but few if any are devoted to solely gazing on the Lord Jesus Christ. Many of these devotionals focus on how we should live the Christian life and are filled with commands and principles. That is not to say that all these devotional materials are wrong or worthless; they are not. The problem is that if you have a command-oriented devotional, it ultimately ends with you all alone with the law, and apart from Christ there is no power to keep the law.

There is no power in the law to transform. "For if righteousness could be gained through the law, Christ died for nothing" (Gal. 2:21). If I focus on Christ, who is my righteousness, I will be changed not by trying to keep the law but by looking at Jesus, who is my righteousness. Faith is manifest in the looking. This may sound strange to you, especially if you were raised in a law-preaching environment. Power in the devotional life to change doesn't come from seeing my failure and trying to be better; it comes from seeing Christ's success and by gazing at Him believe that His success and power can be mine. If we are changed by beholding then it will be essential to make Christ the focus of our devotions and keep Him as such. This is why worship should be at the center of our devotions, for worship is gazing on Jesus and describing with praise and thanks what we see of Him.

You can have a routine of Bible reading and praying that never brings you to the place where you gaze on the Lord Jesus. Remember what the pastor said to my friend Jerry: "For me, doing devotions has kept me from coming to Him only." What did he mean? Devotions that are organized to do so much work, read so much of the Bible, and pray for so many people can put the focus on what you are doing instead of on Jesus and what He has done. Jesus said, "These people honor me with their lips, but their hearts are far from me. They worship me in vain" (Matt. 15:8). If you are looking at the wrong thing, your devotions could be in vain. True devotions are designed to ascend the hill of the Lord, to come into His presence and bathe in the light and glory of Holy God. It is here, in the presence of God, in the light of His glory, that we are changed into His image and empowered to do what He is calling us to—changed by beholding.

For some Christians, telling them to gaze on Jesus is like speaking a foreign language to them. We get nervous when someone tells us, "I saw Jesus" or "Jesus appeared to me." Many Christians have been taught that they can't really see Jesus now but will one day when they get to Heaven. If we can't really see Jesus, why bother looking? This attitude has trained many Christians not to look. If Jesus is invisible, isn't it kind of stupid trying to see Him? If I can't see Him now, why bother trying, for I'll see Him one day in Heaven? We've been trained not to look, and that may be why so few know how to gaze on Christ. Yet Scripture is filled with requests such as, "Show me your face," "Turn your face to shine upon me," "Turn not your face away from me," "Grant me a Spirit of wisdom and revelation that the eyes of my heart might be opened to see the hope of your calling." There is a seeing of Jesus now, one that is by the Word of God and the Holy Spirit, one that is granted by God through His Spirit and of His Son.

There is something we can see of Jesus here and now. This revelation of Christ comes from the word is quickened by the Holy Spirit and shown on the screens of our hearts and minds. You might see Him on the pages of scripture, you might see Him with the eyes of the heart, or the eyes of faith, or even through revelation, but I assure you God wants you to look and see His Son. Like Moses, we are to come into God's presence and remain there, gazing upon Him until we are covered with His transforming radiance and glory. Coming into the presence of the Lord and gazing upon Him is what changes us and causes us to shine with His glory.

When it comes to looking for ways to live a better Christian life, looking on Jesus is not something we think about. You mean all I have to do is gaze on Jesus? The simple answer is yes, but it's so hard to believe, and it may be even harder to do. Just as the moon has no light of its own, so we have no light and can only reflect the light of the Son when we are in position to do so. Our great business is to get into that position, by repenting of all occupations that would take us out of His presence, light, and glory. When we turn our faces to other things, even good things, like Moses leaving the mountain we begin to fade. If we don't turn back to the Lord, our faces will lose their light and glory. We have been taught by some of our teachers that if I do certain things, if I keep the law, if I serve others in ministry, if I share the Gospel, I will shine with the glory of God. This is not necessarily true. The point to be made here is that our works don't make us shine, don't transform us; only the grace of God coming through His glory in the face of Christ Jesus in his presence will make us shine, will transform us. Transformation will come only in believing on, being with, and looking at, Jesus. The works will come, but only after the beholding. Our devotions are the place we go to stand in the light of His glory and begin to reflect His light, His character, His holiness, His power and His glory. What matters in our devotions is not so much the routine as it is the encounter with the living God. Devotions really are spiritual geography, getting into and staying in the very presence of the Lord. "One thing I ask from the Lord, this only do I seek: that I may dwell in the house of the Lord all the days of my life, to gaze on the beauty of the Lord and seek him in his temple" (Ps. 27:4).

What is the desired end of our devotions? Why do we have them? Are my devotions like going to a superstore with my shopping list and checking the items off as I put them in my cart? Are they a place I come to ask God to expand my borders and bless me? Are they a place I come to earn merit by spinning prayer wheels like a Buddhist until God owes me an answer? What we focus on in our devotions lets us know if our motivation is right or wrong. Is my focus me, my ministry, my family, my job or wealth, or is it Jesus? If our focus is wrong, then all our religious gyrations may shade the light of His glory and slow the process of being changed. The desired end is not having God fill my shopping list. The desired end is an encounter with the living God and to gaze upon His beauty.

If strength for the day comes when we gaze on Jesus, wouldn't this include strength for sanctification? Yes! Some of you will find this hard to believe; you may even think it wrong because it doesn't line up with what you have been taught all your life. We struggle with the law and keeping it: I know what to do but can't do it. Many of our teachers are setting the law before us and leaving us with the application: do this and live. What if it's not some self-effort to keep the law that makes me righteous? What if it is just looking unto Jesus, and the looking is the healing or enabling? What if we are really changed by beholding? It might transform the way we live our Christian lives. Instead of putting most of our effort into keeping the law and doing some ministry for God, we might put more effort into gazing on Jesus. The problem is that many Christians don't learn this until they are 56, like the pastor above. We think our transformation comes by our effort to keep the law; we think faith is an exertion of our human strength to obey God. What if faith is as simple as looking at Jesus? What if God's desire in giving us the Word is not so much to learn its rules and regulations as to see Jesus written on every page and then bathe in the light of His glory? This might revolutionize your Christian life; it might revolutionize your devotions. Now power comes not in straining to be good but in straining to see the Son of man lifted up like the serpent in the wilderness that we might look and be healed, be empowered to live the life he has called us to.

Chapter 2

A Borrowed Glow: Moses Shines

 "When Moses came down from Mount Sinai with the two tablets of the covenant law in his hands, he was not aware that his face was radiant because he had spoken with the Lord."
(Ex. 34:29)

OVER THE YEARS, I have used many different devotional guides in my time with the Lord. Richard Ellsworth Day produced one of my favorite daily devotional works. I have worked through this volume several times over the years and have yet to grow tired of it. It has been published under a couple of different titles, but the title I like the best is *A Borrowed Glow*. This is a reference to the means God uses to transform us into His image, yet one we seldom think of when we talk about sanctification. The glow of any Christian will be the reflected light of the glory of God.

When Moses came down from the mountain with His face shining, he had a borrowed glow, and something similar should be happening to us as we draw near to God in our daily devotions. We have the picture of God, who is glorious and shines, and the picture of a human being like Moses, who is nothing more than flesh. Flesh doesn't shine, unless it comes into contact with God, as in Moses's case. If the non-glowing person draws near to the glowing one, they begin to shine, not of their own light but in the light of the one who glows. They glow with that reflected light. The person we borrow the glow from is the Lord Jesus Himself. The means of appropriating that glow is by drawing near and gazing on the one who is the light of the world and the light and lamp of Heaven. The glow is not something we possess; it can only be found in another. The only glow we will ever have is a reflected glow, God's glorious light shining on us and lighting up our life, making us look a little like Him. This means I can glow only by being in proximity to the Lord, only by being in a vital relationship with Jesus, one that includes communication, communion, and cooperation of the parties committed to each another. Keeping oneself in proximity, in relationship, with Jesus then becomes our work and concern, for apart from Him we can do nothing. The goal of our lives should be to draw near to God so the light of His glory will fall on us. This happens when we come by faith to a meeting place with our God. This is the secret place Jesus talked about in Matthew 6. It is our garden where we walk with God in the cool of the day, our place for meeting with our God. This place of meeting is also the place of transformation and empowering.

Personal devotions are a place we go to gaze on this glorious Lord. The first step is looking away from everything that is not God so that we might focus and gaze on Him. In order to gaze upon the Lord we ask God to grant us the Spirit of wisdom and revelation so that we might know Him better. This revelation of God is where the glory of God meets fallen man. The revelation of the glory of God is powerful, and when it falls on men they are changed. The glory of God is His essence, what he seems like. His essence striking man transforms him into the image of Christ. We should ask, as Moses did, "God, show us your glory." We come into His presence by an act of faith, and with unveiled faces we gaze upon Him, to see what we can of that glory. So unique is God's glory that it has the power to change men, to transform them into His image. Moses is but a type and precursor of the new covenant and the glory that can be ours.

Coming to gaze on the Lord will require repentance and faith. It will require you to look away from your sin, your earthly loves and preoccupations by looking to Jesus. This true repentance is turning away from what fills our vision to look at Jesus, and as we do, we are changed. This transformation by looking brings with it a new heart, one filled with the love of God. Now we are able to love God and then our neighbor with divine love. This love becomes the driving force of life and our supreme desire. "Love the Lord your God with all your heart and soul and mind" (Matt. 22:37). How can I be with my love? How can I know Him better? The search for intimacy with Christ will be demonstrated when we draw near to Him in active communion, in vital relationship. Many will not understand what I am talking about here, for they have been taught a fire-insurance type of salvation: Believe this, and you're saved from hell, and one day you will see Jesus when you die. We can know the Lord here and now, we can hear His voice, we can know and experience His love for us. In the relationship, in the communion, in the drawing near Him, we will stand in His glory and be changed to shine like Him, changed into His image.

As Christians, we tend to focus on ourselves, what we need or what we lack. If I want to be a better Christian, what do I have to do? There is no end to the seminars one can attend in the church to have a better marriage, be a better witness, learn how to handle your finances, or how to parent. I have yet to see a seminar on how to look unto Jesus. A great deal of Christian literature being published today could be classified as how-to books or self-help books. There is no end of books or seminars where we learn how to be better husbands, wives, missionaries, pastors, teachers, or whatever else we need help with. Without knowing it, many who would rail against legalism have slipped into it without the least bit of resistance. They have done this by preaching a principle without the Prince. They teach four, eight, or twelve steps to a better Christian life. They are preaching a how-to Gospel and not Jesus. With a how-to Gospel we are setting our vision on rules to live by, principles for church growth, and techniques for a better marriage instead of on Christ. We are taught to do something that doesn't start and finish with Jesus. Looking at how I can be a better Christian, father, mother, teacher, pastor, and so forth, we have looked away from the transforming glory of God in Christ and looked to the strength of our minds to keep the law and change. Because we have made our goal what we want to be (self), we end up looking at ourselves and the principles of change and lose sight of Jesus and drawing near to Him. The result is we have grown dark and lost our borrowed glow. Not only have we lost our glow, we have lost our power for all that God wants us to be.

"When Moses came down from Mount Sinai with the two tablets of the Testimony in His hands, he was not aware that His face was radiant because he had spoken with the Lord" (Ex. 34:29). Moses spends time in God's presence talking with God and receiving the law, and without knowing it comes back shining with the light of God's glory. How did this happen? How did Moses end up shining? Moses didn't have to do anything to shine; there was no law to obey. God didn't say, "Do this, and you will shine." The only thing Moses did was go into the presence of God and talk with Him. Moses was preoccupied with God and the revelation of the law that God was speaking to him, and he came back shining. When he came back to the camp, you could say it freaked the people out. This light so disturbed the people that Moses had to put a veil over His face. Paul speaks about Moses and this shining in II Corinthians 3 and compares it to the New Covenant today. In the Old Covenant the glory was fading; the New Covenant comes with increasing glory and one that is eternal. The glory of the New Covenant is Jesus.

What made Moses shine? Did Moses exert some human effort to shine? Did Moses have a three-step program he followed that made him shine, was he trying to shine? His only obedience was going into God's presence, into God's glory. This transfer of glory from God to Moses was incidental to Moses being with God, a result of being in God's presence and God shining on him. This is so simple, but we have trouble comprehending it. "You mean there is nothing for me to do other than come to God?" It is not nothing to come to God, and you may find that it is one of the most difficult things you do as a Christian. The devil will war against your going into God's presence and standing in the light of His glory. I believe one of the great spiritual battles in the Church is waged here in keeping Christians from going into the presence of God and being alone with Him. All Moses did was go into God's presence and stand there. We don't comprehend it because we see faith as a human effort that when exerted is rewarded by God. We think Moses must have done something by faith that earned him the honor of shining with the glory of God. Have you thought, "The more I obey God, the more I will be like Him, and the greater my faith, the more I will be transformed into the image of Christ"? Or are you changed just by beholding?

Moses's shining was the result of being in God's presence and gazing upon His glory. While God and Moses talked "face-to-face, as a man talks with a friend," there was a transference of God's glory to Moses. This was accomplished by God without Moses's knowledge by the grace of God alone. The story is important because so many of us think that our spiritual change or transformation comes by our obedient responses to God's law. Moses had been obedient to come up the mountain, but the shining was accomplished by God, and Moses received it by being with God. When Moses came down from the mountain, he, being preoccupied with God, didn't even know that he was shining. When we make God the goal of our vision, seeing Him will distract us even from the changes that are occurring in us. We may not know that we are changing, for the change in us is not the goal but God himself.

As Christians, we think our righteousness, our shining, comes from our obedience to the law. Christian, you can keep the law like a Pharisee and never look at God. Many Christians lift their eyes no higher than the law and never see the wonder of God. Some have made a life's work out of looking at the law, and like a Jewish rabbi miss seeing Jesus. What if our spiritual transformation comes not by our obedience but by the grace of God, by being in the presence and glory of God? Moses was changed by being in the presence of God, and he didn't even know that he had changed. You and I will be changed in the same way by coming into Jesus's presence and simply beholding Him. Like Moses you may not even realize you are changing until others tell you. When one is in right relationship, right proximity to God, occupied with God, one can be changed without even knowing it. If this is so, then our gazing on Jesus is all the more important. There was no effort by Moses in his shining. He was simply in the presence of Holy God and received by grace the free gift of God's glory. Moses wasn't the only one in the Old Testament to have this shining experience; I believe Adam and Eve did as well.

As a child growing up in church, I learned the stories of the Bible in Sunday school on flannel graph boards. These were cloth-covered boards on which our teachers would stick paper figures to help tell the story. These figures had a Velcro-type backing so they would stick to the flannel. My introduction to Adam and Eve was via the flannel graph board. What struck me as kid was the fact that they were naked. Back in the 1950s, when I first heard the story, the thought that someone would be naked was shocking to me. Nudity wasn't something you talked about back then. You couldn't have naked figures on a kids' Sunday school flannel graph board, so the artist who made up the flannel graph figures would find creative ways of putting a branch or shrub in just the right place. This pre-fall nudity puzzled me: Why were they naked, and why didn't they realize it? Was it because, like Moses, they didn't know they were covered with the glory of God? When Adam and Eve sinned, they hid from God, for they knew for the first time that they were naked. Was it the sin that caused their glory to fade? There were two types of nakedness for Adam and Eve: pre-Fall nakedness, in which they didn't know they were naked and in which there was no shame, and the post-Fall nakedness, in which they knew shame and hid from God. Adam and Eve not only hid from God in the Garden, they also tried to cover their nakedness by sewing leaves together. What was the difference between the two types of nakedness?

What if they were covered with something pre-Fall that was removed at the Fall? What if they were covered with the glory of God? The Bible says they were naked and unashamed; could it be that they were covered with the reflected glory of God and couldn't see their nakedness? Maybe, like Moses, Adam and Eve didn't know they were shining until the shine was gone. If they did shine with God's glory, how did this happen? The shining comes not by working but by being in God's presence and looking at Him. When they sinned, they knew something was different; they knew they were naked and hid from God. For the first time they didn't want to look at God, or have him look upon them. Now they were afraid of God. God asked Adam, "Adam, where are you?" "I heard you in the Garden and I was afraid because I was naked, so I hid." God asked them, "Who told you that you were naked?" (Gen. 3:11). Sin had brought about a change, but what was that change? Was it the loss of the reflected glory of God because of sin?

The Garden was an observatory, a place where man could look upon God without penalty. We won't know fully what Adam and Eve's pre-Fall existence in the Garden was like until we are glorified in Heaven. Were Adam and Eve the only humans who were able to look at the face of God and live? In this vision of God, were they covered with the reflected glory of God's face? In God's presence there was nothing between them and God, not even clothes, so they could bathe in the light of that glory and be changed to shine in it. I believe the glory of God was their dress. Once Adam and Eve sinned, the vision of the face of God was lost to them and to all men. Moses shining was a type of this loss of the vision of God. When Moses came off the mountain, his face was shining with the glory of God and the people were afraid and had Moses cover his face, for they could not look upon it. When he asked to see the glory of God, the Lord told Moses that no man could see His face and live. So great was one sin that the vision of the face of God was lost to man. With sin, Adam could no longer look into the face of God, for it would kill him.

Could the glory of God have been something so beautiful and bright as to cover any nakedness in Adam or Eve? When Adam and Eve sinned, they knew they were naked and hid from God; was the glory gone? This change in self-awareness caused them to hide in the Garden and sew fig leaves together to cover their nakedness. Could it be that before the Fall, Adam and Eve, looking at the glorious vision of the face of God, couldn't see anything of themselves, even their nakedness in the light of that glory? Adam and Eve had the same reaction you or I would have if a stranger walked in on us naked: You'd grab the nearest thing to cover your nakedness. For Adam and Eve, God walked in on their newfound nakedness, and they were ashamed and embarrassed. They hid and covered themselves to hide their shame, for the glory that had covered Adam and Eve had departed. There are those who have thought that this was the case, that Adam and Eve were covered with glory before the Fall.

In the group of Dead Sea Scrolls fragments known as *Words of the Luminaries* (4Q504) the following passage about the glory of Adam in the garden of Eden occurs: "Adam our father you fashioned in the image of your glory and the breath of life you blew into His nostrils." This reveals what the Qumran community thought about Adam and Eve's Garden dress. The Qumran community thought of Adam and Eve covered with the glory of God. The early Church Fathers made the logical assumption that if Adam and Eve lived in the presence of God, they would reflect His glory. They spoke of Adam and Eve being created in the image of God, and as God was covered with glory, so were Adam and Eve. Many of the Dead Sea writings also compare the shining of Adam to Moses's shining when he came down from Sinai. The rabbinical tradition of Adam and Eve covered with the glory of God was taught by some in the early Church. When sin eclipsed that glory, Adam and Eve lost their garden dress and saw their nakedness and tried to cover it with leaves.

The idea that Adam and Eve were dressed in garments of glory can also be found in some of the ancient writings called targums. Targums were translations of the Hebrew Bible into Aramaic. Along with the translation or paraphrase, the rabbis would give commentary on the scripture. Some of these targums attest to the prelapsarian luminosity of Adam and Eve in the Garden. In some of the targums for Genesis 3:21 where God dressed Adam and Eve in "garments of skin," the translation says, "garments of glory" or even "garments of light." In some later Jewish and Samaritan sources, the story about Adam's luminous garments is often mentioned in conjunction with Moses's story. In one text, when Moses goes up on Sinai, he receives the image of God that Adam had cast off in the Garden (Memar Marqah 5.4). It was as if Moses picked up and put on the pre-Fall garment of glory that Adam had thrown away in the Garden.

When Jesus was transfigured in front of Peter, James, and John, the Scripture says, "As he was praying, the appearance of his face changed, and his clothes became as bright as a flash of lightning" (Luke 9:29). Matthew will say that Jesus's face shone like the sun. Could it be that this shining was what Adam and Eve had in the Garden before they sinned. This is the glory that Jesus laid aside when he came to earth. It is as if Jesus became naked, took off His glory in humility, that He might save the sons of Adam who took off his glory and became naked in an act of sin. Jesus came to restore that which was lost in the Garden not only to save but to cover us again with His glory, and we will begin to put on that glorious dress when we, with unveiled faces, look upon Jesus and shine in the reflected light of His own glory. Then in Heaven that glorious Garden dress will be restored, and we will shine like stars in His presence.

If Adam and Eve wore the glorious dress of God's glory, where did it come from? Was it the result of unhindered access to the presence of God, walking with Him in the cool of the day? The words "walking with God in the cool of the day" connote presence, fellowship, worship, and love. These new creatures were created in the image of God and would have expressed love to their Father as He expressed His love to them. Adam and Eve were a reflection of the image of God. What would it have been like to walk in the unhindered light and love of God? Talk about daily devotions, with devotion being given and received, mingled into a union of love and oneness. What was Adam's business in the Garden? We are quick to say Adam named the animals and tended the garden of God; he was taking dominion over what God had given Him, but this was not the main work. Adam's main work was the free-flowing fellowship with God, maintained in walking with God in the cool of the day. The access to God and the walk with God provided all Adam needed for any work God called him to do in the Garden. God was Adam's first business and the garden second. So great is man's Fall that today we can't even imagine what the Garden experience was like for Adam and Eve.

In Genesis 3 something happened that disrupted this walk that Adam had with God. There was only one law at that time, one thing that God had asked Adam and Eve not to do: don't eat of the tree of the knowledge of good and evil. One rule—but that rule was the test of love for God. Where the Spirit of Lord is, there is liberty (II Cor. 3:17); think about the liberty Adam and Eve had in the garden: the liberty they had in the presence of God. There was no sin there to cloud their vision, no shame or guilt to hinder them from coming to God. There was only one rule, one law. They could eat of any tree in the Garden and they could walk with God in the Garden. There was nothing that hindered them from going into God's presence and talking and walking with Him. There was nothing they couldn't do—except eat from one tree. We know the rest of the story. When they sinned, they hid from God, they hid and tried to cover their nakedness with fig leaves. Adam and Eve had what we are looking for, access to God and walking with Him. Sin separated Adam and Eve from that unlimited access to God. When they lost the unlimited access to God, they lost the glory of God that had covered them. They were banned from the Garden and their walks with God there, and they had to find a new way of looking at God.

We have inherited Adam's sin and add many of our own to it. That sin has fallen on us, and we have to repent of it if we are to walk with God again. After the Fall, God covered Adam and Eve's nakedness with the skin of an animal and in this gave a type and symbol of what he would do for all humankind in sending His son to be covering for us that we might walk again with God in the garden of our love. The walk with God through the Holy Spirit can be restored, and with it access to the glory of God. This might not be to the fullness of Adam's Garden experience, but we can and should know something of this walk with God and the shining of His glory upon us.

Restoration of this Garden walk with God can be accomplished only through the Lamb of God, who takes away the sin of the world. Look at the Gospel (Jesus), and you will see no law. You will see only God's salvation worked out for you in His Son, Jesus Christ. When God asks you to believe (look) on Jesus, He does so that you in looking at Jesus might be changed into His image, wearing the glory of God. Jesus is our Paschal Lamb. When the Passover lamb was slain, it was to be eaten. This would mean that the lamb would have to be skinned first before it was cooked. What was done with the skins of all those lambs, could some of them been made into clothes or coverings? "The Lord God made garments of skin for Adam and His wife and clothed them" (Gen. 3:21). This may have been the first sacrifice, made for Adam and Eve, and their dress could have been made out of the skin of that sacrifice. Figuratively God covers our nakedness with the spotless skin (righteousness) of His Son. He covers us with His glory, the glory of the one and only Son.

Notice what God does here with the sacrifice of His son: He restores to us what was lost to Adam, the vision of the face of God. In this great salvation, God shines the light of His glory—that which made Adam and Moses shine—into our hearts "displayed in the face of Christ" (II Cor. 4:6). Now we can look again at the face of God by looking at the face of Christ. As we look, we will have the dress of Adam and Moses: the righteous dress of the glory of God.

It only took one sin to separate Adam from God. Our sins are manifold, so many we can't count them. Adam's sin was to love and want something else more than he wanted God. This is the heart of our sin as well, wanting something more than we want God. It can be something good, a person we love, a job, something we have a great passion for, even a great ministry in the church. Anything that keeps us from walking with God in the cool of the day will ultimately be a sin. What wouldn't you give up to see God and be changed in the beholding?

When Moses went up on the mountain, he asked to see what Adam and Eve had seen every day, the face of God. God told Moses it was no longer possible for a human to see His face, for it would kill him. Yet in God's grace He knew there was some measure of Himself that Moses could see without dying. God orchestrated a way that Moses could see as much of God as his fallen human body could tolerate, putting him in the cleft of the rock and covering him with His hand; when he passed by, he let Moses see Him from the back. This, along with some 40 days in God's presence, was enough to make Moses shine. The shining, the transformation, came in the beholding, and this is the key. God does the same for us today by telling us to look to Jesus. Looking to Jesus is where God figuratively puts us in the cleft of the rock and has His glory pass by us. In Jesus, God has put all the fullness of the Godhead including the glory that Moses saw, and in seeing Jesus we will see the glory of God in the face of Christ Jesus. Seeing this glory in the face of Christ is what changes us and causes us to shine like Moses.

I know that when we talk about coming into the presence of God and looking upon His glory, we are talking about seeing someone who is invisible. We are talking about something that others can't see, feel, or touch. We are talking about something that is mystery. Many Christians hear this and think, "That's Greek to me," and they can't understand it. That is just the point: It is not something to understand with human reason; it is something that must be revealed by God to us. Paul prayed for the Ephesians that they might have the Spirit of wisdom and revelation that they might know God better. The process of seeking God and beholding Him will come with the gift of revelation that God gives by His Spirit. If you ask as Moses did, "Lord show me your glory," he will answer you. The glory we will see here on earth will be the down payment of the fullness of the glory of God we will see one day in Heaven. The Holy Spirit will lead you to a place where you can stand in the cleft of the rock and see God as Moses did. The glory of God we will see will be in the face of Christ, when we look unto Jesus.

We tend to think of our Christianity in terms of what we do instead of what God does. In our humanness we think our actions are responsible for making the changes in our lives, but is it so? We think of God-given righteousness (sanctification) as a reward for our obedience. If I keep the law, I will be righteous. What if the Christian life is more like sunbathing than keeping a set of laws? What did Adam and Moses do to shine? They came into the presence of God and stayed there and wore the garments of His glory.

What do you do when you sunbathe or get a tan? You must get to a place where the sun will shine on you; you uncover yourself, lie down, and receive the light of the sun, which has a transformative effect on your skin, something we call a tan. You must remain in the light of the sun long enough for it to have the desired effect on your body. If you don't return to the sun again and again, your tan will fade; you will lose the effect of the sun. It is the same for the Christian: We come into the light of the Son, and bath in the light of His glory, which transforms us into His image. Sunbathing is very relaxing because there is nothing I have to do but sit in the warmth and light of the sun. It's very difficult to believe that I am transformed or made righteous by simply coming into God's presence and sitting in the light of the Son. The Son does the work. If we avoid Jesus, our spiritual tan, our glory, will fade. Our Christianity is not so much what we do but what He does in shining the light of His glory upon us, not so much what we do as where we are in proximity to God. Learning how to come into the presence of God and bathe in His glory will be fundamental to your transformation. Can you come with your spiritual beach towel, lie down, and let your soul drink the sunshine of God? Can you learn to relax and bathe in the light, love, and glory of God? I want you to think about your Christian life more like sunbathing than as an adherence to a set of rules.

Notice what is being understood here: It is not by trying to keep the law that we are transformed or made to shine, not by trying to be better, not even by trying to love God more that we are changed. It is by sitting in the life-giving rays of God's glory that one is made to shine. It is so easy that it seems impossible to us, for there is nothing for me to do but look and live, to sit in His presence and soak in the light and love of His glory and be healed.

The Gospel is the first step back to that original covering in the Garden, for the promise and fulfillment of the Gospel is that one day we will be glorified and inherit our parents' original clothing. Like Adam and Eve, we will shine with the reflected glory of God, and this will become our permanent dress in Heaven. Where there is a promise with God, there is a down payment, a deposit, of that which is to come. In salvation God shines the light of His glory into our hearts in the face of Christ Jesus. This is done by giving us His deposit, the Holy Spirit. Our work now is to walk with God the Holy Spirit in the cool of the day and look at Him, and in the looking we are changed into His image. This change on earth can be "in ever-increasing measure" (II Cor. 3:18) as we with unveiled faces behold His glory. Our great business is to look at Jesus, to remain in His presence, to remain in His love, gazing upon the beauty of the Lord all the days of our lives. Here is where the transformation of the Christian happens, in His presence, in the light of His glory. Spiritual Son-bathing is unknown to many who are too busy to come into the presence of God and let Him shine on them. We are busy trying to be better Christians, trying by principles to improve our lives. We are so busy trying to be good for God we don't have time to come into His presence. We are so busy with our ministries, saving the world, we don't find time to come into God's presence and simply bathe in the light of His glory.

Ministry can be a distraction from a life of intimacy with God. We can confuse ministry and relationship with God, thinking they are the same thing. David Wilkerson said in a message in Times Square Church that the demands of ministry had interfered with His times of worship with Christ. Some of us are so busy with Kingdom work we don't have time for the King. Repent, return to Him, or He will remove our lampstand as he said in Revelation 2:5. See your devotions—time spent with God—as the great work of the day, your great business, your first business being to stop and stand in His glory and love.

If your devotions have become a chore you have to get done before you start the real work of the day, you don't understand what your real work is. Your real work is to be loved by God and to remain in that love. Remaining in the love and presence of God is where He shines His glory into our hearts. Part of that glory is God's love, which He also pours into our hearts. With the love given by God, we may love Him and then our neighbors as well. We will want to be with Him and will go to the secret place for our rendezvous. When you come to love Him, the act of being with Him is transformative; we are transformed into the image of Christ and covered with His glory and go forward with Him to the work He wants us to do. Is your great labor, your great business, seeking, beholding, talking, and listening to the living Christ? Is it standing at attention by His throne waiting for a command that may not come for days? Have you discovered the glory of wearing His livery and waiting for Him to speak? Have you discovered the wonder of looking upon the most beautiful person in the universe and being filled with the thrill and wonder of this sight? If not, you may not understand what your true calling is. Our devotional life is not something to get done so we can do some real work; it is the real work, the great business. If this business is done right, with the full heart, you will be covered with glory, and your baskets will be filled with fruit. You will dance as wagons full of the harvest are brought to the Lord of harvest.

This is the great business, daily focusing all our mind and heart and soul on the beauty of God and communing with Him, learning to be intimate with Him, learning what it means to have a real relationship with this living person, learning what a treasure it is to have a friend like Him. Being in God's presence is what makes us glow. God's presence is the place where we are changed by beholding God. The great men of the faith had this in common: They attended the Lord; they entered His courts and spent time in His presence. They knew this time with God was necessary, not optional. Men who don't spend time in the presence of Christ will not have the borrowed glow. They will not have the power they need for the work God has given them to do.

John Bunyan writes of Christians in *The Pilgrim's Progress*, "Now, Pilgrim rose up each morning, a great while before day, that he might keep trysts with His King. Lo, he felt deep the need to do this: for if he came to such a pother in caring for the King's business, that no time remained to gaze upon the King's face, the joy of His salvation did fade away." Let nothing keep you from your appointed "trysts" with the King of glory. Pastor, teacher, elder, church leader, is doing the King's business keeping us from spending time with God, gazing upon His face? Dwight Moody may have been one of the busiest men on the planet in his day, yet he had to have two hours a day with his Lord. Make your most important business gazing on the King's face, and from that gazing go out and shine that light on a world lost in darkness.

Ask what Moses asked of God. Moses said, "If I have found favor in your eyes, teach me your ways so I may know you" (Ex. 13:33). The cry of the Christian's heart should be, "I want to know you, God!" The answer to that prayer is that you will know God. Then Moses said, "Show me your glory." Notice the grace with which God deals with Moses to let him see something of God's glory. "Teach me your ways" and "show me your glory" are prayer request that you hardly ever hear today. Make them yours. "His face was radiant because he had spoken with the Lord" (Ex. 34:29). It is our privilege to speak with the same Lord. Let's speak to Him until we are shining. When we study the Word of God, His Spirit comes and declares His name in our presence. When we study the Word, the Spirit comes and reveals Christ to us from every page. We gaze upon Christ when we look for more revelation of Him in the Scriptures. This is God's way of revealing Himself to us today. Open the Word every day and listen as God reveals His Son to you as He proclaims His name to you. Those who know what it means to gaze on the Lord know something of God proclaiming His name to them by the Spirit. This name touching our ears is one of the ways we behold Jesus and God transforms us into His image and gives us the glow of glory.

The Christian who glows with God's glory has discovered that his or her great need is God Himself. That person comes to Him and imbibes His presence, His glory, and in this way participates in the divine nature. This is what changes and empowers us to do His will. We are changed by beholding. When was the last time you looked at God or just bathed in the light of glory of the Son, and felt the warmth of His fire near you? All things for the Christian fall short of the wonder of gazing upon the King. How many times does He call us to come? He loves for His children to come to Him. He loves like no other, and His love draws us to Himself. In that drawing we are changed. In this nearness to God our heart begins to boil, producing the steam of love that drives us to worship Him and do His will.

God has slain His Son and covered us with the skin of His spotless lamb. He has made us righteous, and now, dressed in this livery, we can come to His throne to find grace and mercy in a time of need. We are told that now we can come with confidence, no longer in our nakedness but dressed in the livery of the court of heaven, the glory of God. True devotions bring us to the place where God will cause all His goodness to pass in front of us, changing us as He does. The goodness of God leads a man to repentance, and true repentance leads a man back to God to gaze upon His glory. It is a place where He will declare His name and reveal His glory to us. In God's presence, His glory becomes our glory. We are changed by beholding and not by working. The unintended consequence of coming to God and standing in God's presence is shining like He does with the light of His glory.

It has been my privilege to know some godly women of prayer. Many of these have a glow about them, a strange beauty. This is not the sensual beauty of the world, a beauty of paint to be put on; it is an alien beauty, one not of this world. A friend of mine called it the "adorning divine." This adorning is the dress of those who have been much in the presence of God. You might call it the glow of holiness, or a borrowed glow. Something happens to the appearance of those who spend much time with God. His glory is reflected on their faces and in their hearts. In the presence of God their attitudes change, and their demeanors are tempered. People could tell that the disciples had been with Jesus, and they will be able to tell when you have been much with the Lord.

In one of the churches that I pastored, it was our custom to have a prayer retreat every year, one for the men and then one for the women. We would get away to quiet place for a couple days to pray and draw near to God. After the prayer retreat, I would have some wives tell me that their husbands were different when they came home. This happened again almost every time we had the retreat. What was happening? Why would they say this of their men? I concluded that these men had been changed by being in the presence of God. We didn't teach men how to be better husbands at these retreats; we had very little teaching at all. Men were being changed by coming into the presence of God, by meeting with God, and their wives noticed and liked the change. They were being changed by beholding.

Many of us are like Adam, hiding from God. Is it any wonder that we have so little power in the Church today or so little of God's reflected glory? If your devotional life is nonexistent, so is your spiritual life. Presenting yourself to God is coming to a spiritual geographical location to meet with a living person. Coming to this meeting place will be the beginning, middle, and end of your spiritual life.

We present ourselves to God not only for inspection but for instruction. Moses received not only the Ten Commandments but the whole law. Presenting yourself to God allows you the pleasure of His company and presence. It is where we see the greatness of our commander and glow in the light of His glory. In God's presence we are changed into His image. Somehow some of His fame falls on us and we carry what should belong only to Him. How can it be that the God of glory would share His fame and glory with us? Oh, what a God, what a Savior! As it was with Moses, so shall it be with us. Our personal devotions will be Sinai for us, the place we will meet with God, hear the law, and behold what we can of God without dying. It will be a place where we changed in ever-increasing measure into the image of Jesus.

When we come into God's presence, all other activities and our conversations with people need to stop. Perhaps you have had an important appointment with someone, a company president or the owner of a large company. The appointment is important, so you dress up and prepare yourself for this meeting. You wash and then dress appropriately for the station or office of the one you are meeting. You may bring something with you to write down what is said. Important meetings have important conversations; they need to be remembered. Everything will be set aside for this appointment. Anything that distracts or gets in the way of meeting with God must go. Presenting yourself to someone requires a place and a time. We must prioritize who we want to be with and when. If God is the most important person in universe, shouldn't we think our meeting with Him is the most important meeting of the day and of our lives? Meeting with God should be the highest honor and greatest glory of our lives.

Finally, we must listen to the commands of God and respond, "For those who are led by the Spirit of God are sons of God" (Rom. 8:14). Moses listened and remembered what God said to Him, and brought it all down from that meeting. Obedience gets us into the proper dress and the proper spiritual geographical location where we can present ourselves to God and he can present or manifest Himself to us. This is where we commune with God face-to-face as Moses did on the mountain and hear what the Lord has to say. Our first obedience is to come to God and be with Him and look upon His glory. From this will come all other obedience to other commands and laws but only after we have obeyed the first.

I believe one of the greatest tragedies of our day is that many Christians do not present themselves to the Lord. They do not see devotional times with the Lord as necessary to spiritual life, so they don't come to God, and therefore they are not changed, nor do they reflect His glory. Many Christians end up living as dead men, without the power of God coursing through their being. Because they are not presenting themselves to God nor seeking Him with all their hearts, they know little or nothing of His manifest presence, nor do they experience God. For many Christians, God is not real. We do not see Him in those devotional times come down in the cloud and stand with us, because we don't go to be with Him, and we are not expecting Him, and we are not asking Him to come. Nothing changes us more as human beings than when we find ourselves in the very presence of God. We must make it our habit to "present ourselves to God." We'll talk more of devotions in a later chapter.

For my youngest son's wedding, he took us to his tailor so we could have a couple of suits cut for the wedding. I was to perform the wedding ceremony, and he of course was the groom. I remember we took all the measurements and tried on several styles of suits. There was the day when the suit was finished, and they handed it to me. They pointed to a room and said I could put it on in there. I went in and took off the old common clothes and put on the best suit I would ever wear. I came out standing a little taller, feeling more confident. When I opened the coat and looked inside, there was a label telling who had made the suit. I thought later, "This is what the secret place is like, a changing room where we take off the old, soiled clothes and put on the fine suit of His righteousness. When we walk out, we will be dressed in His glorious garment. Pulling open the coat of this dress, we see a label that says, "hand-made by the King of kings and paid for with the blood of the Lamb."

In the early 20th century, John Nelson Hyde, the son of an Illinois Presbyterian minister, felt led to begin his lifetime missionary endeavor in the Punjab, in India, now Pakistan. "To the dismay of mission authorities, he devoted most of his time to Bible study rather than language study, displaying the withdrawn intensity of a visionary rather than the engaging demeanor of the traditional missionary" (Richard Klein, *Profiles in Prayer: Praying John Hyde*). John Hyde and others decided there was need of an annual conference for Bible study, prayer, and spiritual renewal. The first conference was held at Sialkot in 1904. Prior to this first conference, Hyde and a friend, Peterson, tarried in prayer one whole month before the opening date. Turner, another friend, joined them for the last 21 days. These three men prayed and praised God for a mighty outpouring of His Spirit. The power of God was definitely on those conventions. One man writing of that first convention said, "I remember how the little company prostrated themselves on the mats on their faces in the Oriental manner, and then how for a long time, how long I do not know, man after man rose to his feet to pray; there was such a confession of sin as most of us had never heard before, and such crying out to God for mercy and help. It was very late that night when the little gathering broke up, and some of us know definitely of several lives that were wholly transformed through the influence of that meeting" (*Praying Hyde*, edited by Captain E.G. Carre). Here was revival falling on the missionaries of the Punjab. This revival worked its way into the society as John and others prayed for one soul a day, then two souls a day, then three, and then four. These men would see the answer to their prayer, and the souls they were asking God about would come into the Kingdom. John was nicknamed Praying Hyde; what a nickname to have! Sialkot became prayed-over ground; it would be different for years. Back in the 80s, when I was in Bible school, one of our instructors told us that missionaries who had been to Sialkot told him that that area in the Punjab was still different. Such was the power of God's touch.

John Hyde and his friends mimicked what happened to Moses when he went to the mountain to be with God 40 days and 40 nights. Though their faces did not glow like Moses's did, they were empowered by the Holy Spirit and had the adorning divine. Hyde and friends went up their Sinai for 30 days and stood in the presence of God, and they returned with their hearts aglow with the reflected glory of God. This touch of God was manifest in the power they saw in their meetings. Very few ministers begin their ministries by seeking God for 30 days. Many of our leaders have yet to learn that we are changed and empowered by beholding. What pastor would not be improved by spending 40 days alone with God?

Learning to come into God's presence and behold Him will be the beginning of turning our attention away from ourselves. Much of our teaching in the Church today is focused on what the individual is to do and not on what Christ has already done. We are teaching our people how they can be better Christians, how they can be better parents or spouses. This self-focus is dangerous and can be misleading, a self-help teaching informed by the self-righteous idea that if you simply teach someone what to do, they will have the means within themselves to do it. Many Christians are frustrated with their spiritual lives; finding the knowledge of what to do provides no power to do it. We have been asked to look in the wrong direction, to look at ourselves and not at Christ.

We have made the faith life something we do instead of everything He does. We don't see faith as a glance at Jesus that heals us and empowers us for service. The true faith life is a life of dwelling in the house of the Lord and gazing on His beauty all the days of our lives. Could it be that much of what we doing for God today we are doing without the Holy Spirit? Are we doing great works without the Holy Spirit in America?

Moses was the governor of a nation of nearly a million souls. Think of the requests that he might have brought to God. Now listen to what he asks of God. First Moses says, "If I have found favor in your eyes, teach me your ways so I may know you and continue to find favor with you" (Ex. 33:13). Moses didn't ask to be a better counselor or judge; he asked to know God, and in knowing God he had all he needed to do the rest. Is this what you are asking God for, or is your prayer list filled with the cares and material things of this world? God responds to Moses and says, "I will do the very thing you have asked because I am pleased with you and I know you by name" (Ex. 33:17). You would think this would've been enough, but not for Moses. Moses pushes the envelope by asking one more thing. "Now show me your glory" (Ex. 33:18). To see the glory of God is everything for the Christian, and this will be our eternal heritage.

How does God transfer His power to us so we may live godly lives? We often think that the power comes to us as we by faith obey some command from God. This is true, but not in the way most of us think. Our logic goes something like this: We have a weakness or a need in our character, so we go to God and ask that it might be addressed: "God, give me power over this sin or help me to love this impossible person." We ask, still looking at the weakness, watching to see if the power comes and we are changed. Many times, we wait and wait and nothing happens, so we get depressed. What if I don't ask for some change in me? What if I ask to see God, to see Jesus, His only Son? What if in the seeing of Jesus I discover that without thinking about my weakness or asking for it to change, I have been made strong in that area? What if our first obedience is to love God and go be with Him? Instead of watching for the weakness and sin to end in your life, look at the one who is all power. You will find the weaknesses of your life are healed in the looking at Jesus.

What if the means of receiving that power was not so much in the asking but was in looking upon Jesus, gazing on the glory of God? What if the obedience God calls us to is to behold the Lamb of God who takes away the sin of the world. Think what a relief this would be, not looking at our frailties and needs but looking at the fullness and sufficiency of Christ. Looking at Jesus frees us from looking to self and our failures. It is in the beholding of God that His glory is being shone into our hearts, and with the glory comes the power we will need to live godly lives in Christ Jesus. God's glory is His essence; it is who God is. When His glory is transferred, so are His nature, character, and power. The shining of this glory is what transforms. When Jesus showed Paul something of His glory on the road to Damascus, Paul was never the same again. He was transformed by the light of Christ's glory.

Adam, Eve, and Moses are types of what God would have for us. He wants us to be those who come regularly into God's presence and reflect His glory, becoming like Him. Our call is to draw near to God, remove our sandals and worship, and then with listening ears to hear the King of kings speak words of love, grace, and mercy.

Recently I received a fancy Swiss watch as a present from someone I love very much. It has a glow-in-the-dark dial. When it first came out of the box, it didn't glow in the dark. I didn't think much about this until one day, living in Arizona, I had it out in the bright sun. I brought it back into the house, and even though it was still daylight I could see that the watch was glowing brightly. I hadn't noticed the glowing before because I had not had it out in the sunlight. This reminded me that this is God's way with His children, to get them into the light of His glory and then make them shine. In order for us to continue to shine we must return to the light of the Son again and again.

Chapter 3

CHANGED BY BEHOLDING

"But we all, with open face beholding as in a glass the glory of the Lord, are changed into the same image from glory to glory, even as by the Spirit of the Lord."
(II Cor. 3:18, KJV)

WHEN I WAS a child, cereal companies would put "prizes" inside the box of cereal. The prizes would be well-advertised on the outside of the box, probably to get children to pester parents into buying the cereal. From time to time, prize-filled cereal boxes found their way to our home. With settling, the prize would usually be at the very bottom of the cereal box. Unable to wait for all the cereal to be eaten, I would dig through the cereal to find the prize buried at the bottom of the box.

One prize I found buried in cereal box was a plastic ring that was supposed to glow in the dark. As soon as I retrieved the ring, I tested its luminosity by finding a dark place where we could see if the ring glowed. I discovered that fresh out of the box the ring did not glow because it had not seen the light of the sun for some time. I took the ring into the sun for a few minutes and then returned it to the dark place, where I found the ring glowed brightly. The ring had no light of its own; it could only absorb light from the sun and release it back. It was dependent on an outside source to give it light. Once it had soaked up enough of the sun, it would glow brightly in the dark. Kept from the sun, the light of the ring would begin to fade until there was no glow at all.

Christian, we are like God's glow-in-the-dark ring. He collects us from all over the world. He draws us into His presence to shine His glory on us, which causes us to glow. When we say "glow," we refer to the transformative work of God to make us righteous, accomplished by shining the light of His glory into our hearts in the face of Christ Jesus. He then set us out in a dark world to draw men and women out of the darkness and into His light. Like that glow-in-the-dark ring, we must be brought back into the light of His glory again and again or we grow dark. If we don't stay in the light of His countenance regularly, our light will begin to fade and we will grow dark. We are those unique creations that God calls into His presence that He might shine on us, and into us, that we might absorb and reflect His glory. This means we will be transformed by that glory, not just to shine, but to be empowered with the life of Christ to live as Christ in this world. This process of coming to be with God and getting into the light of His glory and then shining with His glory must be something we do habitually.

The Christians I have known who reflected much of the glory of God are those who have spent much time in the presence of God, in prayer. There seems to be a direct correlation between the time spent in His presence and the brightness of our shining with His glory and beauty. God shines the light of glory upon those who come into His presence, and they seem to have a glow about them. God's glory is His very essence, what He seems like, in that glory we have all we need for a life of godliness. In God's glory as in Christ are hidden all the treasures of wisdom and knowledge (Col. 2:3). When this light of His glory falls on individuals, they are changed into His image. We too will shine like Adam or Moses when we have seen the King's face. Therefore those who are much in prayer, much in the presence of God, are some of the most beautiful Christians. A life of prayer is one of making Christ our first ministry. What any minister of the Gospel needs most is to be conformed to the image of Christ. "According as His divine power hath given us all things that pertain unto life and godliness, through the knowledge of Him that hath called us to glory and virtue" (II Pet. 1:3). Prayer will become a place of seeing more than a place of asking. "When can I go and meet with God?" (Ps. 42:2). Being in God's presence is the place of transformation, not so much because we ask God to change us, but because the very act of prayer is a step of faith into the presence of God, and being in His presence, with His glory shining on us, is the place of transformation. Spending time in God's presence via the secret place of communion is often overlooked and bypassed, especially when we get busy doing ministry for God. Slowly the glory on us begins to fade, and like that glow-in-the-dark ring I found in the cereal box, we grow dark. This is the first abiding principle: behold and be transformed. To grow you must continue to look.

The way we educate and counsel people today works against Christians by making them think their obedience to the rules or the counselors' suggestions is the way to transformation. Our secular education system works the same way, making us the center of our learning and becoming. This system leaves us alone with the rules of education and our strength and ability to learn and apply them. It teaches us principles or rules to live by, the keeping of which will bring us success. We can then take these principles of learning and build a life, accomplishing our goals, dreams, and desires. All of this can be done without God.

We are told that knowledge is power, so we look to our knowledge as the source of our power to change. If we have the right knowledge, we can transform ourselves into any image we want. This may be the image of a doctor, lawyer, or businessman, or even a Christian minister. There is little difference between our secular education system and our Christian schools, seminaries, and pulpits today. Our preachers and teachers are trained to acquire knowledge and spit it back on tests and papers. If you get enough answers right, you can obtain a degree. In many places, if you want to be a minister you only have to get the degree. With certain churches and denominations, if you don't have a doctorate, you won't be the pastor of a particular church. This puts pressure on pastors to get as much education as they possibly can and causes many to feel deficient without it. We need men who have been much with God and not necessarily so much with the seminary or university. Knowledge in the Christian life is not power; the knowledge of God is power. Growing in the grace and knowledge of God, coming into His presence, is where we will find that power released for us and for others. There is much we might learn in these schools, but if the personal knowledge of God is not the priority, there may be no power to transform the individual into the image of Christ and therefore no power in the pulpit when that person preaches. Being removed from the power and presence of God will not advance the Kingdom of God. Exchanging the knowledge of God for the knowledge of language and ministry practices is not what the Church needs today. The early Church sought men filled the Holy Spirit, not men with shelves filled with university degrees. Without knowing Christ, I can get the best education any Christian college or seminary can give, but I can't get the transforming glory of Christ apart from Him. Therefore some Christian schools, losing the transforming power of Christ, have gone liberal because they have become man-centered and not God-centered. God's method of true education is to get men and woman to simply look at His Son. God doesn't teach some principle to apply; He gives you a vision of His Son by the Holy Spirit, and in looking at Him you are changed. Fix your eyes upon Jesus.

"How many break their brains, and waste their spirits, in studying arts and sciences, things in comparison of no value? Whereas Paul determined not to know anything but Jesus Christ. To know Christ in every point, weather in birth, or life, or death, is saving knowledge. Oh, stand not upon cost, whether pains or study, tears or prayers, peace or wealth, goods or name, life or liberty; sell all for this Pearl. Christ is of that worth that thou canst never over-buy Him, though thou gavest thyself and all the world for Him. The study of Christ is the study of studies; the knowledge of Christ is the knowledge of everything that is necessary, either for this world, or for the world to come. Oh, study Christ in every of the aforesaid respects" (Isaac Ambrose, *Looking Unto Jesus*). Make Christ your main business and your main study; keep your eyes on Him; behold Him, meditate on Him, observe Him again and again, and you will see that you are changed and have power to advance the Kingdom of God.

If I can get an education without the help of Christ, I can build a ministry or church the same way. Without meaning to, we may be teaching people to become self-reliant, to lean on the powers of their own minds. Christian preachers and teachers trained by these schools teach others the way they were taught. They were taught the Bible and the doctrines of the faith, what we call theology. This is what they then teach us. Many of these have knowledge, even good knowledge, but it is not the knowledge of God through a personal relationship. When these men speak from the pulpit, they can give only what they have learned. If that knowledge is of a book and not a person, they may not be pointing you to Christ in their teaching and preaching. Messages will end up being "Do this and live" instead of "Know this person and live." They were taught how to give a sermon or organize a church budget, so they teach what they know. What we are left with are the doctrines they learned, which often come across to us as a set of rules or principles for living a successful Christian life. Without intending to, many end up preaching the law, and the law has no power to save or transform. If our preaching or teaching leaves our students with nothing but the law, we are leading them down the path of self-righteousness. This is the path to legalism, though some of the churches preaching this way would never think they are being legalistic. "No one will be declared righteous in His sight by observing the law" (Rom. 3:20). If the preacher's sermon ends with the law, all he is doing is tying up bundles of burdens and placing them on the shoulders of His people. Old habits of learning and teaching are hard to break.

Some of the teaching from our pulpits sounds like an Alcoholic Anonymous 12-step program; some ministers are actually teaching 12-step programs to recover one's Christian life: three steps to being a better father, four points on how to pray better, and so forth. This puts the focus on us and what we do or don't do. Leaving Christians with laws and principles makes them think that they can keep the law or carry out the principles. We think, "If I just keep the law or principles, I will have the reward of being transformed into what Christ wants me to be. If I keep the laws and principles long enough throughout my life, I will have added rewards in Heaven." When this is how we are being taught, it is only natural that we would be fascinated with the churches' self-help gurus who teach "Do this and live." When we look at our Christian bookstores, we see a never-ending supply of books that read like self-help motivational books. Famous people write books on how they came to Christ and then became successful and tell the steps they took to accomplish their success. We listen because we want to be successes—Christian successes. Some of these men and women have a program or a system they are selling to the Church through books and seminars, some of which can be very lucrative. What if this kind of teaching has no power to transform? We may be turning our people into humanists, encouraging them to use the power within to apply the principles laid out in some message or book as a way to a better life.

During my lifetime I have been to more than my share of seminars and training classes on how to live the Christian life or have a more effective ministry. We have assumed that teaching someone what to do is enough: Now, armed with the steps to success, they will apply them and reach their goal. The only difference between secular teaching and much religious teaching today is that the religious teaching will include a prayer to Jesus for help or blessing. We are not sure just how or when God will help us. With much of the teaching we receive today, we can implement it without God's help and often do. We tell ourselves, "God helps those who help themselves." The thought *I can do this* or *I can become just like the person I read about* is only natural but leads us to the wrong conclusion, especially in the Christian life. Self-motivation, a can-do spirit, or telling yourself to get 'er done is not what Jesus has for you. We may take up the Nike shoe company slogan—"Just do it!"—as our own, and without intending to, we may be turning into evangelical humanists, depending on self-effort or human power. Teaching laws and principles without the Gospel has no power to save, no power to assist us in keeping the law. If we keep looking at the law or principles alone, we'll end up defeated and frustrated or self-righteous and proud. So how do we change? How are we transformed into the image of Jesus Christ? Through hearing and obeying the law? Through the practice of the spiritual disciplines of the Christian life? By obedience to the commands of Christ? How then am I changed, empowered, and transformed into the image of Christ?

Several years ago, I taught a course on worship. One of the books we used along with the Bible was *Gospel Worship*, by Jeremiah Burroughs. Burroughs was Puritan of renown, so loved and honored by other Puritans that they saw to the publication of many of his sermons after his death. The book was a collection of 14 sermons on Leviticus 10:3. Leviticus 10 records the story of Nadab and Abihu, Aaron's sons, offering strange fire before the Lord. They took unauthorized fire, perhaps from their own campfires, put it in their censers, and mixed it with incense and offered it before the Lord. When they offered this incense mixed with strange fire, God was offended, and fire came out from the presence of God and killed them. God was making a statement about human effort in coming to Him. I believe the idea of teaching principles and rules for living apart from Christ is offering strange fire to God like Nadab and Abihu. Many in the Church are choosing the wrong fire to offer to God, and it has had devastating consequences on the Church. There is a right way and wrong way to come to God. The important thing is coming to God the right way.

Strange fire would have been any fire that didn't originate with God. The altar of God was like a giant grill. The sacrifices that were offered there were cooked; some were eaten and others burned up completely. When the tabernacle was built and ready for use, God didn't want men to start the fire on the altar, so He did it Himself by sending fire from heaven. Once God had lit the fire on the altar, He commanded men to tend it in such a way that the fire on the altar would never go out. Any fire used in the censers by the priest was to be taken from that altar. Nadab and Abihu's disobedience was that they found and used a man-made fire, and it cost them their lives. God was making the point that you don't come to Him in your own strength, with your own good ideas, or even your own obedience to the law. You come the way He says, with the provision He has made, in this case with the fire from heaven. We don't come to God with our own good ideas; we don't come with our great learning; we come with the fire from Heaven—the Holy Spirit—and this fire, glory, is gained by looking into the face of Christ Jesus. "The god of this age has blinded the minds of unbelievers, so that they cannot see the light of the Gospel that displays the glory of Christ, who is the image of God. For what we preach is not ourselves, but Jesus Christ as Lord, and ourselves as your servants for Jesus' sake. For God, who said, 'Let light shine out of darkness,' made His light shine in our hearts to give us the light of the knowledge of God's glory displayed in the face of Christ" (II Cor. 4:4–6). The light of the Gospel displays the glory of Christ. God shines His light into our hearts—revelation—by having us look at the face of Christ. We are changed by beholding.

If I am changed by beholding Jesus, then I need to put a priority on worship and beholding Jesus, by making this the first law I obey. This may sound heretical to you because many of us have been raised in law-oriented churches. Notice what Paul adds when talking about seeing the glory of God in the face of Jesus: "For what we preach is not ourselves, but Jesus Christ as Lord." Paul isn't preaching rules and principles to live by; he's preaching Christ. It isn't that I don't obey, it's that my first obedience is to look to Christ. In my looking, I am strengthened and transformed into His image. Now I am free and empowered to obey God's law. Notice that my focus stays on Jesus, not on the law, and the power comes by looking at Jesus and not by looking at the law. For there is no power in the law to save. "For what the law was powerless to do, God did by sending His Son" (Rom. 8:3–4). The power is in Christ alone. God sends you His Son by the Holy Spirit that you might be in a love relationship with Him; and in that relationship, in beholding the one you love, the power of God is transferred from Him to you. Looking at Christ, like looking at the bronze serpent in the wilderness, will be the means by which we appropriate His power and His life to live the Christian life. Focusing on the law frustrates, for no power comes with the law for me to keep it. Legalism, self-righteousness, makes the law the savior. In this scenario, keeping or breaking of the law is all-important, and the focus on the law may distract us from looking at Christ. Jesus told the Pharisees, "You study the Scriptures diligently because you think that in them you have eternal life. These are the very Scriptures that testify about me, yet you refuse to come to me to have life" (John 5:39). The Scriptures were revealing Jesus and the Pharisees could only see the law.

If you are a Christian, there is good chance you are in a Bible study or have been. There is no shortage of Bible studies in our Christian community; we are known for our Bible studies. In our Bible studies we study books of the Bible and discover authorship, history, and background of that book of the Bible. We have studies where we take a Bible character like David and study what the Word says about him. We have Bible studies on the last times and prophecy to the point that what we think about it has divided the Church at times. I dare say in our Bible studies we could be accused by Christ of diligently studying the Scriptures to find eternal life and refuse to come to Christ to have life. Seeing the law, knowing the law, even living the law outwardly will not transform our hearts; only coming to Jesus, beholding Jesus will we find and have life in Him.

I believe what Paul is saying in II Corinthians 3:18 is the answer to how one is transformed into the image of Jesus: "But we all, with open face beholding as in a glass the glory of the Lord, are changed into the same image from glory to glory, even as by the Spirit of the Lord" (II Cor. 3:18, KJV). We are changed by beholding the glory of the Lord. Remember the bronze serpent in the wilderness.

What is the great truth found in II Corinthians 3:18? Paul, contrasting the Old Covenant with the New, says that the Old Covenant—the law—is like a veil over the Jews' faces blocking the view of Christ. Just like the veil that Moses wore blocked the view of God's glory on His face from the Israelites, so the law blocks our view of the glory of God in the face of Jesus. "But their minds were made dull, for to this day the same veil remains when the old covenant is read" (II Cor. 3:14). Notice that the law, the Old Covenant, is called a veil, something that blocks one's sight of Jesus. Much of our preaching today is of the law, principles to live by, so much so that the very sight of Christ is veiled, and we see only the law, which can't help us. The law brought death and condemnation; more than this, it makes the mind dull and is a veil to those who are under it. That veil is removed by looking at Christ, by preaching Christ, by preaching the light of the Gospel.

If Christ is not the focus of our preaching, we may be holding up the law as the means to our transformation. Paul says this kind of teaching and preaching will dull the minds and veil the hearts of our people to seeing Christ. When we look at Christ, this veil is taken away; now we with unveiled faces can look at Jesus, and when we look, we are changed in ever-increasing measure into His likeness, changed not by keeping the law, worrying about the law, testing ourselves against the law, but by looking at Christ. What Paul is saying is that we are changed by beholding, just like the Israelites looked at the bronze serpent in the wilderness and were healed. Jeremiah Burroughs said, "When a gracious heart is in the way of God's worship, it finds the very duty of the worship of God to be strength to it and so fits it for another duty" (*Gospel Worship*, Jeremiah Burroughs) In worship we are beholding Jesus and describing back to Him what we see. The worship is our personal conversation with the living Christ. It is part of our personal relationship with Him, part of our looking at Him, and in this we are changed. This will be a new paradigm for many Christians.

John Piper, speaking at the 2009 conference of the American Association of Christian Counselors on the subject "Beholding Glory and Becoming Whole," had this to say about II Corinthians 3:18: "This is probably one of the most important verses in the New Testament from my understanding about how people change…. The link between the receiving of the life-changing grace and the seeing of the divine glory is the seeing…. It is as if a beam of divine glory shines down into our hearts, and along that beam of seeing comes grace upon grace; there isn't another channel." What Piper is saying is that the means by which God applies His grace to us, His power to us, is by shining the light of His glory on us, and as we see it, we are transformed by the grace that flows through the awesome glory of God. In the glory of God is the grace and power that transforms the individual. We are changed by beholding the glory of God in the face of Jesus. Look at Jesus and live. Therefore learning how to look on Jesus, to worship Jesus, is crucial. Worship is a form of looking, beholding, the Lamb of God, and in the looking comes the transformational power of God.

Paul's apostleship was often in question. Was he really an apostle of Jesus Christ? He answers the question by saying, "Do we need letters of recommendation to you? You yourselves are our letter, written on your hearts, known and read by everybody, written not with ink but with a Spirit of the living God not on tablets of stone but on tablets of human hearts" (II Cor. 3:2–3). Paul is contrasting the writing of human beings with the writing of the Holy Spirit, making a clear distinction between the letter of the law and the letter written by the Holy Spirit on the hearts of men. He makes this same distinction between the law, the Old Covenant, and the New Covenant; one was written by men with ink, the other written by the Holy Spirit on the hearts of men. When we come into God's presence to behold Him, God shines the light of His glory on us and into us, transforming us into His image. In shining His glory, the Holy Spirit comes and writes on our hearts with the ink of His divine glory, His holiness, which is seen in the law. By His writing, the law of God becomes real in our lives. What he writes is obedience to the law as we gaze on Him. Thus we become the handwritten law of God: Just as he wrote that same law on stone with His finger, He now writes it on our hearts, making us the law he writes. He does this when we look on Jesus, His Son. The writing and the changing come in the looking.

The fact that Paul is speaking about the Holy Spirit in the same context as being changed by beholding in II Corinthians 3:18 is significant. We struggle with the concept of the Holy Spirit, and our thinking about Him can be strange at times. When we consider Him, our minds go to thoughts of how to be filled with the Spirit and what that means. There is confusion in understanding the filling of the Holy Spirit. We are taught that when we get saved we are filled with the Holy Spirit. Some will add that we have all the Holy Spirit we will ever get and that we need nothing more of Him. What we have to work out is how the power of the Spirit becomes ours. We are filled with the Spirit when we are saved but struggle with sin and are often taught there are other fillings to be had. These may be called a second filling or second blessing, a baptism of the Holy Spirit, or an anointing. These may be marked with speaking in tongues or demonstrations of power. If the first outpouring of power came with an event—salvation—then new reviving power must come by a second or third event, which we struggle to give names to. We are taught to ask for the Holy Spirit to initiate that reception of the Holy Spirit and power. What if the power comes through beholding? What if one is filled by the Spirit by beholding Jesus?

How do we teach one to be filled with the Holy Spirit? We teach we are filled by the Holy Spirit by faith. First, we must sincerely desire to be filled with the Holy Spirit. Second, we must confess our sins. Third, we should present every area of our lives to God. Fourth, by faith we must claim the fullness of the Holy Spirit by response to His command to be filled and His promise to give us anything that is in accordance with His will. Finally, we must express that faith in the form of a prayer: "God, give me your Holy Spirit." We have put a form to it, and this form may vary in different denominations or churches. We are not saying these things are wrong in themselves but much of this can be done by keeping my thoughts on myself. What is not said—and this is where we want to stand on our heads and look at this upside down—is "Go and behold Jesus." Could it be the filling of the Holy Spirit and being changed by beholding Jesus are the same thing?

In the first part of II Corinthians chapter three Paul contrast the Old Covenant with the New Covenant. He has been contrasting the law written with man's ink (Old Covenant) with one now written by the Holy Spirit on the hearts of men. The Old Covenant came with glory but one that was fading. "Will not the ministry of the Spirit be even more glorious?" (II Cor. 3:8). What is the ministry of the Holy Spirit here? It is the writing on the hearts of men. What he is writing on the hearts of men is the transforming power of God through His glory changing them into the image of Christ. The image of Christ is perfect obedience to the law. He was and is the fulfillment of the law. This transformation into the image of Christ brings righteousness, the power to live righteously. Could it be that this power, the filling of the Holy Spirit, comes when Christ is unveiled, and we look at Him? The Old Covenant came with fading glory that eventually blinded people to Christ. Today, without meaning to, are we preaching the law and blinding our people to Christ? We cover their minds and hearts with a veil of the law or principles to live by, thinking we are helping them to be better Christians. Only in Christ is the veil taken away. Could it be that in our preaching of the law we are not only veiling Christ from them but also veiling the filling and fulness of the Holy Spirit?

Paul continues by saying the Holy Spirit will write something new on you and in you: "Now the Lord is Spirit, and where the Spirit of the Lord is there is freedom" (II Cor. 3:17). Freedom from what? This could refer to the things we often want the Holy Spirit for: freedom from the binding power of sin in our lives. In this context, I think Paul is saying that we have freedom from blindness, the blinding power of the Old Covenant to keep us from seeing Christ. The fullness of the Spirit or the Spirit's work is to rip away the veil and allow us to see Christ as never before. What if the demonstration of the fullness of the Spirit is seeing new revelations of Jesus? Now in the liberty of the Spirit he rips away the veil of the law and we see Jesus clearly. As we behold His glory, we are changed, empowered, filled by the Spirit and changed into His likeness. Being filled with the Spirit is manifest first by a great vision of the Glory of God in the face of Christ Jesus. You're not looking for power to change; you are looking for the face of Christ, and in seeing that face encounter power to change. Paul says this vision of transforming glory is from the Lord, who is Spirit. The manifestation of Christ to us in this dispensation is by the Spirit, who comes with the glory of God in the face of Christ, and in looking at Him we are filled to all the fulness of God with the vision of Christ. The vision of the glory is the filling of the Spirit, which transforms. Here is the power to save and sanctify. The change comes in the beholding, in the seeing.

Paul says, "The god of this age has blinded the minds of unbelievers, so that they cannot see the light of the gospel that displays the glory of Christ, who is the image of God" (II Cor. 4:4). Could it be that the devil is using the law as part of his weaponry to blind unbelievers, and could he be using the same law to blind believers as well? Is the preaching of principles and rules for Christian living blinding our people to their real need for seeing Jesus? What is the answer to this blinding strategy of Satan? Preaching the light of the Gospel. "For what we preach is not ourselves, but Jesus Christ as Lord, and ourselves as your servants for Jesus' sake. For God, who said, 'Let light shine out of darkness,' made His light shine in our hearts to give us the light of the knowledge of the God's glory displayed in the face of Christ" (II Cor. 4:5–6). Preach the face of Christ, which is the Gospel, lift up Christ and let your people see Him, lift Him up like the serpent in the wilderness and he will draw all men unto Himself. The glory of God is part of God; it is His essence. Through this glory comes the transformative power of God as he shines it into our hearts, and this changes us in ever-increasing measure into His image. This shining of the light of the glory of God into our hearts is synonymous with the filling of the Holy Spirit and the fruits of the same.

The "L" in Chicago is the system of elevated tracks that run throughout the city. The downtown area of Chicago is called the Loop and gets its name from a loop made by these elevated tracks in the heart of the city. With the advent of fiber optic cable, miles of this cable have been hung on these elevated tracks throughout the city. Light shines through this cable and transfers information from one point to another. The old method was to use electricity and copper cable. Now, with the fiber optic cable you can transfer many times the information with much less energy or power. With the technology we have today you can take a picture of an object, transfer it into light, and send that light through the cable to a 3D printer and reproduce an exact copy of that object in another location. This is what God does, He translates part of His being into light, the light of His glory, then sends that light through space and time, shines it on us and into us. God's glory, like the light coming into the 3D printer, is translated back into His image in us. The image produced in us is the image of Christ. If you cut off the light that comes into the 3D printer through the fiber optic cable, it can't reproduce anything; it won't work. If we cut off the light of His glory, that glory, the image of Christ won't be reproduced in us. We receive this light by beholding the glory of God in the face of Christ Jesus, just as the Israelites received healing with a glance to the bronze serpent.

For the 25 years I pastored I was bi-vocational, meaning we worked a full-time job along with pastoring. Our trade was ironworking, setting the steel for skyscrapers, bridges and factories. The CTA (Chicago Transit Authority) has a crew of ironworkers that work on the elevated tracks the trains run on throughout the city. I worked for the CTA the last 15 years of my ironworking career. Whenever we would work on a section of the elevated tracks that had these fiber optic cables, we would have to cover them with protective blankets to keep fire and heat away from them. The fire and heat could damage them, and if they were damaged, the light could not flow through the cables. Today we have not protected the cables that carry the light of God's glory to the Church. We have not handled with care the glorious Gospel and have hindered men and women from seeing the glory of God. And the damage done has kept the light of the glory of Christ in the Gospel from shining into the hearts and minds of some believers. Without a recovery of the preaching of the light Gospel we will not see Christ formed in the lives of our people.

This is a new covenant, and it requires new teaching, a different approach to appropriation. Paul goes on to say that his confidence comes not from letters of recommendation but from God Himself. "He has made us competent as ministers of a new covenant--not of the letter but of the Spirit; for the letter kills, but the Spirit gives life" (II Cor. 3:4–6). The old covenant was a code written with ink that would be impossible for men to keep, a code that would judge them and leave them condemned. "If the ministry that condemns men is glorious, how much more glorious is the ministry that brings righteousness!" (II Cor. 3:9). "For the letter kills, but the Spirit gives life." "The link between the receiving of the life-changing grace and the seeing of the Divine glory is the seeing. It is as if a beam of divine glory shines down into our hearts, and along that beam of seeing comes grace upon grace there isn't another channel" (John Piper, speaking at the 2009 conference of the American Association of Christian Counselors). The seeing is primarily done in the act of worship. "When a gracious heart is in the way of God's worship, it finds the very duty of the worship of God to be strength to it and so fits it for another duty" (Jeremiah Burroughs, *Gospel Worship*).

Hidden in these words is the struggle that men face when they are confronted with the law. How can I keep the law? The Old Testament is replete with example after example of Israel's inability to keep the law. It is a history of lawbreakers, failures, and rebellions against God. In Galatians, Paul writes of arguing with the Judaizers, men who wanted to go back to the Old Covenant. They thought salvation was found in keeping the law, and what they didn't realize was that by looking to the law they were blinding themselves to Christ.

Our flesh still battles to try to keep the law and in so doing finds only condemnation and death. So how then shall we live? With the desire to keep the law (self-righteousness) comes a veil that hides the glory of Christ from us. When our focus becomes the law and keeping it, we can lose sight of Christ, and His glory is veiled to our eyes. You might ask yourself what you are looking at in your Christian life—the law or Jesus? Is Christianity a set of rules and regulations to you, or is it a living person? Is my vision filled with rules and regulations or is it filled with the glory of God in the face of Christ Jesus? When we are focused only on the law, we discover our inability to keep it, and our vision of Christ is increasingly veiled. Being focused on the law and struggling to keep it kills us spiritually: "For the letter kills." (II Cor. 3:6)

How do I avoid the struggle with the law? "Who will set me free from this body of death?" (Rom. 7:24). Paul tells us, "Only in Christ is this veil taken away" (II Cor. 3:4). Paul is teaching us that turning to Christ and looking at Him is the only way to lose the veil of the Old Covenant. Repentance is turning from our self-focus, self-trust, and self-righteousness to looking at Jesus. Repentance is turning to the Lord to look at Him, as with the bronze serpent in the wilderness, and never take our eyes off Him once we have started to look. The looking at Christ rips away the veil, and now with unveiled faces we begin to see in ever-increasing measure the glory of Christ and are changed in ever-increasing measure into His image. We look at Christ, and we are healed and empowered. This is beholding! The secret of the Christian life really is looking unto Jesus. Looking unto Jesus will be the secret to your transformation.

It was almost by accident that I learned that the Christian life really is as simple is looking at Jesus. What's even more unbelievable is that my transformation into the image of Christ was based on looking, worship, and not on my keeping of the law. I am not responsible for my righteousness, for there is nothing I can do to be righteous. Jesus, who has begun a good work in me, shall carry it to completion. How does Jesus transform us into His image? He brings us into His presence and has us fix our eyes on Him. When I made Jesus the focus of my life by repentance from my other loves and worshiped Jesus Christ as he deserved, the power and the burden of the law fell away. Keeping the law was no longer my focus. The focus became Jesus: looking at Jesus, loving Jesus, worshipping Jesus, talking with Jesus, and ultimately obeying Jesus. I discovered that when the worship of Jesus became my goal, power to obey His word was forthcoming. When my time and worship of Jesus were diminished, so was the power to overcome sin.

Worship is just another way of saying beholding Jesus. When I set my heart to behold (worship) Jesus Christ, the chains and the burdens of the law fell away. Jesus became my focus instead of the law. The beauty of Christ filled my vision, instead of the bondage of the law. By gazing on Christ, we drink in with our eyes Christ's glory, and in that glory, we have power, fruit, and grace in ever-increasing measure: grace that transforms to us into the image of Christ, grace that allows us to become the fulfillment of the law, grace that empowers us to keep His law. I was keeping the law without looking at the law or even thinking about it. Christ's righteousness was being transferred to me through the seeing of Christ in the act of worship. The righteousness, the obedience, was incidental to seeing Christ. I was in love with Jesus, and when I came to tell Him how much, without me even knowing it I was being transformed into His image. I was being made righteous without trying to be righteous. My ambition was not primarily to keep the law; my ambition was to "gaze on the beauty of the Lord." This looking at Jesus is done through prayer, worship, and the Word. It may not seem like an important distinction, but many Christians are putting the cart of the law before the horse of beholding, and the cart will not pull the horse.

The reason Christianity doesn't work for many today is because they are looking at the law instead of the Lord. We have been taught that if I know what the law is, then I can keep it. We set ourselves on the course of learning the law and then implementing it in our lives. Sadly, this is just what the Pharisees did; they concentrated so much on the law they couldn't see Jesus. Could some of us be doing the same thing, looking at the law and trying to keep it, and missing out on loving and worshipping Jesus, who is our righteousness? We can be blinded to Jesus by setting our focus on the law. You should ask yourself, in your Christianity, what you are looking at—the law, or the Christ? Are you focused on a principle or are you focused on the Prince?

Many years ago, I would attend a Christian seminar that lasted a full week. Thousands of Christians from our area would attend. We would have to sign in and register, get our badges, and collect a notebook that contained all the information covered that week in the conference. The notebook was to be a resource for us to go back to again and again. I have to say that the notebook was beautiful, with many attractive drawings and pictures as well as illustrations that were wonderful. We were instructed in many biblical principles that week and how to apply them in our lives. We carried our large notebooks all week to and from the conference. At the end of the conference, we were encouraged to go home and take on a principle a week and apply it our lives, and then another, and so on until we had worked through the notebook. I remember taking my notebook home and thinking to myself, "OK, let's start with principle one and try to keep that principle for a week before we move on to the second principle next week." After six weeks of trying to be better, trying to do the principles laid out in the notebook, I was exhausted and depressed. It wouldn't be very long before I laid the notebook aside and never picked it up again. What I learned in this conference was what not to do, but the Lord had to take me through it to learn that lesson. The lesson was that there is no help coming from the law to keep the law. There was no power in the law. I also learned that no matter how beautifully you present the law, it is still just the law that has no power to save.

During my long pilgrimage to Christ, one man encouraged me to start each day with the Lord just worshipping Jesus. "Start with the Psalms and read a portion of scripture and address it to Jesus personally. If you have to change a word or two, don't worry about it; just praise the Lord, making Him the central theme of your time." Starting in Psalms, I found what I called my worship Psalms and marked them with a star. I would go through these again and again, and found that these times of worship brought to me a fuller picture of who my Lord was. Each picture became a praise, and the praise quickly turned to thanks. Seeing who God was instead of seeing what I wasn't kept me from getting depressed over my sad state of affairs. I was looking at the glory of God instead of the mess I was. I began to notice changes in my life and behavior as a result of just worshipping God, and at first didn't understand what was happening. I was learning that there is no law in the Gospel, and looking at Jesus brought not only salvation, but it was bringing sanctification to me as well.

John in His Gospel says, "The Word became flesh and lived for a while among us. We have seen His glory, the glory of the one and only son.... From the fullness of His grace, we have all received one grace upon grace" (John 1:16). John is saying what Paul has also said: We were changed by beholding Jesus. John is saying we have received grace upon grace while we beheld Him. We might ask John, "When did you receive grace upon grace?" When we saw His glory, when we worshipped Him, when we loved Him, when we walked with Him. My faith was being exercised by beholding Christ, and I was being changed into His image. I was discovering that "a righteousness from God, apart from the law, has been made known" (Rom. 3:21). The just shall live by faith, and that faith looks like gazing at Jesus.

I would learn more about being changed by beholding when a friend gave me a book written by Joseph Carroll titled *How to Worship Jesus Christ*. This book summarized his life's work: preach Christ, worship

Christ. The heart of Mr. Carroll's preaching and teaching was Jesus. Look at Jesus to be saved, continue to look at Jesus in your sanctification, and finally look at Jesus in your glorification for all eternity. At the institute he founded, the goal was teaching men and women to grow in the grace and knowledge of the Lord Jesus Christ. He taught the importance of developing a personal, intimate relationship with Jesus Christ, founded on never-ending worship. In reading Mr. Carroll's book, I discovered that it is in the act of worship (beholding Christ) that God reveals Himself to men. As we worship Him, God shines the light of His glory into our hearts, and we are changed. For the first time in my life, I was not striving to keep the law but striving to look at the beautiful savior who saved me and just worship Him. Making gazing on Jesus my goal set me free from focusing on my painful, sinful self. As I looked, as I worshipped, I was being changed. It was the greatest period of transformation I had known in my Christian life. The change came not in figuring out how to be better but in looking at one who could never be better. The transformation was not in response to keeping the commands of the law but in looking unto Jesus. I loved being with Jesus and seeing more and more of His glory; there was an excitement in coming to be with Him, for he was revealing Himself to me and in me.

All my life I have struggled with keeping the law, and the more I focused on the law, the less success I had in keeping it. The harder I tried, the less I looked like Jesus. I knew the rules, yet I struggled to keep them. My Christian life was filled with frustration over my inability to keep the law. Our Justification comes by faith, not by working out the law in my life. Learning that we are changed by beholding was a Sabbath rest for me. By faith I was looking at Jesus raised like the serpent in the wilderness. I discovered that as I looked at Him, I had power to live the Christian life in a way I never had before. I found that my focus was no longer on the law but on Jesus, and the transformation just happened. My desire was building this relationship with the living Savior and growing deeper in love with Him. My striving ended, and my rest began as I simply beheld the Lord. I couldn't believe what was happening, for it so was easy. I felt as if I wasn't striving anymore. Beholding Christ was enough; I watched His power flow into my life and change me into His image. It wasn't me doing something; it was me looking at something, at Jesus Christ. As I beheld His glory, I discovered there was power in His glory, and His power flowed into my life as I beheld Him. Finally, for me to live was becoming Christ. I was worshipping, looking, beholding Jesus, and from that alone being changed, empowered to live the life that had always been a struggle before. In another chapter we will see what this looking, this beholding, looks like in a practical way. Our devotions, our worship, are the means of beholding Christ and being changed.

Let me be clear as to what I am not saying! I am not saying that we do not have an allegiance to the law. I am not saying we have no obligation to the law. I am not saying we nullify the law by this faith. Not at all. If we are rightly related to Christ, we should become the law, for this is what the Spirit is writing on our hearts. Just as the starving man must eat first to have strength to walk and work, or a thirsty man have a drink lest he die, we eat and drink of the Scriptures so we may eat and drink of Christ, who is found in them. Jesus said, "You diligently study the scriptures because you think that by them you possess eternal life. These are the scriptures that testify about me, yet you refuse to come to me to have life" (John 5:39–40). Many have studied the Scriptures only to see the law, thinking they have eternal life, and end up only with bondage to a code. Jesus said these scriptures testify of him and that if you come to him, you will have life. There is no power in the law to save or to give life. From this place of seeing the glory of God comes the grace of God where we may keep—obey—the law of God. "Sin is the suicidal exchange of the glory of God for the broken cisterns of created things" (John Piper). "For all have sinned and fall short of the Glory of God" (Rom. 3:23). Could we say that falling short of the glory of God is not seeing God's glory as the answer to my sin? Is it a sin not to behold the glory of God? If the glory of God is the transforming entity in the Christian life, then to not see that glory is sin and bondage. See the glory of God, and be transformed into His image.

In the Old Testament we have the story of the king of Syria sending for Elisha. Elisha's servant had risen early in the morning and gone forth. At that time the city was surrounded by horses and chariots and a great host. "What shall we do, master?" The answer to Elisha's servant's question was to pray this prayer: "Lord, I pray Thee, open his eyes that he may see. And the Lord opened the eyes of the young man; and he saw: and, behold, the mountain was full of horses and chariots of fire around about Elisha" (II Kings 6:13–17). Here we have something that was invisible that is made visible. Elisha had told his servant, "Fear not: for they that be with us are more than they that be with them." Elisha's and his servant's eyes had been opened to see the spiritual realm. God does the same work today, opening the eyes of our hearts that we might see the glory of God in the face of Christ Jesus. The glory of God is all about us as the spiritual horses and chariots of fire were about Elisha and His servant. Our eyes must be opened to see this glory. As Elisha prayed for His servant, Paul prayed "that the eyes of your heart may be enlightened (opened) in order that you may know the hope to which he has called you" (Eph. 1:18). Oh, that we might have our eyes open to see the mountain full of the Father, the Son, and the Holy Spirit coming to our aid. What confidence and assurance must have flooded the heart of Elisha's servant's when he saw the army of God surrounding them. What confidence will be ours when we have this Spirit of revelation granted to us that we might see the face of Christ Jesus.

Why aren't we asking God for more revelation of Himself? Let's say, "God, show me your glory." There is the eminent presence of God, which is everywhere at once, and there is the manifest presence of God, which is specific to a place, time, and person. The manifest presence is that Spirit of revelation Paul prays for in Ephesians. It is the revelation of Himself to an individual. It is our life's work to grow in the grace and knowledge of the Lord Jesus Christ. It is our life's work to seek Him with all our hearts until we find Him. The finding is the revelation of Christ to us through His Spirit. Jesus is a living person who wants to have a relationship with us. He wants that relationship to be the primary one of the Christian's life. He wants us to know Him, to talk with Him, to walk with Him, to gaze on Him—yet for most Christians Christ is dead. He is an icon to hang on the wall, a sculpture hanging in the church, not the risen Lord who is now enthroned in Heaven.

We preach the law to afflict the comfortable, and we preach the Gospel to comfort the afflicted. We should never preach a principle without preaching the Prince. We pastors must preach Christ, who is the power to become every principle in the Word of God. It is our responsibility to raise Christ up like the serpent in the wilderness, and when the law of sin and death bites our congregants, they can look to Christ to be healed and empowered. Pastor, if your preaching is not Christ-centered, then make it so. If you're not preaching Christ, then you may be preaching the law and not the Gospel. If your people are looking at the law, they will find there is no power in the law to keep it. They will find that looking at the law may cloud their vision of Christ. There is no power in the law to change people, and there is no power for spiritual healing. If your preaching is not Christ-centered, your people may be exchanging the glory of God for the law. Paul put it this way: "For I resolved to know nothing while I was with you except Jesus Christ and Him crucified" (II Cor. 2:2). Lift up Christ so your flock may see and in seeing be healed.

When John in the book of Revelation has that door opened into Heaven and sees the throne of God, he describes four living creatures "in the center, around the throne… covered with eyes in front and in back" (Rev. 4:6). Ezekiel uses similar language in his vision of the throne. These creatures who surround the throne in Revelation 4 seem to lead the worship, for when they fall down, the elders and others fall down and worship Jesus. What caught my attention was all those eyes. In the book of Revelation the creatures are covered with eyes in front and back; in Ezekiel's the wheels have eyes all around. Why all the eyes, and why in front and back and all around? If they are moving toward or away from the one on the throne, they will never lose sight of their King. These creatures don't want to take their eyes off Jesus, and they don't have to. Oh, that God would cover us with eyes front and back so that our lives here might be seeing Jesus everywhere and every moment of the day—so if I am moving away from Jesus on a mission, I'm still looking at Him. If I move the right or the left, I'm looking at Him. There is no way I can turn that I won't see Him who is seated upon the throne. Could it be that in heaven we never take our eyes off Him? "Let us fix our eyes on Jesus" (Heb. 12:2). In the looking we become like Him.

"Sink or swim, I go to Him; other hope have I none. I find it very convenient every day to come to Christ as a Sinner, as I came at the first period the word that drew my soul. 'Look unto me' still rings its clarion note in my ears. There I once found conversion, and there I shall ever find renewal" (C.H. Spurgeon). I once was changed—saved—by beholding, and now I continue to behold for renewal, that is, sanctification. Sink or swim, our hope is in looking at the one who bought us and longs to be with us. Look at Jesus and live, for we are changed by beholding. "Think of it! The beauty of Jesus is bestowed upon us by the simple devise of looking at Him, The Living Word, in the Magic Mirror, the Written Word" (*Filled! With The Spirit*, Richard Ellsworth Day).

Chapter 4

BRONZE SERPENT

"The Lord said to Moses, 'Make a snake and put it up on a pole; anyone who is bitten can look at it and live.'" (Num. 21:8)

IN 1976, I was a member of the New England Patriots. It was late summer, near the end of training camp and the beginning of another season, one that would prove to be a pretty good one for us. It was press day, a day when the press has greater access to the players for interviews than after the season starts and schedules get busy. Sometimes you would have a few fans and friends of players mixed in with the group. One of the fans or friends who showed up that day was a man carrying his pet boa constrictor around his neck. Players love to pull practical jokes on one another. One of our players, a real practical joker, knew that one of our defensive ends was deathly afraid of snakes, so he convinced the owner of the snake to go up behind this player and lay the head of his snake on the player's shoulder. Feeling a tapping on his shoulder, the player looked over to see what it was, and seeing the snake, he bolted and hurdled a four-foot crowd-control fence and ran up into the stands of the little stadium where the presser was being held. From the stands he began to scream, "Get it out of here, get it out of here! I'm not coming down until that snake is gone!" The screams and shouts continued until the snake and handler were escorted off the field and out of the stadium.

That day it was only one snake and one frightened man, no bites and no deaths. No one was hurt, and my teammate came down from the stands in safety. What if the snake had been poisonous, and what if the snake had bitten a star NFL player and he had died? The story would have been national news. Now try to think what it would be like to have thousands of poisonous snakes biting thousands of people all at the same time, with many of those people dying.

In the Old Testament, Numbers 21:4–9 records one of the scariest snake stories I have ever read. It's the story of wild and poisonous snakes invading the Israelites' camp, biting and killing people. I don't like snakes and get the chills every time I read this story. This is a story that has fascinated and terrified me at the same time. What would that have been like? Can you imagine the chaos and pandemonium the serpents caused in the camp? Mothers pulling poisonous snakes off their children, husbands trying to save their wives, neighbors trying to help neighbors and then getting bitten when they helped? The terror of the snakes, the bites, and the death of people all around you would make for a most desperate situation. Why was all this happening?

The reason for the Israelites' troubles was that they had grown impatient and were speaking against Moses and God. "Why have you brought us out of Egypt to die in the desert? There is no bread! There is no water! And we detest this miserable food!" (Num. 21:5). The food they were referring to here was the manna that God had provided in the wilderness. God had delivered them from slavery and was providing food for them to eat, and this was the thanks He got. Because of their impatience, grumbling, and ingratitude, God sent poisonous serpents to bite and kill them. When the snakes came and began to bite and kill the people, they cried out to Moses: "We have sinned against the Lord and against you. Pray that the Lord will take the snakes away from us" (Num. 21:7). Moses heard their plea and interceded for them before the Lord. Just making the snakes go away as they asked would seem to be the best policy. God answered their cry but not in the way they asked.

God told Moses, "Make a snake and put it on a pole; anyone who is bitten can look at it and live." So Moses had a serpent made of bronze and put it up on a pole and raised it into the air. "When anyone was bitten by a snake and looked at the bronze snake, he lived" (Num. 21:8). Here is salvation, not from the snakes, but in the midst of the snakes. The people still are getting bitten, but now they have a way to live in the midst of biting snakes. God doesn't save us from the world but in the world. Here is a type of our salvation and how one should live in a fallen, snake-ridden world. Here we have an object to look at, the bronze serpent. Looking at the serpent will cause healing for those who are bitten. All that is required is a glance at the bronze serpent. Those who look at the bronze serpent are expressing faith in God and what He told Moses to do. This is salvation by beholding. They look and are healed. Here we have an important picture of what salvation and faith looks like. Faith looks like beholding.

How would this deliverance work itself out? God provides the means of salvation, tells Moses to make a bronze serpent and put it on a pole, and tells the people that when they are bitten, they are to look at the serpent. Moses does this, and the standard is raised. Many have been bitten and many have died. As the bronze serpent is being raised, people still are being bitten. Once the bronze serpent is up, the people begin to look to it, and those who look are being healed. I'm sure the news of this would have spread like wildfire. The miraculous healings of people bitten by venomous snakes is good news—unbelievable good news. You might hear someone testify, "I was bitten and ran to where I could see the bronze serpent. I looked at it, and I was healed. All you have to do is go look at the bronze serpent, and you will live!"

In the middle of His night discourse with Nicodemus, Jesus uses the bronze serpent in the wilderness to illustrate His teaching to Nicodemus. "Just as Moses lifted up the snake in the desert, so the Son of Man must be lifted up, that everyone who believes in Him may have eternal life" (John 3:14). Jesus is taking Nicodemus back to this story in Numbers to teach him what faith looks like. When Jesus said this to Nicodemus, what picture do you think ran through Nicodemus's mind? This may have been a powerful story Nicodemus had heard growing up in the synagogue. Jesus says He must be lifted up like that serpent in the wilderness, but He doesn't say that whoever looks at Him will be saved. He says instead that everyone who believes in Him may have eternal life. I don't think Nicodemus could have heard Jesus say this without thinking about looking at Jesus as the children of Israel looked at the bronze serpent. The bronze serpent was a type of Jesus Christ, who was lifted up in crucifixion and that looking to His sacrifice gives us life. Is the believing seeing?

Try to see yourself in Israel's shoes. Imagine that on the first day the snakes come into the camp, you get bitten. What do you do? You find where Moses raised the bronze serpent so you can look at it. You find it, look at it, and you are healed. How could you not be excited if you're healed from a snake bite? What would you have to do if you were bitten again the next day? What would you have to do if you were bitten four days in a row? I believe that you would have to go back and look at the serpent again. Say you got bitten and looked and were healed, then you were bitten again, but this time you refused to look at the bronze serpent. What would happen? The looking at the bronze serpent had to continue as long as the snakes were in the camp and you suffered being bitten. Every time you were bitten, you looked at the bronze serpent, and every time you looked you were healed. Faith is an ongoing process, a continual looking to Jesus for all we need.

Faith must have an object, an object that can provide what we can't provide for ourselves. In the story of the fiery serpents, God provides the power for healing and gives it every individual when they believe by looking at the bronze serpent as He had said. God sets an object before them that they can look to for healing. The picture of the snake was so powerful that it still is used in medicine today as a symbol of healing. The looking or seeing was the means of appropriating the healing. Looking at the bronze serpent was the act of faith; if you looked, you lived, and if you didn't, you died. The bronze serpent is a type for the life we are to live now. God has lifted up His Son like the serpent in the wilderness so we might look at Him and be healed and changed. This act of faith, looking at Jesus, will bring to the Christian salvation, healing, and all we need for life and godliness in this life. Looking at Jesus is how we live the life of faith. The writer of Hebrews put it this way: "So we fix our eyes on Jesus, the pioneer of our faith" (Heb. 12:2). Christian, we are looking at many things in the Church today, but I dare say that for many, Jesus is not one of them.

In the serpent story, God's snakebite medicine was infused through the eyes. Receive a dose—a glimpse—of the bronze serpent, and you were healed. This is a picture of faith. Faith is both an action and a receiving. The moment the Israelites looked at the bronze serpent, they received through their eyes the vision of God's salvation, which healed them. In this example, faith and sight are almost synonymous. Looking is believing, and believing is looking. The eyes become the empty hand that receives the salvation of the Lord. To look is to have faith, and having faith, you would look and receive freely the healing of the Lord.

We can see faith as some internal human effort, some human exertion of strength, of thought, of reasoning. If faith is some human power, then how much of that power must we exert to accomplish something? How much faith do I need to be saved, or how much faith do I need in order to be healed? If we think this way about faith, then the exertion of this human energy will be the determinant of my salvation or healing. If I believe hard enough, long enough, I will be saved. If I have enough faith, I can move mountains. But the Israelites were not exerting some human energy to heal themselves. Believing themselves well, they were looking, and when they received the vision of the bronze serpent, something wonderful happened: They were healed. Here we have a new paradigm. No longer is it do this and live; now it is look and live. The implication is that just as the Israelites looked at the snake and lived, so now you shall look at the Son of Man and live. It wasn't enough for them to believe the words Moses said—they had to go and look.

How many times have you had a problem or a need and all you could see was that problem or need? Your prayers were filled with requests about the problem or need. Then you watched to see if that need was being met or taken away. You couldn't see Jesus raised up; all you could see was what you needed. God didn't take the snakes away like the Israelites asked; He gave them a way to live in the midst of them. God wants us to learn to live by looking at His Son. He wants us to make Jesus our great business, the very focus of our lives. We are to keep our eyes upon Jesus and not upon the snakes, waves, storms, and problems of this life. All that we need in life, salvation, and ministry will be found when we gaze upon Christ.

God sets up Jesus on a pole for us in this snake-infested world, and when we are bitten, we only have to look at Him, and we'll be healed. Here we have the means of appropriating the divine life, the power of God, into our lives. For the Gospel is the power of God unto salvation, we looked at the Gospel (Jesus) and the power of God was released into our lives to save us. We continue to look at the Gospel so power may come again and again. This takes us back to brother Jerry's discussion with the pastor about gazing on Jesus. Gazing on Jesus is something we have gotten away from, and what has that cost us? The power of God? We can't believe the Christian life is as simple as looking at Jesus. There must be something for me to do, something more than just looking. Because we can't believe the simplicity of the Gospel, we have moved away from it; we are working, but we have stopped looking at Jesus. The lack of looking costs us the power we need to live the Christian life. It costs us the transforming power of God to change us into the image of His Son. We used to believe "Jesus is the answer," but I don't think we do anymore because we are looking for answers that aren't Jesus.

Jesus said, "Just as Moses lifted up the snake in the desert, so the Son of Man must be lifted up" (John 3:14). Why must Jesus be lifted up, and what does He mean here? Healing for the Israelites came by casting their eyes on the bronze serpent. Healing and power for the Christian today comes by looking unto Jesus. Faith—in the picture of the serpent being lifted up—is synonymous with looking and looking with faith. Jamieson, Fausset, and Brown's commentary on John 3:14 puts it like this: "In both cases it is by directing the eye to the uplifted Remedy that the cure is effected; in the one case the bodily eye, in the other the gaze of the soul by believing in Him."

"Look unto me and be saved" (Isa. 45:22, KJV). Just as the Israelites lived by looking at the bronze serpent, so we will live by looking at Jesus, whom God has lifted up for us to see. Jesus is lifted up so we can look at Him again and again. In the Christian life, there is an abiding principle stated by Jesus: "No branch can bear fruit by itself; it must remain in the vine" (John 15:4). How do we abide in Christ? How do we remain in the vine? We abide, we appropriate the life of Christ, when we look at Him. As the Israelites appropriated healing power by looking at the bronze serpent, so we appropriate life and power for living by looking at Jesus. Isaac Ambrose writes in his book *Looking Unto Jesus*, "Looking to Jesus is the cause of this; the sight of God will make us like to God, and the sight of Christ will make us like to Christ." This is the great lesson of the bronze serpent: Look and live. It is not only look and live, but it is look and become like Jesus. The *how* of looking will be found in our devotional life, when we repent of everything else in our life and spend alone time with our Lord. We look at Him as we worship Him by describing all that He is and does.

This looking unto Jesus will become the process by which we appropriate the power, life, and healing of Christ necessary for living in this fallen world. It should become our spiritual habit, one we continue throughout our lives. Looking will be a large part of our abiding; the looking at Jesus is God's means of attaching us to Christ the vine. We need to learn how to gaze on Jesus, for in that gazing, we have all we need for life and godliness. Through the vision of Christ, God pours His life into ours, and as He does, we are transformed into the image of His Son.

When we learn to gaze upon Jesus, we will see the clouds part and will behold the most beautiful sight in all creation, a sight that will fill us with healing and with the power to live a life otherwise impossible. The sight of Christ will fill us with awe and wonder and stir the passions to joy. Here is the most beautiful sight a soul can ever see. Looking at Jesus—gazing—is the theme of this book. The hope and prayer of my heart is that you will learn to look at Jesus, and if you are looking, to train your eyes to look higher and deeper, wider and farther into the One who is love. You will discover what the Israelites did—that healing, power for sanctification, love, joy for living, and satisfaction of heart all come through the vision of God's Son.

Horatio Spafford wrote the great hymn "It Is Well With My Soul," a hymn born of great pain and sorrow at the loss of four daughters when the ship they were traveling on sank. His wife, who survived the sinking, sent a telegram from England after the event: "Saved alone!" The last stanza of that great hymn starts, "And Lord haste the day when my faith shall be sight." I understand what Mr. Spafford is saying in that verse, that one day we no longer will look through a glass darkly but rather face-to-face. We will have a sight that will allow us to fully see and know our Lord. Some Christians have the idea that we don't see Jesus now but only when we die and go to Heaven. Many who think this way are content to wait until they die to see Jesus. They know the sight of Jesus will come later, so they don't try to gaze on Him now. What if faith is sight? What if believing is a seeing? What if we can see something of our Lord now? What if this seeing is what heals us and transforms us into His image? Would it not be worth any effort to try to see Jesus, to learn how to gaze upon Him now?

Paul prays for the Ephesians, asking God to give them a spirit of wisdom and revelation, and that the eyes of their hearts might be enlightened. Enlightenment speaks of seeing something that was in the dark and which has had light shined upon it that it might be seen. Have you had to go and get a flashlight to enlighten a dark area of your house in order to find something you were looking for? God shines His divine light into the world through His Son that we might see His Son raised up like the serpent in the wilderness. "The people walking in darkness have seen a great light… on those a light has dawned" (Isa. 9:2). What does God want us to see? He wants us to see Jesus. It is the work of the Holy Spirit to reveal Jesus to us so that we might see Him and be saved. Paul wants the Ephesians to see Jesus in order that they might know Him better. He prays that God will send His Spirit to shine the light of His glory into the dark minds and hearts of these Ephesians so they might see Christ. Paul tells us in II Corinthians 3:18 that we are changed into the image of Jesus by beholding Jesus. True faith is about seeing Jesus and gazing on Him continually and in the looking, to be changed into His image.

Remember that moment when you first believed, when you first saw Jesus? What was that like? Was there a striving or a strong effort on your part? Someone had preached the Gospel to you, and you looked at it and were saved. Is there a striving when you ask someone to turn the light on and they flip a switch? It's darkness one moment and light the next, and how did that happen? Do you fully understand how light enters your body and the mind interprets what it sees? I daresay few of us really understand faith, though we have our definitions. When God brought you to Himself, He didn't ask you to do anything but look. "Behold the Lamb of God that taketh away the sin of the world" (John 1:29). With a glance, we looked at Jesus lifted up like the serpent in the wilderness, and the miracle of revelation, the miracle of healing and conversion, began to happen. The snake bites of this life are healed, the poisons of sin in our veins are neutralized, and we no longer are dying. Just because there is mystery here doesn't mean it's not real or powerful or wonderful. We try to tell others what we have seen, but they don't see it; they can't see it. If people can't see Jesus, it doesn't matter what you tell them, for it will be as if you are speaking a foreign language to them. They have to see for themselves—God has to reveal it to them.

The truth is we don't fully understand how we come to see God. Like the blind man healed by Jesus, all we know is that once we were blind, but now we see. This God has shined the light of His glory into our hearts in the face of Christ Jesus. There was a day, a moment, when I saw Him, and I just knew who He was. Remember what Job said at the end of one of his discourses with God? "My ears had heard of you but now my eyes have seen you" (Job 42:5). At the sight of God, Job then despises himself and repents in dust and ashes. The vision of God, given by God, is what brings Job to repentance, and the same will be true for us.

We have our definitions of faith: Faith is personal trust in a person; faith is the proper response to the command of God; faith is the absolute surrender to the will of God; faith is the substance of things hoped for, the evidence of things not seen. Definitions of faith are not faith. It is easy to think that knowing a definition of faith is the same as having faith, but this is not so. True faith must tie the individual to the object of that faith. We tend to see faith as something we do in order to receive something from God. We think those who have the greatest faith will receive the most from God. Recently our pastor stood on the platform waving a hundred-dollar bill in his hand. He called a young girl from the audience to the platform and offered the bill to her and waited for her to take it. He offered it, he waved it, he extended it to her, but it didn't become hers until she received it, which she did with a big smile and returned to her seat. He then said, "She had to believe what I was telling her, and then she had to take the hundred-dollar bill, she had to receive it." This was an illustration of faith: Her faith didn't create the money; her faith didn't make the pastor offer it; her faith could only accept it. God offers to humankind the greatest gift that has ever been offered, but we must believe it is so, we must come as He instructs and simply look at His Son that we might possess the gift He offers.

So what is the empty hand with which we receive the salvation and grace of God? What if that empty hand was our eyes or the eyes of our heart? What if the channel through which God grants us His grace and all He has for us is through the portal of our eyes, our physical as well as figurative eyes—the eyes of our hearts? Faith is receiving the light of God's glory through the portals of our eyes and our understanding. Seeing this light, we receive into ourselves all that Christ is and has for us. It is through this vision, this revelation, that we get to know Him and are transformed into His image.

Let me put it as simply as I can: Faith is looking at Jesus whom God has lifted up like the serpent in the wilderness. Here a glance at Christ will transfer power from Him to us for healing. So let me ask, did you glance at Christ today? Did you make Him your vision, have you made Him your great business? Have you made Jesus the focus of your life? God has blessed us with every spiritual blessing in Christ Jesus, so look and live.

Living in a snake-filled world, you can see the importance of having a daily time when you look at Jesus. We are distracted from looking at Jesus by the snakes from which we are asking God to deliver us. During our devotional times, we look at many things that push Jesus out. They may be good things, but these things won't heal, or give power to transform. Jesus will. The needs of our lives press in, and our prayer times become a shopping list or a wish list of everything we want or need and we look at these and take our eyes off Jesus. It may be that all we can see is the biting snakes and don't take our eyes off them to look unto our healing Christ. What we forget is that what we need is Jesus. For in Jesus, we will find all our supply. The way to receive that supply is not looking at the need—it is looking at Jesus.

You might think that if I'm looking for Jesus alone, God might not know what physical need I have. It is just the opposite. If I'm preoccupied with Jesus and desire Him alone, God will see that I have everything else. Paul says, "He who did not spare his own Son, but gave him up for us all—how will he not also, along with him, graciously give us all things?" (Rom. 8:32). Paul is saying that if God has given you His Son, the greatest, highest, most expensive gift He can give you, don't you think He will give you the trinkets and baubles of this life's needs and give them graciously? Seek Jesus first and you will be seeking all you need. Seek your lesser need first and you may end up empty-handed. God wants to bring us to a place where all we want is Jesus, and then when we have Jesus, we will see that we already have all things.

We tend to want what we want, and often, what we want is not Jesus. When we see Jesus as our great need, what will we ask God for? We will ask Him for more of Jesus. "I want to know Christ and the power of His resurrection" (Phil. 3:10). If I see Jesus as my great need, won't I ask God to satisfy that need? Will I not look to God to give me a greater revelation of His Son? All a snake-bitten Israelite wanted was to see the bronze serpent. God wants us to get to that place in our lives where in desperation, all we want to see is Jesus.

Our faith is our look at Jesus. By this we are saved, healed, restored, empowered. When we look away for a moment, we find we are surrounded by things we can't overcome. When we desire Jesus alone and look at Him, God gives us all the things we were worried about. All of this is ours when we gaze at Jesus. Faith is that simple glance at Christ. God calls us to look again and again, have faith again and again, for without faith (looking), it is impossible to please God. Daily looking unto Jesus is what our devotions are all about.

When we stop looking at Jesus, the poisons from the snake bites of this life will weaken us, then sicken us, and finally cause our death. As humans, we start with a simple look at Jesus, and then we quickly look away. It will never be all right to look away, for looking away leads to trouble. Could the Christian life be as simple as looking at Jesus high and lifted up? Is it true that the power, grace, and righteousness I need to live the Christian life are gained by looking at Jesus? To this we say yes! Our goal in the rest of this writing is to show how, in a practical way, we are to do this looking.

In John Bunyan's *The Pilgrim's Progress*, as Christian the Pilgrim is on his journey, he runs into Piety, who begins to ask him some questions. "And what saw you else in the way?" Piety asks. Christian replies, "Saw! Why, I went for a little further, and I saw one, as I thought in my mind, hang bleeding upon the tree; and the very sight of him made my burden fall off my back (for I groaned under a very heavy burden), but then it fell down off of me." The very sight of Him made the burden fall off. The sight of Jesus will accomplish more for you than a lifetime of striving, dear Christian. Look and live.

"Just as you came to Christ, so walk in Him" (Col. 2:6). So the Christian life will be one of looking to Jesus. We come to Jesus with a glance, and then we think we can turn away and do something different to live a sanctified life. Ask yourself what fills your spiritual vision, what fills your prayers, what you are asking God for. This will tell you something about what your heart really desires. We came to Christ by looking unto Him, and we will walk through all the Christian life by continuing to look at Him. Looking unto Jesus will be the heart of our sanctified life. You will find that the worship of Jesus Christ will become central in your walk, for worship is nothing more than looking unto the Savior and in looking, being changed.

Once we start beholding Jesus, we will never stop, for beholding is living, and living is beholding. The serpents will continue to bite us, and we need to come and look again. Life will become a continual looking at Jesus for the power of His life in this world of death. We will draw life and breath and everything else from Christ as we behold Him. I believe that the step of faith, the trusting, occurs as we behold Jesus. The place of beholding is the place where we let the glory of God shine on us and into us. The place of beholding is what we call our devotions.

Sally and I attended a church for several years and most Sundays, walked out sad and unfulfilled. One Sunday during all those years, the pastor preached a Gospel message to the congregation. We walked out filled with joy at the power of the message and by having looked at what Jesus had done for us. That next week, he went back to preaching the law, and the thrill of the Gospel was lost again. It wouldn't be long before we left and found another church where the Gospel was being preached. Many pulpits won't let their people see what they need—Jesus lifted up.

In the next few chapters, we want to consider what this beholding, looking unto Jesus, looks like in a practical way. Personal devotions are the place where we cast our eyes upon Jesus, where we appropriate healing and find grace, mercy, and power to live, but even more, they are a place where we find our Lord's heart of love. The looking we are talking about is not some impersonal glance at an inanimate object; these are the looks of love. This is the kind of looking that a maiden does when she looks into the face of the one with whom she is madly in love and finds in his eyes that love being returned. This looking is into the face of a living person, one we can see with the eyes of our hearts. This looking is into the eyes of the One who loves us eternally and infinitely more than we love Him. Gazing upon this Lord is one of the great joys of the Christian life. This is the highest honor a human being can have, an appointment with the living Jesus, in a secret place where we can look into His face and find there the love that our hearts so desperately seek.

The only requirement for one to come and look at God is to have the eyes of faith. You can be living in poverty and look upon Jesus. You can be slow of mind and speech and look upon Him. You don't have to have great strength; you can be crippled in mind or body, and you still can look. You don't have to be somebody or be famous to come and look at God. Wealth and fame and great intelligence—things the world admires and desires—often can be impediments to coming and looking upon the face of this most beautiful person. The One we look upon has been given to us as a gift from God. This is not some dead piece of bronze but a living person, the person of Jesus Christ. God doesn't want us to look at what we don't have but to concentrate on what we do have in Jesus. What shall it profit a man if he gains the whole world and loses his own soul? What if you gain the whole world and lose Jesus? What if this living God of glory whispers, "I love you!" What would that do to you in your humble estate, in your poverty? What if you don't have the things of this world but you have Christ? Spurgeon said, "If you travel, remember that our Lord Jesus Christ is more glorious than all else that you could ever see. Get a view of Christ and you have seen more than mountains and cascades and valleys and seas can ever show you. Every mountain gives its beauty, and stars their brightness, but all these put together can never rival Him." The vision of Jesus makes even the poorest man the richest in the world. For in having Jesus, I have everything.

If faith is looking, then an individual who is working without looking is in error, for he has works without faith. We have seen the near destruction of the devotional life of Christians, where prayer and personal Bible study have waned, yet we continue to minister in the power and demonstration of human effort. The works of man cannot accomplish the will of God. "Unless the Lord builds the house, the laborer labors in vain" (Ps. 127:1). The way to the power of God is through faith, through looking at Jesus. This is our daily bread, a daily dining on the vision of Christ, a looking that drinks in the marvelous vision and life of Jesus

The greats of the faith were great because they were constant lookers at the Lamb of God. They started their days with the healing and empowering vision of the living Jesus. This is the call of devotions: to come and look at Jesus every day and see in that vision all you will need. Look and be healed, look and be filled with power, look and be satisfied, look and be comforted, look and be given power over sin, look and have the desire of your heart satisfied and inflamed with love. Look and live today. Looking is believing, looking is seeing, looking is having faith. Start seeing faith as looking, looking as beholding, beholding as worship, and worship as the door of the revelation of Jesus to your heart and mind. The more you look, the more you will see, and the more you see, the more you will want to see.

When did you come to Christ? When were you saved? Go back and think through those days or moments when the great fisher of men caught you in His net. What happened? Maybe you were walking in the woods and God spoke to you as He did to Martin Luther through rain and lightning. Maybe you rose from the back pew of a Baptist Church and went forward on that Sunday night, overcoming the fear and shame because you wanted what the preacher said you could have—Jesus Christ. Perhaps yours was a struggle and battle where you felt you took the Kingdom of Heaven by violence. Maybe silence surrounded you in your car driving down the road, and an imperfect pitiful prayer rose up from your heart and found its way to God, and His glory fell on you. Was that moment all about you, or was it all about Jesus? The first moments of salvation were Jesus breaking into your life. It was His face you saw in those moments, and you looked and lived. Time, the evil of this world, and the trials we have been through try to wipe from your memory the moment when you first saw Jesus. The world, the flesh, and the devil all whisper in your ear and heart that you never really saw Jesus. Walk back into the sunlight of God's Word, walk back into revelation of God by coming into His presence again and gazing upon Jesus high and lifted up as you did in those first moments of your salvation and see if God doesn't do the same thing again. When you look, your weak legs will be strengthened again, your blind eyes will be opened, your withered hands will fill with life, and you will rise up, take your bed, and walk. Your heart again will know the fire of passion and first love you had at the beginning, all in a glance at our beautiful Savior.

What were you doing when you first came to Jesus, when you first beheld the Lamb of God? You were turning your eyes from the mess that was your life to the perfection of Jesus. You were turning your eyes from the snake bites and pain of this life to Jesus high and lifted up. You looked and you were healed, you looked and you were given life, you looked and you were saved. Think now of that moment. What did you do, what effort were you exerting, what energy were you expending? Your eyes were searching the horizon for help and then your eyes met His, and you saw Him and knew that He was real and that you now were saved. He sent His Spirit to be the deposit of His love in your heart. When you think back, doesn't it seem that He was doing everything in that moment? All you were doing was looking at Him and you were healed. What happened in your heart? Didn't it begin to burn within you? Wasn't there love for Jesus such as you had never known? You didn't try to work it up; it was there, fresh and unlike any you had ever known. There was a hunger for more of Jesus while your appetites for other things began to wane. All of this came because someone lifted Jesus up like the serpent in the wilderness and you saw Him and were healed. You looked and lived, you looked and were changed by beholding. If you have grown cold in your love for Jesus, come again and look at Jesus. Read the Gospels and let the beauty of the Savior wash over you and baptize you again with that heavenly fire in your heart. Warm yourself again in the fire of His glory as you did at first faith. Come and look and let Him baptize the altar of your heart with fire from heaven, bringing with it the fire and passion of love for Jesus. Come look at Jesus and live; come and worship Him, for this is what you were created for.

> Lord, I have looked away from thee to gaze upon created things and have lost sight of you. Lord, I have not set watch over the altar of my heart, and by neglect, have let the fire go out. I have been busy at the altars of other gods and have let your altar go to ruin. Forgive me, O Lord, for neglecting Thee! I repent and come to rebuild the altar I have torn down by neglect. Just as Elijah rebuilt your altar in his day and saw your fire fall from heaven, I come to rebuild your altar in my heart and put fresh sacrifices upon it that there may be sweet incense in your nostrils. I come to look again upon thee, the true Bronze Serpent with healing in his wings. I ask that you would be my vision again and fill my vision with the glorious face of Jesus Christ. I call on you now to bring tongues of fire from heaven again and relight the altar of my heart, that the people around me may see fire fall from heaven and cry out, The

Lord, He is God, the Lord, He is God! And you, Lord, would be glorified in the bringing of your holy light to shine on me making me to look like your Son.

This I pray in Jesus's name, Amen.

Chapter 5

FAITH

"Now faith... it means being certain of things we cannot see."
(Heb. 11:1)

WHAT IS FAITH? "Now faith is the substance of things hoped for, the evidence of things not seen" (Heb. 11:1, KJV). I must admit that I have heard this definition all my life and still don't have a good grasp of what it means. We look for definitions of faith and conjure such, thinking that if my definition is right or good, I will have faith. How many messages have you heard on this verse or on faith that were set before you with the admonition "This is faith so now go have it"? Let me add to this definition a couple more. The goal here is not a full theological discussion on the nature of faith, but to look at what faith looks like for many.

Bishop Lightfoot said, "Faith is not an intellectual assent, it is the absolute surrender of self to the will of God, who has the right to command this surrender." Bishop Lightfoot had a protégé named Handley Moule, who went on to be the first principal of Ridley Hall at Cambridge University. He was a student of Lightfoot's and followed him as Bishop of Durham in England. While principal at Ridley, Moule would have speakers such as D.L. Moody and Hudson Taylor come and hold a week of meetings. Moule wrote more than 600 books and commentaries on the Scriptures. He had a great mind, and an even greater heart of love for Jesus as Savior. Moule gave us this definition of faith: "Faith is personal trust in a person." I could add to these many other definitions from men who loved God and end up writing a book on faith, which others have already done. What do you think when you hear these definitions? Where does your mind go? Are these definitions enough to help you grow in your faith, and how would you use these definitions in your life? If I'm to have faith—or more faith—when I read these two definitions, I might think of absolute surrender and personal trust, asking what they are and how to have them. So how do I surrender to God, and how do I have personal trust? I can see faith as something I do alone instead of living by faith in the Son of God. It would seem there is something for me to do. These are but a few of the definitions I have learned growing up in the Church, and they are good, but a good definition is not faith, it is only what it might be. Whatever definition of faith you have, faith itself doesn't become mine until it is gifted to me and placed in object God has commanded me to look at. Now that God has enabled me to believe how do I demonstrate that faith in my daily walk with God?

Many years ago, when I was young and still lived at home, I walked into my brother's bedroom to have a conversation with him. He was lying on the bed, head propped up slightly, motionless, in a deep state of concentration. His gaze was fixed upon the book that was lying at his feet on the end of the bed. His stillness mimicked sleep, but his eyes were still open. I asked him, "What are you doing?" His answer was delayed so long, I was about to leave the room when he finally said, 'I'm trying to move the book with my mind." Telekinesis is the technical term for moving something by using one's thoughts alone. This is not something you see every day, so I was a little shocked by his response. In all fairness to my brother, this was in the heyday of Uri Geller, the famous psychic known for claiming to bend spoons using only his mental or psychic powers. Geller became world-famous and made a good living making people believe he was bending spoons by mental powers alone. I promptly asked my brother if the book had moved yet, to which he replied that it had not. I left him in the middle of his project, but I wondered about the mind and its power to do things like this. I have to admit that I tried the same thing later, away from prying eyes—and the book didn't move.

I believe this idea of telekinesis is how many Christians see their faith. Faith is a believing, a straining of mind and will that levitate a book or, better yet, moves God. This telekinesis concept of faith comes from the way some in the Church teach faith. They teach or emphasize the human side of faith as this human effort, the exertion of a man's will, which when strong enough, moves the hand of God. If I just believe hard enough, I will receive what I ask of God. If we don't get what we're asking of God, it's because we didn't have enough faith, so the answer becomes finding out what faith is and trying to have more of it or taking the faith we do have and strengthening it. The way to have more faith is accomplished by increasing our effort, so we ask more often, we ask with more urgency, passion, and repetition. Much of this exertion comes in the prayer life, where these desires are made known to God. If the desired thing is lacking, we are told to concentrate harder, increase the repetition of asking, pray longer and harder, pray without ceasing, fast and pray, pray until you sweat drops of blood, be persistent and unyielding until your faith becomes a reality. The end of this road often is unanswered prayer and an exhausted Christian.

Some have taught us that you need to believe you already have it and act as if you do, even give thanks for it when you don't have it yet. How often does our faith look and feel like a poor attempt at telekinesis? We camouflage our faith-effort in prayer to give it the air of spirituality. Cloaking this self-effort in prayer and directing it to God doesn't add any power to it. We are taught in Mark 11:23 that if we have faith, we can say to this mountain, "Be thou removed and be thou cast into the sea," and it will happen, yet few of us are in the mountain-moving business. How many times have you been frustrated by your inability to get God to do what you wanted Him to do, to give you what you asked Him for? Why didn't God answer your prayer or give you what you asked for? Was it your lack of faith? Our faith doesn't command God, giving Him orders He must obey. Using your mental powers as a kind of telekinesis to get God to move can end in frustration. Our faith, separated from God, is weak and useless. Our faith alone has no ability to move the hand of God, no matter what our definition of faith is. When Christians don't get what they want from God, they quickly blame themselves for a lack of faith. If the lack of faith is responsible for not having what I ask from God, then increasing that faith, strengthening that faith, will be the answer to the unanswered prayer.

Back in the '70s, I was in a weekly Bible study, and faith was the topic. This teaching on faith emphasized the human side of faith, faith being a human effort that generated some reaction from God. If you had enough faith, you would have material provision. If you had enough faith, you could be healed of any disease. If you had enough faith, you could have health, wealth, and prosperity. The health-wealth-prosperity Gospel was the logical conclusion of the type of faith being taught in this study. Who wouldn't want this kind of faith? I didn't see God, His power, or endless supply in this study; what I saw was my need and my faith as an answer to that need. Why did I want to learn more about faith? I wanted to learn more about faith because I wanted to use faith as the means of getting what I wanted in this life. When there is the slightest separation of God and man, man will find a way to make more of himself and less of God. Man's faith easily can become the focus while the true object of that faith—God—lies diminished. Why was I in this study? Why did I want to learn more about faith? I saw my faith and developing it as a means to acquiring the things I wanted in life. I would have to say that at that time in my life, I wanted many things, but honestly, God was not one of them.

My shallow reasoning went something like this: "I want certain things in my life. I don't have them. The reason I don't have them is I don't have enough faith. So if I can get or have more faith, even a mustard seed amount, then I will have the things I want in my life. I can speak to the obstacles in my life like mountains and trees, and they will be gone. If I have faith, I can ask God for anything, and it will be given." If I didn't have these things, the reason for the lack was my lack of faith. Therefore, learning about faith, or learning how to have more faith, was the logical resolution to my problem. So I thought. What I wanted was a faith that would provide me the finer things in life, not a faith that believed in God and wanted more of Him. How subtle and selfish is the human heart, ". . . exceedingly wicked. Who can know it?" (Jer. 17:9). What I was left with was me, my attempts at having faith, and the failures that resulted. I was learning the hard way that God is not in the business of making me a little god who commands Him. At that time, I would have said that I was believing God for success in my business, but I wasn't believing God; I was believing in my faith. Though I would not have said it then, I was trying to make myself the center of God's attention, instead of making God the center of mine.

With a focus on my faith, the limitations also were mine. What power was there behind this human believing? This Bible study ended for me in disappointment and frustration. In the end, the study group was encouraged to try harder: If you don't have enough faith today, perhaps you will tomorrow: keep believing, keep trying, and don't give up. I don't think it was the instructor's intention, but what came across in his teaching was that faith was a power you possessed and releasing that power would get God to move and accomplish what your heart desired. So often our flesh has an agenda that isn't God's agenda and isn't God.

When a Christian has all this world can offer in the way of family, job, wealth, or status, it is easy for us to think this person also has great faith. Having been a member of well over 30 different churches in my lifetime, I have seen the political power that the rich man has in a church. We tend to see a person's faith and financial blessing as the same thing. If God blesses a man with wealth, then his faith must be strong. So if I can just have the same faith the rich man has, I can have what he has. Because we live in such a rich nation, we tend to see financial success as spiritual success, as faith success. This is because so many Christians really want success in the world and not success with God.

This study on faith was representative of much of the teaching I had received on faith up to that point in my life. The teacher found plenty of support from the Scriptures. Jesus said to the woman with the issue of blood, "Your faith has healed you" (Mark 5:34). When the two blind men came to Jesus and said, "Have mercy on us, Son of David!" Jesus asked them, "Do you believe that I'm able to do this?" When they replied yes, Jesus said, "According to your faith will it be done to you" (Matt. 9:27–29). It is easy to separate the believer from Jesus who made the statement. It would be easy to think that the power to heal came from the faith of those who were healed and not from Jesus. Many studies on faith stop here, teaching, "Your faith has healed you," as if human faith alone has the power to heal. Much teaching on faith today isolates the human faith from God and His divine power to heal. The power to heal is never in our faith—it is only in our God. When we teach on faith, we can seek to make distinctions between parts of things that are one and might separate two things that can't be separated.

Speaking at one of his Ligonier conferences in Orlando, Florida, R.C. Sproul was giving an illustration about the difference between making distinctions between two different things in a theological discussion and actually separating those two things. "When you talk about a man, you can make a distinction between his head and his body, but if you separate the two, you have committed murder." In teaching about faith, we can make distinctions between man's faith and Jesus—the object of that faith—but if we separate them, we have committed theological murder, for faith apart from Jesus is spiritual death. In the study on faith I mentioned above, we were thinking and looking at our own faith so hard that we lost sight of Jesus. We had separated the head of Christ from our body of faith and committed the murder of our faith.

It was over 40 years ago now, while attending an evangelical Christian college, that I was surprised by one of my textbooks. This was in a class preparing men for the ministry, training for future pastors and preachers—a preacher boys' class. The book that surprised me was Napoleon Hill's *Think and Grow Rich*. The book is a treatise on the power of the human being and how that power might be released through something Hill calls faith. "Think," the first word in the title, is the starting point for the human being in his search for success in this life. The thinking and thoughts are human, not divine: "'For my thoughts are not your thoughts, neither are your ways my ways,' declares the Lord" (Isa. 55:8). Hill says, "All thoughts that have been emotionalized (given feeling) and mixed with faith immediately begin to translate themselves into their physical equivalent or counterpart." Many church leaders have had their definition of faith influenced by men like Napoleon Hill. Many in this class I took would go on to be pastors in churches across America. Some may have adopted Hill's definition, thinking it to be biblical. I found many things in common between the study on faith I spoke of above and what Napoleon Hill taught in *Think and Grow Rich*. Let me share some of what Hill taught and see if this doesn't sound familiar to you:

"All through the ages, religious leaders have admonished struggling humanity to 'Have faith' in this, that, and the other dogma or creed, but they have failed to tell people how to have faith. They have not stated that faith is a state of mind, and that it may be induced by self-suggestion" (*Think and Grow Rich*, Napoleon Hill). The inducing of this "state of mind," or faith, is by the power of self-suggestion: I am the genesis of my own faith; I am in control of it. In order to have faith, one can induce it by giving repeated instructions to the subconscious mind. Think repeatedly, say repeatedly, believe repeatedly, pray repeatedly what you want. Now declare it, say it out loud to yourself or others. Have you ever heard of a "name it, claim it" faith? While you're thinking and repeating and declaring what you want, add passion or emotion to those thoughts and desires. Feel it, or believe it strongly, believe it passionately, adding the human energy of emotion to the recipe. With the added emotion these thoughts will "translate themselves into their physical equivalent or counterpart." What I hear Hill saying is that there is a power in our faith to change things, a power capable of translating our thoughts, our visions, our wishes into their physical equivalent, a power that begins with a thought in me.

Here are some of Hill's bullet points on faith from *Think and Grow Rich*:

"Faith is the eternal elixir which gives life, power, and action to the impulse of thought."

"Faith is the basis of all miracles and mysteries that cannot be analyzed by the rules of science!"

"Faith is the element, the chemical, which, when mixed with prayer, gives one direct communication with infinite intelligence."

"Faith is the element that transforms the ordinary vibration of thought, created by the finite mind of man, into the spiritual equivalent."

"Faith is the only agency through which the cosmic force of Infinite Intelligence can be harnessed and used."

Though all of these might not be what some people in the Church are teaching, I think you can see that the Church's teaching on faith has been tainted by these ideas.

Hill continues, "Faith is the head chemist of the mind. When faith is blended with the vibration of thought, the subconscious mind instantly picks up the vibration, translates it into its spiritual equivalent, and transmits it to the Infinite Intelligence, as in the case of prayer." Here is the means of contacting the Infinite Intelligence. It is by the power of our faith that we can transmit our thoughts, prayer requests, to God. Faith is our means of getting the Infinite Intelligence's attention. If God doesn't hear me, is it because I don't have enough faith? If I have enough faith, then I can get God's attention, and then I can get whatsoever I want from God, because my faith can harness and use the Infinite Intelligence—Hill's term for God. Where is Jesus, our Mediator, in all this? If my mind and subconscious mind can contact the Infinite Intelligence on their own, then what do we need Jesus for?

Napoleon Hill is teaching a man-centered, man-powered faith, not the faith of the Bible. Adding to our confusion about faith is the fact that Hill's kind of faith works. It doesn't work in getting to know God or to advance God's Kingdom, but it does work in this world to build the kingdoms of men. God has given to men certain gifts that may be used for Him or for selfish purposes. Men trusting in themselves and using their natural gifts, using the kind of faith Hill teaches, have accomplished great things. They have built great fortunes and businesses and have become the captains of our industries. This kind of man-centered faith also has built false religions and worldwide ministries with millions of followers. If *Think and Grow Rich* was one of the texts in a preacher-boy class, could some of our evangelical pastors have used these ideas of faith to build large evangelical megachurches in America? Are we really building the Kingdom of God, or just building large businesses and organizations? This human-centered faith can be a powerful thing but only as powerful as man, and it will always end in death. Remember what God said at the tower of Babel: "If as one people, speaking the same language, they have begun to do this, then nothing they plan to do will be impossible for them" (Gen. 11:6). The power of man's faith is as no power when compared to the power of God.

If my faith is separated from Jesus, all I'm left with is the strength of my own arm. Self-reliance is a sin very hard to repent of. Self-reliance is really self-righteousness. Self-righteousness is man's attempt to live rightly before God in his own strength. Self-righteousness or a self-produced faith is a power we can use to build churches and ministries when we don't have the patience to wait for God to supply the strength and power. When men don't see power coming from God to accomplish their vision, they may turn to a Napoleon Hill–type of faith where they exert human effort to accomplish their will. Sadly, some in ministry do accomplish their will using their own power and not God's. Just because a work appears successful doesn't mean it is successful with God. Think and grow rich, think and have faith, think and accomplish all you desire: Napoleon Hill faith doesn't really believe God; it believes the self can have a strong-enough faith to accomplish all it desires. The church leader who has a man-centered faith may teach the same to others. Thus, we had this book as a text in a preacher-boys' class.

The Napoleon Hill–type faith is like the magic of the Egyptian magicians: It works without God. It will not work the works of God, but it may accomplish something, even something amazing. God demonstrated through Moses that the faith or magic of these Egyptian magicians was no match for a faith in the power of the living God. Moses's snake devoured those of the Egyptians. The Egyptian magicians used the tricks and power of man to accomplish what they wanted. Many in the Church are doing the same thing today: They use human power and the tricks of business to make it seem like God is doing something. They conjure up things that look magical and call it divine. By the straining of their minds and wills, they build a Christian Tower of Babel. Like the Egyptian magicians, what they do looks amazing, but it's only the sleight of human hands. These men perform acts of faith, using Uri Geller spoon-bending tricks, making it look like some supernatural power. Does my faith move God, or does God move and cause faith in me? If we see faith as an energy, or strength of will, by which we get God to do something, our thoughts about faith are wrong.

Many who have taught us about faith mean well, but their teaching may be so focused on man's side of the equation that they miss the object and power of that faith—Jesus Christ. This separation of faith from the object of that faith leads to false concepts of faith. When our faith is separated from Jesus, we are left with our human effort alone to save us. So much of our teaching and preaching in the Church today is focused on principles to live by: how to be a better Christian, husband, wife, father, or church member or how to have more faith. Churches that would never be accused of being legalistic are preaching law over grace without knowing it. This preaching of law and principles is a natural outworking of wrong concepts of faith. If I have a Napoleon Hill–kind of faith, it is natural to set the how-to principles before someone, encouraging him or her to release the faith within to accomplish those principles. Teaching the principles of faith without the Gospel causes people to look inward at their faith instead of looking outward at the faithful One. There is no salvation in self-analysis and the application of some principle, even human faith, to life. There is no salvation for humankind looking inward at the self-life. "No one will be declared righteous in his sight by observing the law" (Rom. 3:20). Are we teaching faith as a law to be kept, and when we keep it, we have what we seek?

So what does true faith look like? We already looked at the bronze serpent in Numbers 21, where we have a great illustration of what faith looks like. I dare say that the strength or power of the Israelites' faith was of little matter in dealing with the snake problem. If the power was in the faith of the Israelites, couldn't they just have believed they were healed and gone about their business? Might there have been those in the camp who would use their faith as a healing ministry? Name it and claim it? No, looking at the bronze serpent was all that mattered. The power wasn't in the Israelites; it was in God and transmitted to them by looking at the object that God set before them. The power was outside of them and hung on a pole. Once they looked, they were healed, they were saved. Their faith was but a glance at the object of God's deliverance, and by their looking, God's power to heal was released to them.

Wrong ideas on faith have led us to believe that the consequence of not having enough faith is our responsibility as well. If you don't have what you're asking God for, the problem is your lack of faith. This has led to Christians taking responsibility for things they had no control over. If my children are not saved, it's because I didn't have enough faith; if someone I love has died of heart disease or cancer, it's because I didn't have enough faith that they could be healed. There is an army of Christians carrying around guilt that is not theirs to carry, simply because they have wrong concepts about faith. Man-centered faith teaches that we can plant this seed of faith and grow the answers for the things we are praying for. "Name it and claim it" teaches us the power of our spoken word, as if we could speak like God and it would be accomplished. If planting the seed of faith or naming it out loud isn't enough, then add emotion and passion to your desires. Isn't this what Napoleon Hill taught us? We can end up looking like the prophets of Baal dancing, shouting, and even cutting ourselves trying to get the fire to fall from heaven. Though the fire didn't fall that day for the prophets of Baal, they had built a religion with that man-made faith and converted most of Israel. A Korean Christian touring America's churches some years ago was asked what he thought about the American Church. He said, "It is amazing what the Church in America can do without the Holy Spirit." He could have said, "It is amazing what the Church in America can do without true biblical faith."

Much of Christianity in America is what some have called evangelical humanism. It is a man-centered Church dependent on men who are talented, capable, and driven. This church is in love with celebrity, wealth, entertainment, and success: bigger is better. Is it any surprise that our teaching on faith ends up being an exaltation of the human side of faith? If you believe, if you have faith, you can say to a mountain, "Be thou removed." Focusing on the faith you have or don't have can be a distraction from looking at Jesus. A proper faith must be connected to God; it must continually look at God. The life I now live in the body, I live by faith in the Son of God. (Gal 2:20) A man-centered faith loses its desire and appetite for God; it stops waiting on or looking unto Him. There is little need for God when you have talented and capable men who can build and organize. The prayer life is in part a manifestation of the faith life, a manifestation of looking at God. When we see the prayer life of the Church diminished, this is evidence of looking away from God and looking to men. A man-centered faith can leave one looking to self or other men instead of asking God, for help. Maybe this is why counseling has supplanted the preaching of the Gospel in many churches. What kind of power is being released in the Church today, human or divine?

When we preach principles to our people, we must at the same time preach the Prince, or preach Christ. Whenever we preach the law, we must preach the Gospel. The how-to of obedience is to look to Jesus like the serpent on the pole. We look at the Gospel for the grace to keep the law, even grace to believe or have faith. So when someone preaches or teaches about faith, they must at the same time preach Christ. Think about looking at the bronze serpent as an illustration of what faith is like. God wants to bring you into the place where you see faith as looking on Jesus and continuing to look at Him all the days of your life. He wants you to see how glorious He is, and He wants to shine His glory and grace into your life. Jesus wants you to see how sufficient He is. He is so sufficient that simply looking at Him is enough to transform you into His image. The life I live in the body, I live by faith in the Son of God. Now that we are saved the life we live is one of living by faith, placing our faith in the Son of God continually. The Christian life starts with a look at Christ and continues with this looking (faith) until we see Him face-to-face in Heaven. Other terms for this constant looking faith, abiding, communion, fellowship, or a relationship with God.

I want you to think differently about faith. I want you to think of faith not so much as something you are believing but as something you are seeing, something you are looking at. I want you to begin thinking of faith as looking at Jesus. I want you to see faith as a way of seeing. Think about the serpent in the wilderness being lifted up: All you had to do was look and live. Our job is not believing harder; our job as Christians is to look. Looking unto Jesus and faith are the same thing. Faith is looking at Jesus, and in the looking at Him, we receive His grace whereby we are healed, we are sanctified, we are changed. Faith—looking—is the touchstone where the divine power of God becomes mine in simply looking. Adam and Eve looked on God and had shining array. Moses went up on the mountain and looked on God and came back shining. The Israelites looked on the bronze serpent and were healed. Jesus said He must be lifted up like that serpent in the wilderness "that everyone who believes in Him may have eternal life." If Jesus is lifted up like that serpent in the wilderness, what would people have to do to have eternal life? They would have to look at Jesus and live. Believing and seeing might be synonymous in this case, though most people don't think of them in the same way. "Look unto me, and be ye saved, all the ends of the earth: for I am God, and there is none else" (Isa. 45:22, KJV).

The Reverend John Hutton wrote *The Fear of Things* in the early 1900s. The introduction of that work is a chapter titled "The Nature of Evidence." In this chapter, he compares and contrasts seeing and believing: "We have a proverb to the effect that 'seeing is believing.' What we usually mean when we quote it is that the only sure proof that a thing is there is that you see it. The true order everywhere is not 'seeing is believing' but 'believing is seeing.' In every level of things other than the merely physical, this is the order, not that we believe because we see, but we see because we believe.' People from Missouri might put it this way: 'I'm from Missouri, show me!' Thomas, one of the twelve disciples, said, 'Unless I see... I will not believe it'" (John 20:25). Could it be that our believing is looking unto and seeing Jesus? The Greek word *pisteuo* is translated both as "believe" and "faith." Believing, having faith, is the looking, is the seeing: "We see because we believe." For the Christian to see Christ, he or she must believe, and the believing will be the seeing, and in the seeing will be faith to see more. Faith, our believing, is the way we look to see Christ lifted up like the serpent in the wilderness. In this looking, we are healed, empowered, and transformed. This looking then will be the great business of our lives.

While sharing the ideas of this book with a friend of mine, he shared with me that he did not know if he had beheld Christ. His uncertainty came from the fact that we use the word "behold," or "beheld," in a physical visual context. Mainline evangelicals almost begin to sweat when their Pentecostal friends say something like, "I saw Jesus." What do we mean when we say behold, or I have seen Jesus?

Helen Keller was born on June 27, 1880, in Tuscumbia, Alabama. She was born with the ability to see and hear. At 19 months old, she contracted "brain fever," an unknown illness that might have been scarlet fever or meningitis. The illness left her both deaf and blind. Living in this silent dark world, Keller had only her touch to see or understand the world around her. By the age of seven, she had developed or invented some 60 signs to communicate with those around her. The daughter of the family cook, who was near her age, best understood her signs and was able to communicate somewhat with her. In 1886, Keller's mother read an account in Charles Dickens' *American Notes* of the successful education of another deaf and blind woman, Laura Bridgman. The family set out to find out if Helen could be educated like Bridgman. The Kellers sought the advice of a Baltimore doctor, who referred them to Alexander Graham Bell (inventor of the telephone), who recommended them to the Perkins School for the Blind, where Bridgman had been educated. After contacting the school, its director, Michael Anagnos, asked 20-year-old former student Anne Sullivan, herself visually impaired, to become Keller's instructor. It was the beginning of a 49-year relationship during which Sullivan evolved from Keller's governess to becoming her companion.

Anne Sullivan arrived at Helen Keller's house in March 1887 and immediately began to sign into Helen's hand, hoping she eventually would understand that the sign was the name of the thing she was touching. There were weeks of frustration for Helen because she didn't understand that every object had a unique name. Keller's breakthrough moment—her light-bulb moment (beholding)—came the next month, when she realized that the motions her teacher was making on the palm of her hand while running cool water over her other hand symbolized the idea of "water." Water was the breakthrough word. What happened in the breakthrough moment was that Helen saw a connection between Sullivan's signing in her hand and the object she was feeling in the other hand. She learned the name of the object she had felt in her hands and now she could behold the water through the word as well as the feeling. Helen used an alternate sense to understand to behold the world around her that had been closed to her. In our blind state, God comes and signs Jesus into our hands until we understand what He's saying. Now we see Jesus by faith, for faith is a way of seeing Him even though we are physically blind to that world. Beholding the Lamb of God may not be a literal visual experience with our eyes, but the senses we use to see God will make that vision just as real as if we had seen it with our eyes. Helen Keller was "seeing" the water with her sense of touch, just as we will see Jesus with our sense of faith. Like Keller, we may use an alternate sense to see with; it may be that we use the sense of hearing to behold God. "Faith (beholding) cometh by hearing and hearing by the word of God" (Rom. 10:17). It may be that our soul has senses (eyes of the heart) that we do not fully understand. We must remember that we are designed by God and for God first. Part of our design is to be able to see something of Jesus through senses God has buried in our souls. The illumination of this One comes when the light of God's glory shone into our hearts, touches these senses, and we see. God's design includes the ability to see Him, hear Him, and talk to Him and that by faith. The sad thing is that many have been given sight by God to see God and are not using it, so what are they looking at?

When we say believing is seeing, we are not saying that our believing creates the vision; this would be mere schizophrenia. Believing is seeing what already exists. Believing is looking at a real object with the eyes of our heart. This seeing comes when God grants us faith and reveals by His Spirit Christ to us. Once we have seen Christ we continue to look to Him throughout our lives. He becomes for us the healing serpent lifted up for all the camp to see. The looking, the believing, becomes the means of appropriation of the power needed for any and every circumstance in life. This looking is the means of appropriation of the very life of God. As we saw in the Chapter 3, "Changed by Beholding," the observation of Christ, the looking at Him, which is faith or believing, is the place of transformation for the Christian. This is why we need a secret place, a place of observation where we can look at Jesus daily. The Heaven that John looked into was one where saints and angels surround the throne of God gazing on the light and lamp of glory (Jesus Christ), crying out in worship of the same. Heaven will come on earth when the Church becomes preoccupied with looking at Jesus.

Hebrews 11:1 says: "Now faith is the assurance of things hoped for, the proving of things not seen." Andrew Murray comments in *The Holiest of All*: "The visible world is man's greatest temptation to forget God. Faith is the eye with which he can see God." Faith is the eye through which we receive the light of God, the revelation of God, the grace of God, and the power of God. "Faith does not depend for its blessing on the intensity of its effort," Murray says. Our faith doesn't conjure anything; it merely looks at Christ and in seeing him is changed. It is the Spirit's work to reveal Jesus so we may see him and be transformed, healed, empowered. This faith looks to Jesus, who is the prophet of our faith. "He is one that teacheth inwardly, clearly, experimentally, and sweetly; no man can say this, or do this, but Jesus Christ the great prophet of the Church" (*Looking Unto Jesus*, Isaac Ambrose). When we look to Jesus, we not only are saved and granted grace and power, we are taught by the Great Teacher Himself. "I will send you the Holy Spirit who will lead you into all truth" (John 16:13). "For in Him are hidden all the treasures of wisdom and knowledge" (Col. 2:3). Your great business is looking unto Jesus, setting your mind and thoughts upon Him, giving time to pursuing Him, seeking to be in His presence, gazing upon Him continually, and worshiping Him for who He is. When one fills one's eyes with the vision of Christ, one is transformed into the same image—the image of Christ.

John puts it this way in the first chapter of his Gospel: "The Word became flesh and lived for a while among us. We have seen His glory, the glory of the one and only Son, who came from the Father, full of grace and truth.... From the fullness of His grace we have received grace upon grace" (John 1:14–16). They saw Jesus's glory; part of that glory was His fullness of grace and truth, and from the fullness of His grace, they received grace upon grace. The grace comes through the seeing. When we receive grace upon grace, what we are receiving is the very life of Christ. "That you may filled to the measure of all the fullness of God" (Eph. 3:19). The means of reception of the grace and glory and fullness of God in Christ is the seeing. The ability to see the glory of Jesus is a gift from God. The enlightenment of the eyes of the heart is to see the revelation of

Christ, "That you may know Him better" (Eph. 1:15). The seeing will lead us to the place where we know Him better and receive grace upon grace.

Almost 30 years ago, when I began to pastor, the Spirit of God said something surprising to me: "You counsel from your pulpit. If they don't listen and respond to my Word, they won't listen to your chattering." The Lord was teaching me that the preacher's job is to preach Christ, to lift up Christ like the serpent in the wilderness so the people the pastor is addressing can look at Christ and be changed. Your great teaching doesn't change your people, nor does your great counseling. Lifting Christ like the serpent in the wilderness, preaching the Gospel, the power of God unto salvation: This is what will change your people. I think many pastors see the Gospel as the starter program we use to get our people saved and then throw it away. We move from the Gospel to the meat of the Word, the principles of Christian discipline: These are the rules to live by.We move on from the Gospel to teach the principles of discipleship so our people can grow and mature in their faith. Could it be that one of the reasons many in the Church are not growing and maturing in their faith is that we are lifting up rules and principals for our people to look to instead of Jesus. Could our lack of power be because we are not preaching the power of God unto salvation—the Gospel? If we don't lift up Christ, our people won't see Him, and if they don't see Him, they can't be healed. Justification and sanctification come in the same way—looking to Jesus.

When you start preaching five steps to being a better Christian, you have given up on the Gospel, for there is no power in a five-step program. The Gospel is the power of God unto salvation. Preach the word, yes, but Paul, who gave that admonition to Timothy, also said, "But as for me, may I never boast, except in the cross of our Lord Jesus Christ, through which the world has been crucified to me, and I to the world" (Gal. 6:14). "I resolved to know nothing while I was with you except Jesus Christ and him crucified" (I Cor. 2:2). "But we preach Christ crucified, a stumbling block to Jews and foulness to Gentiles" (I Cor. 1:23). Pastor, what are you preaching today? What do you leave your people looking at?

You and I need to stand in front of the Gospel (Jesus) every day, to wash and bathe in the light of His glory. Standing there, you will be healed and empowered for the task of the day. Standing there you will be changed into the image of Christ, which is true sanctification. Pastor, preach the Word, but remember that faith comes by hearing, and hearing comes by a word of Christ. A word of Christ—lifting up Christ, showing your people Christ—will bring forth more faith and more transformation in your people than anything else you can do.

In the New Covenant, we are designed to be like mirrors that stand before him catching the rays of His glory and shining them back upon Him and others. In this way, we glorify Him. Paul teaches us that as we stand beholding and reflecting His glory, we are changed by that glory into the image of His Son. This transformation is our sanctification. As we are made to be like Him, our desire for His glory will grow. If my desire is to look upon Jesus, I need never be disappointed. All my prayers for His name to be glorified will be answered. Once we are set free from looking at the circumstances of our lives and look upon Christ, we can soar in the heavenlies; we can have whatsoever we ask, for we will ask God to show us more of His glory. In seeing Christ, we will have more than anything else we might ask Him for. In this seeing of Christ, we will be transformed into His image and in this will glorify our God in prosperity, poverty, suffering, or even death.

The greatest place of faith is looking, seeing, the Savior. As we stand beholding Christ, He shines the light of His glory upon us and transforms us into His own image. A sinner being transformed into the image of Jesus Christ is the greatest miracle in this world. This change in a person will last for all eternity. We need to hold our gaze on Jesus, like the woman with the issue of blood who would not let go of Jesus until He healed her. Don't be distracted like Peter, who looked at the storm and waves and began to sink. Keep looking at Jesus. What does God want of His children? "To behold the beauty of the Lord all the days of our lives" (Ps. 27:4). He wants us to stare at Him until we shine with His glory. Remember that He is jealous of all your attention. It's just that easy; so easy, we can't believe it. I guess it would take a great deal of faith to believe that I could just look at Jesus and be changed, converted, healed, made righteous, and find power for service and ministry. Yet such is the will of God.

If faith is looking to Jesus, and our churches are not preaching Jesus but 12-step programs, what happens to faith? If faith is looking to Jesus but my personal devotions are filled with the vision of myself, what happens to faith? If my Christianity is all about me and sees only my needs or wants, what happens to faith? Could it be that our lack of power in the Church is because we have stopped looking to Jesus and have no true faith? We have quit believing the Gospel, individually and corporately. We don't believe reading the Gospel or hearing a Gospel message has the power of God unto salvation. We don't believe that when Jesus is lifted up like the serpent in the wilderness, all we have to do is look at Him and we will live. Start looking at Jesus again. We need the Gospel every day, to look at Jesus every morning and trust the Gospel as we walk through the day. As a Church, we need more of the Gospel on Sunday morning from the pulpit so we can gaze and be healed.

Where can we see Jesus? Search every ordinance and duty for Jesus. In the ministry of the Word, tell your pastor, "Sir, we would see Jesus." Oh, that there would be a revival of Christ-centered preaching in America. We see Jesus in the Word of God. This is why we preach the Word. Jesus is the Word made flesh. We study the Word so we may see more of Jesus. When George Muller was asked by a reporter at the end of his life what he would still like to do, he replied, "To read more of the Bible, because I know too little about the excellence of Christ." He wanted to search the Scriptures to find Christ and look on His beauty, His excellence. He wanted to look at Jesus. Much of our Bible study and preaching is focused on everything but the excellence of Christ. We should go to the Scriptures to learn about Christ, to look at Christ on the pages of his Word, to see there the scarlet thread that is woven throughout the whole of Scripture. This scarlet thread written on every page by type and shadow is Jesus.

We see Jesus in the sacraments God has given to the Church: the Lord's Supper and baptism. "This is my body, this is my blood," here is the Paschal Lamb that we are to consume with nothing left over. See Christ administer the supper through his servants, your elders. See the cost of your salvation in Christ, His body and His blood. See Christ in baptism, His death, His burial, and His resurrection, and when the saint goes into the water, his death, his burial, and his resurrection. When the saint is under the water, see God baptizing this one into Christ, just as He did you. When someone goes into the waters of baptism, they are covered with the water, which is a picture of being covered with the righteousness of Christ. See Christ in prayer, for it is Christ that we speak to, it is Christ that we come to, it is at Christ's feet that we lay our worship, our requests, and our burdens. See Christ in fellowship with the saints, for the Church is called the body of Christ. Listen for and look to see the work of Christ in every life. Listen to their testimonies of how Christ found them, spoke to them, and brought them to Himself. When you pray, come and place your petition into the hands of Jesus, and watch as that nail-scarred hand takes it and holds it, knowing that the One who accepts it has bled through that hand to provide the answer you seek.

See Christ in your daily devotions, in your secret place. See Christ in your worship and adoration, where you describe the wonder of who He is and sing it back to Him. See Christ in your daily thanksgiving, seeing that every good and perfect gift comes from Him. See how He cares for you, how He loves you. See Him in the words of the praise offered to Him, His power, glory and eternity, His love and forgiveness. See Christ in your seasons of meditation on the Word, for He is the Word made flesh. See Christ in your daily visits to His palace and His throne room. Look to Him to extend the scepter of acceptance, showing you His desire for you to come and draw near to Him. In this looking unto Jesus, you will be changed into His image; you will become like Him. This is faith!

Hence, what do you desire? Desire to overcome sin in your life? Look at Jesus. Desire to love your neighbor as yourself? Look at Jesus. Desire the fullness of the Spirit? Look at Jesus. Desire revival in your church? Look at Jesus. Desire to preach with power? Look at Jesus. Desire to know God's will? Look at Jesus. Desire to grow in the grace and knowledge of God? Look at Jesus. Desire to love Jesus more? Look at Jesus. Many will say this is too simple and some will call it stupid, but it is God's way of life and power. First, look at Jesus; seek first his Kingdom, and all these things will be added unto you. Faith and looking unto Jesus are synonymous.

Faith, a way of seeing, is received by a glance at Jesus, and now with those glances, I am made to be free, free from distractions that focus on me. Now, in the looking, what glories I see in the beauty of the One who died for me. In the seeing of this beauty, a miracle happens, for in the seeing of the beauty, the beauty becomes me.

Chapter 6

WORSHIP IS BEHOLDING

*"Whoso offereth praise glorifieth me…And I will show him the salvation of God."
(Ps. 50:23, KJV).*

IF YOU WERE to visit George Washington's home at Mount Vernon, you would discover an old key in a glass case mounted on the wall. Beneath it is a drawing of the Bastille, the notorious prison that would become the site of the birth of the French Revolution. The key on the wall at Mount Vernon is the main key to the Bastille. New York City was the nation's first capital. Some months after Washington's inauguration in August of 1790, a reception was held for the new president there in New York City. At this reception, George Washington put this key on display. Afterward, newspapers across the country ran an exact representation of the key displayed in silhouette. Washington considered the key to represent the global surge of liberty: "a token of victory gained by liberty over despotism by another." It became known as the Liberty Key.

The Liberty Key was a gift from Washington's longtime friend, the Marquis de Lafayette, the Frenchman who came to help the United States win their freedom from England. Lafayette also sent a sketch of the Bastille along with the key. Lafayette said in a letter to Washington, "Give me leave, my dear General, to present you with the picture of the Bastille just as it looked a few days after I had ordered its demolition, with the main key of that fortress of despotism. It is a tribute which I owe as a son to my adoptive father, as an aide de camp to my General, as a missionary of liberty to its patriarch." This key represented freedom from the despotism of man's selfish rule.

What is the key to liberty for us as Christians? What would we hang on the wall of our homes to indicate that we are "missionaries of liberty"? If there were to be such a key mounted on the wall in the house of our salvation, I believe that key would be worship, for worship is the act of faith by which the soul looks unto Jesus like the serpent lifted up in the wilderness, and in the looking, the soul is healed of the poison and power of sin. Worship is the key to transformation, for in looking at Jesus, I'm changed into His image. "He has sent me to proclaim freedom for the prisoners and recovery of sight for the blind, to set the oppressed free.… Today this scripture is fulfilled in your hearing" (Luke 4:18, 20). Jesus is the fulfillment of this scripture; by looking unto Him, our prison doors are opened and our captivity is ended.

"Enter his gates with thanksgiving and his courts with praise; give thanks to him and bless his name" (Ps. 100:4).

"Ascribe to the Lord the glory due his name; bring an offering and come into his courts" (Ps. 96:8).

"Sing to the Lord, bless his name; tell of his salvation from day to day" (Ps. 96:2).

Romans 10:9–10 says, "If you declare with your mouth, 'Jesus is Lord,' and believe in your heart that God raised him from the dead, you will be saved. For it is with your heart that you believe and are justified, and it is with your mouth that you profess your faith and are saved."

The declaration of Jesus as Lord is an act of worship declaring His station and power and lordship over all creation including oneself. Remember Saul's (Paul's) first words when Jesus spoke to Him on the road to Damascus, "Who are you, Lord?" Here is true conversion when the heart bows and declares that this one is Lord. True worship is first a heart issue and in order for it to be true, it must come from our hearts first, from a new heart, one changed and transformed by God.

The most common word for worship used in the Bible literally means "bow down." Bowing before the Lord now means responding with repentance and faith to the person and work of the Lord Jesus Christ (Rom. 10:9–10). Such worship (bowing) involves praying to Him, calling on His name, and obeying Him. In order to be true, this worship must come from the heart first, it must be internalized and believed in the heart. Then out of the abundance of the heart, the mouth will speak and declare that "Jesus is Lord." "Let us draw near to God with a sincere heart and with the full assurance that faith brings, having our hearts sprinkled to cleanse us from a guilty conscience and having our bodies washed with pure water" (Heb. 10:22).

We often hear that all of our life here on earth can be an act of worship to the Lord. We take comfort in the thought that everything I do can be an act of worship to God. This may be true in a broad sense but only when the heart is right. This thinking also can keep us from coming to God in actual worship, of coming and gazing on Jesus. By actual or real worship, I mean worshiping God with praise adoration, psalms, hymns, and spiritual songs. It is carving out time in my day when I do nothing but declare in word and song and praise the wonder of the Lord. This worship is looking at the wonder of the glory of God in the face of Christ Jesus and singing to Jesus of His worthiness, holiness, and love, literally bowing before the God of the universe in worship as well as words. Thinking that all of their life—the work they do, the children they raise, or the ministry at Church they are involved in—is their worship, many Christians don't or won't stop and actually worship Jesus in their day. Christians can think that if all their acts and activities are worship, then specifically worshiping Jesus with time, attention, and psalms is not necessary. I think this is why the devotional lives of so many Christians are a desert place, and the altar of the Lord in their lives lies in ruin. We must come again and intentionally worship Jesus on a daily basis like looking unto the bronze serpent in the wilderness and being set free from the poisons of this life.

When I was a child, one of my Christmas gifts was a microscope. This microscope did not have a built-in light source, but it had a mirror with which you could find the light and reflect it on the slide. The mirror was set on a swivel so no matter where the light was, the mirror could find it and focus it where needed. Whenever I used that microscope, the first thing I had to do was find the light and then move the mirror to focus on that light. Many times, I had to move the whole microscope to capture the light. Once I had the light perfectly focused, I could see what was on the slide. Worship is like the mirror on that microscope. Worship focuses us on the light of God's glory, allowing that glory to shine upon our hearts and faces, changing us into His image. Then once we are changed, we reflect that light back onto Jesus and into a dark world where it is needed.

Worship is the key that will set us free from the despotism of sin and its slavery. It is one of the great keys to a successful Christian life. Worship is the natural by-product of beholding, of looking at something that is wonderful and beautiful. Worship is putting into words what we see of God's beauty and glory and adding to it thanks and praise. Worship is the means we use to bring glory and honor to Jesus. Worship by its very nature is the preoccupation with another to the exclusion of oneself. If God's highest concern and chief end for which he created the world is His glory, then our chief end is to be preoccupied with that glory. Being preoccupied with the glory of God is where we will find our greatest happiness, our highest joy. Preoccupation with the glory of God is the heart of worship. "The Westminster Larger Catechism says that man's chief end is 'to glorify God and enjoy him forever,' but we shall then know that these are the same thing. Fully to enjoy is to glorify. In commanding us to glorify (worship) him, God is inviting us to enjoy him. God is most glorified in us when we are most satisfied in Him" (John Piper, *A Peculiar Glory*).

Many of us have the wrong picture or understanding of what worship is. C.S. Lewis writes in *Reflections on the Psalms*, "The miserable idea that God should in any sense need, or crave for, our worship like a vain woman wanting compliments… Even if such an absurd deity could be conceived, he would hardly come to us, the lowest of rational creatures, to gratify his appetite. I don't want my dog to bark approval of my books. " God does not need our worship, nor does He gain or grow by it. If God was like that vain woman and wanted compliments for her own sake, then worship would become a burdensome duty. God is not like some despot who wants men to grovel at His feet, making much of Him and humiliating them. God doesn't call us to come and worship Him to humiliate us. He also doesn't call us to worship because He needs something from that worship, for He needs nothing. God calls us to worship Him so we might see who He is and in seeing Him, be filled with joy at the sight of His beauty. God gives worship as one means of coming to love Him. He calls us to worship Him so that in seeing something of the glory of God, we then can be changed by that beholding. Worship is not spinning some prayer wheel of evangelical faith or the reciting of empty chants and songs. How many times have we prayed the Lord's Prayer and it was empty of meaning and love? Worship is not some work I do to get to God; worship is the act of beholding the beauty of God and speaking the wonder of that beauty back to Him, with praise, glory, and thanksgiving. It is the empty hand of faith that receives the glory of God and in so doing, reflects and offers some of that glory back to Him.

If there is no interpersonal relationship with God, then all my praise becomes as a sounding brass or a tinkling symbol. It is empty because it speaks of nothing that is known to me. When God shines the light of

His glory into our hearts, we begin to speak from a position of knowing. "My ears had heard of you but now my eyes have seen you. Therefore I despise myself and repent in dust and ashes" (Job 42:5–6). In worship, God reveals Himself, and the One we had only heard of we now will see. Our worship is an expression of love to God for revealing Himself to us and becomes the enjoyment of our relationship with Him. Worship is speaking words of love to God.

Consider again Leviticus 10, where Nadab and Abihu offered strange fire to the Lord, man-made fire. Many Christians believe they can offer "strange fire," man-made worship, fulfilling certain duties and then placing them on the altar of God. Worship as a duty of human effort is an offense to God and lives under His potential wrath. The altars of our hearts must have the heavenly fire fall on them in true conversion before our worship, our offerings, will be acceptable to God. Much of our worship today is man-made. We have worship services, worship teams, worship music, and individual times of worship called devotions, but all of these are empty if there is not first fire from heaven poured out on us in conversion. We are but keepers of the flame called to not let the flame go out. If we are not careful, we can become like Nadab and Abihu, offering our man-made fire to God. Our worship is our enjoyment of God. Do you find worship of God enjoyable?

C.S. Lewis continues in *Reflections on the Psalms*: "But the most obvious fact about praise---whether of God or anything—strangely escaped me… I had never noticed that all enjoyment spontaneously overflows into praise… I think we delight to praise what we enjoy, because the praise not merely expresses but completes the enjoyment; it is its appointed consummation."

Worship is the consummation of our enjoyment of God. It is the consummation of our love, the enjoyment of our love: "My lover is mine and I am his" (Song 2:16). The chief end of man is to glorify God and to enjoy Him all the days of this life. These two become one in worship.

While riding motorcycles with some friends through the desert, we came upon the Ivanpah Solar Electric Generating System, a solar thermal power plant in the Mojave Desert. We saw a tall tower surrounded on all sides by a field of mirrors. I later learned that there are 173,000 of these mirrors called heliostats, which focus the light of the sun on that tower, which contains three power plants. The sight of thousands of acres of mirrors surrounding these towers was incredible. These heliostat mirrors direct the sun's light and heat to the central towers. The receivers then generate steam to drive steam turbines. The position of the sun changes during the day, so the mirrors must move to follow the sun. The exact adjustments of the mirrors are fully automated, with each mirror having sensors and tracking systems that allow it to stay focused on the sun. Worship is our tracking system that keeps us focused on the Son, reflecting His glory, and it is in reflecting this glory that power is produced in us and we are changed.

Worship, being focused on the Lord, produces a holy steam, or power, in the individual to transform him or her into the image of God. When a pot is set on the stove and heat applied, there is a reaction between pot, heat, and water that causes the water to boil and give off steam. True worship brings the believer into the presence of God by the Holy Spirit, and the reaction of the human heart to the presence and glory of God produces a boiling in our hearts, giving off the steam of our love and adoration for God. In this interaction with God, He pours out His love into our hearts, which causes them to boil, giving off the steam of love back to Him. Worship is speaking our love back to God. One of the by-products of this love reaction is the steam that is released in the form of worship as expressions of love to God. The steam is the praise and worship that comes from that fiery interaction with God. It is natural, as effortless as the steam that rises from boiling water. If you put a pot of water on the fire, it will boil and give off steam. When God by the grace of His salvation puts the believer in His presence, shining His fiery glory on that person, the heart will boil, giving off the steam of love, worship, and praise. The reason there is so little worship today is that Christians are not focused on the glory of God, nor are they standing in His fiery presence. ". . . [H]is eyes were like blazing fire. His feet were like bronze glowing in a furnace" (Rev. 1:14–15).

Oswald Chambers said, "Worshiping God is the great essential of fitness. If you have not been worshiping, when you get into work you will not only be useless yourself, but a tremendous hindrance to those who are associated with you." Worship is beholding or looking at the one being worshiped. It is in beholding Jesus that we are changed into His image. Worship will be the act of faith by which I look unto Jesus and, in the looking, receive the glory of God, which contains the transforming strength and power of God for the ministry He calls me to do. If I have not been looking (worshiping), there will be no power and I will be a hindrance to those I minister with. It is in the act of worship that the believer receives the grace of God through the glory of God in the face of Christ Jesus. You are not a worshiper because you say you are; you are a worshiper when you worship. "Yet a time is coming and has now come when the true worshipers will worship the Father in spirit and in truth, for they are the kind of worshipers the Father seeks" (John 4:23). It will be part of the work of the inhabiting Holy Spirit to turn your heart and mind to look upon Jesus and pour out worship of the same. Worship puts my focus on Jesus, who then heals and empowers me to live like Him before Him and the world.

It is important to remind ourselves here of the necessity of new birth or salvation. "For God so loved the world that he gave his one and only Son, that whoever believes in him shall not perish but have eternal life" (John 3:16). God offered His only Son as a sacrifice for you, for your sin. It is that sin that has kept you from seeing the glory of God in Christ Jesus. You were created for God to glorify Him, to worship Him, to be with Him. Sin, inherited and committed, has broken that supreme relationship. If you believe on Jesus, that relationship can be restored, and you can be reunited with your Heavenly Father. "Look unto me, and be ye saved, all the ends of the earth" (Isa. 45:22, KJV). Turn your eyes to Jesus and look like the Israelites did to the bronze serpent, and you will live. Christ calls you to Himself this day. Will you come, will you repent, will you believe, will you look and be saved?

Worship is the key that unlocks the door upon which Jesus is knocking. Remember what He said: "Here I am! I stand at the door and knock. If anyone hears my voice and opens the door, I will come in and eat with him, and he with me" (Rev. 3:20). God's response to the worshiper is to reveal Himself, then to love the worshiper, and then to come in and sup with him. We begin with worship and end up having dinner with Jesus, who loves us more than any other being in the universe. This speaks of fellowship and the enjoyment of our Lord. When the door opens, Christ comes in to be our dinner guest, and we have the pleasure of His company. We will be satisfied with His unfailing love. As we have dinner with Him, fellowship with Him, he changes us into His image. This is the enjoyment of what should be the supreme relationship in your life. Many who believe in God never really worship Him and never find that enjoyment of a personal relationship with Him.

God's means of transferring His righteousness to man is by using the conduit of His glory and person of His Spirit. Worship positions me in the stream of that light so that I might look at Him until I look like Him. This is why when God saves a man, He brings him into His presence and desires to keep him there. When we are in His presence, the light of His glory will continue to shine on us and transform us into His image. One of God's promises for the coming of the New Covenant was that He would write His law on our hearts. The writing of the law upon the heart is accomplished by the Spirit, not by man. The writing of the law upon the heart is the picture of the heart being changed into the image of the law, into the image of Christ, who is the fulfillment of the law. How does God write the law on the heart of the Christian? By the Christian beholding, gazing upon, the Lord Jesus Christ, by seeing Christ, with the aid of the Holy Spirit. "In a little while you will see me no more, and then after a little while you will see me" (John 16:16).

"I did not see that it is in the process of being worshiped that God communicates His presence to men. It is not of course the only way, but for many people at many times the 'fair beauty of the Lord' is revealed chiefly or only while they worship him. Even in Judaism the essence of the sacrifice was not really that men gave bulls and goats to God, but that by their so doing God gave Himself to men" (*Reflections on the Psalms*, Lewis). "But thou art holy, O thou that inhabitest the praises of Israel" (Ps. 22:3, KJV). God desires that we worship Him because He wants to reveal Himself to us. We worship because He is worthy of all our praise, but in that worship, He reveals Himself to us; we see Him, and in seeing Him, we will want to worship Him more, and as we do, we are changed by standing in His glory. The revelation of Himself to us will include the revelation of His love for us. The Psalmist says, "Satisfy us in the morning with your unfailing love, that we may sing for joy" (Ps. 90:14). The singing for joy comes from hearts heated to a boil by the fiery presence, glory, and love of God. Worship is the enraptured soul declaring its love for Christ. In speaking forth its love, it is enjoying the one loved.

Griffith Thomas, one of the founders of Dallas Theological Seminary, said, "Revelation and worship are the foundation of everything." Remember what C.S. Lewis said: "I discovered it is in the act of worship that God reveals himself to man." If both of these men are right, then we should have a self-perpetuating cycle. You worship, and God reveals His glory to you. You see the fresh revelation of God, and you worship or glorify Him even more. Then again, there is even more revelation, and you worship and glorify Him even more. Thomas is saying that these two are the foundation of everything in the Christian life. Just as we come to salvation through the revelation of Christ by the Spirit through the Word, so we continue to walk with Christ by the revelation of Himself by the Spirit through the Word. With every revelation comes the joy and love of the Lord, and out of that love and joy, the heart is caused to sing the glory of the One giving the joy and love to us. Worship brings fresh revelation of Christ and keeps our salvation fresh and new. This fresh revelation of these mercies is new every morning—or they can be if we go and look. This revelation of the glory of God in the face of Christ is what causes us to grow in the grace and knowledge of the Lord Jesus Christ and transforms us into His image.

Paul prays for the Ephesians something he wants them to know. He wants them to know the love of God. Paul's prayer goes like this: "I pray that out of his glorious riches he may strengthen you with power through his Spirit in your inner being, so that Christ may dwell in your hearts through faith. And I pray that you, being rooted and established in love, may have power, together with all the saints, to grasp how wide and long and high and deep is the love of Christ, and to know this love that surpasses knowledge—that you may be filled to the measure of all the fullness of God" (Eph. 3:16–19).

Worship is counting the ways God loves us. Before the foundation of the world, He chose us. He carried a line of righteousness and the message of salvation through history to us. He prophesied One who would come and set us free, the Messiah. He came and took on flesh that He might keep the law for us and offer that perfection as a sacrifice for our sin. He died, was buried, and rose again for us. He ascended into heaven for us to prepare a place for us where one day, He could bring us to be with Him. Open the Word and read of His love on every page. Take every love token He has given and offer it back to Him with praise. Let Him come and inhabit that praise and be with you. Oh, the love of God! How does He love me? Let me count the ways—and you will find that it will take an eternity to count them all. Counting the ways He loves us is a part of our worship. Counting the ways God loves us will be a way of enjoying the love of God.

Paul is praying that we might understand how much God loves us; let us count the ways. First, we must have help to understand how great the love of God for us is. So great is God's divine love, we need the help of the Holy Spirit to understand something of its greatness. "You may have power, together with all the saints, to grasp how wide and long and high and deep is the love of Christ" (Eph. 3:18). The size of this love is beyond the boundaries of our understanding. Paul tells us this love is so great that it surpasses knowledge; it is beyond our understanding, yet there is something of this love we can know. His love is beyond time, for He has loved us before the foundation of the world and chose us for Himself. His love is eternal and will never end. His love is so big, there is no place I can run and hide from it, for no matter where I go, His love was there before me and will be there when I leave. Surely, goodness and mercy—and we can add love—shall follow me all the days of my life. He has loved us in His Son, in His incarnation, in living His perfect life, and in going to the cross. He has loved us in His death, in His resurrection, in His ascension, and in His enthronement above. He will love us in His return when He bids us come and meet Him in the air or in ripping open our graves to meet Him in the sky. He will love us with a feast in Heaven, the marriage supper of the Lamb, and with a return to the new earth to rule and reign with Him. You could spend the rest of your life and all eternity considering how He loves us and never find the end of it. Will you not let your heart burst forth in the worship of the lover of your soul?

Yet there is something more. How could there be any more? Paul says, "And to know this love that surpasses knowledge." Paul doesn't just want us to know facts about the size of this love. He wants us to experience this love by experiencing the lover, God Himself. The wonder is that we can. Here is where many fall short: They know intellectually that God loves them, but they have never experienced that love personally. Experiencing the love of God is the highest and greatest experience a human being can have. Yet we have traded away this great experience for the trinkets and baubles of this world and of the evangelical Church. Worship will unlock this door to God and the fullness of His love. In the power of this relationship with God, one is freed from the gravity of other competing loves. In the act of worship, God reveals Himself to men as the God who is love. In knowing and seeing something of this love, we will see that this is a living person who loves us and desires to live with us. Our hearts will be flooded with the love of a living person, and we will be transformed by it.

Paul is praying that we will see, with the assistance of the Holy Spirit, the immensity of the love of Christ. The revelation of this eternal, perfect love brings forth more praise and worship, which brings forth more revelation. It is hard for us to believe Jesus is so in love with us. How can it be? He not only loves us but also wants to dwell in our hearts, to be one with us. Paul wants us to focus on God's love, not our own. More than this, Paul wants us to experience this love of Christ. From the revelation and the fullness of the love of Christ will come joy unspeakable, for which we will praise and worship God more, guaranteeing more revelation of that love. When that love is revealed to us and in us, we will be transformed into that love. This means we will be able to love God and others with the love of God poured into us by His glory.

Subjective truth never delivers; objective truth delivers. One of the clearest pictures of this is Peter walking on water. Jesus, who had been praying, decides to join His disciples, who are out in a boat fighting against wind and wave. He is coming to them by walking on the water. When the disciples see Him, they think it's a ghost and are terrified. Jesus lets them know that it is He. Peter says, "Lord, if it is you, bid me to come to you on the water." Jesus's response to Peter's request is "Come" (Matt. 14:28–29). Peter gets out of the boat and walks on the water toward Jesus. What must that have been like? Up to this point, Peter is performing a miracle by looking at Jesus. Peter then changes his focus; he sees the wind and the waves; these were the elements that were causing the problem, preventing the boat from arriving at its destination. Looking at subjective truth (the problem), Peter begins to sink and cries out, "Lord, save me!" Jesus reaches out His hand and catches Peter. Here again, the focus is on Jesus. When they get into the boat again, those there with Him worship Him, for they have seen something of His glory (Matt. 14:23–33).

When I look inward—at the wind and the waves—I see my failures and ask what to do now, how to walk on that water. I look at the Word of God for the answers regarding how to live in the storm. I see some answer about how to live, and I look at it instead of Jesus. I focus on my failure, my sin, and then I focus on the law that says don't do that sin. Where is the help? It's like someone telling you not to see a pink elephant in your mind, and the more you try not to see the pink elephant, the more you see it. If all that I can see is my sin and the law, then as with the pink elephant, I can't get them off my mind. There is no power in me to change, and there is no power in the law to change. I have nothing that can deliver me—subjective truth. "I do not understand what I do [self-focus], for what I want to do, I do not do, but what I hate, I do. And if I do what I do not want to do, I agree that the law is good. As it is, it is no longer I myself who do it, but it is sin living in me. I know that nothing good lives in me, that is, in my sinful nature. But I cannot carry it out. For what I do is not the good I want to do; no, the evil I do not want to do—this I keep on doing. What a wretched man I am! Who will rescue me from this body of death?" (Rom. 7:14–24). This chapter of Romans can be very depressing. It is one that most Christians are quite familiar with. The answer to the spiritual depression in this chapter of Romans comes in the next chapter of Romans. The answer is not looking further inside to find more sin, nor even in digging more into the law to find more rules to keep. The answer to man's need is outside himself; it is a new law, the law of the Spirit of life. Worship focuses not on internal sin, nor on the law that declares what not to do. Worship focuses on the objective truth that will deliver me—the Spirit of life. My deliverance, righteousness, and sanctification are not to be found in me; they are to be found only in my Savior, Jesus Christ. We have forgotten the Gospel in all our counseling and principles for spiritual growth. We have forgotten what the Gospel is—the power of God not just for salvation but also for sanctification. We have forgotten to look at Jesus lifted up like the serpent in the wilderness in order that we might be healed, empowered, and transformed into the image of Christ. Worship is looking at the perfections and power of Jesus and by the miracle of God's transforming power, seeing them, they become mine in Christ. Here is my power, here is my perfection, here is my ability to overcome sin, in Christ, and these are mine by an act of faith, worshiping and beholding Him.

Here is the point we want to understand: If I am justified by faith and not by works, then how am I sanctified? By faith! Could faith be as simple as looking unto Jesus like Peter walking on the water? Could it be as simple as looking at the bronze serpent and being healed? Could the Christian life be as simple as looking at Jesus and being transformed? We can't believe it because we really find it hard as humans to believe that we are saved by faith and transformed into His image by faith and nothing else and that faith could look like a simple glance at Jesus. Worship is me glancing at the glory of Christ and praising Him for what He has done and will do in me. Worship is preoccupation with the Gospel. Worship is that step of faith where we look at Christ and live again and again. Worship is one of the ways we look at the Gospel—at Jesus—and are being saved. Many today have quit looking at the Gospel. They have quit worshiping Jesus and lost any power they did have.

Jeremiah Burroughs, writing in *Gospel Worship*, said something that changed the way I thought about my approach to God and my need for Him: "Again, as natural conscience gives no strength to do the duty, so it does not make a duty to be strong to the soul. That is, there's no strength gotten by the duty. One is not by one prepared for another, 'but the way of the Lord is strength to the upright' (Proverbs 10:29). That is, when a gracious heart is in the way of God's worship, it finds the very duty of the worship of God to be strength to it and so fits it for another duty." What was Burroughs saying here? It is not obedience to God's law that strengthens the soul for its duty. Power doesn't come to us by trying to obey some law but when we look to Jesus with our praise and worship. Faith that fills its vision with the glory of God in worship will find that worship to strengthen it, empower it, and transform it. We think that my obedience or even my attempt to obey is what causes God's power to be released to me. Does God reward those who try to obey Him with more power? When that gracious heart is in the way of God's worship, beholding God, worshiping God, he finds the worship (beholding) to be strength to it. How often is our focus in the wrong place—on the law and whether I am keeping it or not. "When the gracious heart is in the way of worship," focused on God, worshiping and admiring God, glorifying Him for who and what He is, then God gives the power that transforms the life. Burroughs restates what Paul writes in II Corinthians 3:18, that we are changed by beholding Jesus. Though they use two different words, I believe they are saying the same thing, for worship is a way of beholding Jesus. Beholding and worship may be synonymous and the way to power in the Christian life.

Walking in the way of worship, I can offer my love back to God as I see all that He has done for me. The language of worship can become the language of love, describing His beauty, His strength, and His power. Describing the wonderful character traits of the one we love is a way of offering our love to Him. We praise the one we love and love Him in the praise.

As we have already said, Paul mentions in II Corinthians 3:18 that we are changed by beholding this Jesus Christ. I believe it is proportional: The more we behold, the more we are transformed into the image of God's Son. Paul says that as we look at God's glory, we are being transformed into His likeness with ever-increasing glory or measure. Worship changes our focus from our internal sin and failure to Christ's perfection, holiness, and righteousness. Worship is looking at the glory of God, and in seeing that glory, God gives all that is needed for life and godliness here on earth. The answer to our sin and failure is to gaze upon the perfection of Christ and His inability to fail. The answer to our sin is to gaze on the Gospel. Looking at His glory, we receive grace upon grace. Worship puts us in the place to do this, the place to be changed by the beholding.

There are many things we can do in our devotions: We can pray for others, for the sick and lost, and for those who are weak in faith. We can confess our sins and ask for forgiveness from above. We can pray and ask God to open mission fields and save the lost. We can pray for our ministries and churches, and we should. But what we should do first and most often is take the key of worship that will set us free from bondage to this earth, and soar in the heavenlies with our Savior. And as we speak love to Him, we find that we are changed into His image. Part of that transformation will be power to do His will in a lost and dying world. Your worship of Jesus will do more for people around you than anything else you can do.

What do you know about worship? Have you given yourself to the worship of God? Do you sing to Him the praise that He deserves? Do you find your post as the cherubim and sing without stopping: "Holy, holy, holy" to the praise of His glory? You will find that your worship is the moment in the day when you stop and look at the bronze serpent so you will be healed and empowered to walk through the day without the poison of sin in your life. Will you take time from your busy life to worship Jesus, to be a service to Him so you may be transformed into what He would have you to be, and then find your place to serve Him and others?

In the late 1980s, I went back to school full time, with a wife and four small children. God called us to go to Bible school. I had much to learn in Bible school, but not all the lessons that God wanted to teach us came from the classroom. One day, I was studying, preparing for some tests and writing some papers that were due. I would often listen to Gospel music while studying. One day, my youngest son asked if he could come in and sit with me. I told him almost scoldingly, "You can come in, but you have to be quiet, for your daddy is studying." He came in and sat in the chair to my right and just sat, such stillness being very unusual for him. One of the songs I was listening to moved me deeply, and I began to weep. By this time, I had almost forgotten about my little son sitting there with me. I turned to see how he was doing, and to my surprise, I saw big tears rolling down his face. This little man could not hear the music I was hearing, the music that was moving my heart to tears. Why was he crying? This young boy loved his father, and when he saw his father cry, he cried. He was transformed by being in his father's presence. Being in his father's presence, he was sharing his father's heart. He was sharing his father's emotions. When we come into our heavenly Father's presence, He shares His heart with us; He shares with us His joy; He shares with us His life. As with my young son, God uses the love He gives us to draw us into His presence, and there He reveals His heart to us. Seeing something of that heart, of His glory, we are changed. Worship is the little child asking his father if he can come and sit with Him and being in His presence, share His heart, and change into His likeness. Come, then, and worship the Lord in the beauty of holiness.

In the almost 20 years I played football, I only had one true championship. We had won the championship and headed to the locker room for interviews and the celebration of our victory. We were wild with exuberance. Our owner was a billionaire and something of a wine connoisseur, so he had Dom Perignon champagne for drinking a celebratory toast. What we didn't know was that he had bought two kinds: cheap champagne for spraying all over each other and Dom Perignon for a true toast to one another for the victory. Some of the guys had taken the Dom Perignon and were spraying it, wasting it by pouring it over one another. One of the staff came in screaming, "That's Dom Perignon! Don't waste it like that. Use the cheap stuff!" His cries were of little use as we continued to spray the Dom Perignon on each other in celebration. We were jumping into one another's arms and loving one another with our praise and thanks over this great victory. We were high-fiving each other and screaming with joy. Few people get to experience something like this, and it's one reason the TV people like to get their cameras into the locker rooms for these celebrations. I sat in that locker room as long as I could, for I knew this might never happen again in my life. What I didn't know then was that this celebration was worship. In that champagne shower, praise and jumping up and down, hugging each other, we were worshiping together. We were enjoying one another's company with a joy we had not known before and seldom would again. Our King is a victor, and He has won the greatest victory and made us a part of it. We are called to come and celebrate that victory with the champagne of praise and the shouts of joy, to embrace our victor, to carry Him on our shoulders, and thank Him for winning the game, which we never could.

For many, the key is hanging on the wall behind glass. Break the glass, take out the key of worship, unlock the door to gaze upon the One who has won the victory for us, and worship Him with song and praise. "Lord, I was a loser, but you brought me to your team. Though I could do nothing to win the victory, you weren't ashamed to make me a part of your team, not ashamed to let me play. Now I share in the victory and glory that is yours, and you have made it mine. How can I ever thank you for winning for me?" Come join the celebration; come with worship and praise, sing the songs of victory, and embrace the Victor with your worship.

Chapter 7

OBSERVATORY FOR GOD

"God did this so that men would seek him and perhaps reach out for him and find him, though he is not far from each one of us. 'For in him we live and move and have our being.'" (Acts 17:27–28)

THE FIRST WRITTEN record we have of a refracting telescope is of Hans Lepperhey's patent that he filed in 1608 for his instrument "for seeing things far away as if they were nearby." News of the invention soon was heard of throughout Europe, leading other scientists to begin experimenting and improving the device. Galileo was one of those men improving the telescope and turning it to the skies to study the heavens. We have a record of how astronomy has continued to improve and increase the power of telescopes over the last 400 years. With these improvements, astronomers have discovered things never seen with the naked eye. They also have discovered ways of eliminating the things that would distract from what they wanted to see. Much of what they did for hundreds of years was eliminate distracting lights and find thinner air by moving to the tops of mountains to reduce the atmospheric distortions of what they wanted to see. They finally put these observatories out in space where there is no air or atmosphere to distort what they are trying to see.

In the 1960s, scientists put the first telescopes in space to remove interference caused by the atmosphere. The pictures that came back encouraged larger and more sophisticated space observatories. In 1990, NASA sent up the Hubble telescope, which had some problems with its lenses that had to be addressed in subsequent Space Shuttle flights. Once it was repaired, the pictures that were sent back were beautiful beyond description. There was no comparison with what had been seen before. In 2021, the Webb telescope was launched to give us an even better view of space. Astronomers wanted to reach into the depths of space to seek and find what might lie hidden there. They have given themselves to this task for over 400 years. You might say that they have given themselves wholeheartedly to that goal. Think of the work and effort that has been put into seeing objects in the heavens. Think of the billions of dollars that have been spent in this pursuit. If we would put but a portion of that effort into building an observatory for seeking and finding God, what would be the result and what would we find?

As we looked at Adam and Moses, we saw that they both had places where they would go and look upon God. We used these two because when they saw God and were in the presence of God, they were changed by His glory. The shining wasn't because of some effort they put forth; it was because God was shining His glory upon them. You and I will never shine or live righteous and godly lives by self-effort. It will be the result of God's grace manifest to the seeking heart that looks on Christ and longs to be with Him. Adam had the garden where he walked with God in the cool of the day. Here was the first "God observatory," and as Adam and Eve observed God, they were changed and had the glow of His glory. Moses went up on the mountain, spent 40 days observing God, and came back shining with God's glory. He also had a tent of meeting where he would go and talk to God as with a man, face-to-face. Adam and Moses met with God and walked and talked with Him, and the result was that they were shining with His glory. Just as the astronomer has a dedicated place to observe the heavens, we need a place we can go and observe our God, unhindered by the lights and atmosphere of the world, a place where we can gaze on the beauty of the Lord—a God observatory.

My eldest daughter, Katie, married a young man from New Zealand. He had been working in the United States but was transferred back to New Zealand in 2014. We didn't know how long it would be before we would see Katie, so we decided to go to New Zealand for a summer Christmas. Christmas of 2014, we packed our bags and headed Down Under to celebrate with them in Auckland.

This Christmas experience was very different from any Christmas we had ever celebrated before. Christmas in New Zealand is in the dead of summer, as their seasons are the reverse of ours. New Zealanders use their Christmas vacation to go to the beach or to go camping or hiking in the mountains; it's a national summer-time holiday. That being the case, it seemed as if the whole nation was on the road.

We celebrated Christmas in Auckland and then headed to the South Island for a five-day motorcycle tour that gave us a taste of the diversity of that island: the dry western slopes covered with grapevines, the snow-capped Southern Alps, the rich, dense rainforest of the western side of the island. We caught the short flight from Auckland to Christchurch, where we picked up our motorcycle. The first stop on our tour was Lake Tekapo, where we spent our first night on the South Island. Lake Tekapo is a remarkable turquoise-colored lake in the Southern Alps that gets its intense milky-turquoise color from the fine rock-flour (ground by glaciers) suspended in the water.

One of the best things about Lake Tekapo's scenic location is that it is far away from the lights of major towns and cities. The isolation and flat plains provide beautiful clear skies that offer unparalleled views of the stars and planets. The area was named the world's largest International Dark Sky Reserve in June 2012. This means that the skies are almost completely free from any light pollution, making it one of the best places in the world for stargazing. As a dark sky reserve, the town of Lake Tekapo has rules concerning exterior lighting for homes and even for streetlamps. Having lived most of my life in the Chicago area, I knew something about light pollution. Even on the clearest of nights, we could see only the brightest stars and a few of the constellations. I was looking forward to seeing the stars unhindered by competing lights.

I was troubled as we pulled into Lake Tekapo, for it was an overcast day with no break in the clouds. I thought to myself, *I've flown halfway around the world to get here, and I'll only be here one night, and now I won't be able to see the night sky at all.* Having arrived late in the afternoon, we settled into our bed-and-breakfast and then got something to eat. Everything in Tekapo is within walking distance, so we walked down to a restaurant and had dinner, then walked around town, and finally back to where we were staying to settle in for the night. Our room had a sliding glass door to the backyard, and I found myself looking out of it all evening to see if the clouds had cleared away. Finally, at about ten o'clock, I gave up and went to bed, doubting whether I would ever see Tekapo's starry night. The night we arrived was to be optimal for star-gazing because there was no moon that night. Tekapo was one of the darkest places I have ever been. When we turned the lights off in the room, I couldn't even see my hand held right in front of my face.

Still hoping to have a chance to see the stars of Tekapo, I got up at about two o'clock in the morning, went to the sliding glass door, and looked out. There they were! The clouds had blown away and there in the clear black sky were the stars as I had never seen them before. I was in awe. As I looked at this awesome display of stars, I realized that compared to these stars, I had never seen stars in my life. It was so amazing that I had to wake up Sally so she could see them as well. (By the way, waking up Sally in the middle of the night is not something that you do lightly.) Together we looked at the night sky like young children, as if we were seeing the stars for the first time. We saw stars, clouds of stars, and shooting stars with a brightness and intensity that we had never known. Like two thirsty souls, we drank in the view of what God had created, thinking that the heavens really do declare the glory of the Lord. This was the high point of the trip for me. I didn't want to go back to bed. This was the greatest star show I had ever seen, and I probably will never see its like again.

To view this glory, we had to get to a place where there were no distracting lights. If you would see God, you will need a place to gaze on Him (behold Him) where there are no distracting (competing) lights. It occurred to me shortly after seeing the stars in New Zealand that most Christians have heard about God, but they have not seen the bright glory of God because there are too many competing lights in life. These competing lights have drowned out our vision of His glory. Most have not known that there is a place they can go and see God, to see His glory, and be driven to wonder, love, and praise. Most have stopped at knowing there is a God and have missed the adventure and wonder of "gazing upon the beauty of the Lord." I thought I had seen the stars, but when I saw the stars that night in Tekapo, I realized I never had. Many Christians have seen glimpses of God's glory, only to have it drowned out by the lights of this world.

Like an astronomer, we should build a place designed to see God, a place dedicated to looking at God. The observatory we build may be called the secret place, a quiet time, or daily devotions. Your observatory should have a dedicated place or location where you go for the express purpose of looking at your God and for meeting with Him. It will be your workplace where you do the great business. Observing God will be your main work. Everything else you do in the day will be less important and significant. Your observatory will have your telescope "for seeing things far away as if they were nearby." Your observatory and telescope are for seeing the unseen God. Your telescope is the Word of God through which we look to see the God of the Word, and the Holy Spirit who reveals and magnifies that vision of God. The vision and revelation we see there will be the work of the Holy Spirit, who reveals Christ to us through the Word of God.

Listen to Jesus's words as I believe He was talking about an observatory where we might see God: "And when you pray, do not be like the hypocrites, for they love to pray standing in the synagogues and on the street corner to be seen by men. I tell you the truth, they have received their reward in full" (Matt. 6:5). Notice that the hypocrites' goal wasn't to see God but to be seen by others. Could it be that the only observation you want is to be seen by others doing your Christian deeds? "But when you pray, go into your room, close the door and pray to your Father, who is unseen" (Matt. 6:6). Few build these observatories, as they have been told they can't see God because He is invisible. Few build them, for all they really want to see is them-selves and their conditions here on earth improved. Some think, *Why should I build an observatory to see someone who is invisible?* Many are defeated before they start. "But when you pray, go into your room, close the door and pray to your Father who is unseen. Then your Father, who sees what is done in secret, will reward you" (Matt. 6:6). Here is a picture of going into an observatory. The religious leaders were praying in the streets in order to be seen by others. They were distracted by what men thought of them and how their performance was in front of an audience. Your observatory is not for others but for you and God alone. In this observatory, God is the first observer; He sees who comes to the secret place and what is done in secret. When you go into the closet, you close the door to the distracting lights of world, and you are alone in the dark with your Father. The Father sees you when you come in and knows what you want before you even ask. He knows what you are looking for, and He knows if you are looking for Him. Jesus says, "He will reward you." We think the reward is what we are going to ask for—things of this world. I say the reward is seeing the unseen Father; the reward is a vision of Christ. When the lights of the world are shut out, slowly but surely the light of the glory of God will begin to shine in when you are looking for Him.

"The disciples came to Jesus and asked, 'Why do you speak to the people in parables?' He replied, 'The knowl-edge of the secrets of the kingdom of heaven has been given to you, but not to them. Whoever has will be given more, and he will have an abundance. Whoever does not have, even what he has will be taken from him. This is why I speak to them in parables: Though seeing, they do not see; though hearing, they do not hear or understand'" (Matt. 13:10–13). Knowledge of the secret things was given to the disciples, and that same knowledge can be given to us who believe. Whoever has will be given more and will have abundance. The secret things of the Kingdom are given in the secret place, in the secret observatory. Jesus goes on to say to His disciples, "But blessed are your eyes because they see, and your ears because they hear. For I tell you the truth, many prophets and righteous men longed to see what you see…" (Matt. 13:16). Just as the Father sees you when you come into the secret place, it is His desire that you see Him. The gift of seeing God, the gift of the secret things of the Kingdom of God, has been given to us. The question is: Will I receive this gift and see the glory of God in the face of Christ Jesus? It is God's desire that you see Him. He has sent the Spirit with the gift of wisdom and revelation that you might know Him better. Won't you come and just look at Jesus? This seeing is just the beginning of a life of seeing with greater clarity the wonder and glory of Christ. Will you build an observatory to see the greatest vision a man or woman can ever see? And will you go in and look every day at the glory of God in Christ? Building your observatory can be synonymous with building your relationship with Christ.

What makes a good spot for observing the night sky? You will need clear skies, where no clouds block our vision. You need a dark place where there is no competing light. These competing lights steal away the glory of the stars you want to see. Astronomers look for special places to look at their stars—places away from cities and their bright competing lights. They look for places that are at high altitude so there is less atmosphere to affect or distort the images they are looking at. Just as the astronomer needs a special place to see the stars at their best advantage, you need a place to go and look upon God that is free from distracting lights and the atmosphere of the world. Like the astronomer, you need to build a place where you can gaze upon the Lord without the distractions of the world—a place you go to do your work of observing the Bright Morning Star.

What are the competing lights we need to get away from so we might see the Glory of God? One of the lights that drown out the light of God is need. How many times have you come to gaze on the Lord only to see or think about what you want or need? There is no end to the needs we will have in this life, whether imagined or real. There is no end to what a person may want, for the flesh can never be satisfied. J.D. Rockefeller, being the richest man in the world in his day, was asked, "If you could have anything, what would you want?" He is said to replied, "Just a little more." Philosopher George Santayana said, "Only the dead have seen the end of the war," and I think we could paraphrase his quote by saying, "Only the dead have seen the end of need." We must repent of ourselves and our selfish desires for anything other than Christ. There will be no end of need and lust for the things we think are needs, as long as we live. Our loved ones will get sick; we will always need more food and water; we will have health concerns throughout life. If we allow it, this never-ending need will become all we see, and we'll never turn our telescope to look at Christ. Filling our vision with self and the things we want and need in this life will eclipse the light and glory of God.

Herman Melville writes in *Moby Dick,* in a chapter titled "The Sermon," of a message preached by Father Mapple. His text was Jonah 1:17: "And God had prepared a great fish to swallow up Jonah." Jonah was in rebellion and was running from God's command to go to Nineveh to preach to those people. We know the rest of the story. In the message, Father Mapple says this: "But all the things that God would have us do are hard for us to do. Remember that he oftener commands us than endeavors to persuade. And if we obey God, we must disobey ourselves; and it is in this disobeying ourselves, wherein the hardness of obeying God consists." The great competing light of self and what we want must be disobeyed; our plans must be disobeyed; our wants and desires must be disobeyed. We must look away from these things. We must set them aside and block them out if we are going to see something of the glory of God. The desire to see God must become the first desire. This self-disobedience the Bible calls repentance. If we would see the light and glory of God, we first must look away from the lights of what the self wants. These are often good things, yet things that are not God. Repentance is not just turning around and obeying a law of God; it is turning around and looking at and relating to Jesus. Until my life is taken up with looking at Jesus, it may be that I have never really repented of looking at myself. The first obedience will be answering God's call to look unto Him.

If you were to describe what you observe in your daily devotions, what would that be? Take a tape recorder into your secret place and record your prayer. Most of us we would have to say after hearing our prayers that we were at the center. The things we desire and need are what we are praying for. Personal desire fills our prayers to the point that God is drowned out. Most of what we talk about is me, my, and mine. We might even pray about ministry and spend our time and thoughts there. Ministry can be a subtle way of looking at self—what I am doing for God. If we would call this an observatory, the only thing being observed is ourselves and even what we are doing for God. Until we repent and turn away from the bright light of self, we will never see the healing light of God's glory. As Father Mapple said, this is hard—hard to be done with self and want only God. If we turn away from self and its desires and look at Jesus, the light of His glory will begin to shine through, and we will see what few have seen—the glory of God. We are delighting in ourselves and what we are doing and in what we want. God wants us to "Delight thyself also in the Lord; and he shall give thee the desires of thine heart" (Ps. 37:4, KJV). If we delight in and desire God, He will give us that desire, He will give us Himself, and we will see something of His glory.

To see the Lord, you must repent of your sin and look upon His face. I have not included individual or particular sins or made them the focus of this writing. The reason I have not done this is that we are all sinners. "For whoever keeps the whole law and yet stumbles at just one point is guilty of breaking all of it" (James 2:10). We are guilty of breaking all the laws. "There is none righteous, no not one" (Rom. 3:10). You and I are monsters of iniquity. As Christians, we should see what monsters we are by the difficulty we have at looking at the most beautiful thing in the universe—Jesus Christ. We don't look because we really don't want to look. We don't look because we really don't want Jesus. We want what we want and hope Jesus will give it to us. There are other things we want and want to look at, and, in our sin, we flee and hide from the vision of God, just as Adam did in the garden. When you try to gaze solely upon the Lord, you will find it difficult—even impossible—without true repentance. The world, the flesh, and the devil all will war against you coming to gaze on the beauty of the Lord. If the enemy can stop you here at the beginning, he has won the war.

If you are going to see God, first you must decide this is what you want to see. Next, you need an observatory, a place where you go to see (observe) this great phenomenon—God. Like the astronomer, this is a dedicated place with the singular purpose of seeing one thing—God. This place must be free from the clouds of sin, of wanting to see anything but God. Sin unrepented of will keep you from seeing God. Go quickly to God and confess that which the Spirit of God reveals to you. He will be faithful and just to forgive us our sins. Keep short accounts with God. In this way, we deal with our known sins. The Psalmist not only asks forgiveness of his known sin but also those that might be unknown to him. "But who can discern his errors? Forgive my hidden (unknown) faults" (Ps. 19:12). We are habitual sinners and sin so much that sometimes we can't tell if we are sinning or not. Confess what you know and that which you may have missed. Be careful not to linger here looking at your sin. Some have been trapped by the devil to keep looking at themselves and their sin and never get to looking at God. Remember, as you see something of the glory of God, you will see His forgiveness for your sin as well.

This observatory is also a place where the competing lights of this world have no interference with our looking at and seeing God Himself. The clouds of sin and the desires for the vanities or lights of this world will drown out any vision of God. As the atmosphere of earth keeps the astronomer from seeing stars with great effect, so the atmosphere of the world will blind us to the glory of God. The atmosphere around us will affect how we see God. Let me give an example: In our day, sensuality is something we don't think of as being sin or something that would keep us from seeing God. Sensuality is relating to or involving gratification of the senses and physical—especially sexual—pleasure. Sensuality has to do with gazing on the fallen beauty of this world. The atmosphere of our day is extremely sensual and particularly sexual. The vision of and delineation of the feminine form is everywhere. Everything in our culture is sexualized. Sensuality will include other beautiful things this world offers, things that are not evil in themselves but have a beauty that pulls our eyes away from looking unto Christ. This sensuality blinds one to the spiritual world and cools the heart of passion for God. You may find that you have to throw out the sensual things you have been looking at if you really want to see God.

When you work with steel, sometimes you have to heat it up to bend it. As an ironworker, I would heat the steel until it glowed red, and when it was red enough, I knew it was ready to bend. I might touch that red-hot steel with another piece of cool metal, and where I did, that spot would go black. What happened when I touched it was that the heat was being pulled out of that spot by the cool metal, and cooling, it would grow dark. I would have to heat it up again to get it to bend. Sensuality is like touching that hot spot with a cold piece of metal: it draws the heat out and blackens the metal. When sensuality touches the heart, it will quench the flame and blacken the heart of passion and love for God. Sensuality draws our eyes away from Christ to the temporal beauty of this world and cools the heart of love.

Let me add that you don't want to bring your electronic devices into your observatory. The device itself can be a distraction or temptation to look away from God. Once you start with your phone or computer, you may not be able to stop, and the time you wanted to look at God soon is stolen away. Your observatory should be electronic-device-free. In some homes, parents will collect their children's phones in a basket so they can sit down together to share a meal and conversation with one another without being distracted by their phones. Being present or being there for those at the table is what is important. We will have to be present for God and undistracted from gazing at Him if we are going to see Him.

When astronomers sent telescopes into space, they found out how much the invisible atmosphere of the earth had distorted the things they wanted to observe. The emptiness of space is more conducive to our telescope use. Holiness is like the emptiness of space in our quest to see God. Holiness takes us outside the invisible atmosphere of this sinful world and separates us from it. This is laying aside the unclean things of this life before coming into the presence of the Lord. Holiness will help us to see with greater clarity the great vision of His glory. Without true repentance, no man will see God. If you are holding on to some pet sin in this world, or if you have the desire to gaze on some beauty of this world before God, you must repent of it until your only desire is to see God Himself. The atmosphere of sin in this life will keep you from wanting to see God. It will keep you hiding like Adam in the garden, covering yourself with the fig leaves of the world to hide you from God.

With the aid of the Holy Spirit, you need to develop a sensitivity to the things around you. Be sensitive to sin in your life; sensitive to the sensuality of the world, which easily can draw our attention away from God; sensitive to the Holy Spirit, who will lead us to observe God and reveal Him to us. The devil often uses the most beautiful things of this world to distract us from God's beauty. These beauties may not be sin in themselves but beautiful enough to keep us looking at them and not looking at God. When you come into a dark room out of the sunlight, you can't see for a while. Then slowly your eyes adjust, and that which is in the dark can be seen. It is like this with God. You stand in the distracting lights of the world, and coming into the closet, you may not see God at first, but if you continue coming, the eyes of your heart will adjust and you will begin to see the glory of God. You not only will see God's glory, you will begin to see the things of the world that fell on the lens of your telescope like dust and blocked your view of God. You will learn that you have to wipe that dust away (ask for forgiveness of your sins) in order to clear your vision of God. You may discover that God will have you set aside good things, beautiful things, things you never would consider sin, so you can see Him.

When it comes to seeing God, we need a dust-free environment where not even the smallest particles of the world will be let in. It may not seem like much at first, but the dust of tiny sins can slowly settle on the lens of our telescope and build up, clouding our view of God until it is eclipsed completely. Are the lights of this earth drowning out or blocking the light and glory of God? Is the sin in your life keeping you from seeing God or even trying to see God? Who shall ascend the hill of the Lord? He who has clean hands and a pure heart. Holiness should be the atmosphere at your observatory. The higher up the hill of the Lord we go—with clean hands and a pure heart—the clearer our view of the glory of God.

For the Christian, having a place to observe (behold) the glory of God is fundamental and necessary for spiritual life. It is fundamental because the power I need to live Christ's life in the world comes by looking at Him. Our observatory may be called different things, but the purpose of this place is seeing God and in seeing Him, communing with Him, exchanging devotions or tokens of love. This observatory of God must be a place where the glory of God has little or no competition from distracting lights. Remember the line from the old hymn: "And the things of earth will grow strangely dim in the light of His glory and grace." As we come to this tent of meeting with God every day, we must extinguish all other lights as we enter. A friend of mine once told me that he would not allow many people into his secret place, his observatory. He didn't want the contaminations of those who did not have that heart seeking after God in this sacred place where he would meet with God. Is the place of your devotions—your observatory—a sacred place to you?

God's chief concern, his chief end, is His glory. If that is so, then our chief end or goal is that glory as well. Moses cried to God, "Show me your glory." Man's chief end is to glorify God and enjoy Him all the days of our lives. We are to be occupied with God's glory, seeing that glory, worshiping that glory, and as we do, we will be changed to reflect it and look like it.

Our preoccupation with God and His glory will be seen in our daily coming to Him to gaze on the beauty of the Lord. If we are changed into His image by beholding (II Cor. 3:18), then we must continue to behold until nothing is left to change. As we gaze on the face of Christ, He will pour His glory into our hearts, transforming us into His image. It is very hard for us to believe that we are changed by just looking at Jesus. Isn't it interesting that most of our quiet time or prayer time is taken up with looking at ourselves and what we need instead of looking at Jesus? Fix our eyes on Jesus. Observing the life and face of Jesus is what our devotions are all about. We need to look at Jesus on a daily basis. We need to look and live, look and be transformed.

I want to make a distinction here between having devotions and having an observatory where I behold the glory of God. Our premise from the beginning of this book has been that we are changed or transformed into the image of Christ not from obedience to the law (earning grace) but by beholding the glory of God. Earlier, we spoke of our friend having a conversation with the pastor, asking him, "Do you think the average church member knows how to gaze on the Lord?" Part of that pastor's response was, "Doing devotions has kept me from coming to Him only." I believe what this pastor was saying was there can be a difference between devotions and seeing (beholding) God. The purpose of our devotions is not some empty routine of Bible reading and prayer in which we look for some promise of God to claim. The purpose is not to give our lists of wants and needs to Jesus. The purpose of our devotions is to see God in all His glory and, bathing in that glory, be changed into His image. "For God, who said, 'Let light shine out of darkness,' made his light shine in our hearts to give us the light of the knowledge of the glory of God in the face of Christ" (II Cor. 4:6). The light of His glory gives us the knowledge of who He is and transforms us into His image.

Just like the astronomer, when we build our observatory, we must decide what to look at. Think about the early astronomers like Galileo, who had to decide what they wanted to look at. Galileo would turn his telescope to the skies to look at the stars. We must decide what we want to see and point our telescope at that object and observe it. Most Christians keep their telescope pointed at things on this earth and our life here. What if we turned our telescope and focused it on the Bright and Morning Star? For the Christian, there is no better sight, no better object for us to look at than Jesus. We will have to turn our telescope away from ourselves and the problems of our day. Our times with the Lord can be stolen away by the various fires or emergencies burning in our lives. When these erupt, all we see are the smoke and flames of the fires that cloud out any vision of God. If I would observe God, I must decide to look at God. You must make God the goal of devotions. We will have to look away from our lusts and desires, no matter how innocent they appear. You might even have to look away from your ministry. Focus your telescope on Jesus, fix your eyes on Him, and let the magnifying power of the Holy Spirit bring Him into focus. If you set your heart on this, just as I looked into the night sky of New Zealand and saw new glories in the heavens, you will see new glories of the Savior. If we don't make God the goal, the circumstances and emergencies of life will be all we see. If you have no goal of what you want to see, you will hit it every time.

At the heart of our Bible are the four Gospels. Have you ever wondered why four? We have four written observations of the life of Christ. This written revelation is what theologians call special revelation, that which God has breathed out through those who wrote the Gospels. It is the revelation of His Son to us. John writes in his Gospel, "The Word became flesh and lived for a while among us. We have seen his glory, the glory of the one and only Son, who came from the Father, full of grace and truth… from the fullness of his grace we have received one blessing after another" (John 1:14, 16). John saw the glory of One full of grace and truth, and He poured out on them one blessing after another. I don't think we go too far when we tie the seeing of Jesus and the pouring out of grace together. John goes on to say that no man has seen God, but we have seen God, the only Son. I think what John is trying to say is that Jesus is the definition of God that a human being can see and understand. Look at Him as John did, see His glory, and receive grace upon grace. God shines His glory into our hearts as we look upon the face of Jesus. In seeing Jesus, you will see much of what you have been asking for disappear and you will learn that all you ever really needed was Jesus. In this, we will be changed, not trying to change, but changed by beholding.

These four observations of Jesus we call the Gospels. My New Testament teacher in school told us that Mark's Gospel was like a series of snapshots, pictures of the life of Jesus. Reading it was like taking out the photo album of Jesus's life and looking at the pictures. You can learn much by looking at old photos of someone. These snapshots are over two thousand years old but are just as good today as when they were taken. In the Gospels, we have four photo albums to look at to see the glory of Jesus, full of grace and truth. Looking at Jesus's life history, His birth and growth to manhood, His ministry and His cross, how He overcame death and the grave and ascended into Heaven will be transformative and slake the thirst for all other desires.

Looking on His face, we will have the glory of the knowledge of God; we will know Him and become like Him. What do you think God wants you to look at?

The Gospels have a table of contents made up of four pictures: the King, the Ox, the perfect Man, and the Eagle. These four pictures are seen when the throne of God is seen in the books of Ezekiel and Revelation. We see strange creatures surrounding the throne with these four faces. reflected from the throne of God. This table of contents allows us to look at different facets of Jesus's life. If you want to see something of the King and His Kingdom, read Matthew. If you want to see something of the suffering servant, look at the Ox in Mark. If you would see the perfect Man who would then be a spotless sacrifice for your sins, look at Luke. If you would see one who soars above all other creatures, look at the Gospel of John and see the Eagle. "Learn of me" or "learn from me," Jesus said in Matthew 11:29. We will begin to see that there is no end to what we might see or learn about Jesus. "Jesus did many other things as well. If every one of them were written down, I suppose that even the whole world would not have room for the books that would be written" (John 21:25).

Many Christians make a habit of devotions that have no vision of Jesus. There is no vision of Jesus because people aren't looking for Jesus. The lights of need and pain block out the glory of God. They are looking for answers to problems and needs and can't see Jesus written throughout the Scriptures. We don't see Jesus as the answer, so we aren't looking at Him or for Him. We are looking for how we might be better Christians. We are looking for how we might overcome sin. We are claiming some promise that will fill a need in our life, and miss what we really need. We are asking God for everything but Himself. Moses asked God to show him His glory. You will know you have an observatory when what you are asking for is more of God. Turning our vision to the Lord and gazing on His beauty will have a transforming effect on your life.

We can start with the Gospels, but the Old Testament is full of His beauty as well. On the road to Emmaus, Jesus opens the Old Testament to the two disciples He is walking with. "And beginning with Moses and all the Prophets, he explained to them what was said in all the Scriptures concerning himself" (Luke 24:27). Oh, to have heard this homily and to see the glory of Jesus throughout the Old Testament. Here is the scarlet thread throughout the Scriptures that points to the fulfillment seen in the Gospels. "Look unto me, and be saved, all the ends of the earth; for I am God, and there is none else" (Isa. 45:22, KJV). The looking is the key, and in looking, we are saved and changed.

The habit of many is to open the Bible and read so many verses or use a devotional text and get a good promise from Him. Then there is prayer to commit the day and work to Him. The devotional ends up being something about me, the prayer for all I need and want. This habit can be empty and have little or no vision of Jesus but lots of vision of problems, needs, and even death. If our visions are of negative things, we grow weary and depressed. When devotions are full of me and empty of God, they can end negative and depressing. What a way to start the day. Therefore, many stop having devotions altogether.

When I was in Bible school, J. Oswald Sanders came and spoke to us students. He spoke that morning from I Corinthians 9, where Paul talks about having a right to be paid for the Gospel but denying himself such that he may offer it free of charge. The important thought in the chapter is giving the Gospel—doing anything, suffering anything, to preach the Gospel (Jesus) to others. "For when I preach the Gospel, I cannot boast, since I am compelled to preach. Woe to me if I do not preach the Gospel!" (I Cor. 9:16). I mentioned Sanders's book *The Incomparable Christ* in the chapter on worship and how reading through this book and looking at Jesus was transformative to my devotions. My devotions were becoming my observatory, the place I would go to look upon Jesus. As I read a chapter a day, I would see something new about Christ and worship Him for that particular glory. My focus was on Jesus and Him alone. I was surprised by the changes that were occurring in my life. I wasn't working on me. I wasn't thinking about me or my problems. I was just looking at Jesus. For the first time in my life, sanctification was being worked out in me—not through my striving, but in simply looking at Jesus. I worked through that volume many times over the years and saw the same results. Sanders was preaching the Gospel to me through this book, and by reading and looking at Jesus, I was being changed. As I read through this volume, I began to look for other books that were just about Jesus, but I found that there weren't many. Look for those books and devotions about Jesus so you may look and be changed. I was beholding the glory of God in the face of Christ Jesus, and by the looking, I was being changed. Jesus is the Gospel, the power of God unto salvation. When we look unto Him, we are healed. Set your telescope on Christ and look at this Bright Morning Star.

After working through *The Incomparable Christ*, I saw that my attention and my focus in the secret place, in my observatory, had to be on Jesus. I would spend time in the Gospels and just look at the pictures of my Savior and what He had done for me, until I wept. The Bible I carry is over 40 years old now, and when you look at the edges of the pages, you will see—starting in the Gospels and running to Romans—that they are yellowed, cracked, worn, and torn. These pages are more worn than any others in my Bible because this is the place I go again and again to observe the Lord. Fixing your eyes on Jesus is the great business for which you will have the greatest return.

Along with the Gospels and books like Sanders's *The Incomparable Christ*, I discovered another volume that dovetailed perfectly with those books. It was a little volume by Joseph Carroll, *How to Worship Jesus Christ*. This volume taught me that when I look at Jesus, I can take what I'm seeing and turn that observation into worship. I saw that worship was the natural outcome of my daily observations of Jesus. Now I was not only seeing Jesus but also enjoying what I was seeing with the outbreaks and praise and thanksgiving. The joy of seeing and being with the Lord gave way to songs of praise and thanksgiving that became the heart of my communion with Him.

We hear stories of men and women who pray for hours and wonder how this could be possible. I believe these individuals have seen the glory and beauty of God, something so beautiful that you never grow tired of it. The beauty of God can have a powerful effect on a person, one that is transformative. This beauty will have its full revelation in Heaven, and we will have an eternity to look on Him who bought our salvation and is our salvation.

Start by asking yourself what you are thinking about in your devotion times: Is it mostly about you or is it mostly about God? What do you pray about? What answers are you looking for from God? If the answer to that question is you, then turn your attention away from self and begin to focus primarily on God Himself. Worshiping God is the main tool we use to change our focus from self to God in our devotional times. When the Lord was first drawing me to Himself, the Spirit of God impressed upon me to stop praying for myself: "I know what you need before you ask me," referencing Matthew 6:8. The problem was that when I started with me and what I needed, I couldn't get to who Jesus was and what He already had done for me. I couldn't lift my eyes from self and see the glory of what had been provided for me in Christ. The habit of self-occupation is a difficult one to break. For many, prayer is talking to God about what they need when it should be talking about God, who He is, and what He has done for us.

It sounds self-defeating not to pray for yourself, but God wanted me to learn that self-focus in prayer was defeating. He wanted me to come and think about Him, to worship Him, to see who and what He is and has been on my behalf. In my devotions, I would look at God and begin to worship Him. There were days when I never got to my prayer list and never asked Him for anything. I felt guilty because I had been taught that prayer was asking God for things for myself and for others. I was taught to keep a prayer list and check off the answers to my prayers. Those with such prayer lists often bragged about how many answered prayers they had seen. If I wasn't asking God for things, then how could I have answers and show how spiritual I was? I felt that my prayers were responsible for the advancement of the Kingdom of God and that if I didn't pray for Kingdom stuff, I was shirking my responsibility. God wanted me to stop praying for myself so the clouds of self-preoccupation would blow away and I might see the glory of God. When I began to see His glory, I began to change without even trying to change and without thinking about what had to change in me. Now my prayers were more about God and less about me. II Corinthians 3:18 was being worked out in my life. When I was taken up with worship, I found that most or all of my prayer would and could be about God. Those who want to see God will find that most of their prayers are filled with God.

Making God the focus of my prayer also was a way of asking God for Himself: Lord, show me your glory. It is a way of possessing God or participating in the divine nature. It is making Him your desire and filling your heart and mind with the knowledge of God. It is a way of seeking Him with all our hearts and not giving up until we have what we ask of Him.

"Now Moses use to take a tent and pitch it outside the camp some distance away, calling it the 'tent of meeting'" (Ex. 33:7). Moses had a place to see the glory of God, but he had to get to a place outside the camp, away from distractions and the pollution of people. Moses would enter the tent, and the pillar of cloud would come down and stay at the entrance while God spoke with him. This is visual: The cloud came down, and God came down, and there He would meet and talk with Moses. The people would stand at the entrance of their own tents and watch this, and when the cloud came down, they would worship this God. If there was a place on the earth where you actually could meet with God and talk with Him face-to-face as a man speaks with his friend, what would you give to get there and meet with Him? A place where God would speak to you, answer your questions, command you, lead you, or just bless your heart with His word and with His presence: Would you travel the world and make any destination your end in order to have this time with God? This meeting place is your divine right as a son or daughter of God. If you will take the step of faith to set up a tent outside the camp, God will come down in a cloud of His glory and meet with you there as He did with Moses. This will be your observatory.

If you have a tent of meeting with God, not only will it stimulate love for God in your own heart, it will stimulate and promote worship in others. As the Israelites watched Moses meet with God, they worshiped at the sight. Your meeting with God and your vision of Him will promote the same in others. This is the beginning of revival. Your personal revival (vision of God) may help produce revival in others. Like early astronomers, you may help other people set up an observatory where they too may go and gaze at the light and lamp of glory.

Astronomers make a life's work out of what they observe. They spend their days looking at the heavens. They spend their strength and their lives thinking of ways to better see the stars and invent equipment that will help them do so. Think of the hours of work that went into the research and development of the Hubble telescope: the years of development, the design, the engineering that had to go into its creation, system after system thought of, designed, and created, then tested, and backup systems put into place in case one fails. Think of the billions of dollars it cost to build it and then launch it into space. It boggles the mind. Think of the millions of man-hours spent to accomplish this task. Why did they do this? To see farther into the universe and to see more of the universe than humans ever have seen before. In the end, they accomplished their goal and have left us with outstanding pictures of things previously unseen—things no man ever saw before. Yet in all of this work, many of these individuals never saw the God who spoke those stars into being.

What effort are you willing to expend in order to build your observatory so you may see and find God? "If you will seek for me with all your heart you shall surely find me" (Jer. 29:13). Now ask yourself the question: What effort, what time, what part of your life are you willing to sacrifice to see God? If a secular man is willing to pour out his life to see what God has created, what should we be willing to spend to see its Creator? The astronomer's job is to gaze at the stars. The Christian's job is to gaze upon God in all His glory. We should find time every day to look at God and His glory and be just as fascinated with Him. Do you have an observatory?

For astronomers, the observatory is their workplace, and they spend their workdays looking at the heavens. We need to build observatories where we make our work seeing God with all our hearts and upon finding Him, gazing at the beauty of the Lord. This is our great business. This will sound strange to many—for we have been taught that we can't see God—but they don't know that God desires that we would have His Spirit of wisdom and revelation so we might know Him better. I want you to think about your devotional place as an observatory where you, like an astronomer, spend your workday conducting experiments to see the glory of your God better.

Few men and women will wholeheartedly seek God. Few will do whatever they must do to establish, to build a secret place—a secret observatory—where they meet alone with God. The ones who do will find God, they will see God, and discover glories beyond description. In the secret place, we learn the deepest intimacies of God's heart. It is where we discover that the love of God is a real entity, and when it is poured out upon our hearts, we are satisfied as with no other love. In your observatory, you will see wonders that the world only dreams about. Standing in the glory of God, you will discover that God's glory is saturated with all the fruits of His Spirit, with all of His character traits, with His love, with His righteousness. Seeing the beauty of God will hold you spellbound for hours, and time will seem to stand still. As you look at the face of God, you will be changed into His image. As you look into the face of the eternal One, time will seem to stand still. This is why some can spend hours in God's presence and it only seems like minutes.

Can you imagine someone going to the Grand Canyon only to stay in their room and never see the wonders of the canyon itself? When asked if they have been to the Grand Canyon, they can say yes, but in reality, all they saw was the inside of a hotel room. A television, a bathroom, and a bed are nothing compared with the beauty of that natural wonder. Many Christians are like this, saying they have been to see God, but they have never opened the door of their dull devotions to step out into the splendor, glory, and beauty of God. If they would move from the small room of devotions to gazing on the beauty of the Lord, they would be in awe of His beauty and not want to leave His presence. Devotions would become a place to run to instead of a place to run from. The reason devotions are so boring for some and non-existent for others is because of a wrong goal. For many, the goal of devotions is to be a better Christian or is something to do to fulfill one's duty to God. Devotions like these will be nothing more than sitting in your room at the Grand Canyon and exchanging the glory of the room for the glory of the canyon. Do not deny yourself the glorious sight of God, His love, and presence. Or, as Paul said in Romans 1:23, ". . . and exchanged the glory of the immortal God for images made to look like mortal man and birds and animals and reptiles." What might you be exchanging the glory of God for?

We have tended to see this shining of the light of His glory into our hearts as a one-time event when God gives us a dose of His glory and we are saved. Believing this may be why many are kept from growing in the Lord, for they seldom or never behold His glory. Just as the earth receives a daily dose of light from the glory of the sun, which causes things to grow, so we need a daily dose of light (glory) from the Son in order to grow spiritually. Remove a plant from the light, and it will die, for we are God's planting, His trees of righteousness who flourish in the light of His glory.

The goal of our devotional time is to encounter the glory of God. Encountering the glory of God and encountering God are the same thing. When this happens, you are changed and you are affected by the living God. He speaks to you, He loves your heart, and He grants you a word of encouragement that fills you to overflowing. By shining His glory on you, He shines grace upon grace on you. He commands you and leads you. You encounter Him in such a way that, like Job, you cry out, "I know my redeemer liveth" (Job 19:25, KJV). Here is assurance of salvation. This gazing (beholding) has been lost in many of our devotional times with the Lord. We have not been taught that we are changed by beholding the glory of God. We have "exchanged the truth of God for a lie, and worshiped and served created things rather than the Creator" (Rom. 1:25). Some of those created things may be church buildings, ministries, and even people here on earth.

For the average Christian, Jesus died two thousand years ago and lives in Heaven. In order to see Him, we would have to go back in time or wait to die and see Him when we get to Heaven. In the meantime, we believe that He exists, so we try to do the best we can and hope that one day we will see Him. Can I really see Jesus today? Can I have an intimate relationship that is filled with fellowship and joy? Will He speak into my darkness, will He shine the light of His glory into the blackness of my life? The answer to these questions is yes and amen. This should be the normal Christian experience, but for many Christians this is foreign and for some even absurd. Many Christians don't know this is something they should be doing and experiencing.

For many of us, prayer time is talking to God about ourselves, as the focus has become me, my, and mine. Like that old Wednesday night prayer meeting, being focused on human beings doesn't deliver or transform the individual. Many in the Church today don't know how to pray because their teachers and preachers don't know how to pray. We need to cry out to the Lord like the disciples of old: "Lord, teach us to pray" (Luke 11:1). Several years ago, our small church invited a speaker who had shared conference platforms with some of our nation's top preachers and teachers. Frankly, we were surprised he decided to come. The occasion was our annual prayer conference. He told me at that time that he had never been asked to do a prayer conference. This surprised me. As you go back and study Church history, the closer you get to revival, the more you see things like prayer leagues, prayer unions, and active powerful prayer meetings. Perhaps this is one reason we have not seen powerful nationwide revival in our day. The apostles of old had to "give themselves to prayer and the word" (Acts 6:4). Maybe we are not seeing transformation in the lives of our fellow Christians because they are not seeing and asking for the glory of God in prayer.

Prayer and the Word are two parts of the telescope with which we see God. Prayer is a dialogue, not a monologue, which is why prayer without the Word of God is no prayer at all. Whenever the glory of God is revealed in scripture, God is there speaking. It was so at the birth of Jesus, as it was at His baptism, as it was on the Mount of Transfiguration, where God was speaking with the burst of His glory. When God shines the light of His glory into our hearts and allows us to see the face of Christ Jesus, He will speak. His primary way of speaking to us is through the Word of God. It is then our place to listen and respond to that speaking. When God reveals His glory to you, He will speak and use the Word of God to make it clear. But more than this, in the Word He will make the vision of Himself clear, and in seeing this vision, you will be changed. We have reduced our times with the Lord to reading some little pamphlet for five minutes, hoping that some two-sentence snippet will feed our souls and give us power to get through the day.

Can we turn our observatory into the Mount of Transfiguration, where we see Christ transfigured and glorified? Can the living God come and inhabit our prayer rooms? Can God come and shine the light of His glory on us and make us shine like the stars? He desires to fill you to all the fullness with God. If these truths were but half true, wouldn't they be worth risking everything for?

Prayer is not a monologue but a dialogue. A dialogue is two persons having a conversation. We were taught as baby Christians that we must pray and read the Word if we are to grow spiritually. Prayer and the Word together are prayer. Prayer is that conversation or dialogue with God, and there can be no dialogue without a two-sided conversation. Prayer that does not have the expectation of God speaking into those moments is not prayer at all. If your prayer life is a monologue, then you have not experienced what God intends for you in prayer. And if your prayer life is a monologue, it probably is filled with self: me, my, and mine. When you read the Word of God in your prayer time, are you hearing from God? And then what do you do with God's speaking? Do you listen, do you respond, do you obey? If you're having a conversation with an individual and they ask you a question, what do you do? You answer them. If they ask you to do something and you love them, what do you do? You do what they ask. Prayer is a conversation with a living person, so stop and listen for His responses.

When your prayer is filled with worship, you actually are speaking about the glory of God. Just as there is power for transformation in the glory of God, so there will be transformation for you and others as you declare the glory of God in the person of Christ in worship in your prayer. You will be declaring God's glory and see it again throughout your prayer, and others who hear you will see it as well.

You will note that I have not focused on giving you some form of devotional procedure. I want you to construct an observatory, a tent of meeting, like Moses, a place where you will go to meet with God (behold God) outside the camp, not some form or formula that becomes a dead habit or lifeless ritual. This is to be a place where your vision is filled with the greatest view in the universe—the glory of God in the face of Christ Jesus.

Leviticus 6:12 (KJV) says, "And the fire upon the altar shall be burning in it; it shall not be put out; and the priest shall burn wood on it every morning, and lay the burnt offering in order upon it." Devotions are keeping the fire of God going so there may be divine fire in our lives. We need to tend this fire daily, making sure it doesn't go out. We serve God at our altars, where we offer the sacrifices of praise, for He is worthy. Don't let the fire go out. Watch the fire of your love and keep it burning by coming and looking at the fire of heaven. You must make preparations to keep the fire going. The wood must be cut, stacked, and stored. We have been given the fire of heaven to start the flame of our altar. Don't let the fire of heaven go out. The fire on your altar came from heaven, and the fire in your heart came from heaven, so don't let it go out. Watch for the rain of this world and evil to put it out. "It shall not be put out" (Lev. 6:13, KJV).

Through the years, coming to this observatory, this quiet time, has been both a struggle and a glory. It has been empty and it has been full; at times, it has been nonexistent. Many Christians fight the same battle, struggling to be consistent in having devotions, a quiet time, or time with the Lord. For years, this quiet time was about me and what I was doing. I would try different ways of having devotions; I would try different devotionals and different translations of the Bible. I would try different ratios of prayer to Bible reading. I tried different times of day, sometimes morning and then sometimes night, just before going to sleep. God used all of this to draw me to Himself so even if I wasn't what I should have been, or my devotions weren't what they should have been, God still used them. I see it as following the tracks of the sheep to find the shepherd. The breakthrough came when I changed the focus of this quiet time from self-observation to God-observation. When I changed the focus of my telescope from me to God, I saw wonders in the heavens that I had never seen before, and these times took on a richness they never had. I finally saw that my devotions were an observatory where I looked through the telescope of prayer and the Word to see something of this beautiful Savior. The wonder is that when you see something of the Savior, you will be changed in the beholding.

Plato tells the Allegory of the Cave in his work *The Republic* to compare "the effect of education and the lack of it on our nature." Written as a dialogue between Plato's brother Glaucon and his mentor Socrates, the story is narrated by Socrates. In the story is a group of people chained in the cave and looking at a wall that faces away from the entrance of the cave. This wall is all they can see. Behind them is a second wall, behind which puppeteers stand, which prevents their shadows or presence from being seen. Behind this second wall and the puppeteers is a fire that casts a light so that when the puppeteers lift shapes and images above their protective wall, a shadow is cast onto the wall of the cave, which the prisoners can see. For the prisoners, the shadow show becomes their reality. They think this is the real world, and it is the only world or reality they will ever know. The puppeteers can make this world anything they want. They can fill it with deceptions and lies and they teach the dominant doctrines of the time and place. They also speak with ventriloquist-type voices so the shadow images on the walls seem to speak to the captives in the cave. The prisoners never know that the images they are seeing are but shadows of real things that exist outside the cave. Few humans ever escape the cave, as it is not an easy task. Today, many of our pulpits are filled with puppeteers who propagate the doctrines of our time, putting shadowy images in front their people instead of preaching the glory of God in the light of the Gospel.

Plato then says: Suppose someone should drag a prisoner by force, up and out of the cave, all the way into the light of day. First the prisoner would be angry and in pain because of the bright light of day. Then his eyes slowly would adjust to the sun, and he would begin to see real people, not just shadows on the wall. Eventually he would be able to look at the stars and moon at night until finally he could look upon the sun itself. Only then could he reason about it and learn what it is. Now he has seen the real world in the light and glory of the sun, compared to the false shadows he had thought were real. With this newfound knowledge of the real world, the prisoner wants to go back into the cave and tell others what he has seen. When he goes and tells those still held captive in the cave what he has seen, they don't believe him. They think his journey into the light has harmed him (pain caused by the light) and they should not undertake such a painful journey. Plato notes that if the prisoners in the dark cave could have, they would have killed this one—or anyone who would try to drag them out of the cave and into the light. This is just what people did to Jesus. He went into the prison and darkness of man's sin and told them that He is the light of the world. Comfortable in the dark, the prisoners wanted to kill Him and eventually did. They loved the dark and the half-truth shadowy messages they were seeing and hearing, and they didn't want to be dragged out into the light of the glory of God. They wanted to stay in their prison in the dark.

Many in the Church are like those prisoners in Plato's cave. They are seeing shadows on the walls of their churches being preached by puppeteers who won't drag their people out into the bright light of the glory of Christ by preaching the message of the Gospel. They love the ear-tickling shadowy messages of something for me instead of everything for Christ. They would rather look at shadowy messages on the walls of their prison than be dragged out of the cave into the light of the glory of God. Some only see shadows of God and never come into the light of His glory. They don't want to make it their business to gaze on a light that not only frees but also transforms the individual into something new. They don't even know that they can look at the light of the glory of God, so they remain chained in the darkness of their cave, seeing only shadows and half-truths about the God of light and glory, whereas His Son has come into the cave declaring, "I am the light of the world" (John 8:12). Don't let the devil keep you chained in the prison of his dark cave; rather, come out and look upon the light and glory of the Son, and shine with the same glory.

Isn't this what happened to the Apostle Paul (formerly Saul), whom Christ dragged out of the cave of darkness to shine a light on him brighter than the noonday sun, changing him forever? Paul then went back into the cave to tell his fellow prisoners what he had seen, that they might see it as well. Those prisoners who loved the darkness eventually killed Paul for his message of the light of the Gospel, just as they killed Christ. Are you still in the cave? Jesus calls to you today. He is walking through the darkness of your cave, calling you to come and follow Him out of the dark into the light of His glory. Won't you follow? Won't you come out and gaze into the light of the Son?

Though we cannot look at the sun with our naked eyes without injury, astronomers have learned how to look at it without doing damage to themselves. They have turned their telescopes to the sun and learned much about it. They have discovered sunspots and solar flares that burst forth the glory of the sun into the universe. Won't you turn your telescope to see something of the glory of the Son and be changed by beholding? "But for you who revere my name, the sun of righteousness will rise with healing in its rays. And you will go out and frolic like well-fed calves" (Mal. 4:2).

Chapter 8

THE GOSPEL

 "For I am not ashamed of the Gospel, because it is the power of God that brings salvation to everyone who believes: first to the Jew, then to the Gentile. For in the Gospel the righteousness of God is revealed—a righteousness that is by faith from first to last, just as it is written: 'The righteous will live by faith.'" (Rom. 1:16–17)

I LOVE TO read history. I remember on one of my historical adventures reading of an artist who would stand on his head to look upside down at what he wanted to paint, to get a fresh perspective. Apparently, he could see things upside down that he could not right-side-up, or at least added elements. That different perspective aided him in seeing more of what was there, and then he copied it down. Recently I read of another artist, Tom Nachreiner, who holds weekend studio workshops teaching artists to paint upside down. Tom doesn't have them stand on their heads but takes pictures of their subjects and turns the pictures upside down. An American impressionist whose studio is in Delafield, Wisconsin, he explains: "I teach upside down so that teaches people to see the shapes rather than the subject matter." It was his upside-down technique that intrigued and surprised many of the 20 artists who registered for workshops.

What if we turn the Gospel upside down and look at it from a different perspective? Come stand on your head with me and let's take a fresh look at the Gospel. As we look at it upside down, the added perspective may cause us to see something that you've never seen before about the Gospel. Let's look at it in the light of our theme, "changed by beholding." When was the last time you thought about the Gospel or took a good look at it?

Endless books and theologies have been written about the Gospel. In the Church we have fought and battled over what the Gospel is for 2,000 years. In the first century, Paul wrote the letter to the Galatians, clarifying the Gospel he preached to them because some people among them had started to preach a different Gospel. The Reformation was a battle over the Gospel, which the Roman Church had perverted and turned into a work to be done by man. Luther and other reformers returned to Paul's message of justification by faith alone. The five *solas* of the reformation are facets of the Gospel and state that Christians are saved by grace alone, through faith alone, in Christ alone, as revealed by Scripture alone, to the glory of God alone. During the Reformation there were different camps espousing different ways of looking at the Gospel, Arminianism on one side and Calvinism on the other, taking their names from the names and theology of their leaders. These battles remain with us even today. I remember walking down the aisle of my church many years ago with a copy of John MacArthur's *The Gospel According to Jesus Christ* and getting a hate stare from a leading member of that church. There was a battle going on between Easy Believe-ism and Lordship salvation, which was really an old battle about the Gospel. Though I believe it is important for our theologians to fight the battle over what the Gospel is, it is not our goal to refight it here. In light of what we have been speaking about throughout this book, our goal is to get people to look at the Gospel, at who Jesus is.

What is the Gospel? "Now, brothers and sisters, I want to remind you of the Gospel I preached to you, which you received and on which you have taken your stand. By this Gospel you are saved, if you hold firmly to the word, I preached to you. Otherwise, you have believed in vain. For what I received I passed on to you as of first importance: that Christ died for our sins according to the Scriptures, that he was buried, that he was raised on the third day according to the Scriptures, and that he appeared to Cephas, and then to the Twelve. After that, he appeared to more than five hundred of the brothers and sisters at the same time, most of whom are still living, though some have fallen asleep. Then he appeared to James, then to all the apostles, and last of all he appeared to me also, as to one abnormally born" (I Cor. 15:1–8). The Gospel according to Paul in its simplest form is the death burial and resurrection of Jesus. Paul simplifies the Gospel even more when he says, "For I determined not to know anything among you, save Jesus Christ, and him crucified" (I Cor. 2:2). When Paul says this, he is not excluding the burial and resurrection; his statement is shorthand for the Gospel. The cross has become the symbol of our Christian faith. The cross is the Gospel reduced to a single symbol.

Notice that Paul says that this Jesus—crucified, buried, and risen—appears to the Apostles, to more than 500 brothers and sisters, and then Paul Himself. His appearance to Paul was after Jesus's ascension to heaven. Having the Gospel correct—the death, burial and resurrection of Jesus—is important, but the appearance of Jesus to these men, the sight of the risen Lord, is what made all the difference in their lives and was the thing they witnessed to until their deaths. These appearances (revelation) of Jesus to the believer have been continuing for over 2,000 years now. He may not appear in a physical body as He did to the Apostles and the 500, or in a great light as He did to Paul, but the revelation of Jesus to the believer is what happens when a person hears the Gospel and believes unto salvation. The work of the Holy Spirit is to reveal and make Christ real to the believer. It is not just knowing the Gospel facts; it is seeing the Gospel, who is Jesus. Having the Gospel correct is important, but it is meaningless if that Gospel is not revealed to the individual by the Holy Spirit. It is in the believing and seeing of Christ like the serpent lifted up in the wilderness that I am changed and transformed into His image. Jesus is still appearing to men and women today. Has He appeared to you?

We have four books at the beginning of the New Testament that are called the Gospels. These four books give us the accounts of the birth, life, and ministry of Jesus up to and including crucifixion, burial, resurrection, and ascension. These Gospels give us the written revelation of Jesus and His work on man's behalf, what He taught, the miracles He performed, the way He dealt with people, the giving of His life on the cross as a sacrifice for our sins. These Gospels are a biographical portrait of Jesus. When we preach the Gospel, it is from these pages that we find our message. So we preach Christ and Him crucified, buried, and risen. There is no difference between the Gospel Paul just mentioned and the four Gospels in the Bible. We preach the Gospel from what is revealed to us in Scriptures. But the Gospel is not just some history recorded in the

Bible. The Gospel is a living person whom we can know and with whom God has called us to be in fellowship. Jesus is the fulfillment and manifestation of the written revelation of the Gospel in the Bible. When Paul gives us his definition of the Gospel, he adds the phrase "according to the scriptures." Before Paul had his Damascus Road experience, he was Pharisee and something of a Bible scholar, but that knowledge of the Scriptures, the law, had not led him to a knowledge of Jesus Christ. The Gospel became a reality for Paul when he met Jesus, the living Gospel, on the road to Damascus. When Paul saw Jesus, he was transformed by that vision. It is by preaching what is written about Christ from the Scriptures that the power of God is released and the living Gospel is revealed to the believer. Believing in and seeing that revelation of the Gospel, the believer is changed into the image of Christ and healed of the disease of sin and its power.

In Luke 4, we have the story of Jesus going to the synagogue and taking the scroll and opening it to Isaiah 61:1–2 and reading, "'The Spirit of the Lord is on me, because he has anointed me to proclaim good news to the poor. He has sent me to proclaim freedom for the prisoners and recovery of sight for the blind, to set the oppressed free, to proclaim the year of the Lord's favor.' Then he rolled up the scroll, gave it back to the attendant and sat down. The eyes of everyone in the synagogue were fastened on him, He began by saying to them, 'Today this scripture is fulfilled in your hearing'" (Luke 4:18–21). Jesus is not only proclaiming the good news, He is the good news. He is the one who gives freedom to prisoners, sight to the blind, delivering the oppressed, and forgiving sins. Jesus is the good news, the fulfillment of the Gospel.

I want to make a distinction between the Gospel as a doctrine or written revelation and the Gospel as the living person Christ. I can believe the doctrine of the Gospel—the death, burial and resurrection of Christ—and not believe in or have faith and trust in the living person of Christ. This may seem like a subtle difference, but I assure you it is an important one. "You believe that there is one God. Good! Even the demons believe that—and shudder" (James 2:19). There is a believing that will not save, or what might be called a devil's faith. Agreement with or intellectual assent to the written Gospel or doctrine will not save; only faith in the living Gospel, Jesus, will save. We are called to look at Christ as Paul did and live, live in a new relationship with the living Christ, who is the Gospel. If we don't know Christ, we don't really know the Gospel. Faith in Christ, seeing or beholding Christ, is transformational, it is salvation and entrance into a relationship with the living Jesus. There is a difference in believing something *about* Jesus and having faith in Jesus as a living person and knowing Him personally.

The Gospel in its essence is the death, burial, and resurrection of the Lord Jesus, but it is more. You can add the perfect life he lived here on earth so we would have a perfect sacrifice for our sins. You could add His incarnation, virgin birth, and ascension into heaven. You could add the work that Jesus is doing now in intercession on behalf of those He came to save. You could add to that the rule of the universe even now from His throne in Heaven. To understand the Gospel fully, we will have to understand the height and depth and width and breadth of the love of God, all manifest in the person of His Son, and to do that will take all eternity. Do you see the Gospel as a doctrine, or do you see it as the living person Christ?

Hence, what do we preach? We preach the Gospel as revealed in the written Gospels and all of Scripture. We preach the death, burial, and resurrection of Jesus. Paul puts it this way: "For since in the wisdom of God the world through its wisdom did not know him, God was pleased through the foolishness of what was preached to save those who believe. Jews demand signs and Greeks look for wisdom, but we preach Christ crucified: a stumbling block to Jews and foolishness to Gentiles, but to those whom God has called, both Jews and Greeks, Christ the power of God and the wisdom of God" (I Cor. 1:21–24). Most evangelical churches and preachers have the Gospel according to scripture right, and it is what we preach when we preach the Gospel. The problem is that we preach it to the lost, and we should, while not seeing it as being the main message we should preach to the saved.

Looking at the Gospel right-side-up, we see it as something we preach to the lost in order that they might be saved. We see it as the genesis or catalyst for salvation. We preach the Gospel to the lost so they might be saved, and once they are saved, we preach and teach the laws and principles for Christian living, which will take them on to Christian maturity. "For everyone that useth milk is unskillful in the word of righteousness: for he is a babe" (Heb. 5:13, KJV). We can see the Gospel as the milk of the Word, as something we must move on from to the meat of the Word, the principles and disciplines of Christian living. Our Christianity thus goes from a look-and-live Gospel to a do-this-and-live Gospel. The rules for Christian living may distract men from looking unto Jesus and keep them from being transformed by beholding Christ, who is the Gospel. In preaching these rules we may be veiling Christ to those we're preaching to.

There are no principles in the Gospel, no rules for us to follow and keep. We are only to believe the Gospel. What law did you keep when you came to Christ and first experienced this salvation? Did you try to clean yourself up and look more righteous so Jesus would select you? Did you work to reform yourself, doing away with bad habits and chronic sins, and was this enough to have Jesus accept you? No, you just believed what Jesus had done for you on the cross and in this belief, you were saved and made one with Christ.

The Gospel says nothing about loving my neighbor or how to love my wife and children. There are no principles for Christian growth in the Gospel. The five *solas* of the Reformation address the fact that there are no rules or principles in the Gospel, that salvation is by Christ alone, revealed by the Scripture alone, by God's Grace alone, through faith alone, to the glory of God alone. "For it is by grace you have been saved, through faith—and this is not from yourselves, it is the gift of God— not by works, so that no one can boast" (Eph. 2:8–9). We think that after we have looked at the Gospel, which is Jesus, we can look away to rules and principles to live by. When you look at Jesus, the Gospel, all you see is Christ and the work He has done on your behalf, what He has accomplished for you. You see the free gift of God in his Son; you come and eat and drink without price. You can't do, you can only look and receive; you can only believe.

There is no law here to keep; there is only the grace of God manifest in His Son, who is given to you as a gift. When I say there are no rules or law in the Gospel, I mean there are no rules for you to keep or changes for you to make so you might be saved; this has been done by Christ. There is the sense that in Christ I keep the law by believing in Him. In the Gospel we confront the grace and mercy of God and can only hold out the empty hand of faith to receive what He has done for us in Christ. What we receive is not only what He has done in the past, we receive the living Christ by His Spirit as well. Jesus's command was to repent and believe the Gospel, and I not only believe what He has done in the past, I believe and trust Him for what He will do today in me and through me. Our work is not to look at the law and try to do it, but to look upon Jesus and, in the looking, find the grace and life of Jesus being poured out on us and into us. We are not changed by learning the principles and trying to do them but by looking at Jesus and being transformed into the law as the Spirit writes the law on our hearts. We will preach the law, but the answer for our failure to keep the law perfectly is not trying harder to do what it says but looking at Jesus so there may be power for me to keep the law. If we preach the Gospel properly, all we are left with is the vision of Christ, and when we repent and believe and behold that vision, we are changed into the image of Jesus, who is the perfect fulfillment of the law.

"Once saved, always saved" is a comforting doctrine I was raised with in the churches I grew up in. "Once saved, always saved" speaks of eternal security. It speaks of the complete and finished work of Christ on our behalf to do that which we cannot do for ourselves. It teaches that once you're saved there is nothing you can do to lose your salvation. His salvation is eternal; therefore, it can't be broken or nullified. This salvation is by grace through faith and not of ourselves. Teaching this doctrine has led to certain conclusions that may not be right. This has even seeped into some theology according to which "it is possible, even probable, that when a believer out of fellowship falls for certain types of philosophy, if he is a logical thinker, he will become an unbelieving believer. Yet believers who become agnostics are still saved; they are still born again. You can even become an atheist; but if you once accepted Christ as Savior, you cannot lose your salvation, even though you deny God" (*Apes and Peacocks or the Pursuit of Happiness*, R.B. Thieme). If the Gospel I know is doctrinal and not relational, then a person can end up with this kind of thinking. What this suggests is that you begin with the Gospel to get saved, and that one-time experience with the Gospel is sufficient for salvation even if you stop believing in Christ. Even if your experience looks and feels like that of an unbeliever, you are still saved. I believe this kind of teaching and thinking on eternal security can leave us with the misconception that I only need the Gospel one time in my life when I come to Christ in salvation. It is a Handi-Wipe Gospel: Use it one time and throw it away. Then after you are saved, if you want to grow as Christian you look for the principles and laws of Scripture by which we can live the sanctified life. But this is not something that you have to do, so many Christians don't. I believe the reason many Christians don't see sanctification worked out in their lives is they think they have all that God wants to give them in praying that salvation prayer, and they no longer pursue the Gospel.

R. B. Thieme sees the Gospel as something in the past. In that past Jesus died; in the past I believed and accepted Jesus as my Savior. Looking back and believing that historical moment is enough for salvation even if there is no change in the life. If the Gospel becomes just a history to believe instead of a present and perpetual experience and union with the living Christ, then there will be no power to change the individual. Just believing historical facts about Jesus doesn't save. The living Jesus saves, or all historians who believe that Jesus was a historical figure might be saved. Many Christians use the Gospel one time and then throw it away, for they think salvation has been accomplished and now they can take the next steps to sanctification but they don't have to. Thieme's theology breeds the subtle idea that believing the Gospel is one event, and then growing in my faith to maturity is another event or several events, taking a person to spiritual maturity. It is the thought that once a person is saved, they need something more than the Gospel to continue their Christian life. They need to learn the principles for Christian living, the principles for sanctification. The Gospel goes from look-and-live Gospel to a do-this-and-live Gospel. This idea that there is something more I have to do now to be sanctified encourages the individual to look for something more than the Gospel.

If we see the Gospel as the starting point of our Christian life, it makes us want to look on to something else, to the deeper truths of scripture, leaving the Gospel behind. Now that I am saved, what do I do to live the Christian life? So once someone is saved, we move from preaching the Gospel to preaching the how-to's of the Christian life: how to be a better father, mother, Christian, evangelist, giver, and how to love people. How-to preaching can quickly take our eyes off Christ and put them on law and trying to keep it. It can take our eyes off Jesus and put them on our performance and on the principle that says, "Do this and live." Because there are no principles, no laws, no rules in the Gospel, other than repent and believe, we think if we don't preach the how-to Gospel (law), our people won't know how to live. So we separate the Gospel from the principles of holy living and teach the principles, thinking our people will be able to work them out. I love the saying that goes, "We afflict the comfortable by preaching the law, and comfort the afflicted with the Gospel." I believe much of our preaching today is afflicting the comfortable with the law, and we stop there. We have forgotten that we can only then comfort those with the Gospel. "I do not set aside the grace of God, for if righteousness could be gained through the law, Christ died for nothing" (Gal. 2:21). "But that no man is justified by the law in the sight of God, it is evident: for, the just shall live by faith. And the law is not of faith: but, the man that doeth them shall live in them" (Gal. 3:11–12). The only hope one has for keeping the law is to do what one did when coming to Christ the first time, and that is to believe the Gospel.

The power to become the law is found in Christ alone, and the way for the Christian to live out the principles and rules of Christianity is not just teaching them the rules but by preaching Christ or the Gospel. We have seen that we are changed by beholding Christ; the Gospel is Christ, and when Christ is preached and seen by those we preach to, they will be changed. When we do preach the law, it is but a schoolmaster to afflict the comfortable and then to lead us to look unto Christ for the power to keep the law and for the comfort that power brings. God's way is not preaching the rules to live by so your people will know what to do and then do it. God's way is preaching the Gospel—His son—and getting people to look at Him. This will transform them into the image of Christ. They will be transformed into the principle or rule that Scripture speaks of, not by knowing the principles so much as by knowing the Gospel, which is Jesus. In the preaching of the Gospel, lifting up Jesus, the power of God is released. This power is released for the lost and the saved alike. We don't go on from the Gospel to something different, more or better. We should never move on from the Gospel, and yet this is what has happened in many churches today. Our need will always be Christ and gazing on Him again and again. When some other truth clouds the vision of Christ, we are moving in the wrong direction.

But you say we must preach the whole counsel of God, and I would agree. So when we preach the law or some principle for Christian living, we must come back to the Gospel and look to Christ first for the power to live out whatever the law tells us we are to do. Power for the Christian comes in relationship or union with Christ, who is the Gospel. We can preach about surrender or dying to self, but there is no power in us to do this. Our surrender, our dying to self, can come only when we first look to Christ. It is by looking unto Jesus that we have the power we need to live out the commands of Scripture. It is in looking unto Jesus that we are transformed into the image and righteousness of Christ. The application for any rule or principle that we find in Scripture is to flee to Christ and gaze upon Him. Preacher, the application for any and every message you preach should be look at the Gospel, should be look unto Jesus. This application of looking to the Gospel repeatedly will be our vital relationship and union with the living Christ.

When I was young, I had some doubts about my salvation, doubts fostered by sinful behavior and the lack of power in my life. When sharing my doubts with pastors and teachers, I would hear, "Did you believe Jesus died for your sin? Did you believe He rose from the grave? Did you believe he ascended and sits on the throne of heaven today?" To all the above I would answer yes. Then they would tell me, "If you believed, you are saved." I was told to look back to the event of my salvation, to the day I accepted Christ as my Savior. I was looking back and getting reassurance from something I had done many years before. The focus was on my belief, on my decision, on something I did when I came to Christ, instead of being on Christ in the present. It was like the Gospel was something I used in the past to get saved, and that one-time look was enough.

This mentality keeps the Gospel in the past or ties it to our conversion, or the beginning of our Christian life, and leaves it there. If the Gospel was what I used to get saved, then what do I use after that to grow in faith and relationship with Christ? We use the same Gospel; we come to Christ again to believe Him and behold Him, and in the beholding, power is manifest in our lives to become whatever the law says I should be. We see the Gospel as the road to salvation but then quickly look for other roads to sanctification or spiritual growth and maturity. We then preach the principles of Scripture, what we call the meat of the Word, by which we might grow to maturity. We think that maturity comes not by the Gospel but by knowing the principles of Scripture and then keeping them. The principles of Scripture are just another term for the law. Here is the problem, for no one will be made righteous by the law. So could we be preaching the wrong thing to our people? What should we be preaching? The same thing we preached to them when they first got saved? Should we continue to preach the Gospel? This will sound foreign to some. It will be like standing on your head and looking at the Gospel again upside down.

What if the Gospel is not just the beginning of the Christian life but also the middle and end? What if the Gospel is the bronze serpent on the pole to which we look again and again to be healed of the snake bites of this life? What if the Gospel is what I am commanded to look at to keep the law? What if the Gospel is Jesus? What if the Gospel is the living bread, the bread of heaven that we were instructed to ask for daily? What if the Gospel is the sap I drink from the vine on a continual basis. What if the Gospel is not a one-time touch but a continual meal or feast to be consumed? What if the Gospel is the living water, water we need daily, or we'll die of thirst? What if the Gospel is what we preach to cause our people to mature in their faith? When the Gospel is preached and seen, power is released by God for our transformation. If the power of God is released in the preaching and believing of the Gospel, is it any wonder there is so little power in the Church today? There is little preaching of the Gospel in many of our churches. No wonder we have no power in the Church and so many of our members live snakebit and poisoned lives. We have lowered the bronze serpent, and our snakebit congregants have nothing to look at for healing. If we have moved away from the Gospel, we have moved away from the power of God to heal all our diseases and transform us into the image of His Son. Paul Washer says, "So many people think that the Gospel is for lost people. The Gospel *is* for the lost people. But it is even more for the converted people. The more you and I understand about what truly happened on the cross, the more you and I will be driven to serve Christ—not out of legalism, not out of some fear or dread, but simply out of joyful appreciation. Look what He did for me!" (HeartCry Missionary Society, https://heartcrymissionary.com). I would add to Paul Washer's thoughts that not only will I be driven to serve Christ, I will be transformed into an obedient servant of Christ in beholding the Gospel. The Gospel is the power of God unto salvation, unto transformation, including what we call sanctification.

I talked in a prior chapter about building an observatory in which we look at Jesus. Our churches should be a continuation of our personal observatories so when we come together we can corporately observe Christ. We should be looking at the glory of God in the face of Christ Jesus. We should be preaching Christ, who is the Gospel. Would you say you have heard the Gospel from your pulpit a lot this last year? What has happened to the Gospel preaching today? Are we preaching and teaching the Gospel? Do we see it as central to the life of the Christian and the Church? Are we saying today as Paul did in his day, "But as for me, may I never boast, except in the cross of our Lord Jesus Christ, through which the world had been crucified to me, and I to the world" (Gal. 6:14)? Our churches should be observatories of the Gospel where we fix our telescopes and eyes upon Christ, the Gospel, and look at His wonder. It is by looking at the wonder of Christ, at the Gospel, that we are transformed into the image of Christ. What are we looking at today? Personal spiritual gifts and how we can plug ours into the local church, three- or four- or twelve-step programs on how to improve ourselves and our lives, learning some love language, or how to be baptized by the Holy Spirit, Toronto-type blessings, speaking in tongues; you fill in the blank. What is your pastor preaching from his pulpit? Is it the Gospel?

The true Christian doesn't just start with the Gospel and move on to something else. The true Christian stays eternally focused on the Gospel. What I mean by this is that once you have fixed your eyes on Jesus, the Gospel, you never take them off the Gospel. The Gospel is not a one-time stop for the Christian. The Gospel is the serpent on the pole that we look to for healing every time one of the serpents of this life bites us. The Gospel is what you come to look at every day in your devotions. The Gospel is what you worship. The Gospel is your path to Christian maturity and sanctification. You are called into a relationship with the living Gospel, who is Jesus. As long as we are on this earth, there will be serpents, and they will bite us, and we will need to look for healing at the bronze serpent on the pole, who is Jesus Christ. The devotional life is one where we spend our life looking at Jesus and are being changed. We position ourselves to view Jesus lifted up like the serpent in the wilderness so we may keep our eyes on Him continually, for we will need to look at Him to live every day of our lives.

The Gospel is not just a historical event that I believe in order to be saved. The Gospel is a living person with whom the Father calls us into fellowship. My fellowship with Jesus is fellowship with the Gospel, a living in relationship with the Gospel. This fellowship is ongoing, for my need of the Gospel is ongoing. The Gospel (Jesus) has to be central in the Christian's life, for this is the believer's fundamental need like air, water, and food. The Gospel will become the very air we breathe for our spiritual life. The Gospel is Jesus, and the fellowship I am called to with this one will be eternal.

In his book the *Supremacy of God in Preaching*, John Piper tells this story: "Years ago during the January prayer week at our church, I decided to preach on the holiness of God from Isaiah 6. I resolved on the first Sunday of the year to unfold the vision of God's holiness found in the first four verses of this chapter. 'In the year that King Uzziah died, I saw the Lord sitting upon a throne, high and lifted up; and his train filled the temple.' So I preached on holiness of God and did my best to display the majesty and glory of such a great and holy God. I gave not one word of application to the lives of the people. Application is essential in the normal course of preaching, but I felt led that day to make a test: Would the passionate portrayal of the greatness of God in and of itself meet the needs of people? I didn't realize that not long before this Sunday one of the young families of our church discovered that their child was being sexually abused by a close relative. It was incredibly traumatic. They were there that Sunday morning and sat under the message. I wonder how many advisers to us pastors today would have said: 'Pastor Piper, can't you see your people are hurting? Can't you come down out of the heavens and get practical? Don't you realize what kind of people sit in front of you on Sunday? Some weeks later I learned the story. The husband took me aside one Sunday after service. 'John,' he said, 'these have been the hardest months of our lives. Do you know what has gotten me through? The vision of the greatness of God's holiness that you gave me the first week of January. It has been the rock we could stand on.'" I would say John Piper was preaching the Gospel, for Paul tells us in II Corinthians 4 that God shines His glory, the glory John Piper was preaching about, into our hearts in the face of Christ Jesus.

There is no deeper truth than that of the Gospel. This is why Paul prayed that his readers would be strengthened with power by the Spirit, to grasp how wide and long and high and deep is the love of Christ. The love of Christ is the Gospel. The dimensions of the Gospel are measureless, eternal. How could there be any end of teaching or preaching on the Gospel? It is in Christ, the Gospel, that we find not only salvation but also every spiritual blessing. The power we need to live the Christian life is found in Christ. The power for transformation and maturity is found in the Gospel. The Gospel is the manifestation of Christ to us by the Spirit through the Word. "He will not speak on his own; he will speak only what he hears…. He will bring glory to me by taking from what is mine making it known to you" (John 16:13–15).

John Piper was not preaching on grief, or how to handle abuse; he was preaching on the glory of God. He was not preaching on what to do if someone wrongs you, and he wasn't preaching on forgiveness. He was preaching on God's holiness and glory, and I would add that he was preaching the Gospel. He discovered that preaching on the glory of God was enough to meet the need in the hearts of those parents suffering under the burden of what had happened to their child. He lifted the bronze serpent of God's glory in that service, and those parents looked and were being healed of their serpent's bite. "For we do not preach ourselves, but Jesus Christ as Lord, and ourselves as your servants for Jesus' sake. For God, who said, 'Let light shine out of darkness,' made His light shine in our hearts to give us the light of the knowledge of the glory of God in the face of Christ" (II Cor. 4:5–6). The knowledge of the glory of God—the holiness John Piper was preaching about—shines forth to us from the face of Christ. It is hard to teach about God's glory without Christ being in the picture. As we look at and imbibe the light of that glory in the face of Christ, we are changed into His image. Preaching Christ changes people; it sanctifies the church.

Dwight Moody preached to millions of people on two continents. If you read his sermons, what you find is that he preached a lot of Gospel messages. He saw revival on two continents, preaching the simple message of the Gospel. The churches he preached to were revived with the Gospel. Moody said he would preach to the churches for two weeks to get them saved and then would preach to the lost people the saved church would bring in. The secret of Moody's success and power was preaching the Gospel.

Moody had an assistant named J. Wilbur Chapman, who went on to lead his own evangelistic campaigns in America and around the world. Moody called Chapman "the greatest evangelist in the country." In 1877, while in school, Chapman went to Chicago to hear Moody preach and went to the inquiry room after the meeting to be counseled by Moody himself, and he came to Christ. Chapman went on to preach evangelistic campaigns with Moody until he went out on his own. At one time, along with his own campaigns Chapman oversaw the work of fifty-one evangelists working in 470 cities. Many of these evangelists are unknown to us but well known to God. Preaching the Gospel was the heart of their work. Much of this preaching was to saved people who were transformed by seeing Christ again when the Gospel was preached.

When Wilbur Chapman started preaching his own evangelistic campaigns, he needed to hire an advance man to go into the cities and organize the crusade. He hired a man named Billy Sunday, who went on to preach his own evangelistic campaigns. Sunday became the most famous evangelist of his day, building tabernacles across America and calling men and women to walk the sawdust trail to Christ. The works of Moody, Chapman, and Sunday were directly related, touching one another and spanning three generations. It was as if they were passing the baton from one to the other. God was using the evangelists to preach the Gospel to the lost as well as the saved. The effect was to save sinners and revive the Church.

Chapman trained Billy Sunday in the way and work of evangelism. "What Sunday learned early on was that the evangelistic meetings were inextricably tied to the local churches; they were successful only when seen as extensions of these local bodies. If the pastors were ministered to, encouraged, and revived spiritually themselves, they in turn could inspire their churches to unite with other churches and seek spiritual renewal within their ranks. From there they could reach out and confront nonchurch people with Christ's claims and promises and then follow that up with prayer for growing churches, more dedicated members, and a morally transformed community" (*Billy Sunday and the Redemption of Urban America*, Lyle W. Dorsett). Perhaps we are seeing Moody's influence here. What did Billy Sunday preach to the preachers? The Gospel, until they were revived and able to inspire their churches to seek spiritual renewal. The Gospel was what was needed, and it was preached to the saint as well as the sinner.

When these evangelists came to town, to whom were they preaching? As we said, these local campaigns were not possible without the help of the local churches uniting to support the crusade. The local churches supported the campaign with their attendance as well. What would they hear? They would hear the Gospel almost exclusively. That Gospel would have a reviving, transforming effect on them. Some of the church members got saved and others rededicated their lives to Christ. Many were revived in their love for Christ. The power was in the Gospel being preached. "And I, if I be lifted up from the earth, will draw all men unto me" (John 12:32, KJV).

When I was young, we would have revival meetings for two weeks in the spring. An evangelist would come, and for those two weeks we would get the Gospel every night. I can remember the pull the Gospel had on me as I walked the aisle more than once, hearing an invitation to come to Christ. The preaching of the Gospel had a purifying effect on me individually and on the church. Preaching the Gospel released the power of God on the saved as well as the lost. Preaching the Gospel drew the lost to Christ and the wandering saved back to Christ. It was like the whole church experienced a violent shaking when the Gospel was being preached.

There is a scene in Dante's *Inferno*, Canto XII, of a place where the path Virgil and Dante have been taking has been wiped away by a great earthquake and the landslide that followed. The path is covered with the debris and rubble of this great landslide, and loose gravel causes Dante's feet to slip and slide, becoming an impediment to his travel. Dante is told by Virgil, his guide, that the last time he came this way the path was open. Then Virgil says, "Before His [Christ] coming who the mighty spoil bore off from Dis, in the supernal circle, upon all sides the deep and loathsome valley trembled so." What Virgil was telling Dante was that when Christ died on the cross and the earthquake came, it shook not only the earth but went down into hell itself and shook the foundations of hell, causing landslides there. Hell trembled with the work of the cross, and then Jesus went into hell and carried off the spoil. I remember reading this for the first time and thinking about the earth-shattering power of the Gospel. "To this end was the Son of God manifested, that he might destroy the works of the devil" (I John 3:8). The work of the cross does violence to the work of the devil, and preaching the cross or the Gospel has the same earthshaking power today it did back then on the lives of all who hear it.

As I grew older, I watched as two weeks of revival services became one, and then five days, and then an extended weekend. Then the revival meetings were gone. If you still have them, rejoice. How many of our churches have evangelistic meetings in the spring anymore? How many of our churches still preach the Gospel to their people? Is there a correlation between preaching the Gospel and power in the Church? Could it be that the more Gospel we preach, the more power will be released—power to change our lives and then power to move into the community to reform it? In the lives of Moody, R.A. Torrey, Chapman, and Sunday, we have three generations of evangelists preaching the Gospel to the Church and the lost in campaigns all over the country and around the world. All these men were primarily evangelists, which means they primarily preached the evangel, the good news of the Gospel (Jesus). They were not ashamed of it and never thought it was beneath the Christian to hear it again and again. They saw something of revival and reform in the society. Churches were filled and on fire for Christ.

Chapman and others developed Bible conference grounds for summer conferences so attendees could hear more preaching and have days of retreat. Chapman helped develop Bible conference centers in Winona Lake, Indiana; Northfield, Massachusetts; Montreat, North Carolina; and Stony Brook, New York. Chapman had a home in Winona Lake, Indiana, for a time, and Billy Sunday took over that home and lived there himself. Billy Graham made his home in Montreat. Christians went to these places to spend their vacations sitting under the Word of God and learning to draw closer to Him. Spending one's vacation on drawing closer to God: Is that what we see today?

In twelve years of school, I attended twelve different schools. My father was in construction, and we moved from town to town as the jobs ended and new ones began. When I was in the third grade we found ourselves in Wichita, Kansas. We always found a church and attended regularly. During our stay in Wichita an evangelist named John Haggai would come to town and hold meetings. Our church would go and support the meetings. Though only in the third grade, I went with my parents and sat under this man's preaching. Even at that early age, God was dealing with me, calling me unto Himself. I felt the pull and power of Gospel on my life. John Haggai was a graduate of Moody Bible Institute, as were his father and mother. John's life bore the stamp of men like Moody, Torrey, and Chapman, all of whom had ties to the same school. Dr. George Sweeting was a classmate of John Haggai and was the best man at John's wedding. He pastored and did the work of an evangelist before becoming pastor of Moody Church and then president of Moody Bible College. I share this to give you some idea of the of fire in men like these, who have served God throughout my lifetime, men whose lives were given to declaring the Gospel, men who were not ashamed of the Gospel of Jesus Christ.

John Haggai preached a message to the Southern Baptist Convention in which he said, "God help us to reappraise and to re-emphasize the place of the pulpit in evangelism. Revitalized pulpits in our land with the proper emphasis on evangelistic preaching will bring a new day spiritually and socially within our drink-hazed, lust-crazed, gold-glutted borders. Forbid, O God, that we should minimize the place of the pulpit in evangelism." The sermon brought national headlines and invitations for John to preach around the country. It was at this time that John left the pastoral ministry to become a full-time evangelist. Notice what he is saying to the pastors of that day: Where is the Gospel in your pulpits? Could it be that he saw the Church moving away from preaching the Gospel to preaching things that have no fire or power in them? I would add that preaching Christ or the Gospel is just what our pulpits are for, to the saved and to the lost.

In the late 1960s and early 1970s, I attended several week-long conferences at the Winona Lake Bible conference grounds in Indiana. At that time one of the last of Billy Sunday's wooden tabernacles was still standing and being used for the main meetings. One night in that tabernacle I heard God's call on my life to surrender my life to preach the Gospel. I guess you could say I walked the sawdust trail that night. As I write this, I wonder how many lives like mine were touched indirectly by the works of men like Moody, Chapman, and Sunday, sitting in places they had established for the purpose of preaching Christ and Him crucified. Let me share a little of what happened after I walked the sawdust trail that night.

It was late spring of 1971 when I made that commitment to follow Christ and preach his Word. Before this conference I had played football in high school and was recruited by a college in Illinois and granted a four-year scholarship. When I returned from the conference, I called the school and told them I would be renouncing my scholarship and going to Grand Rapids Bible College and Seminary to prepare for ministry. I had contacted the school in Grand Rapids to see how to apply and what they needed from me. During this time the pressure to go and play football instead of answering this call to follow God increased. Some of those close to me couldn't understand how anyone could forfeit four years of paid education to go and be a preacher. The school in Illinois called me and asked me to come out again and talk with them first; they said I owed them that at least, so I went. During that visit they said I could work for God there and that they would help me start a Fellowship of Christian Athletes chapter on campus to do God's work while I played football. In the end I played football instead of going into ministry. It would be 16 years before that football journey was over and I heard God's call again in my life.

As I've already explained, when I came out of football, I started a business by buying a seat on the Chicago Board of Trade and trading commodities. During these years at the Board of Trade, God was doing a new work in my life, drawing me ever so tenderly back to Himself. My parents were attending a church in Indiana that we had attended since 1968. A friend of my parents who had been widowed met and married a woman who had been on staff at a small Bible school in Greenville, South Carolina. She and my mother got to be friends and ended up as prayer partners. This lady had brought with her the tapes of some of the teachers at that school and had given some to Mom to listen to. One day after a visit to Mom and Dad's, when walking out the door, I saw one of these tapes on the counter and asked my mom about it. After a brief description, I asked if I could borrow one to listen to, as I had an hour-long commute into Chicago. As I began to listen to this preaching, God was doing a work in my heart and drawing me back to Himself. I was listening to at least two hours of preaching and teaching a day, and often more. Listening to those tapes was igniting a fire and love in my heart for Christ again. What was I listening to?

I didn't realize until years later that what I was listening to was the Gospel. The tapes were primarily the preaching of Joseph Carroll, who had traveled the world preaching the Gospel and founded this school in Greenville, South Carolina, in the early '70s. One of Mr. Carroll's fellow teachers at the school would tell us years later that Mr. Carroll really only had three or four messages, and all were basically the Gospel. Hearing them, I was looking at Jesus, and in the looking, a change was happening in my life. My spiritual life was being rekindled as I listened to the Gospel, and I was seeing power manifest in my life to break the power of sin. "For the kingdom of God is not a matter of talk but of power" (I Cor. 4:20). Power, particularly the power over sin, was the missing element in my life. The power of the Gospel was transforming my life as I was listening and looking at Christ. When you begin to see Jesus, the desire of your heart changes and you want to know more about the One who died for you. You want to grow in the grace and the knowledge of the Lord Jesus Christ. It became clear to me that God was calling me to get training and preparation for the road ahead, and the school in Greenville would be the one we attended. I have to admit there was a lot of doubt and turmoil in my life at this time, for I had just established my business, bought a new home, and finally gotten settled.

With all this happening so fast and with the doubts I was having, I decided to go have few quiet days with the Lord, praying and seeking His face and His will, to be sure I was hearing from Him. As I was considering where I might go for a couple of days, thoughts of Winona Lake came back to me, and I thought I could go there and hear some preaching and pray and be sure of God's will. Winona Lake was just a few hours' drive, so off I went. When I arrived, the conference that week was Christian magicians and clowns. I thought there probably was not much for me there, so I walked the conference grounds talking with the Lord.

This was 1987, and the Billy Sunday Tabernacle was still there, but it had been condemned and was boarded up. Though I didn't know why at the time, I was drawn to the Tabernacle and began to walk around it. For some reason I felt as if I was to go in, but there was no opening that wasn't locked or boarded up. Finally, I saw a window that was boarded but the corner of the plywood was loose, so I pulled it open and dived in. There were the wooden benches the sawdust trails and the platform just as it had been 16 years before. I went down to the front benches and sat and prayed and worshipped the Lord. Though I didn't realize it then, the Lord had brought me back to the very place where I had said I would follow Him and serve Him, no matter what that meant.

After some time in the front row, I went up to the platform and stood in the pulpit looking out over the empty tabernacle. I can't describe fully the next moments, as it felt as if the weight of God fell upon me. I can remember holding on to the pulpit, thinking, "If I let it go, I will fall to the floor," so great was the weight upon me. I remember that my knees bent under me, and my head dropped and bowed in the presence of God. Here again I renewed the promise I had made 16 years before with no one in attendance but the Lord and me. In that moment came these words: "Where is the fire in my pulpit?" I must admit that at the time I didn't understand the question. Here was the pulpit from which men like Wilbur Chapman and Billy Sunday had cried out to crowds of people, not only in Winona Lake but around the country and around the world. What did they preach? They preached the Gospel; they preached Christ and Him crucified. Could it be that the missing fire was and is the lack of Gospel preaching in God's pulpits across our country?

Several years ago, I was teaching through Romans and read this: "First I thank my God through Jesus Christ for all of you, because your faith is being reported all over the world" (Rom. 1:8). Here was a church that was famous for its faith throughout the world. Oh, that this could be said of us! It would be like someone today addressing a letter to some large church in America that was well known throughout the country. The question came to me: "What do you teach Christians who are already famous for their faith? Paul said, "For we do not preach ourselves, but Jesus Christ as Lord" (II Cor. 4:5 NIV). "For I resolved to know nothing while I was with you except Jesus Christ and Him crucified" (I Cor. 2:1). Paul wanted to keep the first things first. Pastor and Christian, do you want to know nothing but the Gospel? What did Paul teach or preach to these Christians famous for their faith? The Gospel! The book of Romans is perhaps the greatest treatise on the Gospel ever written and some think one of the finest things ever written by a human being. No matter your spiritual location, your greatest need is that shining of the Glory of God into your heart in the face of Jesus, the Gospel. This is the answer. We seem to be preaching many things that are not Christ, and our people are starving for a grand and glorious vision of Christ. I believe there is a famine for the preaching and hearing of Gospel today.

As a young Christian, I used to say, "Jesus is the answer" to which some smart aleck would say, "What's the question?" Jesus is the answer to any question. What is your problem as a human being? Jesus is the answer. You were made for Him, and any lack of fulfillment, or sorrow, or addiction, sin, hatred, anger, and anything else you can think of are solved and resolved in Jesus. God's healing process for your soul is to stand you in the glory of His Son and shine His glory on you and change you into His image. No matter my circumstances, if I shine—reflect—the glory of God, I'm doing what He created me for. That may be in abounding or being abased, in life or death, in peace or war. Being changed into the image of His Son is God's goal for me. Beholding His glory is one of the ways I glorify Him, and seeing His glory, I'm changed into His image. We will see God's glory in the face of Christ Jesus, who is Gospel.

The Disciples saw the glory of the Gospel and were changed. "We have seen His glory, the glory of the One and only Son.… From the fullness of His grace we have received one blessing after another" (John 1:14, 16). Here is the beginning of our thought, changed by beholding: "We beheld His glory." From the fullness of His grace—free and unearned—we received grace upon grace. Think about the great proportion of the New Testament that is given to the Gospel—four of them. Do you think God the Father wants us to gaze on the Gospel, i.e., Christ?

Jesus said He was to be lifted up like the serpent in the wilderness and would draw all men to Himself. Can a saved man be drawn closer to the Lord? Preach the Gospel: "Give your text and make a shortcut to the Cross." Jesus died for you! What is your problem today? Start with the Gospel. Say to yourself, "Jesus died for me," repeat it, read it. Jesus died, bearing my sin away. Jesus loves me, this I know. How? Jesus died for me; here is the Gospel. Desire to know nothing in your pulpit, pastor, but Jesus and Him crucified. Jesus rose for you and is alive now and is speaking to you if you just come and listen and look at the glory of the Lord. It shines today. Ask God to show you the face of His Son, Jesus.

Paul said, "I am not ashamed of the Gospel, for it is the power of God unto salvation" (Rom. 1:16). Salvation is not just justification; it is also sanctification. You are not just saved, but you're *being* saved. You'll need to hear and see the Gospel at every step of your Christian life. If I want a deeper spiritual life, I need the Gospel, for in the seeing of the Gospel the power of God is released and revealed to save you from whatever trap you may find yourself in. The righteous will live by faith: "I have been crucified with Christ and I no longer live, but Christ lives in me. The life I now live in the body, I live by faith in the Son of God, who loved me and gave himself for me" (Gal. 2:20). If the Gospel is the power of God, then preach the power. What do I need to be saved from? My sin, yes, and then what after that? Here we can add everything that happens to Christians: hatred, evil habits, anger, bitterness, greed, pride? How do I find the power to overcome these? In the Gospel. What is the Gospel? Jesus is the Gospel. Preach Jesus and make Him central in your pulpit. Let people see the glory of Christ. Teach your people to turn their eyes upon Jesus, looking into His wonderful face, and watch as the things of earth will grow dim in the light of His glory. Pastor, understand that your people need to the see the glory of God in the face of Christ Jesus, and in seeing this glory will be transformation. Preach the Gospel. "He who did not spare His own son, but gave him up for us all—how will He not also, along with Him graciously give us all things?" (Rom. 8:32). The Gospel is God's greatest gift and it includes everything else. Preach the Gospel, get your people to look at Jesus, and in finding Jesus they will find everything else they need for life and godliness.

We don't believe this is so, and we have moved away from preaching the Gospel. Counseling, psychology, and many other things are pressing in. In many places we are teaching a works Gospel. "If you do *x*, you will be delivered from your problem." We are teaching twelve steps in the Church of Jesus Christ today. Is this anathema? We must be careful here that we don't make bundles and tie them on the backs of our people. We don't need to learn the law better; we need to learn how to gaze on Jesus better. In viewing, beholding, our Jesus, we are changed. Pastor, teacher, are you preaching Christ, are you helping your people to see Christ and be healed? Are you lifting up the bronze serpent of Christ on Sunday morning from your pulpit so your people can be healed of their snake bites? Are you teaching them to look at Christ, to flee to Christ and gaze and be healed? Or are you making bundles of laws and tying them together and putting this great load on the backs of your people?

Gospel preaching is Christ-centered, Christ-focused preaching. Subjective truth never delivers; objective truth delivers. Preaching the law is subjective; it is preaching what I should be doing, or what am I doing wrong. There is no power here to help those you are peaching to. Preaching the Gospel, Christ and Him crucified, is objective truth. It is preaching what Christ has done, what He alone has accomplished for us. It is preaching the endless supply of His sufficiency. Let your people see the objective truth that will set them free. Let them see Christ. When you preach a principle, preach the Prince, the answer and the power for keeping the principle. Lift Jesus up like that serpent and tell your folks to look and live. However many times you fall, get up and look; when you're bitten by the serpent of sin, go and look at the bronze serpent, who is Christ. Faith for us amounts to looking at Christ. So just look and live. Even when you find it hard to believe, go look at Jesus. If you think it is too easy, do it anyway. Look and live. "If you have the faith of a mustard seed, you can say to this mountain be gone and be cast into the sea" (Matt. 17:20). Here is mustard seed faith, casting a glance at our beautiful Savior so you might be changed and set free.

The great men and women of faith put themselves in a position to see Jesus every day of their lives. Their work became looking—worship—and they started every day at the throne of grace to gaze on God's greatest gift—Jesus. "I keep asking that the Father may give you the Spirit of wisdom and revelation, so you may know Him better" (Eph. 1:17). It is God's desire to give you the Son by His Spirit. His Spirit will help you to see the Son better by the power of revelation. As Christ is revealed to you, so is His power, so is His glory, and in the presence of that power and glory you are changed by beholding. The power of God comes through the seeing of the Son, and helping you to see the Son—revelation—is the Holy Spirit's work.

Behold your God and live. Look and look again at Jesus and be changed. If we are not preaching the Gospel, it is because we don't believe the Gospel is the power of God unto salvation. Many have believed, as we said before, that the Gospel is just the genesis of our Christianity, and then we move on to obeying the laws and principles of Scripture. Expository preaching is important, and what we should be doing in our pulpits, but expository preaching is not the goal; Christ is, and if my expository preaching hides Christ in any way, we have a problem. The goal is God and His glory. Not that there is anything wrong with expository preaching. We glory in it and do it. The point is being honest with what our goal is in our preaching. Is the goal to get through so many books of the Bible or it is to reveal Christ to those we teach? The goal of expository preaching should be to get people to see Jesus. Preach Christ and Him crucified. Find the scarlet thread of Christ everywhere in scripture and draw it out for your people. All of our messages should end with Christ being lifted up for our people to see and then be healed. We study the Word of God that we may see and know the God of the Word. We study the Word of God so that Christ may be revealed to us.

Moody, much used of God, was simple in his preaching. He used the same sermon many times and thought that it took several times preaching it for the sermon to become good. He was rough on the English language, but here was a man much used of God in this country and in England. There was power in his preaching, the power of the Holy Spirit to bring forth streams of living water from this man's belly. What did Moody preach? Christ. He put forth the simple Gospel, and the power of God was released. Oh, that we preachers would trust the Gospel again and loose it from our pulpits.

Pastor, do you feel that preaching the Gospel to your people is simplistic or naive? Don't the saved in our congregations need something more? Don't they need the meat of the Word? Don't those sitting in your congregation need the deeper truths? Once we have preached or taught the Gospel, we feel pressure to move on to these deeper truths. You may think I preach the Gospel to get them in the Kingdom and then I preach great truths of the Christian life—the meat of the Word—so they might mature in the faith. If you were to stay with the Gospel, some in our congregation might ask the question, "Where's the beef?" Feeling this pressure, our teaching moves on to counseling, teaching about divorce, or end times, what a spiritual family is, the deeper life, sanctification, love, or something on self-esteem. There is the misconception that if the people I'm preaching to are saved, they don't need the Gospel again; they need some deeper teaching that will lead them to maturity in Christ. Many of the churches I grew up in preached the Gospel occasionally and then hit it heavy in the spring with our revival meetings. The Gospel is deeper life teaching. It is the road to sanctification, to maturity, so preach it. Want more power in your church? Preach the Gospel. "For God so loved the world that He gave His one and only Son" (John 3:16). What are you teaching and preaching, pastor?

One of Spurgeon's biographers wrote a chapter titled "Christocentric." What do you think was Spurgeon's focus? Give your text and take a shortcut to the Cross. "They demanded of themselves what they expect in every Christian, the evidence that all actions begin and end with the warm, sweet presence, living yet. The Puritans were Christocentric men. They rejected with contempt this ceremonious homage, which other sects substituted for the pure worship of the soul; they aspired to gaze full on his intolerable brightness, and to commune with him face-to-face. Like old Fleetwood, the only bitterness of soul they knew was when Jesus hid his face from them" (*The Shadow of the Broad Brim*, Richard E. Day). Spurgeon, "the Prince of Preachers," would not be a good example of today's expository preacher. His pattern wasn't to go verse by verse through a whole book. He could seem topical in his preaching at times, but that topic always came back to Christ. "The motto of all true servants of God must be, 'We preach Christ; and him crucified.' A sermon without Christ in it is like a loaf of bread without any flour in it. No Christ in your sermon, sir? Then go home, and never preach again until you have something worth preaching" (*Spurgeon on Preaching*). What would happen in our churches if we just preached the magnificence of the Gospel every week? What is the Gospel but the serpent on the pole so men might behold the intolerable brightness of Christ and be changed?

If beholding Jesus is the way of transformation, then not only does our preaching need to be Christ-centered, we need to make our devotions Christocentric. If our devotions are filled with me and what I need, filled with my ministry, filled with my lost children, filled with my poor health, will there be any power released? Shouldn't our devotions have more of Christ and less of us? Shouldn't we be looking at Jesus and worshipping Jesus more in our devotions? When we are occupied with Jesus in our worship, when we lift praise to Him, when we exalt His character and His nature and describe who He is, we are preaching the Gospel to ourselves. This worship, this declaration of His name and His wonders, this Gospel will be powerful and transformational in the life of the Christian. It will be as if I am preaching the Gospel to myself every morning. As I look at Jesus, as I worship, as I declare who He is, I am preaching to myself the power of God unto salvation. Power will be released in the declaration and in the looking at Jesus every morning. We do this as we worship Jesus and describe who and what He is to ourselves and back to Him in praise and thanksgiving. The power of worship is that we are looking at the Son and praising Him for all that He is and what He has done, and in this looking, we are changed into His likeness. Worship focuses specifically on the Jesus who is the Gospel and enjoying the view of the glory of God in the face of Christ. God wants us to look at His Son repeatedly, until we look like Him. If we are to love Him first, then shouldn't our devotions be about Him first and about us second? Making Christ our focus will start in the secret place. Love the Lord your God with all your heart and soul and mind, love Him by looking at Him, by looking to Him.

Think about your prayer life. Would you say the preponderance of your devotional time is taken up with Jesus or with you? When the focus of our prayer life becomes our problems and needs, we find we are asking God for many things that are not Him. When your focus becomes Jesus, you will find that you are asking God for fewer things and spending more time describing Jesus in worship. Your prayers will become worship. Describing Jesus in worship, meditating on, praying the Gospel, will be a powerful experience, one of deliverance and transformation. When your focus is right, you will find you are praying Jesus; you are praying the Gospel. This Gospel prayer will not only transform you but in corporate prayer will transform others as they hear and see the Gospel you are praying out.

You will find no joy or fulfillment in what you lack. Your problems and deficiencies do not lift your spirits or encourage your heart. You will find no power over sin in looking at yourself. Looking at these things can be depressing. Looking at your needs and problems will not empower you for service. Yet this is where many of us spend a great deal of our time in our devotions. If you see only need, obstacles, and pain in your prayer time, then it is easy to get disappointed in your devotions and begin to move away from them. It is easy to be constantly disappointed when all I see is need. One thing to remember is that there will never be an end to need until we arrive on that golden shore of Heaven. No matter my need today, I can always have Jesus, gaze at Jesus, and find hope and power to live in the snake pit of the world.

Recently I have watched the Billy Graham crusades of the past on cable. I have been impressed with the power of the messages and wondered why. I watched the greatest evangelist of our time and thought maybe it's because he was such a great preacher. As I listened, I realized I haven't been hearing this much from our pulpits. I missed the sweet simple messages about Jesus and what he had done for me. As I watched, I began to weep, for I realized that what made the messages powerful wasn't the man but the message itself. Billy was preaching the Gospel, simple yet powerful, the power of God unto salvation. He was holding up the bronze serpent. I looked, and healing was happening in my soul. I saw again that I needed the Gospel; I needed to hear it again and again. I need to look into the narrative and see Christ crucified for me. I have been saved for many years, but this old heart needs to hear again the message that transforms. Oh, Church, how far have we strayed from our great need of the Gospel? Oh, that God would raise up sons of thunder again to give themselves to this simple message and pour the balm of Gilead over the hearts of the people listening. Where is the fire in my pulpit? Oh, that we would come and desire nothing but Jesus from our pulpits, that we would desire Him in our times of devotion and that our prayers would be filled with the wonder of who He is and what He has done. Oh, that we might say, "For me to live is Christ."

A friend of mine recently asked, "If you had one message for the Church in America, what would it be?" I told him I would preach the Gospel. If our great need as individuals is to look at Christ, then our great need as a congregation is the same, to look at Christ. In the congregation this will be accomplished by the preaching Christ or preaching the Gospel. Just because a man is preaching the Bible doesn't mean he is preaching Christ. Some think we preach the Gospel to the lost to get them saved, and once they are saved, we teach them principles of how to live the Christian life. Preaching these principles or the law may veil Christ to those we are preaching to. We have moved from preaching the Gospel to preaching the law and wonder why our messages aren't transforming the lives of people. The lost man needs the Gospel to get saved; the Christian needs the Gospel to continue to be sanctified. Thinking his pews are filled with Christians, the average pastor preaches very little of the Gospel. We are saved by looking unto Jesus, and then we turn away from looking at Jesus to learning some principle or law. We need to preach the Gospel to the lost, the sick, and the mature in the Church to get her well and keep her well. Christian, when was the last time your pastor preached the Gospel to you? When was the last time he lifted up Jesus like the serpent in the wilderness that you might look and live? When we start preaching the Gospel to the Church again, she will be healed, she will be saved, and I believe revived.

Let me remind you what I said in the chapter on worship: "Again, as natural conscience gives no strength to do the duty, so it does not make a duty to be strong to the soul. That is, there's no strength gotten by the duty. One is not by one prepared for another, 'but the way of the Lord is strength to the upright' (Prov. 10:29). That is, when a gracious heart is in the way of God's worship, it finds the very duty of the worship of God to be strength to it and so fits it for another duty" (*Gospel Worship*, Jeremiah Burroughs). What was Jeremiah Burroughs saying here? It is not obedience to God's law that strengthens the soul for its duty. Power doesn't come to us when we obey some command of God; power comes when we worship God by filling our vision with the Gospel. Faith that fills its vision with the glory of God in worship will find that worship, that beholding, will strengthen it, empower it, and transform it.

"And I, when I am lifted up from the earth, will draw all people to myself" (John 12:32).

Chapter 9

WAITING ON JESUS'S TABLE

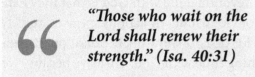

> "Those who wait on the Lord shall renew their strength." (Isa. 40:31)

THE FIRST TIME I went to Disney World I couldn't believe the lines waiting for the rides. The lines were so long that they would organize you with ropes to control the flow of the crowd so that it wouldn't flow out in the walkways and clog pedestrian traffic. They would have signs telling you how long you could expect to be waiting before getting on your ride. It was nothing to have a 45-minute- to an-hour-wait for a ride and sometimes longer. Since waiting is such a large part of the rides at Disney that created something called Fast Pass where you could reserve your place in line and do something else like eat snacks or even get in another line for a different ride while you wait. You could actually be waiting for two or more rides at the same time, oh joy. Because I hate to wait so much, I have never been back to the Magic Kingdom. It wasn't so magic to me.

For most of us waiting is something we hate to do. There is a nothingness, an emptiness to waiting that seems wasteful of our time, and therefore our lives. When we have to wait, we can easily get aggravated and angry. Have you ever had to wait in line at a restaurant and got so aggravated you left and went to another restaurant only to end up waiting even longer for a meal? We can feel helpless, anxious, frustrated, and angry in our waiting. After all our waiting if we don't get what we have waited for, we can feel cheated or robbed. Hidden in this reaction to waiting is a high self-image: "Don't you know who I am? I shouldn't have to wait for anyone!"

Husbands, have you ever had to wait for your wife? This is enough of a phenomenon in marriage, that Don Sampson and Wynn Varble wrote a song titled "Waitin on a Woman." The song was recorded by Brad Paisley and included in his 2005 album, *Time Well Wasted*. How many arguments or tense moments have couples had because one party was waiting on the other. The song tries to turn the negative of waiting on a woman into positives. Waiting to meet her, waiting for her at the altar, waiting for her to have a child, and finally waiting for her in Heaven.

I believe one of the reasons so many Christians fail to maintain a devotional life with God is that they hate to wait on anyone, even God. This is not something we would say out loud, but our actions speak extremely loud what we say can't be heard. When the thing we have waited for doesn't show up, the disappointment can drive us to stomp off, slam the door, and never return to spending time with God. We leave because we think that we had waited too long, or the waiting made us believe what we are waiting for is never going to come. This impatience with God can lead some to think, *This prayer stuff doesn't work.* If God isn't going to answer me, why bother coming to Him at all? We forget the Israelites waited for 400 years to be delivered from Egypt.

Another reason for the failure is that we're waiting for the wrong thing. What if we are waiting for something that God doesn't want us to have, so He never gives it to us. These could be good things, but good things can often get in the way of the best things. We can think that if I just wait long enough, put in the waiting work, God will have to answer me. We can see waiting as a means to end, asking God for something, plus waiting, equals getting what I ask for. If I wait long enough, God will see my waiting and reward it by answering my prayer or giving me what I want. This would be a misunderstanding of what it means to wait on God. We can confuse waiting with importunity. We can see waiting on God as a means to an end, but what if waiting on God was the end itself? Impatient, disappointed, and angry with God, many Christians have stomped out of their devotions never to return. Having a wrong perspective about what it means to wait on God can lead to failure in our relationship with the Lord.

If you had an appointment with the King of England at ten o'clock and he showed up at twelve, you wouldn't greet him with, "Your Majesty, you're late; why did you keep me waiting?" Because of his station all his time is more important than yours. Therefore, whatever he's doing, even if he was intentionally making you wait for him, it would be for your good. Because of who he is even waiting for him becomes the most important thing you could do with your day. Most of us would tell and retell the story of having to wait for the king and how he was two hours late. After meeting him the waiting would be insignificant and forgotten. One might boast to their friends, "Can I tell you about the day I met the king of England?" If that could be true of an earthly monarch, how much more would it be true of waiting for the King of kings and Lord of lords?

Waiting can seem passive and so unproductive, sitting in a chair doing nothing. What if waiting wasn't unproductive? What if waiting was one of the most productive things you could do. What if waiting wasn't passive but something active? Some of this will depend on who you are waiting for. What if you were to discover that waiting was the highest and most glorious thing a human being could do? What if you discovered that waiting on God was not a means to an end but the end itself? What if waiting on God was something He wants you to do?

Occasionally you will hear of a waiter receiving an exorbitant tip. The last story I heard was of a waitress receiving $10,000 for serving two glasses of water to a patron and person with him. The story of large tips makes the rounds of local news and often go viral on the Internet. The common thread in these stories is someone is waiting on a client, and another person is being waited upon. In the midst of all this waiting the one waited on decides to wait on the waiter by giving them a gift. Out of these brief encounters of service come these great gifts, which make great stories. I think there is a lesson for us here.

If this is how unjust men treat one another, how will the God of glory treat those who wait on Him? Will not the God of glory out tip any unjust man or woman? Will He not pour out from His great treasury for those who wait upon Him? Remember, this God knows your needs before you ask Him. This God will satisfy your needs from His great treasury in heaven. This God is more generous than any man living.

Many see devotions as a place to ask God for things and then wait until He answers. What if the opposite were true? What if prayer was the place where we ask Jesus what He wanted and waited on Him to bring it to Him? What if the goal of prayer was not so much Jesus serving you but you serving Jesus? What if the object, the goal, of prayer was Jesus and His desires and not yours or some need for your ministry? What if the goal was to please Jesus by bringing to Him our service of praise and worship? Remember the large tip we talked about earlier came not by asking but by waiting and serving.

The English word "wait" has two basic meanings. The first, is the idea of passing time until something happens, which is the passive side of waiting. The second is to wait at table, or to wait upon someone who is dining, bringing them their food and drink. Most Christians' prayer life is like the first of these meanings; we ask God for something and then sit back and wait for God to serve us and answer our prayer. Christians can even grow angry with God because they have had to wait for something a very long time or didn't get it. We act as if we are in restaurant and had to wait a very long time for our food, only growing angrier the longer we wait. This is because we see our devotional life as Jesus waiting on us instead of us waiting on Him. What if we begin to see waiting on Jesus as serving him?

Waiting is not something most people enjoy. We can find it boring, distasteful, and inconvenient. Having to wait in traffic has driven people to a new psychosis, road rage. When we see lines outside the door of our favorite restaurants we drive on by. We have waiting rooms in hospitals, doctors' offices, even at our oil change place. These waiting rooms try to ease our pain with magazines, TV, coffee and treats. This kind of waiting is passive and entails very little activity. Though there will be elements of this kind of waiting in our prayer lives it isn't what we want to think about now. I want to think about the second part of the definition of wait. To wait upon someone, to serve them as a waiter at their table.

Think of your prayer life as if you are a waiter in a restaurant and Jesus comes in and is sitting at one of your tables. "That ye may attend upon the Lord without distraction" (I Cor. 7:35). What does it mean to wait upon the Lord, or to attend to the Lord? What does that look like? If we look at how waiters serve people in restaurants, we may learn something about how to attend upon the Lord.

Here we should take some stock in our prayer life by being honest with ourselves. "To thine own self be true." Is your prayer life a series of request to God for things you need or want? Are you waiting for what you want, or are you waiting upon Christ's table? Are your desires the goal of your prayer life, or is it Jesus and what He wants? Is Jesus there to serve you in your devotions, or are you there to serve Him? If your devotions are all about you, they can be very boring and disappointing. Boring and disappointing devotions are easily quit.

Consider with me for a moment a waiter in a fine restaurant and how he conducts himself around his tables. It is not a habit of mine to dine in fine restaurants, for I cannot afford them. In my lifetime I have been in a few where the waiting was superb. Let's consider how good waiters do their job so me might apply similar principles in our waiting on the Lord.

Before clients ever show up the waiter prepares for their guests. Before they arrive, there is bathing and cleaning to make one's self most presentable. This will include grooming, makeup, and hair for the wait staff. In finer restaurants there is a dress code and a uniform, which is detailed and neat. There may even be an inspection of the server's dress by the chef. Before service there is often a meal prepared for those serving so they will have plenty of energy to serve those who come to their tables. In some cases, the restaurant will know who is coming and what they have ordered in the past or even what they will order that day. The waiter's focus is on those they are serving. The job is to lay aside their own wants and needs to meet the wants and needs of those they are waiting on.

In the brief time that he has he will try to get to know as much as he can about his clients. Is this a birthday party, anniversary, or some other kind of celebration? Where are you from, and how did you hear about us? Is this your first time with us? If it is a place of some quality during this initial repartee, he may take the napkins from the table and lay it across their lap, as he puts the menu into their hands. Part of the waiter's job is to make those he is serving feel comfortable about where they are and who is taking care of them. In this way the waiter builds trust with those at his tables. If this trust is strong enough, those at the table might commit their choice of wine and dinner into the waiters' hands.

With the table settled, and napkins draped on the laps, the waiter offers the specials for evening to the table. This can be a rather long discourse describing specials of meats, vegetables, sauces, soups, and salads all from memory. Now it's time to order drinks and appetizers, all of which will be done again from memory, with table talk mixed in. The waiter must take care to concentrate on the one speaking making sure they get the clients order correct. With background noise this can be difficult requiring the waiter to draw near to the one ordering so they can hear. Waiters will tell you it is very hard work, and they often go home exhausted at the end of the shift.

After the table is settled in with menus and napkins the waiter will begin with drinks and appetizer orders. The drinks will usually come first and after preparation the appetizers. Once the drinks and appetizers are served, there may be a lapse of time before ordering the main entree. A good waiter watches the table to see when it may be most appropriate to proceed with ordering the main course. You may see the waiter cruise by the table several times with no interaction just checking on the status of the table and see if anything is needed or if they are ready to order. If those at the table are having a good time with free-flowing conversation and laughter, he may wait before getting their entree orders. What's happening at the table is the most important thing and not to be interrupted just so the waiter can get his job done. The waiter will inconvenience himself to satisfy the desires of those he waits on. When ready the waiter will take the entree orders often without pen and paper. When you think of the number of things that has to be remembered with each order this is impressive. Some high-end restaurants record all their customers' orders onto the computer for future reference. In this way the waiter may anticipate the client's choice without them having to say a word.

In the 1970s my wife worked for a brief time for Oral Roberts University in an assisted living facility. Sally worked as a waitress in the dining hall, where she would take the orders and then serve the table. At this facility you couldn't use paper and pencil to write the orders down; you had to memorize the entire order and deliver it to the kitchen. Having to memorize everything nearly drove her mad. Just think about how many ways you can prepare eggs. Along with this, what kinds of toasts, side dishes, and drinks. Everything was done to take away the stigma of living in an Old Folks Home. All the extra work by the wait staff was done to make the inhabitants feel more comfortable, at ease, and at home. She was there to wait on them and make their life easier and more comfortable.

The waiter is there to listen. A good waiter is a good listener. Restaurants can be noisy places, and the waiter must listen with concentration and care to the clients. The noise of the restaurant and even conversations going on at the table may compete with the person's order he is trying to take. He may have to draw near to hear them or ask them to repeat what they just said. People who are soft spoken or have accents can be hard to understand. The waiter's primary mission is not talking but listening for the orders of those being served. If we are talking all the time, something many Christians think is prayer, we won't hear from the one we are waiting on. The most important things said will be the requests of his clients at the table.

Many Christians who come to Jesus never shut up; they have their own agenda and won't stop talking until they are sure that Jesus knows all about it. Prayer, we have been told, is talking to God, so some think if they are not talking, it can't be prayer. What if prayer is also listening to God, and what if it is more listening than talking? "Do not be quick with your mouth, do not be hasty in your heart to utter anything before God. God is in heaven and you are on earth, so let your words be few." (Eccles. 5:2) Let your words be few and listening much. Don't be so busy telling the Lord what we need or want, that you can't hear Him give you

His order. Learn to wait on God's table by becoming a good listener. Do we listen to the Word more than we talk to God? Shut up and listen for God.

The choices for food made by those at the table are called orders. Those orders are taken to the kitchen, where they are obeyed by the kitchen staff and prepared. When prepared that order will return to the one who ordered it, ready to fulfill their desires. Your devotions are the place where you come to serve at Christ's table. You come there every day to see what He desires, to take His order, and see that it is filled to His specifications. Even with the order taken, filled, and delivered to the table, the waiter's duties are not yet done. He will check to see if the order is filled properly or if anything else is needed. Now he continues to wait by keeping an eye on the table to see if there might be anything else needed.

If the waiter is good, you can get their attentions with just a glance of your eye. When your eye catches theirs, they will respond and approach the table. Catching the Lord's eye and knowing there is something He wants is a place of maturity in the Christian's life. Wait upon the Lord and learn His subtle glances.

As a waiter serves at table, there is an active watching of the table. He may not be seen doing this, but he watches. As dinner is consumed, do those at the table have any needs? Is the water glass empty, what do the drinks look like? Can the appetizer dishes be removed? Are they done with their dinners? Are they ready for dessert and coffee? The Waiter looks at the table and analyzes what is going on in order to anticipate the needs or desires of those sitting there. One of the ways you know you have a good server is that you don't have to ask for very much, for your waiter has anticipated many of your needs.

After the dishes have been cleared the waiter may take a crumber from his vest pocket and scrape the crumbs from the table. This is a small thing but has always impressed me when I see a waiter do it. He's cleaning up my crumbs from the table in preparation for dessert and coffee. All this effort is focused on those being waited on. It is an active waiting.

I was in a restaurant in California that had live music playing for the guests. That night it was a jazz saxophonist belting out some mellow tunes. After playing for half hour, he got up and began to move around the restaurant stopping to serenade at each table. When he stopped at our table we all stopped our eating just to listen because his playing was so good. He had nothing to do with our orders or bringing our food, but he was an important part of the service that night. I thought of how kings and rulers in times past would have singers entertain while dining. What if Jesus calls you to wait on His table by singing praises to him?

Would you think of this as waiting on Him? I think this is why worship is so important; it is our way of serenading our Lord as He dines.

When the waiter goes home after a day's work they are exhausted, because their total focus has been on the needs of others to the deprivation of their own. Now that they are off duty they can begin to think about their own needs. After serving others for hours they may be starving and get something to eat. They may finally get the rest and sleep they need. Most Christians have devotions so they can get something from Jesus; they come to let Jesus serve them. They want Jesus to serve them instead of taking care of Him. When we come and wait on Jesus to serve Him, we are doing what we were created for. Waiting on Jesus we find our fulfillment, purpose, and satisfaction in meeting our Lord's needs. Waiting on Jesus we may find that all we wanted and needed are being satisfied without asking. We are not saying that Jesus has needs that we can meet, for He needs nothing. We want you to see waiting on Jesus as something that is more than just wasting or passing time.

I want you to think of your devotions as if you were a waiter in a restaurant where you work. I want you to think about Jesus coming to your table every day. Think about what you would say to Him and what your service to Him would be. Somewhere we have gotten the idea that our devotions are all about us, me, my, and mine. Your devotions are not about you; they are about Jesus and what He wants. Your job is taking His order every day. Have you ever seen your devotions in this light? Devotions are about caring for Him and serving Him. A waiter can't be concerned about his needs while waiting on others.

Fine restaurants will have a group meal before what they call service so the wait staff will have energy to serve. When Jesus comes to your table to be served your needs are not the important ones. "Thy kingdom come, and thy will be done on earth as it is in heaven." "When did you give me drink, when you have done it to the least of these?" When you are totally devoted to waiting on someone else there is little thought of self.

I have known my share of people who have the gift of hospitality. These find their joy not in receiving but in serving and giving to others. For the Christian we too shall find our true joy in serving the Master as He sits at table and allows us to serve Him. Here we find our worth and our honor, here we find our high place. This is why worship (service) is so important to the Christian. We serve the Lord by first paying all our attention to Him (worship) and then waiting on Him for His order, and then we carry that order to and from the kitchen and place it before Him.

Remember when Jesus said, "Suppose one of you had a servant plowing or looking after the sheep. Would he say to the servant when he comes in from the field, 'Come along now and sit down to eat?' Would he not rather say, 'Prepare my supper, and get yourself ready and wait on me while I eat and drink; after that you may eat and drink'? Would he thank the servant because he did what he was told to do? So you also, when you have done everything you were told to do, should say, 'We are unworthy servants; we have only done our duty'" (Luke 17:7–10). The point of the story Jesus tells is that we have reversed the roles in our devotional times with the Lord. We come expecting Him to make our supper, seat us at the table, and then serve us before the Master eats. We make ourselves the focus and our needs the theme. Oh, the high honor of waiting on the Lord with no expectation of something for me. The pure honor of serving the Lord is enough everyday whether He gives blessing or suffering. Here in the waiting, we have the grace of His presence and the grace of His words even if they are only orders. Watching and serving our Master will be transformational for us. As you grow in the Lord you will see that the service of waiting on the Lord looking unto Him is the place of greatest blessing, for in the looking (waiting) we are changed into His image.

Waiting on others there will be moments that seem empty and quiet. That inactivity can be mistaken for laziness. G. Campbell Morgan had this to say about those quiet empty moments: "Waiting for God is not laziness. Waiting for God is not abandonment of effort. Waiting for God means first, activity under command; second, Readiness for any new command that may come; third, the ability to do nothing until the command is given." Ready at our station as we wait upon the Lord it may appear we are doing nothing, and the devil may even accuse of such, but we are activity under command. "Wait for the Lord; be strong and take heart and wait for the Lord" (Ps. 27:14). It may seem as if nothing is happening in your waiting, but you are actively serving your God. Even if we are only watching His table, that watching will be transformational to our lives.

In the Scripture we have a memorial to one who waited upon Christ in the proper way:

> When one of the Pharisees invited Jesus to have dinner with him, he went to the Pharisee's house and reclined at the table. A woman in that town who lived a sinful life learned that Jesus was eating at the Pharisee's house, so she came there with an alabaster jar of perfume. As she stood behind him at his feet weeping, she began to wet his feet with her tears. Then she wiped them with her hair, kissed them and poured perfume on them.

When the Pharisee who had invited him saw this, he said to himself, "If this man were a prophet, he would know who is touching him and what kind of woman she is—that she is a sinner."

Jesus answered him, "Simon, I have something to tell you."

"Tell me, teacher," he said.

"Two people owed money to a certain moneylender. One owed him five hundred denarii,[a] and the other fifty. Neither of them had the money to pay him back, so he forgave the debts of both. Now which of them will love him more?"

Simon replied, "I suppose the one who had the bigger debt forgiven."

"You have judged correctly," Jesus said.

Then he turned toward the woman and said to Simon, "Do you see this woman? I came into your house. You did not give me any water for my feet, but she wet my feet with her tears and wiped them with her hair. You did not give me a kiss, but this woman, from the time I entered, has not stopped kissing my feet. You did not put oil on my head, but she has poured perfume on my feet. Therefore, I tell you, her many sins have been forgiven—as her great love has shown. But whoever has been forgiven little loves little."

Then Jesus said to her, "Your sins are forgiven."

The other guests began to say among themselves, "Who is this who even forgives sins?"

Jesus said to the woman, "Your faith has saved you; go in peace." (Luke 7:24–50)

This sinful woman was waiting on Jesus. She makes Christ the focus and looks to His needs. The theme of the story is forgiven much, love much; forgiven little, love little. Jesus said, "As her great love has shown." Because of her "great love" she came to serve. She waited on Jesus, she washed His feet with her tears, and wiped them with her hair. Wiping Jesus feet with her hair was a service of humiliation, but not a burden to the heart lost in love. Her crowning glory was to pour out her perfume upon His feet. She would not give that which cost her little. Alabaster was brought to anoint Jesus's feet. Perhaps you have come and anointed Jesus's feet with the perfume of your tears, or the alabaster of your praise. Oh my friend, how can we not wash His feet with our tears when we remember what He has forgiven us of. He forgives and doesn't hate. This woman being forgiven much, loved much. How much have you been forgiven of? How much do you love and serve? Have you made your devotion times about waiting on Jesus or Jesus waiting on you? Have you come to wash His feet with your tears, to wipe them with your hair? Do you go and anoint his feet with the perfume of your love and praise?

For many of us Christians our devotional times have become a place where we sit at Jesus's table and say to Him, "Come now, Jesus, prepare my supper and get yourself ready to wait on me while I eat and drink." We come with our shopping lists, with our orders, as if the only thing that matters to Jesus is getting us what we ask for. We see Jesus as our waiter and think we can command Him, "Fill my glass, give me another piece of lamb." If Jesus doesn't jump when we ask or give us the service we expect, we get angry with Him. Many Christians have fallen away from their devotions because Jesus won't treat them as the king or queen of the universe. We come and sit down before him in our devotion time and try to make Him the waiter. We begin snapping orders at him and expect Him to run and fill them. Would He not rather say, "Prepare my supper, and get yourself ready and wait on me while I eat and drink; after that you may eat and drink"? Our devotional times should be places where we prepare supper for the Lord. We prepare for the Lord a meal of praise and worship and set it before Him. It should be a place where we come to serenade our King, singing whether He notices or not. We see that His cup is full of the wine of joy and gladness and thanksgiving. Then we step back and watch as our King sups and sips of His cup we have prepared for Him. We glory in the fact that we might give to Him some small service after all He has given us. We have been called to be waiters at the table of the King of kings; to serve Him, to wait upon Him is the highest honor a human can have.

"Would he thank the servant because he did what he was told to do? So you also, when you have done everything you were told to do, should say, "We are unworthy servants; we have only done our duty." We love rewards and trophies in America. We look for rewards in our work and in our sports and in all areas in our lives; unfortunately, many of us do in our Christianity as well. Some preachers hold the rewards of Heaven before their people as motivation to live a better Christian life. "If you don't work hard for God, you won't have any rewards." I believe our expectation of receiving rewards in Heaven is evidence of a self-focused life, not a Christ-focused one. The real reward is being in His presence, and being there we will be changed into His image. Here is the tip the King of kings leaves when we have served him at his table: He transforms us into His likeness.

If you are only devoted to yourself and the doing of your will, your devotions will be a desert place. This is the same thing as seating ourselves at Jesus's table and expecting Him to serve us. We begin to think of answers to prayer as a reward, that Jesus rewards us by answering or giving us what we ask for. Would you exchange every answer to prayer for an opportunity to serve the Lord at the table? Would you give all your desires away to have the one desire of waiting on Him? In our devotional lives we are to see ourselves as unworthy servants who have been called into the very courts of Heaven to serve at the King's table. If we never saw a single answer to our prayers but stood by Jesus's table waiting on Him and for Him, this will be worth more than the whole universe. This service and livery make the pauper a prince and a rebel a son. There is no reward that can best this. The greatest reward of all is to be in the presence of the King of glory. Nothing will match this in status, prestige, or reward. Our eternity will be one where we are paying full attention to the Lord and his needs and desires. Heaven will be running with joy and abandonment to fulfill our Lord's heart's desires and longings. One of the wonders of Heaven will be getting lost in His desire and His will.

Nehemiah was cupbearer to the King Artaxerxes, who was known as the King of Kings, Great King, King of Persia, King of Babylon, Pharaoh of Egypt, and King of Countries. You could say he was a big shot in the ancient world. A cupbearer was an officer of high rank in royal courts, whose duty was to pour and serve the drinks at the royal table. Because of the fear of plots to assassinate the king such as poisoning, the cupbearer was a thoroughly trusted person. He would sometimes be required to swallow some of the drink before serving to demonstrate that it was not poisoned. The cupbearer's relationship with the king often gave him a position of great influence. The position of cupbearer was greatly valued and given only to a select few throughout history. Nehemiah was Artaxerxes's cupbearer. This office would put him in the presence of the king daily.

In Nehemiah 2:1–10 we read, "In the month of Nisan in the twentieth year of King Artaxerxes, when wine was brought for him, I took the wine and gave it to the king. I had not been sad in his presence before, so the king asked me, 'Why does your face look so sad when you are not ill? This can be nothing but sadness of heart.' I was very much afraid, but I said to the king, 'May the king live forever! Why should my face not look sad when the city where my ancestors are buried lies in ruins, and its gates have been destroyed by fire?' The king said to me, 'What is it you want?' Nehemiah was a servant in the king's court and would test and serve the wine to Artaxerxes. One day while serving the king noticed that Nehemiah looked sad, and he had never been sad in the king's presence before. 'Why does your face look so sad when you are not ill?' Nehemiah tells Artaxerxes that the reason he is sad is because his hometown lies in ruin. After hearing this Artaxerxes asks Nehemiah, 'What is it you want?' Nehemiah prays and then answers the king. 'If it pleases the king and if your servant has found favor in his sight, let him send me to the city of Judah where my ancestors are buried so that I can rebuild it'" (Neh. 2:5).

When Artaxerxes asked Nehemiah, "What is it you want?" he not only asked but provided all that Nehemiah would need to rebuild the cities' walls. He also sent a retinue of armed guards with him to protect him on his journey. All that Nehemiah would need was provided and all this because Nehemiah was in the place of waiting on and serving the King. You may think that your times of just waiting on the Lord are unproductive. You may find in your service that one day the King turns to you and asks, "What is it you want?" Is not the King of Glory able to give you exceedingly abundantly more then you ask or think? This not from asking but from serving from waiting before the Lord.

Here we have a situation that is something like ours when we come into the presence of the King of Heaven. Nehemiah has a job to do for the king; he was there to make sure the king had wine and wine that had not been poisoned. Nehemiah was serving in this capacity daily, and the king noticed his countenance was sad and asked, "What do you want?" It was not Nehemiah's primary purpose to go and get something from the king; he was there to serve. While Nehemiah was serving the king, the king saw a need in Nehemiah and asked what he might do. Now the king acts and makes his servant his focus. The service from the king comes while Nehemiah is waiting on the king.

The king then asks Nehemiah, "How long will your journey take, and when will you get back?" What the king desired was his presence and wanted to know when he would be back. Our king is so much greater than any king that has ever lived and can do so much more that any earthly king. Our God wants us to come and serve Him, wait on Him, for he knows that for us to be in His presence is what's best for us. As you serve him, you may find He asks you what He might do for you.

Waiting on Jesus's table and waiting for Jesus to return are I believe the same thing. Setting your heart to wait on Jesus daily may be the same as looking for His second coming. Looking, waiting, or watching for Jesus is being the wise virgin. It is about being prepared and watching for the bridegroom's coming. The way to be prepared is to look a little every day. When we wake in the morning and go and wait on the Bridegroom, we are in the perfect position to see His second coming. We are being wise virgins with lamps in hand and cruse full of oil. The daily watchers (waiters) are the ones who will not be caught unaware and won't miss the Bridegroom.

Waiting on Jesus can be very hard. When Joseph was in prison not knowing if he would ever get out there must have been some hard days. The Israelites waited for over 400 years to see God's promise of deliverance fulfilled. Paul's various imprisonments may have led to doubts and fears and times of wondering if God was ever going to answer his prayers. Our waiting on Jesus is not passive but active with gazing, praise, thanks, adoration, worship, and listening. Our waiting on Jesus is an active service, paying attention to Him by gazing at Him, whether He speaks to us or not, whether He answers our prayers or not. Waiting on God is something we have been commanded to do many times in Scripture but not without promise. "But they that wait upon the Lord shall renew their strength; they shall mount up with wings as eagles; they shall run, and not be weary; they shall walk and not faint" (Isa. 40:31). It is in this waiting, looking at Jesus to serve Jesus, that we are transformed empowered to continue to serve at Jesus's table.

In 2009 Richard Gere and Hollywood made a film called *Hachi: A Dog's Tail*. The movie was based on a true story of Japanese professor Hidesaburo Ueno and his Akita dog named Hachi. Mr. Ueno got Hachiko in 1924. Professor Ueno would take the train every day to the University of Tokyo and then return home by the same. These two developed such a bond that Hachiko would go the station and wait for his master at the end of each day, and they would walk home together. In 1925 Professor Ueno died of a cerebral hemorrhage and never returned to the station. After Professor Ueno's death, Hachi would continue to return to the station and wait for his master every day until Hachi himself died on March 8, 1935. Hachi and his unrewarded loyalty became something of a national phenomenon. While he was still alive, he became a national celebrity, appearing at functions around the city. One day Hachi was discovered dead on the streets of Shibuya. Hachi was honored with a funeral, complete with headstone. The name of the station where he waited was changed and is now called Hachiko Entrance/Exit. A bronze statue was erected at the station as well; this was done while he was still alive, and he attended the ceremony. After he died, he was stuffed and placed in the National Science Museum of Japan. It seems almost tragic for Hachi to wait for his master all those years, and he never showed up.

Hachi's master never did return, and his expectations were unfulfilled. He had faith that his master would return, so he would go to the station every day and wait for him. Many Christians have waited daily for their master to return only to die in their waiting like Hachi. Were they fools? No, their waiting wasn't in vain, for as they waited they filled their vision with their Master watching to see what He might need or want. Remember there is a difference in waiting on something you want from Jesus and waiting on Jesus for Himself. We will discover that waiting on Jesus is also serving Jesus. In our waiting on Jesus, He will shine His glory on us and we will be changed, changed by beholding, changed by serving in his presence, changed by waiting on him.

The silences of God are worth more than all the oration and gifts men of this world can offer. If He is silent, He is still present, He is still God, He is still saving us, He is still preparing a place for us, He is still interceding for us. If He is silent, His glory can still shine on us. If He is silent His love is still being manifest toward us. God's silences are not a manifestation of His inactivity or of inabilities. He is just being silent. In that silence, we have the abundance of His word. Read the love letters he has written to you again and again and revel in his love.

Having built an observatory to gaze on our Lord, like the astronomer, we study the Bright and Morning Star. We watch and wait on him. The great lesson we will learn is that the waiting and gazing and seeing the Lord is the great reward. It is the place of transformation for us.

What do you love apart from God? "The Bride loves naught, rests in naught and finds relief in naught; whence a man will know by this if he have indeed love toward God.... Namely, if he be content with aught that is less than God" (Works of St. John of the Cross). Come then, Bride, worship and serve the Lord with gladness, wait upon His table, and serve Him with all your heart, for He is worthy. In all your waiting and serving you will give constant attention to Him and will gaze at Him and in this waiting, you will be transformed into His image.

Chapter 10

Devotions, Tokens of our Love

Webster's Collegiate Dictionary has these definitions for the word "devotion":

1. Love, loyalty, or enthusiasm for a person, activity, or cause.
2. Religious worship or observance.

Devotion(s) are love from the heart of God, given to us without limit, with which we may love God in return, and love God with a perfect and holy love. The place where we are to meet with God, observe God we call our daily devotions, but for many Christians a daily time with God has little experience of God or His love. We have been taught what we should be doing in our devotions instead of what God will be doing. We are so busy with our devotional techniques, trying to have correct devotions, we become like Martha working so hard that we don't have time to just sit at His feet like Mary and enjoy His presence and what He has to say to us. For many Christians, devotions are devoid of God. Any devotion time spent without God present will be nothing more than time spent alone with yourself, and the fullness of that time can be no greater than what you are and what you bring to it. All true devotion times begin and are sustained by the devotion and love of God. As Christians we have been taught that Christianity is a personal relationship with God, yet for many, God is impersonal and unknown in their devotions. We have talked about beholding Jesus and the transformation that will come as we look at Him. Our personal devotions will be the greatest place of looking at God and enjoying our relationship with Him. Our devotions will be a place of discovering intimacy with God, of knowing His love and then loving Him with the same in return.

Martin Luther's famous treatise *The Babylonian Captivity of the Church* dealt with the seven sacraments of the Church. In the heart of this book Luther describes the Church having turned the Gospel into a work to be done instead of a grace to be received. Luther said that the Church had turned the Gospel into the Mass and made it a work to be done to gain Heaven. The same thing could be said about some of our devotions today. What should be a place to receive the free love, grace, and fellowship of God has become a workhouse for salvation: working through our prayer list, praying for world missions, praying for our ministry, being a prayer warrior, and standing against the powers of darkness where we live, praying for the lost in our Jerusalem, Judea, and uttermost parts of the earth, praying over the sick and needy, praying for revival, praying over the needs and wants in our own lives and the lives of others. Then we take time to read a chapter or section of Scripture and maybe memorize a verse or two.

Do not misunderstand me: I'm not saying that we shouldn't be doing these things I have just listed. The problem is that we find it hard to just focus on our Lord with praise and worship and talk to Him as we would with any other living person. We can think that our devotions are just asking God for stuff. Reciting our endless lists of requests can become impersonal, as we speak without end and don't stop to listen to Christ or wait on His presence with us. By making these prayer targets the focus, we can miss fellowshipping with the risen Christ by the Holy Spirit. We can miss gazing upon the Lord.

The Church in Luther's day had taken the free gift of God's grace and turned it into a work to be done to gain Heaven. Ask yourself if you see your devotion time as a place to receive the free gift of God's grace—the Gospel—on a daily basis. Do you see it as a meeting with someone who loves you and whom you love or as a place of duty and spiritual work? Have we taken what should be a free gift from God, His love and

His company, fellowship and presence, and turned it into a work to be done for Him? Remember when we quoted the pastor who said, "For me doing devotions has kept me from coming to Him only." Are we taking the free gift of God's grace and company and turning it into a work we do alone? Could it be that we suffer devotional fatigue because we find ourselves separated from God in our devotions? For many, devotions are a one-sided conversation where you are the only one talking, instead of trusting God to come and speak and reveal Himself and His love. Do you see devotions as a tool to gain some merit with God or as a place you go to be a better Christian? Or do you see it as place you go to receive the free gift of Christ's devotion, a place to go to receive the Gospel?

If we are changed by beholding, then shouldn't our devotions be primarily beholding Christ and, in that beholding, discover something of the love He has for us. Part of the change or transformation that will happen to you as you behold Christ will be going from thinking you are unloved to knowing you are loved, as you experience something of His presence and company. As we behold Christ, the glory of God shines into our hearts, and part of that glory contains the love of God. We experience that love when we behold Christ fixing our eyes on Him. You not only learn that you are loved and accepted, you also will be changed from an unloving person to one who loves God and others as you behold Him. We call our times with the Lord devotions, but many devotional times have little to do with devotion and love and much to do with routine and self-effort. The devotion that is first in our devotions is the devotion or love of God. When you make these times with the Lord a place of gazing upon Him, what will be revealed is the love God has for you personally. Remaining in the love of God will be transformational for you and your times of devotion. With the love of God revealed, you will see that these times of devotion are more about relationship and fellowship with Him and less about the prayers you pray for others. Devotions for the Christian are first discovering the devotion God has for us.

In Ephesians 3:17, Paul wants the Ephesians to know the love of God and prays this for them. "I kneel before the Father…. I pray that out of His glorious riches He may strengthen you with power through His Spirit… to grasp how wide and long and high and deep is the love of Christ, and to know this love that surpasses knowledge." As H.C.G. Moule says in his Commentary on Ephesians, "Here is an object eternally transcending, while it eternally invites, the effort after a complete cognition. Forever there is more to know." "Surpasses knowledge" means that it is so big that you can never learn all about it. Just when you think you have learned all you can about the love of God, He opens the door of revelation and shows you there is more to learn. The height, width, breadth, and depth of this love is without end. God wants so much for us to know His love, He sends divine help. I pray that He may strengthen you with power through His Spirit in your inner being, so that Christ may dwell in your hearts through faith.

Paul is telling us that God doesn't just give you love and leave you to figure it out. God is granting you the Spirit of wisdom and revelation to understand and know this love. God gives you a person, Christ, who is love, to dwell in your heart expressing that love to you and empowering you to express that same love back to God. The first and greatest command is to love the Lord our God with all our hearts and souls and minds. Before this love comes to dwell in our hearts, we have only the love of man, which is spent primarily on ourselves. Now with the help of the Spirit the love of God is revealed to us, and we are empowered to love God. The love God wants us to know is His love, a love that is so big we can never find the end of it. A love that is filled only with me can only be as big as I am and no more. God takes a tiny human heart and fills it with His fullness by causing His Son to dwell in our hearts by His Spirit. Here the finite and infinite can meet in the heart of a man or woman born again of the Spirit of God. Now that heart can know the love of God and being flooded with it can love Him and others.

When I went to Bible school, I had bought a home that we had to remodel and clean up before we could live in it. This house needed much work. The work we needed to do wasn't finished when school started, so we couldn't move in yet. We were granted permission to live in the dorms on campus until our home we finished. These dorm rooms were one big open room with a bath and walk-in closet that had a door on it. Having my devotions, I would go into the closet and shut the door to be alone with the Lord. One day in that closet the Lord granted me a word about His love that I have never forgotten.

Having played football on all levels—high school, college, and pro—I had learned what it meant to work hard for a goal and then achieve it. I had brought that same thinking to school to work hard for God and then whatever ministry He would call me to. Just as I had worked hard to earn accolades in sports, I thought I would have to do this with God as well. In football the highest award I could earn was to be All-Pro, something I never achieved. If I couldn't be All-Pro in football, maybe I could be All-Pro with God by working hard for Him. That morning God said to me, "David, you are already All-Pro with me; I can't love you any more than I do." God's love is not determined by our actions but by His love alone. When He sets His love on us, it is without hesitation and without limit. God was saying I was trying to earn something that can't be earned but can only be received by faith. So it is with all who come to know the love of God. I'm sure many of you could share a similar experience, a day when God revealed something of His love for you that had a profound effect on your life.

The heart of the Reformation battle for Luther could be summed up in the phrase "justification by faith alone." God's part is to do everything we need for salvation; our part is to believe it, to receive it by faith. Many Christians are still fighting the battle of justification by works in their devotion times. You may have turned your devotions into a work you do to get closer to God, or work you do to gain merit with God so he will answer your prayers. If you turn your devotions into a work to be done for God, they can become exhausting and something that can wear you out until you stop having them. You can see your devotions as a place you go to work for the love of God more than as a place you go to drink of the free love God has for you. We call them devotions because here the love of God is manifest, not because we first loved Him but because He first loved us. We call them devotions because it is first of all God's devotion expressed to us. God expresses His love to us by giving us His Holy Spirit. He pours out His devotion into our hearts by the Holy Spirit and grants us the power we need to love God and others with this *agape* love. The goal of our devotions is to know God and in knowing Him, to know His love. Our devotions should first be about building a relationship with God. By our looking upon Him—worship—He reveals Himself to us and in that revelation reveals His love to us.

John gives a discourse on love in I John 4: "Dear friends, let us love one another, for love comes from God" (I John 4:7). The love of our devotions comes from God and is obtained as we look at Jesus. When we say look at Jesus or looking unto Jesus, this is a synonym for believing or having faith in Jesus. If love comes from God, then we must go to God to receive this love by faith. John is not saying love one another first, and you will have the love that comes from God; he is saying love comes from God and can be mine only by faith, by looking unto Jesus. "We love because He first loved us" (I John 4:9). God is the genesis and first cause of all true love. He is the fountain we must drink from if we are to know love and be able to love Him and then others. We can love properly only when we touch the hem of Christ's garment, and the virtue of His love goes out of Him and into us.

John continues: "Everyone who loves has been born of God and knows God." John is saying that those who love have been born again and know God. The powerful transformation of new birth is required for someone to love God and their neighbor. This salvation comes when we look to Jesus like the serpent lifted up in the wilderness. Part of that salvation is the gift of God's experiential love to us and through us. Having

God pour out His love into hearts can be a very powerful experience, leaving some people wondering what just happened, others in tears. Some believers testify to the fact they knew they were saved because for the first time in their lives they felt loved and wanted to love others. The regeneration of our being—salvation—includes a new heart, a heart that knows the love of God and loves with the same. Just as we were born again by looking unto Jesus, so we continue to look and have faith in Christ, that we may be filled again and again with the love of God. We are filled with the love of God by having God love us.

John continues: "This is how God showed his love among us; He sent his one and only Son into the world that we might live through him" (I John 4:9). Here is the great offering, the great price God paid that we might be saved. We can see the Gospel as something in the past. God loved me at the Cross by giving His Son as a sacrifice for me, so we look back to the past and believe something that happened in history. We believe that God loved us by offering Jesus to die for our sins. We believe that by believing the Gospel we'll be saved. We believe that we were loved by God in this act. I would never want to diminish in any way the unbelievable love of God manifest to us at the Cross. What we don't believe, or have trouble believing, is that the same man who went to the Cross is alive now and wants to be in a loving relationship with us, that this risen Lord can and will express His love to us as a living person. When we touch the Gospel, Jesus, by looking at Jesus we get to know Him, and in knowing Him we get to know His love for us, not just the love He had back then at the Cross but the love He has for us now, one that He is expressing now and that can be known. We will see how great the love of God was in giving us His Son as a sacrifice for our sin, but now we will see that God gives us a living Bridegroom. God demonstrated His love toward us in that while we were yet sinners Christ died for us, and He continues to demonstrate His love by allowing us to be in union with His Son. In the Gospel God demonstrates His love; in looking at and fellowshipping with the living Jesus we appropriate that love and live in a love relationship with Him. In this relationship we can bath in His love daily.

People can think that the circumstances of their lives reflect the love that God has for them. Bad circumstances are interpreted to mean God doesn't love us, while good circumstances mean God loves us, but this is not necessarily true. You could be the richest man in the world and never know love. You could be the poorest man in the world and know love. A life without love is misery to the soul of man. God can manifest His love to us in any circumstance. He can do this in good times or in the worst of times. God's love is beyond circumstances. Knowing God, who is love, growing in a personal relationship with Him, is the door to knowing and experiencing the love of God. If Jesus is alive, we can know Him and can experience the love coming from this living person. Isn't it wonderful to think that no matter my circumstances, good or bad, I can know the love God has for me in midst of them, and I can have fellowship with His living, loving Son?

The love that comes from God it is not some entity separated from God. God gives you His love by giving you Himself. John tells us that when we look at Jesus and are born again, "God lives in us and His love is made complete in us. This is how we know that we live in Him, and he in us: He has given us of His Spirit" (I John 4:13). When we say the Christian life is a personal relationship, it is because the salvation we have comes in a person. God gives you His Son by the Spirit to become a part of you, to live in you, and you to live in Him. This Holy Spirit will bear witness to us of this love by making Himself known to us. There is a living person dwelling in you and with you. You are not far from God, but so close that you are one. Paul says that God shines the light of His glory into your hearts in the face of Christ Jesus (II Cor. 4:6), and the shining of the light of His glory into our hearts is synonymous with giving us His Spirit. You will have a knowledge of the Holy Spirit being in you and with you, for He will convict, lead, guide, counsel, comfort, instruct, teach, and love. Here is the personal relationship, a living person, who is love, given to live in us and commune with us. In this communion we experience the love of God and are empowered to express the same love back to Him.

"And so, we know and rely on the love God has for us" (I John 4:16). Those who have been born again should know and experience the love of God. Is this your experience? If we are honest, we would have to say we are constantly tempted to think that God doesn't love us. When we experience the various struggles and trials this broken world brings us, the devil comes and whispers, "See, your God doesn't love you." The first thing here is to know the love God has for us. This is the personal experience of the love of God. Our observatory is to be a place we go to meet with a living person who is made real to us by the Holy Spirit and then to experience the love of this living person. It is this experience of the love of God that we rely on to build our faith so we will come to Him for more of Himself, more of His love, which is the first great need of our lives. We move from knowing the love of God to relying on this love. First, we rely upon the love of God as manifest in the work of the Cross to pay our debt and forgive our sins, and in this reconcile us with Himself. As Christians, we rely upon the love of God to do the work of justification for us where our sin is dealt with so we can come and fellowship with a holy God. With this work done, we are called into fellowship with the personal God who will satisfy the unfulfilled longings of our hearts with His love, a love He wants us to know. This love is given to us as we look at Christ, as we receive Christ. As human beings we want to know we are loved. When we look to Jesus, He expresses His love to us and slakes the thirst for love we have in our hearts. Once our hearts are satisfied with his love, they are freed from seeking this love in the wrong places, and loving the wrong things. Now we can come and drink freely of His love in ever-greater measure. Now, finding the answer to our hearts' need in His love, we find a satisfaction, a fulfillment that brings rest and peace. After we have known the love of God, we rely on this love-to-love others rightly. I have no true love apart from God, for no good thing dwells in me. Now in relationship with Christ, being loved by Him, I can appropriate His love and with a new heart love Him and others rightly. The Christian relies on the love of God to satisfy his or her need to be loved and then to appropriate this to love God in return.

"God is love. Whoever lives in love lives in God, and God in them" (I John 4:16). God is love; what a definition of God. When you think about God, what do you think He is like? When you think about God, do you think about God being love? As already noted, we struggle with this idea that God is love and loves us because the devil is constantly telling us that He doesn't. John is speaking of a living relationship with God. Whoever lives in love lives in God and God in him. Living in love is synonymous with living in God. This is the supreme love relationship. John is describing the Christian life as living in the love of God, living in love with God, and God and His love living in you. Would you say this is a description of your life? Would you describe your life as living in love, living in the love of God? If someone described your life, would they say you're in love with God? Think about that for minute: God wants you to live in the life-giving shower of His life and love. God wants you to experience his love. God wants to live in you. Who can love like God? Who can thrill the heart of man like God? God designed your heart to find its full joy and satisfaction in His love alone. What is it like to live in this boundless love? This is the highest experience a man or woman can have. This is the greatest adventure of life: to know God and His divine love. This is what we are called to. Do you know the love of God? Why is it that most devotion times have little experience of the love of God? Shouldn't these times be a place of experiencing the love of God? I think John is saying that since God is love, you can't know love or live in love without living in God and God living in you.

When I was in high school, in the late '60s, we had to sign a pledge before we could play on the football team. Written out in the contract were the things we were to abstain from that the coach thought would be a distraction from playing football. One of the items on the list was that we would not date girls during the season. "Moonstruck" is a term used to describe someone who is insane, or loony in general, but it's most often connected with the idea of being lovesick or romantic and irrational. It stems from an ancient belief that the moon could actually cause insanity. The thought behind it was that when someone falls in love, they become so focused and distracted by that love relationship that they act crazy. Many Christians don't know what it means to fall in love with Christ, for they don't live in the love of God. There should be a sense that when the love of God is manifest to us, we become God-struck, and that love changes us forever. When the world sees us in this condition, love-struck with God, people may think we are crazy. Are we falling in love with Christ to the point that our hearts are swept away and no good for anything but Him? It is possible to live in the love of God and find that He is more wonderful and exciting than any person you have ever known or ever set your heart and affections on?

"This is how love is made complete among us.… In this world we are like Jesus" (I John 4:17). Living in the love of God, we must look unto the one he sent as a demonstration of that love, Jesus, His only Son. As we continue to look at Christ with unveiled faces, we remain in the love of God, and we are changed into the image of Christ in ever-increasing measure. In the looking we have both the love of God and His transforming power. This love manifest to us by the Spirit causes us to keep looking at Jesus and to keep loving Him. As we live in this love relationship with Christ, we begin to look like Jesus. The love of God is made complete in us when we are transformed in ever-increasing measure into the image of Christ. In the looking, I am loved by God and can experience His love, and I am granted love, which I then use to love God and others. In the looking, I am changed into Jesus's image. How will you ultimately know that you are being loved by God and are living in that love? In this world we are like Jesus.

All devotion is first devotion from God to us. We are called to remain in this devotion. "Keep yourselves in God's love" (Jude 21). Paul prays that we might know the love of God (Eph. 3:19). Let us remain in God's love by coming to Him daily, bringing the offerings of our devotions to Him by worshipping Him. God then pours out His love into our hearts by the Holy Spirit so we can then love Him with a divine love. Here is the great business, dwelling in the love of God and finding as I do that my heart is changed and I now love God and others. Why don't we run to the secret place to be loved by God? Why don't we live in the love of God? Is it our lack of faith? We should be consumed with the love of God and our relationship with Him in our devotions. Many Christians' times of devotions have nothing to do with love and much to do with labor. Remaining in the love of God and remaining or continuing in your devotions can be one and the same.

We are so self-centered and concerned about what we are doing in our times of devotion, we almost never ask what God is doing. One of the hurdles we have to overcome is thinking that somehow in devotions we can earn some merit whereby we turn God's attention to us. This puts the focus on what I'm doing instead of what God is doing. You should never have devotions without thinking about and praising God for what

He has done, is doing, and will do in the future for you. There are many who are having what I would call Godless devotions. This self-orientation causes many to forget God, who should be the focus and purpose of our devotions. Knowing God, knowing His love and living in that love, is to be our goal. We can ask for many things and never ask for God Himself. Have you ever been disappointed because you asked God for something and didn't get it? Were you asking for God, were you asking for a greater revelation of Himself, were you asking to see His glory? If you have had the revelation of God, was it a disappointment? How is it that we have so quickly exchanged the glory of God for created things? Let's think first about what God is doing during our devotions instead of what we will be doing.

Before we ever existed, before the world ever existed, God was making decisions about us and what would become our times of devotion. "For he chose us in him before the creation of the world to be holy and blameless in his sight. In love he predestined us for adoption to sonship through Jesus Christ, in accordance with his pleasure and will" (Eph. 1:4–5). Before there was a world, before you existed, God chose you to be holy and blameless in His sight. He chose you to be with Him. When we have devotions, we tend to see it as us coming to be with God. We see ourselves as searchers who have traveled a great distance to find a hidden treasure. There are those elements and pictures in Scripture that clearly point to the fact that we do seek after God—asking, knocking, and finding. But before we existed, before we ever sought after God, He was choosing us and then came to seek and to save us.

Our self-centered perspective can't see any farther back than our own beginning, and we really can't see back that far. Our earliest memories begin when we are two or three years old. God has been thinking about you before there was a world for you to live in. He chose you to be a His possession, to be adopted as His child, to be with Him. He chose you to be one with Him through Jesus. He chose to pour out His love on you and into your heart. He chose you to be in relationship with Him, to know Him and His love. Way before we existed, God was making decisions that would affect the place we call devotions. Your heritage begins with the choice of God, with Him deciding something about you before there was a world. How significant is God's decision about you if it predates the world? There is a sense that God has been waiting for eons for you to show up and spend time with Him, for you to be to the praise of His glory. The genesis of your devotions predates the book of Genesis.

"Then God said, 'Let us make mankind in our image, in our likeness'" (Gen. 1:26). Here we have the picture of God having a conversation with Himself. The three persons of the Trinity in conversation decided to make man in their image and likeness. Thinking about this conversation to make Adam makes me wonder, Did God have a conversation about you or me when He chose us before He created the world? Could it be that our names were spoken between the persons of Godhead before there was a world? In the courts and councils of God, your name was spoken in the choice He made for you to come to be with Him. The love of God for you and toward you began in a place and time we cannot find with our minds, and it may have had no beginning, for He has no beginning and His thoughts about you may have been from eternity past.

God didn't just choose us all those eons ago; he knew there would be a Fall and the repercussions of that Fall and that it would be an obstacle to your devotions, and what would be needed to overcome that obstacle, that sin. The way of rescuing you was worked out before it was needed, worked out before you existed. Revelation 13:8 says, "And all that dwell upon the earth shall worship him, whose names are not written in the book of life of the Lamb slain from the foundation of the world." The salvation, the redemption, needed and provided by the Lamb of God, was worked out and provided for you from the foundation of the world. This salvation, this road to God, was paved before it was ever needed. This is what God was doing before there was a world, before you ever existed. The author of salvation had written the book long before it was needed. God was actively working to get you to Himself before the world existed.

This God who loves you more than you can understand does not rest with choosing you. Jesus taught us that "[n]o one can come to me unless the Father who sent me draws him" (John 6:44). God the Father enables us, or draws us to Himself, taking no chance that you might remain lost, taking no chance that you would miss being with Him. We know that He uses the Word of God activated by the Spirit of God to reveal the Son of God. He speaks and calls our name, He shines the light of His glory into our hearts, and He pours out His love into our hearts by the Holy Spirit. He has set men in our path to speak the Gospel to us so we might hear the Gospel, believe it, and be saved. We will know the fullness of His enabling power someday, but much of it will remain a mystery until we are home in Heaven. He performs the miracle of opening our blind eyes that we might see that which is invisible to others. He not only opens our eyes to see, He opens our ears that we may hear His sweet voice and His calling for us to come unto Him. We feel the mysterious gravity of His love and enabling power to pull us out of orbit around those planets of death and bring us into orbit around the Son of life.

It would be impossible for us to know fully what God has done in enabling us or drawing us to come to Him. It is good to go back and remember where you were when the Gospel found you. Remember how it came to you. Remember when you first heard and how your heart was drawn out to Christ. Remember the message that was preached and the voice of Jesus coming through the preacher as he was pleading for you to come to Christ. Perhaps you were alone, sitting in the darkness, when you heard the voice of God in that still small way saying, "This is the way, walk ye in it." Maybe you experienced the love of Jesus flowing from His heart to yours, and you had never known this kind of love before. When His love fell upon you, there was a love in your heart for Christ you had never known, and you wanted to know Him and love Him more. God's enabling caused you to fall in love with Jesus, and this love changed the course and path of your life. You knew one thing: You loved Jesus for the first time with all your heart. The fire of that love hasn't gone out, for many waters can't extinguish love and many rivers can't wash it away. The testimony of every Christian is a testimony to the enabling power and love of God to draw men and women to Jesus. The Scripture says that they overcame the devil by the power of their testimonies and the blood of the Lamb. Our testimonies will reveal the ways God enabled His children to come to His Son.

We, like the children of Israel, are pilgrims, strangers in a strange land. Just as the children of Israel wondered in the wilderness, we too will wonder in our temporary wilderness until God calls us home to Himself. Israel had a guidance system while they wondered in the wilderness. The Tabernacle contained the throne of God (the Ark of the Covenant) and over that Tabernacle was the presence of God manifest in the pillar of cloud by day and the pillar of fire by night. God was in their midst; God was Emmanuel to them. All Israel had to do was look out of their tents at the pillar of cloud or fire to see whether it was moving, and when it began to move, they packed up and moved with it. When the pillar stopped, they stopped, and if the pillar remained for a month or more, they remained and did not move until God did. Guidance was made easy for Israel: They had only to look at God. There is a sense that we get our guidance the same way, by looking to God every day to see if He is moving or staying put. Your calling in life will never be anything more than following God and moving when He begins to move and stopping where He stops. Whatever that might be, you will never go alone, but always following Him to where He is going and joining Him in what He is doing. In our devotions God will manifest Himself to us as a living person we can trust and follow. "For those who are led by the Spirit of God are the children of God" (Rom. 8:14).

We don't have to wait to die to see Jesus. His name is Emmanuel, God with us. This God is with us today. You can be with Him today. You can enjoy Him today. As the title of one of Francis Schaffer's books says, "He is there and He is not silent." Come and enjoy the speaking God and fellowship with Him. Let nothing deter you from entering into the promised land of fellowship with God. Let nothing deter you from coming into His presence and touching the face of God. Don't stop seeking, don't stop pressing into God until the reality of His presence is yours.

In Zephaniah 3:14–17 the prophet tells us what else God is doing during these times of devotion. "Sing, O Daughter of Zion; shout aloud, O Israel!… He has taken away your punishment" (Zeph. 3:14–15). The news is so good, and this God is so good, our response is to sing and shout and rejoice with all our hearts at what He has done. "The Lord has taken away your punishment, he has turned back your enemy" (Zeph. 3:15). It is a wonderful thing to meditate on the love of God in the taking away our punishment through the gift of His Son. In taking away our punishment God performs perhaps His greatest miracle. To take away our punishment, God can't just say that we do not deserve punishment, for He is just, and the punishment, once ordered, must be carried out. He looked for a scapegoat to bear the punishment and asked His son if He would be this scapegoat. Jesus says, "Not my will but thine be done" (Luke 22:42). "But he was pierced for our transgressions, he was crushed for our iniquities; the punishment that brought us peace was on him, and by his wounds we are healed" (Isa. 53:5). God propitiates His own wrath by pouring it out on His Son, His lamb. He takes away our punishment by punishing another. Jesus took our punishment, and now we can come to Him debt-free, for our punishment has been paid, poured out on another, and has satisfied the wrath of God. Now I can come without condemnation, for my punishment and sentence have been served by another. All glory to the Lamb who has borne our punishment and given to us the ability to come to God and receive what we don't deserve. This He did so you could come and fellowship with Him. Won't you come?

When we are saved, we find we still sin. Because we are still sinners, because we still fail at times, we can have a natural dread of God. We have the dread of a child who must stand before his father, caught in the act of doing wrong. There are times when we don't want to come to God, for we dread that He might punish us. We can see the bad circumstances of our lives as God punishing us for the wrongs we have done. When we come into His presence knowing who and what we are—sinners—there is this dread or hesitance because of the fear of the judgment and justice of God that we deserve. We instinctively know we deserve to be punished for the wrong we have done. I think this knowledge of being sinners can hinder some from coming to God, for fear of His retribution. We are afraid we will get what we deserve instead of the grace we don't. We think we don't deserve His love and mercy but deserve His wrath and anger, which is true. That punishment that we all dread has been taken away; that punishment that was rightly meant for us has been taken by another: Jesus, our Savior. "Then I saw a Lamb, looking as if it had been slain, standing at the center of the throne" (Rev. 5:6). John saw the lamb that was punished so our punishment could be removed. In looking at Jesus, we will see the lamb who was slain to remove our punishment. Look on Him and see where your punishment has been carried out, a punishment and can't be required anymore. See that your sin has been covered by the blood of the lamb, and God says that your sentence has been carried out in full. Now I am set free from the fear of getting the punishment I deserve. Now I can come and get what I don't deserve, His unmerited favor, His overwhelming love. There need be no fear or dread or hesitance in our coming to Him. God tells us, "All this I have done for you in my Son. Won't you believe it and come unto Me?" This is what God has done and is doing in our devotions that we might come to be loved by Him.

As a child, I was fascinated by fire and loved to play with matches. We lived in a neighborhood where all the houses were exactly alike. It was a post–World War II subdivision that was built in a hurry to meet the housing demand of all those soldiers who returned home to begin their lives and families. These were small Cape Cod one-story, two-bedroom homes. On the back of each home was a small tool shed for storage. One of the houses near us was abandoned, so I went into the tool shed and was playing with matches and started a fire. I was caught by some of the neighborhood kids, who put the fire out and literally dragged me home. When they turned me loose, I ran into our house and found I was all alone, so I locked the doors, hoping to keep out the punishment that was surely to come. Eventually I unlocked the door and faced my mother, who said, "Wait until your father gets home." I didn't want to see my father, for I knew the punishment would be bad. Hiding in my room I heard my father enter the house and then he called me out to speak with him. I remember walking slowly to him, as one might walk to the gallows. I stood before him and waited to hear my sentence and receive my punishment. To my surprise, he didn't say anything about the fire, and then what he said shocked me. Bouncing a new beach ball, he said, "Hey, would you like to go to the beach tomorrow?" My dread turned to joy and wonder at how my evil could be forgotten and I would be rewarded with a great day at the beach. There was no dread or separation from my father any longer. Without knowing it, my earthly father had taught me one of greatest lessons about my Heavenly Father: that He can forget and forgive my sin because of what Jesus has done for me. Because of Jesus's work, we can go and enjoy a day at the beach with our Heavenly Father. "In His love he will no longer rebuke you" (Zeph. 3:17).

After the prophet tells us our punishment has been taken away, he tells us, "The Lord is with you" (Zeph. 3:15). Because He is with you, there is no fear of harm, because He is with you, He becomes your protector, and He will be mighty to save. In this short passage he says this twice: "The Lord is with you." He wants them to understand this and believe it and live as if it were so. Think about your times with the Lord, your times of devotions: Do you believe the Lord is with you? Do you believe He will come and be with you in these times we call devotions? If someone saw you having devotions, would they see someone who acting as if God was there with them? Would your actions convince them that you believe He is present with you? Christian, the Lord, the King of Heaven, is with you. Did you hear what the prophet said, "He is with you"? This is the hardest thing for us to get through our heads, and this is something the devil fights against, for if the Church really believed God is with us and can be seen, the impact on it and then the world would be dramatic. Meditate on that fact over and over again as you come to God in your times of devotions: God is with me!

The prophet now gives us even more of what God is doing during these times of devotion. "He will take great delight in you" (Zeph. 3:17). As Christians, we don't expect God to be good; we don't expect Him to come and be with us, even though He tells us repeatedly that He will. We doubt these things, and if Jesus were walking on Earth today, we would probably hear Him say, "O ye of little faith." One of the hardest things for us to believe is how good our God is. When God should be angry with us and punish us with eternal fire and separation from Him, He takes delight in us. Have you ever watched a grandparent get out pictures of a grandchild out and begin to pass them around? This is a person delighting in someone. Watch grandparents' faces as they talk you through such pictures; that look is the look of delight. Listen to them as they describe what a child is doing and how well; this is delight. Listen as the bragging almost puts you off, almost makes you wish you hadn't asked about the grandchildren. Can you even imagine what it is like to have God delighting in you? Will He not delight in your coming to Him? Will He not delight in having a relationship with you? Believe this and enter into the delight of God by coming and fellowshipping with Him.

God is so delighted in us, he wants to show us off to the worlds, both seen and unseen. "Have you seen what my son or daughter is doing?" We see something of God's delight in a person in the story of Job. "Then the Lord said to Satan, 'Have you considered my servant Job? There is no one on earth like him: he is blameless and upright, a man who fears God and shuns evil'" (Job 1:8). Here is the proud father showing off His son. After the baptism of Jesus, "A voice from heaven said, 'This is my Son, whom I love; with him I am well pleased'" (Matt. 3:17). God broke through and spoke to the earth about His son, one in whom he was delighted, one with whom He was well pleased. It is difficult for us to believe that God is just as delighted in us as He is with His Son. God places us in His Son so when He sees us, He sees the completed work of Jesus and delights in us. Because of the great work of Christ on our behalf, it is true. Meditate on this fact, believe it, and enter into the fullness of this reality. Come and walk in, live in, the reality of God's delight for you. Can you imagine God delighting in you in this way? We know how often we fall short and think that

God will be ashamed of us. The wonder of the work of Christ on the Cross for us is that it turns the wrath of God into delight for His children. Come unto Him and enter into His delight through the work of Christ on your behalf. During your devotions, God will come there to delight in you.

"He will quiet you with His love" (Zeph. 3:17, KJV). When our children were little, they would often get restless and fuss. You would check the particulars: Dry, fed? If these were covered, then we used the last resort, which was to quiet them with our love. We would pick them up and rock them and talk to them, trying to soothe whatever might be bothering them. Would you come and let God take you in His arms and rock you until you're quiet? Do you believe He can do such? Come unto me, and I will give you rest, He says. I can tell you that I have been held by God during some of those dark stormy nights. I have felt His loving arms around me and moved to His rocking motion until my heart was quieted and my fear was gone. If you come to Him in devotions, you will know the quieting love of God. Let not your heart be troubled.

The prophet tells us that God now does something more: "In his love he will no longer rebuke you but will rejoice over you with singing" (Zeph. 3:17). God is so delighted in us and so rejoicing or glad to be with us that He sings over us. When I first read this, I was sitting in my back yard by a mesquite tree we have. In the top of the tree was a cardinal, and he began to sing with all his heart. I love the cardinal's song. Just then it hit me: This is what the Lord does over me. He is so glad to be with us, He loves us so much, He breaks into song, a song of rejoicing. When God comes to our times of devotion, he comes singing as well. We are so busy trying to be something to God, thinking about ourselves in our devotions, that we have missed the glorious song of God being sung over the child He loves with all His heart. us: "This is my beloved son in whom I am well pleased" (Matt. 3:17). He glories in His work on our behalf and rejoices over what He has accomplished in us. The next time you come to be with your God, think about Him holding you like a mother holds her child, and the great God singing a lullaby to you. The songs He sings will melt your heart as nothing else can. We are so busy trying to be something and do something for God in our devotions, we never stop to listen to our God as He sings the song of gladness over us. "Arise, come, my darling; my beautiful one come with me" (Song 2:10). God sings over us. Think about a time and place where you were so happy in fellowship that you sang together. God comes and sings to us, sings and rejoices over us; let us join His song and sing along with Him.

There is something else God does during our devotions: He gathers the fruit of His garden. He gathers the fruit of love, joy, and praise. "I have gathered my myrrh with my spice. I have eaten my honeycomb and my honey. I have drunk my wine and my milk" (Song 5:1). He hovers over us and gathers the praise of His loves, His saints. Like a farmer gathers his apples, grapes, or other fruit, so Christ comes and gathers the fruits of His secret gardens he has planted. He then glories over His harvest like a farmer with wagons filled to the full with the harvest. He takes what he has gathered and consumes it. In this way God dines on, consumes, the love of His people, their fellowship and praise. It is in this way we can be a pleasure to Him. When we think of how often we are hurtful to Him, what a joy to find a place where we can bring Him pleasure and joy. If God has done all this and is doing this even now, why would we avoid being with Him and hearing Him sing a song over us?

God plants us in His garden and causes us to grow into a new creation, one watered with His love and care. He grafts us into the vine of His Son, and we begin to produce the fruit of that love and care. He then comes to His garden and dines on the fruit being produced there. God is the husbandman who prunes the vines who tends them so they might produce the best fruit, and fruit abundant. He loves His garden and enjoys its produce. From this garden of love comes the flowers that when pressed become the perfume that we pour out upon Him to sweeten our union with its fragrance, the fragrance of love.

The whole course of the Christian life is started and maintained by an attitude of repentance and faith. Turning from looking at ourselves to looking at the Lord is repentance. Filling our vision with God instead of self and its wants and needs is the beginning of repentance. As we turn to the Lord we will know and experience the love of God. This is the high point of this earthly life and should be a place where we live, not just visit occasionally. Your devotions should be a place where you experience the devotion of God, a place where He will come and wash you with His love as the bride in Ephesians 5, where he will teach you how to love by loving you. Your devotions should be a place where God reveals who He is and what He is like as he did for John, showing him that God is love. The first reason for beholding Christ is to know Him and grow in the grace and knowledge of our relationship with Him. Growth in this relationship will be a growth in the knowledge of the love of God.

Your devotions can be a banquet hall for the love of God. "He has taken me to the banquet hall, and His banner over me is love" (Song 2:4). It is a place He has prepared for you even before the foundation of the world. It is a place of rest, not of labor; a place of faith, not of works, lest any man should boast. It is a place to dine with the King and enjoy His fellowship, to sup with Him and He with you. God desires we live in His love, dwell in His courts, gaze on His beauty and dine fellowship with Him. Remember, gazing on this beauty is transformational. Could it be that your devotion times are dead because you don't believe that God will reveal Himself to you, or that He rewards those who diligently seek Him? Is it hard for you to believe that the God of the universe wants to fellowship with you and love you today? Remember, if I am saved by faith, then how am I sanctified? I am sanctified by the same faith. Believe and be sanctified, believe and dwell in the presence of God, believe and find the love of God poured out on you, believe and have faith that God can and will manifest His love to your heart today, He will come and manifest His presence to you, He will inhabit your praise. He will comfort you with His words, "I am with you, I will never leave you nor forsake you" (Heb. 13:5). He will come and pour out His love into your heart by the Holy Spirit.

When faith grows cold and love dies, the enemy of works often moves in to take the heart captive, leading her away to Babylon. Works and the traditions of works can replace faith and love in our religious life. Have we made our devotions a work, a routine by which we despoil our most precious possession? What is that most precious possession? The manifest presence and love of God and the free invitation to come to God to be loved by Him most deeply. "My lover is mine and I am His" (Song 2:16). Do you believe there is a holy place, secret place, where God will meet with you, talk with you, love you, and lead you by His Spirit? Do you believe that you have a divine appointment with God your Father, who waits for you to come? Do you believe that all the earning of right and merit has been done by another? Then set aside a sacred place and time to meet with the Lord, a time to look at Him and trust Him to come and be with you and to express His love to you and in so doing change you into His image.

Have the love and presence of God been a mystery to you? Do you feel you are in the dark when it comes to the love of God? Are you busy trying to work your way to God? Have you filled your life with ministry, church, and other good things to earn a place at the right hand of God? Do you feel like you're screaming at God trying to get His attention, but He doesn't look at you? In the story of the Prodigal Son, you have the picture of the father looking for the son and seeing him while he was yet a long way off. The father then runs to the son in Jesus's story. Don't you think God will do the same thing for you today? God your Father was looking for you before you ever thought about looking for Him. He saw you a long way off, before the world began, and ran to you and kissed you. He put a robe on you, a ring on your hand, and sandals on your feet. He called out to the servants, "Kill the fatted calf that we may be merry, for my son was lost and now is found." This God is the same yesterday, today, and forever. He still comes and wants to celebrate with all His children who come home from their rebellions. Our Father wants to feast with those who return home to Him. He wants to manifest His love to us and make His presence known. What God has for us can't be measured: "That Christ may dwell in your hearts through faith… that you may be able to comprehend… the width and length and depth and height, to know the love of Christ which passes knowledge" (Eph. 3:18–19). This is not something we have to wait for and die to attain; this is ours now by the Spirit of God. To be filled to the measure with all the fullness of God can be ours today, if we will just believe, if we will just behold Christ. Devotions are the place to begin the process of experiencing being loved by God. Believe God for the manifestation of His love to you today, and when it is manifest, you will be freed to love Him in return.

Too many Christians think of their devotions as a grocery store where we bring our shopping lists to find and buy what we need from God's store. We think of our prayers as the currency of exchange in God's store: If I don't have what I'm asking for, I bring more currency, more prayer, and surely, I will have it. But all the money in the world can't buy what God gives away free. We must learn that everything that comes to us from God can never be bought, can never be earned, can only be received freely. We think if we cry out all day and night, and even fast, we will be heard for our great effort. Devotions for many have become shopping trips to God's store to get things we need or want. Like the Children of Israel, we are not satisfied with the bread of heaven and cry out for something else, for something more. Instead of dining on the bread of heaven we are "lusting exceedingly in the wilderness" (Ps. 106:14, KJV) for something that isn't the bread of heaven. God often brings what we cry for and then brings leanness to our souls. Be careful what you ask for if it isn't God.

So many Christians start devotions that fail. I believe one of the reasons so many fail in their devotions is they are all alone in them. There is no experience of God, no knowledge of His presence or of the ministry of His Spirit. There is little or no communion, communication, or fellowship with the living God. We come and offer our requests like a Buddhist spinning a prayer wheel; there is nothing personal about it. We find ourselves alone, and the only voice we hear is the echo of our own. Finding ourselves alone, we find our minds and hearts set on "What shall we eat, or what shall we drink, or what shall we wear?" (Matt. 6:31). Finding ourselves alone in our devotions can be evidence that we are not seeking God and that we are still focused on ourselves and have not repented to look at and have faith in God. Think about your devotions. What is the focus? Is it God, or is it just you?

In Romans 8:35, Paul asks the question, "Who shall separate us from the love of God? Shall trouble or hardship or persecution or famine or nakedness or danger or sword?… For I am convinced that neither death nor life, neither angels nor demons, neither the present nor the future, nor any powers, neither height nor depth, nor anything else in all creation, will be able to separate us from the love of God that is in Christ Jesus our Lord" (Rom. 8:35, 38–39). If nothing can separate us from the love of God, then why do so many of us feel separated from the love of God? Why don't we experience the love of God more? If nothing in this fallen earth or in this dispensation of time can separate you from the love of God, come to Him and let it fall on you. There is unmeasurable love for you now, here, in the sanctuary of your love, the secret place of your love. If God's love is not yours, is it because you are still lost in your sin? Is it because of your lack of faith? Is it because of your unbelief? If God says nothing can separate us from His love, then what is keeping us from the love of God? Are my self-righteous works keeping me from the grace and love of God? If I don't have the love of God, is it because I'm looking for something else? Could it be you are worshipping at the shrine of some lesser god, where you have set up an idol and have not repented of such? Do we think that those who have the love of God have earned it or deserve it? Can I do something to earn the love of God? Are you too busy doing something for God, trying to earn a love that is given away for free? If you can't earn the love of God and He gives it for free, why not come to Him by faith look unto Jesus and receive as much of it as you can? If this love is priceless, can't be bought, and nothing can separate us from it, then it should be yours.

Luther said in *The Babylonian Captivity of the Church*, "For no one would dare to make the mad assertion that a ragged beggar does a good work when he comes to receive a gift from a rich man." In our devotions we should be like a beggar coming to God's house and begging for food that we might live. The beggar has no rights, he has no merit, and has earned nothing. The beggar has nothing he can exchange for what he asks; he can only live on the grace and mercy of the one he asks for help. If we don't come and beg, we won't eat, and we'll die. The Christian life is one of constant begging (believing) for food (love) from God. This begging is the place of faith. It is looking unto Jesus and in looking receiving the life-giving free gift of His love. Our work is to receive the love of God; all you have to do is receive it by faith. Here we dine on the daily manna, the bread of heaven, Jesus Himself. If we could see our devotions more as a soup kitchen, where we dine as beggars on the love of God, I believe it would turn our devotional lives around. The Church needs to eat in God's soup kitchen daily, we need to partake of Him daily. We will never be anything more than a crippled Mephibosheth invited to eat daily at the King's table. When will we stop trying to pay for a meal that is priceless and simply enjoy the rich fare of God's table? Oh fool, just accept the invitation of God and enjoy dining, feasting, celebrating, and making merry with Him. This is what awaits us in our devotions: more of God's grace, more of God's mercy, and more of God's love—more of God. When will we learn to enjoy being with God?

Massimo Buttura is one of the world's top chefs. His Osteria Francescana, a three-Michelin-star restaurant in Modena, Italy, has been listed in the top five of the world's top fifty restaurants and has been named best restaurant in the world. People get reservations for his restaurant months in advance, traveling to Europe and making Massimo's Osteria a part of their trip. Massimo started a charity called Food for Soul. You might say it was a soup kitchen, but it looks nothing like any soup kitchen you have ever seen. Massimo called on architects, artists, and interior designers to create a beautiful space within which homeless and needy people would eat. He didn't just want to put some food on a plate and shove it in front of someone. Massimo wanted to surround them with beauty and art to affect their souls as well as their stomachs. At one of his "soup kitchens," a replica of the Last Supper has been painted on the wall. He called on some of the best chefs in the world to give their time to prepare new and creative meals for people who couldn't pay. Those who come to this soup kitchen don't go through a line with a tray collecting food as they walk through. At Food for the Soul, needy souls are seated at a table set with linen, china, glassware, and silverware and are served their meal by waiters. Paupers are treated like kings. The establishment feeds the needy but does it with gourmet meals. The food they serve in this soup kitchen people would pay hundreds of dollars to eat. Massimo says, "Good food and art shouldn't be for the wealthy alone. These things need to be for every man but seldom are." Giving needy, undeserving people the best of food, a beautiful place to eat, and walls covered with beautiful art builds dignity in them and gives them a sense of worth. Massimo says he has found that treating people with this kindness has a positive effect for change in their lives. It is a way for Massimo and his friends to show the poor and needy that they have a place at the table of this community.

When I heard about Massimo's Food for Soul, where people come to eat a meal they could never afford, I thought, "Isn't this what God has done for us?" God has opened His soup kitchen of grace where we the starving and destitute of the world can come and eat for free. He has prepared a table for us in His presence. We come to God and partake of a meal we could never pay for consisting of the bread of heaven. As sinners we are destitute; we have nothing with which to buy bread or earn a seat at His table. We are starving for what we need most and can't find on our own. We see a sign that says food for the soul, we walk in, and find God has prepared a table for us full of food, the richest fare, fit for a king. This place of His grace is decorated with the beauty of the Lord, with the glory of the Lord. We sit at His table and wonder at this king and His goodness to share his banquet, to share His company with us. We begin to be merry together. God shares with us His presence and His love, and the greatest gift of all, His Son, who is the Passover Lamb, the bread of heaven. "Take and eat, this is my body." We become consumers of this God and of His love. Our devotions should be a place of feasting with God, of feasting upon God and becoming "partakers of the divine nature" (II Peter 1:4). Remember what Massimo said: "Giving needy, undeserving people the best of food, a beautiful place to eat, and walls covered with beautiful art builds dignity in them and gives them a sense of worth." Sitting with God in His banquet hall will produce change in us through our simply looking upon and dinning with the Lord. By faith we partake of God, of His divine nature, of His love. My beloved is mine, and I am His. We used to hear, "You are what you eat." That old adage speaks of our body becoming what we eat. What do we become if we partake of the divine vision, the divine nature? We become more like our God.

In Christianity we never graduate from God's soup kitchen. We will never be at a place where we don't need to come to God and eat and drink for free. "Ho, everyone who thirsts, come to the waters; and you who have no money, come buy and eat. Yes, come buy wine and milk without money and without price. Why do you spend money for what is not bread, and your wages for what does not satisfy? Listen carefully to me, and eat what is good, and let your soul delight itself in abundance" (Isa. 55:1–2). Here is bread that satisfies, abundance we can have without money, without price; here is where we become consumers of God, consumers of the bread of heaven. "Now Eat your bread with gladness and drink your wine with a joyful heart, for it is now that God favors what you do" (Eccles. 9:7). We will never graduate from God's soup kitchen and get to the place where we feed ourselves. What we need can only be freely given to us, never earned. We'll be dependent on God forever. Devotions should always be a place where we come again and again to partake of the free gift of God by faith. The kitchen is open; come and drink and eat without price. Come and eat in the soup kitchen of God's grace, mercy and love. His kitchen is for the undeserving, the poor, the lame, the weak and broken of this earth. Only the proud can't eat here, for they want to work or pay for what they get. Here is a mystery: You can't pay for what God has for you. You can only come and open your mouth and eat and drink of Him freely and without price. This speaks of relationship, of participation in and partaking of another, a living relationship based upon knowing each other and becoming one.

As we have said, for many Christians, God's place in our devotions is doing what we want. We have made the God of glory a genie, and by rubbing the lamp of our devotions we hope to get three wishes. When you make your life the focus of your devotions, a darkness will begin to fall over them. The reason for this is that God, who is light, is not the focus, the thing desired. "For Thou wilt light my candle: the Lord my God will enlighten my darkness" (Ps. 18:28). Jesus said, "I am the light of the world." When we seek God alone and bathe in the light of His glory, our devotions will have an illumination that will cause us to shine like Moses coming down for the mountain. The light of His glory will fall on the scriptures, and we will see Jesus in them as never before. We will have new and deeper revelations of our God and Jesus Christ, His only Son. We will have the glory of God shone into our hearts in the face of Christ Jesus. Devotions will be about getting more of God instead of checking off our prayer requests, about spending time alone with God. God first gives you Himself. "And this is eternal life, that they may know You, the only true God, and Jesus Christ whom You have sent" (John 17:3). Our devotions should be like standing in the shower of God's love. Our devotions start and end with the revelation of God and His love for us. It is this love, this devotion, that God reveals to us again and again in our devotions. What would it be like to be loved by God every day, to come into His presence and enjoy His company?

What are devotions for most of us? For most Christians devotions are the routine of spending some time each day reading God's Word and saying a kind of rosary of prayer. In some of these devotions God is not even a thought on our minds. Some of these devotions are an empty routine filled with our idle chattering. There is no conversation with a living and loving person, no awe of the living God, who is willing to come and be with us. What should devotions be? A place where the glory of God is shined into our hearts, and seeing this glorious God we fall and worship Him for humbling Himself to come and be with us. We worship Him for His devotion to choose us before the world was made, His devotion to write the salvation we would need to get back to Him, His devotion to call you to Himself and reveal Himself to you, to give you His one and only Son on the cross, to give you His Spirit to comfort and counsel you, to live in you. Our devotions are us looking at Jesus, and in our looking, His devotion becomes ours. We will know this love by meditating on, worshipping, and beholding Jesus.

Why are devotions for the Christian one of the great battles in the Christian life? Why do we struggle here to maintain a consistent time with God? If someone is having devotions, there is the possibility that God will reveal something of Himself and change that person's life.

"For our struggle is not against flesh and blood, but against the rulers, against the authorities, against the powers of this dark world and against the spiritual forces of evil in the heavenly realms" (Eph. 6:12). We need to understand that there are real spiritual entities that come against us in a war of attrition to kill this contact with God. If you are having devotions, don't stop, continue, but put your focus on Jesus and keep it there until you are changed by looking at Him. If you are not having them, then begin, and by so doing, begin to war against these spiritual forces coming against you.

Devotions are the miracle by which God pours out His love into a human soul and then allows that soul to love Him with a perfect love. God breaks the grip of the individual's self-centered love and replaces it with the divine, supernatural, holy, pure love of God—a new heart. Now, with this perfect love, that soul is drawn into union with the living God, drawn into the very love circle of the Trinity. This is the highest experience that a human being can have, yet the devil has covered it with a veil so devotions have become a boring laborious duty to be done, gotten out the way, so you can get on with your day. You don't bring your love to God, for that would never be acceptable; human love is not required or desired in the courts of Heaven. God has to do a new thing, must give a new birth, a new heart, and regenerate us to bring us to the place where we might bring acceptable love into His courts and lay the gift of that sacrifice on the altar of His praise. This is just what He does in salvation. The presence and work of the Holy Spirit is to break us of our self-centered worship and allow us to look at and worship Jesus and be changed by our beholding.

We have many devotional books and daily guides, but few are devoted solely to gazing on the Lord Jesus Christ. Many of our devotionals today are focused on how we should live the Christian life and therefore are filled with commands to righteousness. That is not to say that all these devotional materials are wrong or worthless; they are not. The problem is that if you have a commandment-oriented devotional, it ultimately ends with you. Am I keeping this law, am I doing this or that, or am I failing in my Christian life? The focus becomes me, not Christ. Here is the problem: If I focus on what I am or am not, it won't help me to change. If I focus on Christ, who is my righteousness, I will be granted the power to change. It sounds too easy. You mean I don't have to try to struggle and wrestle like Jacob with God? I think the real wrestling is with the idea that all I have to do is walk into God's soup kitchen and dine on the free fare of God's table. Power in my devotional life to change doesn't come in seeing what I am; it comes in seeing who He is for me. We are changed by beholding. Therefore, it is critical to make Christ the focus of our devotions and keep Him such. This is why the worship of Jesus should be the center of our devotions, for worship is a form of beholding Jesus. The desired end of devotions is not having God review my shopping list and filling it. The desired end is an encounter with the living God.

Once we enter the love of God, seeing what He has done to bring us to this place of love and worship, we will see transformation in our lives. Once we have been born again, loved by God, and learn to live in that love and rely on that love, we can bring that new and right love to God. Now our devotions are not just God loving us, but we turn our new hearts upon God and actively love Him in return. Our devotions become the place to meet with our true love; each of us brings the gift of our love for the other. Now that we have the love of God and see that we don't have to earn it and that it will never run out, we are free to love God. Now I can come and place the tokens of my love at the feet of Christ, who loved me unto death. Now it not just what I get out of my devotions but what Jesus gets out of our devotions as well. Now we bring to Him the devotions of thanks or praise and worship. We bring to Him the sacrifice of a broken heart. "For the sacrifice that is pleasing to God is a broken and contrite heart" (Ps. 51:17). We like the widow bring the two mites from our purse, a small gift but our all (Luke 21:1–4). Now we can add to our devotions the joy of giving to Jesus.

Now you can begin to think of your devotions more like the woman with the vial of alabaster who breaks it and pours it over the feet of Jesus (Matt. 26:6–13). Jesus had forgiven her of many sins. She came with gratitude to Jesus and worshipped Him with her tears and her hair and her perfume. She was looking at Jesus and worshipping him unashamed as others looked on and criticized her. She was loving Him for loving her. She stood at his feet, weeping, and wet his feet with her tears. Then she wiped them with her hair and kissed them and poured perfume on them. She was pouring out devotion on Jesus. Why, because she had experienced something of the love of Jesus. I believe all devotions start here, start with the love of God to forgive our sin and our not being able to believe it is so. We come with what we have and pour out on Jesus the tears for our sin, washing His feet and wiping them with our hair of humility. We come and love Him with the perfume of our thanks, anointing him with it. I don't think we ever get past the wonder of the love of God to forgive us our many sins. You may find that all you can bring to Jesus in your devotions is the tears of your sorrow for your sin and the tears of joy that He forgives you. Pour them out on Jesus, for they are precious to Him. Some of the old mystics talked about the prayer of tears. I have known the Lord for many years now, and still wet His feet with my tears over the sin in my life that He has forgiven. Bring your tears, bring your hair, and bring your perfume and gaze on the Lord and wash the Lord's feet and dry them with your hair and in this way wait upon Him.

Recently I heard a pastor talk about devotions and ministry as being bifurcated. As he mentioned this bifurcation it was almost with a tone that we shouldn't get stuck on the devotion and worship side but should get out there and do ministry. It was like he was saying, "It's OK to pray, but let's not get stuck there." Today the Church hasn't gotten stuck in devotions, and I would say this the problem; our preoccupation is not with Christ and His worship but with ourselves and our desires, even with our ministries. Some are so busy with church and ministry, they have little time to be with God alone.

In the Gospel of John (John 12:1–8) we see the story of Mary anointing Jesus's feet and wiping them with her hair. Judas Iscariot objects and says, "Why wasn't this perfume sold and the money given to the poor? It was worth a year's wages." Judas didn't really want to have this to give to the poor; he wanted the money so he could steal some it. How many times have you been tempted to take the time you would have anointed Jesus's feet with your love and give it to the poor in some service or ministry? We can see our time with the Lord as a waste of that time, time that could have been better spent in serving others. This woman was adoring Jesus Christ by anointing Him with one of the most precious things she had. Pouring this out on Jesus wasn't practical at all, nor was it focused on the ministry of taking care of the poor; it was just focused on Jesus. How many of us would think that spending much time with Jesus, pouring out the perfume of our lives, is a waste? I would dare say that pouring out worship on Jesus wastefully is just what is needed today. Making Jesus central in our devotions and central in our lives will bring about change in us and prepare us for service when we finally do leave His feet to go to serve others. Today many of our pastors are focused on the poor, the needy of the world, and have left Jesus's side to take perfume meant for Him and pour it out on the world as casting pearls before swine.

It's important to notice what Jesus said here, for it seems selfish. "Leave her alone." What is Jesus saying here? "Leave this woman alone; she has been occupied with me, loving me." After years in ministry, I have seen too many pastors who see loving Jesus as serving in the Church in some capacity. We must be careful as pastors and leaders that we don't exchange the glory of God for service to people, that we don't flee from Christ in order to wait tables. The loving worship and tender care of Christ, pouring perfume upon Him, is the priority for the Church. We've moved away from worship that we might be sellers of perfume instead of pouring it over Jesus. If our devotion to Christ is right in our lives, then whatever ministry Jesus calls us to will have its proper place and power. Ministry will not be a problem but a great harvest of fruit that comes from this union with Christ.

Notice what Jesus says next; it almost sounds cold and heartless. "The poor you will always have with you." In the Church we have developed an incorrect view of who God is and what He wants. We have thought at times that Christ's priority is the poor and needy. This is because we have an incorrect view of who God is and His priority. God's first concern is for His glory, and we are to make His glory our first concern. We demonstrate this when we come daily to do just that with our praise and worship. We have become human-istic, human-centered, in our religion. We see service to humankind rather than Jesus as the priority. Here Jesus is making the point that He is the priority and worthy of the lavish gift of this woman "wasting" her wealth on Him. He is worthy of your perfume of love daily. He is worthy to have you waste time on Him that might have been spent helping others. Does Jesus get your first love, your best love, or is that being spent on others?

I was in the eighth grade in Gary, Indiana, on December 3, 1967, when we heard the news that Dr. Christiaan Barnard had transplanted the heart of a deceased young female accident victim into a middle-aged man suffering from coronary artery disease. The patient lived only 18 days before dying of bilateral pneumonia, but the transplant was hailed as a major medical triumph. In less than two weeks Christiaan Barnard performed his second transplant. The rest is history. God likewise transplants His own heart into us. He cuts out the old diseased heart and gives us a bright, shiny new one. With the new heart comes the love of God. "I will give you a new heart and put a new spirit in you; I will remove from you your heart of stone and give you a heart of flesh. And I will put my Spirit in you and move you to follow my decrees and be careful to keep my laws" (Ezek. 36:26–27). God creates in us a new heart, for the old heart is dead and dying. In this heart is a new type of love, the very love of God. Now with this new heart we no longer offer "strange fire" but the very fire of heaven. Remember that the altars of the Tabernacle and the Temple were ignited with fire from heaven. Jesus must touch our hearts with His holy fire, the Holy Spirit, igniting them to love. He transplants that holy fire and love into us, so we can love God and then our fellow man. Jesus prays, "I have made you known to them, and will continue to make you known in order that the love you have for me may be in them and that I myself may be in them" (John 17:26).

There are no end of devotional books or daily readings with which to guide our devotional time. Having a devotional book and reading a selection out of it in the morning may not be the same thing as meeting with God and experiencing His love and fellowship personally. Many of the devotional guides become nothing more efficacious than going to church and lighting a candle. The routine can become empty, dry, lifeless, and for some people, just boring. The routine is so empty that many Christians find no meaning there and may wonder why they do it. Many would say, "I just don't get anything out of it." Word of advice: Look for devotionals that have Jesus at their center. Look for books that lift Him up like the serpent in the wilderness. When we see Jesus lifted up, it will be transformational to our devotions. "Thus we read that looking up to Jesus, or lifting up the eyes to Jesus, goes for prayer in God's book. 'My prayer will I direct to thee,' saith David, and will look up' (Ps. 5:3, KJV). Faith in prayer will often come out at the eye. Thus, Stephen looked up to heaven; let us look up to Jesus by calling on Him; now this calling on him contains prayer and praise" (*Looking Unto Jesus*, Isaac Ambrose). Isaac Ambrose is saying the act of looking unto Jesus goes for prayer in God's book. The act of looking to Jesus is prayer. If your devotions are not filled with the experience of the love of God and fellowship with Him, you are missing the mark, missing what should be the goal of our devotions.

In 2005 an Ellis Research did a survey for *Facts & Trends* of pastors and their prayer lives. The survey found that the average time a pastor spent in prayer was 30 minutes a day. During that time, a typical pastor spent twelve minutes with prayer requests, eight in quiet time, seven giving thanks, seven more in praise, and five confessing sin. The top five things they prayed for were individual congregation members' needs, the congregation's spiritual health, wisdom in leading the church, spiritual growth for the church, and personal spiritual growth (*Facts & Trends*, May 6, 2005). Notice the average is 30 minutes a day for pastors. These statistics speak more of empty routine than of a love affair with Jesus. In some churches pastors spend more time with their mistresses than with the Lord. Is it any wonder we don't see revival in the Church?

The tokens of love we bring to God can be small and almost insignificant things like the widow's mite. Sally and I went to school in the small town of Macomb, Illinois. One of our treats was to go to the Lamoine Hotel downtown and go into the coffee shop and get a maple frosted Danish and cup of coffee, about all we could afford back then. We still talk about those moments today, how we enjoyed each other's company while dining on that giant maple frosted Danish with coffee. Forty years later, all we have to say is "maple frosted," and we are both swept back to those school days and early love. That was a special moment of fellowship and communion between us. The maple frosted Danish became the love token of those days. I dare say that I could bring Sally a maple frosted Danish today, and it would bring tears to her eyes. It isn't the Danish but what it represents—the love and communion of those moments together. We can think that the tokens of love we bring to God have to be big things. Have you ever thought how small a thing even giving your whole self to God really is? Start by thinking of small gifts you can bring to God, tokens of the love you have for Him. It might be as small as just spending an hour alone with Him and let love grow from there.

When you fall in love with Jesus, you will share precious moments alone, unique moments that will be represented by some token of your special love: a word He has spoken to your heart, a verse, a gift that He gave you, a comfort He has poured out on you, the shining of His face upon you. The greatest token may be His manifest presence to you: "I am here!" In the moments you share with Jesus, you both will find tokens of love and communion. "I want you to have this in remembrance of me." Didn't Jesus leave His Church with a memorial supper, a token of His love, that could be eaten with the express purpose of remembering all that Jesus had done for us? Walking with Jesus, you will have a collection of these tokens and remembrances of your love together, tokens of His love by which you know you are loved. And if you will offer them, He will have some as well.

One spring my mother was driving back to Chattanooga from Indiana and thought and prayed as she got close to the city, "Wouldn't it be wonderful to see the pear trees in bloom?" She made that last turn around some mountain, and when the city came into view, there before her were hundreds if not thousands of pear trees in full bloom. As she passed tree after tree, she rejoiced, for she knew this was not a random accident. She knew that the timing of all things was in His hands, even a trip to Chattanooga. She knew that Jesus, whom she loved and who loved her, could bring forth this floral symphony to salute her as she came home. Jesus had presented her with flowers on a vast scale, and it was something she enjoyed immensely and would never forget. She saw her life intertwined with Jesus's life and knew that He is not only a savior but the lover of her soul, her beloved. The timing of the pear trees and her travel was not an accident but an intention of the God who loved her. There are no accidents with God, and there won't be any in your relationship with Him. She never forgot that moment, and after that, whenever the Lord would do something special for her, she would simply call it a pear tree.

Though you will never be able to keep up with Jesus and the expressions of His love, you too can bring tokens of your love to Him. In our moments alone, in your moments of worship and thanks and of loving communion in the secret place, you can exchange glances and gifts of love. "Let us go early to the vineyards to see if the vines have budded, if their blossoms have opened, and if the pomegranates are in bloom, there I will give you my love" (Song 7:12). When you come to gaze upon our Lord, you can bring tokens of love to lay at his feet. You can strew His way with palms and cloaks and cry hosanna to him. When you come to be with the Lord in your devotions, do you think, "Here is a place I can love my Lord and bring some token of love to him"?

Many years ago, I learned how powerful a small token of love could be. A dear friend of ours helped us pack our house for a move. The circumstances were such that we had to be in the city we were moving to before I could get all the arrangements finished and pack our house for the move. I didn't know how we were going to get it all done. Our friend came forward and said she would pack our belongings. I don't know how she did it. I hate to think of where we would have been without her help. Some months after our move, we returned for a visit to the city we had moved from, wanting to thank our friend Sally, and I bought her some roses. We went to see her, and the roses had arrived before we did. When I walked into her house, I was greeted with a bear hug like few I had ever received. She squeezed me tightly and then she took both of my arms, one in each hand, and with tears running down her face, she said to me, "David, I'm fifty-four years old and no man has ever bought me roses." These roses touched this person's heart, and this was a lesson to me about the power of the small thing to make a difference in the lives of people around us. The roses were a token of our appreciation and love for the kindness shown to us, but they moved her to tears.

Our personal devotions are the place we come to present our love to Jesus. We bring our love tokens to Jesus for all He has done for us. It is hard for us to imagine the depth of the love He has for us. This secret place with God is where we celebrate our love with the exchange of gifts, tokens of the love of our hearts. This token may be our thanks and praise, a poem or a song, a love letter you have written the Lord. John and Charles Wesley wrote thousands of hymns, love songs, to the Lord. When we come to be alone with Christ, we have a safe place where we can declare our love to Christ, even if that declaration might seem silly to someone else, He will come and receive that love. When was the last time you told Jesus how much you love Him?

If we take our human relationships for granted, we can do the same thing with our divine relationship. We think to ourselves, "I live in the presence of Almighty God. I am never apart from Him. Why then do I need to bring to Him tokens of love? I know I love Him, He knows I love Him, and I know He loves me, so why do I need special times with God? Why do I need to continue my devotional time with my God? Why do I need to continue to have dates with my God? Relationships are about relating to each another, about interaction, communion, and communication with each another. If there is no relating, if there is no inter-action or communion, then is it a relationship? There are marriages in which two people live in the same house but have no relationship, no communion or communication with each another, no exchange of love. Proximity to someone is not a relationship, yet that is all some Christians have with the omnipresent God. It may be easier to take an invisible person for granted than it is one who is visible. If you have a track record of taking visible people for granted, then ask yourself how you're doing in your relationship to the invisible God. Relationship will manifest itself as a reality, in giving and receiving the tokens of love.

One day in my time with the Lord, His word to me was, "David, you have never brought me roses." It was a strange word to me, and at first, I doubted that it was the Lord, thinking this was just a thought that had popped into my head. Over the next few days, it kept coming, but I didn't know what to do with it. Finally the Spirit said, "Why don't you treat me like a real living person?" I thought about that and how I was treating the Lord. I asked Sally if she would get me some roses on her rounds. She asked what they were for, and I told her I believed the Lord wanted me to give them to Him. This she did, and the next morning as I came to be with the Lord, I presented the roses to Him. Other than the roses there was nothing unusual about the morning; it was a sweet morning of fellowship with the Lord, and the roses were an expression of my love to him. I thought how true it was that so often I didn't treat my Lord as if He were a living person, as if He were there with me, watching me, loving me, helping me. I was reminded of the woman who poured out her perfume on Jesus and how He accepted this and enjoyed the gift. I hoped the Lord would find some pleasure in what might seem a silly act to some.

The roses stayed on my desk, and since I live in the desert, they dried in perfect form and shape. Only a tinge of color has been lost. As of this writing, several years have passed since I gave them to Christ, and they are still there, speaking of my love to Him. As He has preserved those roses perfectly, He will preserve our gifts of love to Him and never take them for granted. Devotions are about devotion, about love. So let there be love in your times with the Lord. See your devotions as a place you come to love and be loved by Jesus.

Chapter 11

THE FIRST OBEDIENCE

*"The time has come,"
he said. "The kingdom
of God has come near.
Repent and believe
the good news!"
(Mark 1:15)*

THE GREEK WORD *euangelion*, which is translated "gospel" or "good news" in most of our English translations, can have several renderings. *Euangelion* can be translated to mean bearing a message, a good message, or an unbelievable message. Imagine you were living in the Middle East before the time of Christ and a great king and his army were coming to conquer your nation or city-state. You knew back then that to lose a war to another king and nation would mean that life as you knew it would change forever and not for the good. In those days to lose a war to another king could make all the inhabitants of your city and nation the property of the conquering king. If you could not escape, you might be caught in the war as your city was attacked, pillaged, and burned. You and your family could be sold into slavery, carted off to some foreign country to live at the whims of your new owner, never to see your loved ones again. Worse yet, you might face the excursioner's blade and be killed—only after you had watched as all your family was killed before you. Your land and possessions would be taken away, and all you had worked for and built could be lost in a moment. You would wait under the dread of this coming terror. Your king would go out and meet this invading army and do battle to defend your way of life. What would happen? You would pray to God and ask that you and your family be delivered and that the king and his army would be successful. Maybe you would consider your alternatives and think about packing and what escape route you might take. You would wait in the silence and dread with your family huddled around you, finding it hard to do anything but wait for the news to come from the battlefield. "Any news, any news from the front?"

Then on the horizon a runner would come from the battle, panting and sweating, dirty with the dust of the road, and many gathering around him to hear the news. Stopping to catch his breath, surrounded by a crowd waiting on his words, he would say, "I bear a message from the king! We have won the battle! The enemy has been turned back, and we have a victory!" This would be good news, great news, unbelievable news. At one moment you were considering all to be lost and what the terrible consequences of losing the battle might mean for you and your family, and now you hear all is not lost and the great terror has been removed. Your city and houses will not be burned, you will not be sold into slavery, your children won't be ripped from your arms, and you won't be killed. This is what is meant by good news, by the word "gospel." The Gospel is good news that is so good, it is hard to believe it. The dread of coming judgment is gone, and your enemy has been defeated. The Gospel is so much more than good news from the battle front. The Gospel is Jesus.

When Jesus says repent and believe the Gospel, He is saying believe something that is almost impossible to believe: "Believe the message I bring of good news." Believe you don't have to conquered and imprisoned or be blinded by your captors; you can be free to live in the power, freedom, and victory He has provided for us. Believe that our king has won the victory for us and we can now live as sons, as princes. Believe that you can come into the very court of the king and fellowship with Him. Believe that a way has been made that we might know Him and love Him and have access to His presence. Believe that all our sin and shame has been forgiven and the punishment taken by Jesus. Jesus then gives us His righteousness so we can live with Him. Believe that in this Gospel message we are given sight so we may see Christ, who is the Gospel. Believe the Gospel and walk with Christ by His Spirit and know Him in a personal way. Believe that He will write the law on our hearts by the Holy Spirit, transforming us into His image and giving us His righteous dress. And this is just the here and now. Believing the Gospel, we will live forever with our Savior. If we believe the Gospel, when we die and are buried that body shall be made new and rise again to live a new life in a new body in Heaven and on the new earth. We will get to do life over, but this time do it perfectly. With the Gospel I can live in fellowship with God.

Is this good news to you? What are we to do so all this can be ours? "After John was put in prison, Jesus went into Galilee, proclaiming the good news of God. 'The time has come,' he said. 'The kingdom of God has come near. Repent and believe the good news! (Mark 1:14–15). What is the work to do? Repent and believe the Gospel. "Then they asked him, 'What must we do to do the works God requires?' Jesus answered, 'The work of God is this: to believe in the one he has sent" (John 6:28–29). When Jesus says "Believe the good news" and then "Believe in the one he has sent," these are the same thing. Jesus is the good news that God has sent to humankind. Jesus is the Gospel. Our work, our first obedience, is to repent and believe in the one God has sent. Believing the Gospel, believing the one He has sent—Jesus—will be our first and ongoing obedience.

The first obedience that God calls for is to repent and believe—have faith—in Jesus. In II Thessalonians 1:8, the Apostle Paul puts it this way: "He will punish those who do not know God and do not obey the gospel of our Lord Jesus." For Paul, obeying the Gospel is believing in the one God has sent. When we think about obedience to God, we usually think about keeping the laws or rules we find in Scripture, like the Ten Commandments. However, our first obedience is not to a law but to a person: We are commanded to have faith in Jesus. In obedience to the Gospel we are saved and brought into fellowship with Christ. Now that we are saved, what must we do to perform the works God requires? We continue to do that which we did at first: We continue by repenting and believing in the one He has sent. Our first obedience becomes a continual obedience, a continual believing in the one God has sent. His name is Jesus.

Have you ever ordered a toy or piece of furniture that arrived at your home unassembled? You open the box, remove all the contents, and then look for the instructions. There, in a plastic bag among countless mini-pieces, screws, bolts, and nuts, you find the instructions. Some brave souls will start out without glancing at the instructions, but I have learned the hard way that it is always better to read the instructions and walk through the steps they give, or you get into trouble. When you open the instructions and after you read through seventeen warnings to keep these parts away from your dog or children, you'll come to step one. "Do this first," followed by a second step and a third and so on. If you get the steps out of order, you can get into trouble and may have to undo what you did to put them in the right sequence. These steps toward assembly build on one another; you can't do the second without having done the first. They must be in the right order.

In the Christian life we have an instruction manual called the Bible. It can be very intimidating when we see all the instructions, all the rules. This instruction manual is what we teach and preach in our churches; it is ever before us. We are taught that we should read and meditate upon the Word, that we should study it, and this we do. We look at the laws—instructions—and then ourselves to see if we are living up to God's standard. We see where we fall short and try to repent and obey the law anew. We are told that if we obey God's laws, we will be blessed. As with the instructions to assemble the furniture, we start with step one and then quickly move on to steps two and three and four, seldom looking back to step one. We are constantly seeking new commands and new teachings from the Word of God.

God's Word isn't like the instructions to assemble a piece of furniture. With God's instructions you start with step one but you never stop doing step one. This is where many get lost, for they see the instructions of God as progressive: Do step one, then two, and so on. But God's instruction is like this: Start with step one, stay with step one, keep doing step one, and never stop. Now add step two to step one, doing both together. God's instructions are more like a chain: Step two is linked to step one, and three to two, and so on. You may have a very long chain of instructions—commands—but if the first link is broken, then all that hangs upon it will come crashing down. If that happens, we must go back and establish the first link again. The first link in the Christian life is the most important, and if it is broken, then all my obedience to other rules will end in failure. What is that first chain link for the Christian's life, the first step, the first instruction and command to be obeyed? Repent and believe the Gospel, have faith in the Gospel, to look unto the Gospel. The one He has sent, this is Jesus.

In Matthew 22 Jesus is confronted with a question intended to stump him. "Teacher, what is the greatest commandment in the law?" This must have been discussed over and over by the Pharisees, with arguments by the great rabbis being quoted along with Scripture. Jesus answers quickly and simply, "Love the Lord you God with all your heart and with all your soul and with all your mind. This is the first and greatest commandment." As Christians, when we hear this, we think the first thing we are to do is to love God with all our heart, soul, and mind. This is the first and greatest command, so it must be what I am to do first. If I were to ask you, "How do you love God, how do you keep this commandment?" what would you say? Some might say by keeping His commands, for Jesus said the one who loves him will keep His commandments. Others might say we love God by serving Him in some ministry. I believe it is just here that many Christians get into trouble. After having believed the Gospel, they look away from Christ and look to commands of Christ and ministry to demonstrate love for God. Christian, if I look away from Christ to the law or ministry, I will find no power to do either. If our first obedience is right, we will do both the commands and ministry but not as a first obedience. The first obedience is to obey the Gospel, to believe in the one God has sent, and to continue to believe in this one until He brings us to Heaven.

Nowhere in the New Testament does Jesus command us to love God. In the Matthew 22 the passage we just quoted, Jesus is answering the question about what the law says in the greatest commandment. The law says love God. We know that the law is powerless to help us keep it. "For through the law I died to the law so that I might live for God. I have been crucified with Christ and I no longer live, but Christ lives in me. The life I now live in the body, I live by faith in the Son of God, who loved me and gave himself for me. I do not set aside the grace of God, for if righteousness could be gained through the law, Christ died for nothing!" (Gal. 2:19–21). The life I live in the body, I live by faith in the Son of God. My first obedience is to believe, have faith in, and look unto the one God has sent. This first obedience brings Christ to live in me and by His powerful life keep the law through me. My first step in my Christian life will be the same as my last step: to live by faith in the Son of God. How quickly we take our eyes off Jesus and put them on the law or some ministry and wonder why our spiritual strength waxes and wanes.

In our devotions we should be like a beggar coming to God's house and begging for food that we might live. Jesus is the bread of heaven, and we need to come and dine on Him, believe in Him daily, or we will find we suffer from malnutrition. If we don't come, we won't eat, and if we don't eat, we'll waste away. The Christian life is one of constant begging (believing) for food (love) from God. This begging is the place of faith. It is looking unto Jesus and in looking, receiving the life-giving gift of His life, love, and grace. Our work is to believe in Jesus and in that believing, receive everything we need for life and godliness. Here we dine on the daily manna, the bread of heaven, Jesus Himself, and find power to keep all the other commands that follow believing in the one God has sent.

As Christians we tend to think more legally than relationally when it comes to God. Jesus taught us, "If you love me, you will obey what I command" (John 14:15). When we hear these commands, we can run to obey them without looking unto Jesus. What can we forget is that we can no more keep the law than we can create a world, without first running to Christ. I can search the Scriptures for the commands, but they provide no help or power to keep them. We search the Scriptures for Jesus's commands and put them on our list of things to do and obey. This list can quickly become large and overwhelming. When we find a command, we say to ourselves, "I am going to keep this command," and with our best effort we set out to do just that. But we find this road to obedience can be very difficult and often frustrating as we look at the laws of God and try to keep them. Our attempts to do this, to love Jesus by keeping His commandments, often ends in failure and frustration. We examine our lives against these laws to see where we have succeeded and where we have failed. We find we are often returning to the same law again and again, trying harder and repenting more, hoping that we will succeed. It is just at this point that we begin to learn how frustrating the Christian life can be. It is easy to turn away from Jesus and look at the law alone. When I was a young Christian and would share Christ with others, often the discussion would get around to the rules of Christianity. My Christianity was identified by the rules I was supposed to keep. Unbelievers who never kept any of the rules of God seemed to know what rules were to be kept. We would often hear, "I thought you were a Christian. You're not supposed to do that." I must admit many of those rules I wore on my sleeve. "We don't smoke, drink, or chew or go out with women who do." Raised a Baptist, I was known for what we didn't do. Keeping the law at least outwardly was our way of loving God, but it usually ended in failure and frustration. Most us don't see the believing in the one He sent as the way we grow in our relationship with Christ.

When you think about obedience to God, does your mind go to keeping a set of rules or to believing in a loving person? We are apt to see obedience to God as obedience to the Ten Commandments or other rules we find in Scripture. Obedience to a set of commands can be sterile and impersonal. Setting our eyes on the law can often end in self condemnation, for in looking at the law all we will see is our failures. When you think about obedience to God, are you focused on rules to keep or a ruler to love? Listen as Jesus speaks to a Church long ago and far away: "I know your deeds, your hard work and your perseverance. I know that you cannot tolerate wicked people, that you have tested those who claim to be apostles but are not and have found them false. You have persevered and have endured hardships for my name and have not grown weary" (Rev. 4:2–3). This sounds like high praise. Who could ask for anything more? This is where many Christians find themselves: giving themselves to good deeds, hard work, perseverance, standing against wickedness, and enduring hardships and not growing weary. If you were to stop there, it would sound like this church is doing great. Yet…

"Yet I hold this against you: You have forsaken the love you had at first" (Rev. 2:4). They had forsaken their first love and replaced it with something else: their good deeds and hard work. The first link in the chain was broken. "Consider how far you have fallen! Repent and do the things you did at first" (Rev. 2:5). What were the first things they had done? They had repented and believed the Gospel. From this first obedience they came into relationship with Jesus and experienced His love for them and the love He provides for us to love God. They had been treating Jesus like a living person, not like some rules to be kept. They were relating to, believing in, someone who was alive, with communication, communion, and fellowship. Believing and being with this one was the obedience, and being His friend was the goal. Remember, the first command is to repent and believe the Gospel.

It was 1969 when I saw for the first time the woman I would marry and spend my life with. I was just 15 at the time. It was at a wrestling meet, and she was sitting in the stands with one of her friends. I had never met her, so I walked up to her in the stands and said, "Hey, what are you doing this weekend?" To which she responded, "Oh, nothing." Then I said, "How about you and me getting married this weekend?" Her response was, "Sure." I never thought she would be the one I would marry and spend my life with, but she was. That was over 50 years ago, and our relationship has been based on love and never on rules. We never had a written contract or code that we would follow. We never had a prenup or any rules for our marriage. What we had was a love for each other. When we found ourselves in trouble, we would go back to that first rule to love. We have treated each other like real, living persons who have hearts that can be hurt or thrilled. We have opened space in our lives for each other. We have lived every day together. We have loved, we have worked together, we have suffered together, we have walked through life as one person. To see one is to see the other. We have had children, raised them, and walked through the struggles of parenting, and we have pastored churches together and served the flock of Christ. All of this we have done without rules and regulations being the focus, for the focus has been love for the other person. We have grown in the knowledge of each another over these 50 years by being together. In the same way Jesus's call to repent and believe is a call to a love relationship, not a legal code.

Were there rules? Yes. There were things we would never do to each other, boundaries we would never cross. But the rules were never the focus. The person loved was the focus, with the goal of growing in love and intimacy. I think this is what Jesus is saying here: "You have been busy with rules and regulations, with the business of church and ministry, and you have forgotten that I'm here and want to love you and be loved by you." He wants us to be with Him, to relate to Him, to adore Him, to sing praise and thanks to Him. Jesus uses the illustration of marriage to describe our relationship to Him, but instead of seeing the most beautiful person, we see rules, regulations, and ministry. To all that, Jesus says repent and return to your first love, to the first command: "Believe in me, and there you find my love and the love to love me with." Over the years with Sally, one of the first things spoken almost every morning is "I love you." Shouldn't this be something we say to our Lord every morning?

Hudson Taylor was the father of the China Inland Mission. His biography, by his daughter-in-law, should be required reading for all Christians. Here was a man who lived his life as if his God was alive and walked by his side. Hudson Taylor went out to China without any outward signs of support other than what his God had told him. Hudson's first obedience was to be with the living God. God spoke to Hudson: "My presence will go with you and I shall give you rest." God never leaves His children alone but always goes with them. The children of God will find in the end that God has always gone with them: His name is Emmanuel. Like the Children of Israel in the desert, Hudson didn't need anything but his God walking with him and going before him. As you study the lives of men of faith, you find they have this in common: They know the living God and have made room in their lives for Him as if he were a real, living person. Hudson Taylor's obedience to believe Christ led to the great work God did in China, and it is still going on today.

How did Hudson know what to do and when? His life of faith began before he ever went out to China. His life of faith began in the secret place with the Lord. If you would be a man or woman of faith, that life of faith will begin for you in the same place, the secret place, or in a secret meeting with Holy God daily, something we call devotions. Coming to meet with God daily will be your first obedience every day. This coming is repenting and believing the Gospel, believing in the One He has sent. The first obedience answers the call of the Lord to come away with Him. This first obedience is a way of making Jesus your priority of the day. It is a way of choosing Him first in your day, making Him your first appointment of the day. This first obedience will be answered every day. "Come unto me, come follow me." Practically this obedience is worked out by coming to meet with God privately in the closet as Jesus taught in Matthew 6. Those who respond daily to the Lord's call will find a reward there, guidance and power to keep the commands that are spoken to them.

Christianity is a love relationship with Jesus Christ, and growth in that relationship with Christ will be the growth in knowing who He is. It will be growth in my intimacy or closeness to Him. Growth in this relationship with Christ gives me everything I will need for life and godliness. "His divine power has given us everything we need for life and godliness through our knowledge of Him" (II Pet. 1:3). The means of appropriating all we need for life and godliness is through knowing Him, through building a relationship with Him and getting to know Him better. The development of this personal relationship with Jesus is the delivery system for all we need in the Christian life, all we will ever need for righteousness, fruit of the spirit, power over sin, and power for ministry. That Jesus is infinite means his supply is infinite, able to meet every need one might have. Our place is to look upon Him and live. In looking upon Him we will find His love and also our love for Him as we believe and look upon Him. Power to keep the law, guidance, and knowledge of His will come in knowing him personally in believing in Him, in believing He is there for us.

Our individual devotions are the place we come to love God to be with Him. How many times have you heard the Christian life described as a relationship? Yet how many treat Jesus as if He were alive. They don't meet with Him, they don't talk to Him, they don't listen to Him or love Him with their words or presence. They may be busy with steps two, three, and four, but they have forgotten step one, and therefore the chain breaks and all their good deeds come falling to the ground. There are people who say they love you but don't want to spend any time with you or have anything to do with you. Is this love? If we are changed by beholding, then a face-to-face meeting with God is where one grows in the grace and knowledge of the Lord Jesus Christ. Our first obedience is to this secret rendezvous with God. God has always had a place to meet with man. It may be an altar, a tabernacle, a temple, a closet, or some alone place, but God wants to meet with and be with His people. The first obedience is to believe He exists and stand in the glory of God as we behold Him. "And without faith it is impossible to please God, because anyone who comes to him must believe that he exists and that he rewards those who earnestly seek him" (Heb. 11:6). Our work is to believe in the One God has sent, to believe He exists and rewards those who earnestly seek Him. This will be manifest daily as we come to behold Jesus, and in the beholding, we will be transformed into His image. This looking unto Jesus will give us all we need for our relationship with Him and then with others as we walk through our day. This first obedience will be repeated daily for the rest of our lives, for it is the first link on which the chain of our Christian life will hang.

What is your first priority, your first obedience in your day? If it is Jesus, shouldn't He be the first person you look at, the first person you talk with, the first person you love and serve in the day? How is it that we have gotten to the place where we say we love Jesus and totally ignore Him? There are some Christians who haven't talked with Jesus for months or even years. Is this love? What kind of love is this that ignores the one loved? Christianity is a union with Christ; it is falling in love and staying in love with Him. It is in our daily look at Jesus that we are empowered for the work of the day. As we look, we will learn and know something of the love of God. If your life is not progressing in the knowledge and love of God, it may be because you are looking in the wrong direction.

God doesn't call anyone to Himself without desiring the closest friendship. God has called us to know Him and in the knowing find all we need for life and godliness. In II Peter 1:3, Peter says, "Who called us by His own glory and goodness?" God's calling on your life is first to Himself, to be one with Him. When Jesus says come, he means come to Him. Hudson Taylor had followed God into the secret place daily, long before leaving for China. Your walk with God will start in the same place every day. If you don't obey God and come to this secret rendezvous, you won't know God, and the rest of your obedience may not matter. Before any work, before any law, before any ministry, or job, God saved you that you might know Him and grow in that knowledge.

When I played football, we would have team meetings where we would prepare our strategy to defeat our opponent. Missing this team meeting was one of the worst things you could do. It showed that at a critical moment you found something else to do while the whole team was forced to wait for you. Missing this meeting showed you had your priorities somewhere else. The person who missed the meeting demonstrated by his absence that his first obedience was to something other than the team. If you missed this team meeting, there would be a cost: public shaming and a fine. Missing your meetings with Christ will show that your first obedience may be to something else. The penalty may be loss of power and transformation in your life because you are not meeting with Christ.

Why was the China Inland Mission so successful in evangelizing China? It was said of Hudson Taylor that the sun never rose on China without finding Hudson Taylor on his knees worshipping his Lord. Hudson Taylor made the team meeting every morning. Seeking God every morning was the secret of his life and ministry. Often this meeting would be held in the corner of some crowed inn with people crowed in about Him. There, Hudson would light his candle to read the Scriptures and fellowship with the Love of his life. This was Hudson's first obedience every day and would be all of his life. If you walk with God, you will have to answer His first command to believe in the One He has sent. By believing in Jesus, looking unto Jesus, you will find the love you need to love God and the power to do what He commands. This is accomplished by going to be with Jesus and looking at Him like the serpent in the wilderness. This will be a daily event, daily obedience. Nothing in your life or ministry will be more important than the time you spend with God every day. This will be your first obedience, your first appointment, your first call every day. It will also be where you're empowered for the work of the day as you are changed into His image by coming to behold Him.

One of the books that Hudson Taylor wrote is telling. He wrote a small commentary on the Song of Solomon called *Union and Communion*, which I think reveals much about the man. I first discovered this book in my Bible school library. The Song of Solomon is a precious love letter to His bride. This song speaks of the depths of intimacy and love with the King. It is a picture and type for our relationship with Christ and can be a guide to intimacy with Him. Hudson's relationship with Jesus was the source and power of his life. I believe his first obedience was to his Lord and tending his love relationship with Him. His understanding of Christianity was as a marriage to the perfect bridegroom, Christ. From his marriage with Christ (relationship) would come many spiritual children, those saved in China as a result of the union with the One he loved.

When the children of Israel were in the desert for 40 years, their first act every day was to look at God. God represented Himself in the pillar of cloud by day and pillar of fire by night. When the cloud went up and began to move, they followed. When the cloud stopped, they stopped. The key was keeping an eye on the cloud, or we could say keeping an eye on God, looking unto God. You might imagine an Israelite going outside his tent in the morning and wondering what the day would bring. All he had to do was look at the cloud and it would tell him what the day would bring, travel or rest. So it is with the Christian: We go outside our tent and look to God every day to know what we will be doing this day. Looking unto God is our team meeting every day where we first love Him and then get the instructions for the day.

Study the lives of the great men and women of faith, and what will you discover? You will discover that many of them were masters of this first obedience, of following Jesus into the secret place. You will discover they were those who lived a life of intimacy with their Lord. These men and women knew about the secret place and found their Lord there daily. It is the call to all whom the Father draws to His Son: "Come and be alone with my Son, be intimately connected to my Son." Jesus is the bridegroom; we are the bride. Our devotions are the bed of love that gives birth to the children of God. We might ask ourselves how so many children are being born apart from intimacy with Christ. Could it be that many of these children are illegitimate? Could this be why so many of these children fall away, for they were never conceived by God but came out of human effort alone?

When Paul was converted on the road to Damascus, he was blinded by a great light. Men traveling with him led him to a house in the city. It was to this house that God would send Ananias to heal his blinded eyes. This Ananias did after arguing a little with God. When God gave Ananias the address, He also gave him this interesting note: "He is praying." I believe that with true conversion comes a praying heart. Paul's first obedience was to follow the Holy Spirit into a conversation with Jesus Christ, whom he had just seen on the Damascus road. Conversion is a union with Christ, and prayer is the means of communicating with Him. Those who are born again of the Spirit of God pray, even without instruction. Prayer for the Christian is as natural as breathing is to a newborn baby. For now, it will suffice to say that the Spirit of God will begin a conversation with you at your new birth, one that will last forever. This conversation with God may be part of what we call devotions and is our first obedience daily.

Jesus is alive and never gets enough of his children, and he desires their presence again and again. He wants to be with them every day and walk with them throughout the day. This first obedience is our first response to the person Jesus Christ. As Christians we are "first responders" to Jesus. His command to His people is the same today as 2,000 years ago: "Come follow me." You might put it this way: "Come be with me." Saints throughout the years have understood this and obeyed. "Arise, come my darling, my beautiful one, come with me" (Song 2:10). You will hear this same command as the Lord draws you to Himself. We call it a first obedience, for it is the first command he gives to those who will follow him. This command is not only the first, but it is continuous. You will be responding to the Lord in the same way all the days of your life. Our first obedience will be manifest every day as we come to believe in Him and be alone with Him in our devotions.

More than anything, Jesus wants you for Himself. He wants to be alone with you to reveal who He is and to demonstrate His love to you. "And our fellowship is with the Father and with His Son" (I John 1:3). If you have grown tired of meeting with Jesus, if you have stopped following Him into the secret place, go back to where you remember your first love. Return to this first obedience, to this first love, and come away with Him. If following Christ into the secret place is not the foundation of your Christianity, then the first link of your chain may be broken and all your works may be falling to the ground.

If Christianity is a relationship with a person, then our devotions are the framework upon which we build that relationship. When we come to God in our times of devotion, we are seeking Him first and not something else. If we meet this one and get to know Him, we will understand Christianity, and if we don't meet Him, we won't understand it. This relational aspect of Christianity is what makes it different from other religions. Without a living relationship to God, our devotions become nothing more than ancient pagan practices. The ancient pagans would offer a devotion to their gods, with the hope of propitiating their gods' wrath or meriting some favor from them. They thought that if they would bring their god enough gifts and sacrifices, he wouldn't be mad and just might hear them. They thought that by giving their gods gifts, they might persuade the gods to do the same in return. The relationship with these ancient gods seldom went beyond this contractual level. There was no real knowing of these gods in a personal way. There was no real knowing, for they were not real gods.

Sometimes as Christians we treat our God like one of these pagan gods. We think that our devotions can appease God's wrath, or cause God to grant us some favor. If I just pray long enough or hard enough, God will have to grant my petition. If you see your prayers as offerings to appease your God, then you could never pray long enough or hard enough to appease Him. We must remember there is no work we could do to appease our God's wrath. This has already been done by Him through His Son. Nor is there anything we can do to earn merit or His favor. This has already been done by the Son as well. All we have to do is live in the favor and merit that the Son has purchased for us. When God calls you to come, there is nothing for you to do but come and be with Him. By coming and following Him to the secret place we will live out the acceptance that has been accomplished for us and live in the favor that Jesus has granted us. Your first obedience will always be a rendezvous with Jesus every morning. "Come and see a man who told me all that I ever did" (John 4:29). What riches of fellowship and knowledge of God await those who believe that God has paid your admission price into His presence and into the favor and love of His heart. "Come unto me all you who labor, and I will give you rest" (Matt. 11:28). Remember to use the key of worship to unlock the door to intimacy, for in the act of worship God reveals Himself to the worshipper.

Some Christians have exchanged the glory and warmth of a living person for the coldness of a code. They never see the glory of God in the face of Christ Jesus, for they only see the rules they need to keep. To what is our first obedience? Our first obedience is to a living person, not a set of rules or doctrines. God's first command to us is, "Repent and believe in the one He has sent." I think we can safely say that "Come follow me" is synonymous with believing. Devotions are about believing what Jesus Christ has accomplished for you, believing that He wants a relationship with you. God is looking for a personal relationship with you. Jesus wants to be treated as a living person, but many Christians treat Him as if He were still dead in the tomb. When you became a Christian, were you introduced to a person, or were you introduced to a bunch of rules? Remember, when the disciples were following Jesus, the New Testament had not been written. In the beginning it was simply a group of men and women obeying Jesus's command to come and follow Him, and in that obedience, they were with Him. After His ascension they would be led by His Spirit. Our first obedience is to a person who will command us to come and follow Him, to come and be with Him. Are you in a relationship with Jesus today?

I believe one of the reasons so many of our young people are walking away from the Lord today is that they were introduced to a set of rules, a code of ethics, a religion, and nothing more. They have never met Christ or heard Him say, "Come and follow me." They only have a relationship with a written code or religious system. They know the Christian code of ethics, but many have never had that formal introduction to the living God. We have settled for hearing our children pray a prayer or walk an aisle, outward signs only. How many Christians have really met the living Christ and continued to meet with Him daily. God is calling us to come to Him and speak with Him like Moses did, face-to-face. A religion of rules will have only the power of condemnation. It cannot deliver, and it cannot save. There is a big difference in knowing the rule book and knowing the Ruler.

I am not saying that your first obedience is to independently love God, for you are not capable of this. I am saying that your first obedience is to look at Jesus first for the love and power to keep the first commandment every day. The look—faith—is enough for you to be healed of your lack of love and will grant you the love you need to keep the first command to love God with all your heart. It may seem like semantics, but it isn't. I must come by faith continually to trust Jesus for all I need to be to Him and others. The beauty of His system is that it is not my obedience that is the main thing; it is my faith that looks unto Him, and in the looking comes the power for loving and serving Jesus.

The Moravians were a group of Christians who fled persecution in central Europe. A wealthy count opened part of his estate, where they eventually settled and built a community they called Herrnhut. They experienced one the greatest outpourings of the Holy Spirit since Pentecost, leading the world into foreign missions and lighting the fire of revival in the Church. The Moravians' motto was "The Lamb has conquered. Let us follow Him." Our first obedience is to respond to this living person who is Christ, to follow the Lamb who has conquered. We will never forsake the law, but we must remember the I keep the law by believing in the One He has sent. If you see your Christianity as do's and don'ts, or as rules to live by, you may be looking in the wrong direction. Your first obedience is to look to Christ and be healed of all your sickness and weakness. Your first obedience is to walk not by the law but according to the law of the Spirit of life, to walk in relationship with Jesus by his Spirit, to walk and live with the living person Christ. This living person Christ will lead you into the secret place, the place of devotions and will never stop calling you there, or calling you to Himself.

Oswald Chambers said, "We consider what we do in the way of Christian work as service, yet Jesus Christ calls service to be what we are to Him, not what we do for Him. Discipleship is based solely on devotion to Jesus Christ, not on following after a particular belief or doctrine." Our first obedience is to the living person Jesus Christ, not written code. Our first obedience is to sit at His feet like Mary and listen, not be rushing around in the kitchen wondering why everyone is not helping us. Our devotions are the place we come to believe in Christ, to believe He exists and rewards those who diligently seek Him. We love him by believing in Him, we love with song, praise, and thanks. We love Him with our time and presence. We then love Him with our obedience, and then our neighbors. When you look at your Christianity, do you see it as something legal, do you see a ministry, or do you see a person you are madly in love with? If you find yourself alone and beaten up in ministry, without Christ, turn around and run back to Him. You will probably find Him waiting for you at your place of devotions. Your true growth in ministry will come from growth in intimacy and union with Christ.

Your love is to and for Christ alone, and that will never change. All our lives, the first obedience will remain the same. It doesn't matter what work God calls you to; your first obedience will be to believe in Him and to look at Him, to come and be with Him, to come and walk and talk with Him daily. Jesus wants your habit to be what His was, to get alone with God daily. "Very early in the morning, while it was still dark, Jesus got up, left the house and went off to a solitary place, where he prayed" (Mark 1:35).

In Italy they have the Italian tradition of Passeggiata, a gentle stroll. As evening falls and the harsh sun hides its face, thus cooling the air, the evening ritual begins. Passeggiata allows those walking to talk with one another or with those they pass. It is a time to socialize with friends and neighbors, enjoying their company and the glories of the day. Italians tend to dress up for Passeggiata, as it is a time to meet people. Older folks may just sit in front of their houses or at a restaurant and talk with those who pass by. Our devotions with God are like Passeggiata, a gentle walk and talk with our Savior, and something we do every day. This is what Adam did when he walked with God in the cool of the day.

If you are going to climb Camelback Mountain in Phoenix, one of the trails you can take is through Echo Canyon. If you stand in the canyon and yell, you can hear your voice come bouncing back to you. Devotions for some are like standing in Echo Canyon. There is only one voice there, and it comes bouncing back to the one who spoke. It is difficult to have a conversation with an echo; all that is heard is what has already been spoken. Devotions for many Christians are like Echo Canyon: All they hear is their own voices bouncing back to them. The emptiness of treading the devotional path alone wears many out. Therefore, countless Christians no longer talk with God. There was no interaction with a living person, no finding of another in the devotions. For many Christians, devotions have become a valley of despair, where they are alone with themselves without God and without hope.

Jesus knocks on the door of our lives and says, "Come follow me." Every day He will knock and call for us to come and follow. All you must do is open the door and take a gentle stroll with a person who loves you more than anyone else does. As you two walk together, you will talk, sharing the events of the day and the cares of your hearts. It is also a time to share the love you have for each other. Your believing in the one He has sent will be manifest in those times we call devotions. Our devotions should be as easy as answering the door when someone who loves you wants to take a Passeggiata with you, as easy and enjoyable as having a walk and talk with a friend. "I have something I want to share with you. Will you walk with me?"

Italians will dress up for Passeggiata, as we should for the Lord. By dressing up, we mean a time of preparation for being with the Lord. It is a time when we dress our hearts and minds to be in His presence. I have read of saints who would never have devotions without getting properly dressed and making sure they looked their best. I was told the story of a lady who would stop at a mirror she had in her house that was on the way to her secret place and check to see how she looked. She wanted to make sure she looked her best before she entered her Lord's presence. Some will think this silly, but if you really believe you are meeting with the living God, won't that change how you act in your coming to Him?

This appointment with God is the highest and greatest appointment of the day. It is the first step after believing in the One He has sent. Meeting with God is the greatest thing that can happen to any of us. Did it happen for you today? Just repeat this phrase, "I met with Almighty God this morning." Stop and just think about that statement. A mere mortal can have the privilege and pleasure of the company of Almighty God. He can have a Passeggiata with God, just as God and Adam walked together in the Garden in the cool of the day. Why, if we have this high privilege, would I not want to take advantage of it? Do you walk and talk with God?

I want you to see your devotions as developing the habit of obeying the Gospel by saying yes to God and coming to be with Him. God is an extreme person of habit. He never changes. He loves taking these walks with His children, and once started, He never stops. God will ask for other obediences to His word or to some ministry, but He will never ask you to stop coming to be alone with Him, asking you to come and love Him. God wants you to come and be with Him. He wants to be the focus of your life and of your devotions. You will discover that this devotional walk with God will be the most satisfying thing you do in your day. I have often come to God in my devotions with a shopping list of requests, only to discover they have been forgotten when I am bathing in the pool of His love. Many times the things that I wanted to ask for and didn't were answered without asking. You will find that the more time you spend with this God, the more you will have the desires of your heart, without having to ask. You will find that all your desires become Him. Our greatest request will be to ask for more of Him. When we say yes to God and open the door of devotions to Him, He will walk into our lives and reveal Himself to us. In this revelation of God, we have everything from God. God can't give us any greater gift than Himself. God's revelation of Himself is the heart of our devotions, the great goal. Having this, you have all, and not having it, you have nothing. Like the walk on the road to Emmaus, Christ will reveal who He is from the Scriptures, and our hearts will be warmed within us.

To have this walk with God, we must turn away from whatever we are doing with that time in the morning. Turning to God is your first obedience every day. Turning to God, we have to turn away from whatever may be occupying that time or space. You may choose more sleep, or you may choose to plan your day, or you may choose to think about other things. If we choose God, we must disobey ourselves. Herein lies repentance from self to loving and obeying God. Here is our first obedience. Do you really want God, or just what he can give you?

Recently, I went to Glacier National Park with three men I love. The first day of our visit we drove on the Going-to-the-Sun Road. The road was covered with clouds of mist, and we saw nothing of the glories of that road and the mountains and valleys and rivers that were there. We could see only a few feet in front of our car. The next day we drove it again, but this time there were no clouds, and there were no words to describe the grandeur and glory of what we were seeing. It was difficult to try to take it all in. Vista after vista kept moving our eyes from one glory to another. We traveled the same road but had two different visions—one clouded and hazy, the other clear and glorious. This is how it will be as you take the Go-to-the-Son Road. Some days may be cloudy and hazy, and you see nothing of the glories of Christ. Don't give up, and keep taking the road until the skies clear and you see glories you can't describe and wonders that move your eyes to try to take in all that God is and has for you. When the clouds clear away in your devotions and you see something of the glory of God, you will find only one word coming from your mouth to describe the indescribable: Glory!

My father raised rabbits when I was in college. I had a younger sister still at home who liked to get the rabbits out of the cage and play with them. One day I heard a scream coming from the rabbit cages and saw my little sister running back to the house. As she got closer, I could see that her hand was bleeding. I surmised that she wanted to play with the rabbit, and the rabbit didn't. The rabbit she grabbed turned and bit one of her fingers, which was bleeding profusely. Surprisingly, while running back to the house she never let go of the rabbit that bit her. Many Christians are just like my sister: They want to play with the world and get bitten and still won't let go of the world. What we will learn as we walk with Jesus is just how great life can be when we let go of the rabbits that bite us—the world and our other loves—and grab on to the living God. What is your morning now filled with? Would you gain if you exchanged your rabbit for the glory and presence of God? I have learned over the years that Jesus doesn't bite.

Setting down our rabbits is just another way of saying "repent." No one comes to Christ without laying down that old life and its loves or turning from its sins. To follow Jesus, we must set down, or give up, the rabbits we love and cling to. This laying something down, our sins, to pick up the love of Christ will be the repeated pattern of our life. It is the first obedience, to repent and believe the Gospel. Here is our daily repentance, our daily cross, death to the old life and relationships and sins that we might gain a new life, a new love whose name is Jesus. We tend to see our crosses as a huge sacrifice, a death to self where our lives are martyred. We tend to see this as a painful experience, a torture. We may see it as giving up a job and a way of life to find another, and the catastrophic effect that can have on our lives. What if our daily cross was not an instrument of torture but of freedom? What if it was something that killed my old life so I could live a new with Christ? What if it is God's instrument to set us free from selfish desires and all the things we want in this life that compete with God for our time and attention? Part of God's work in the Gospel, is to crucify our old nature with Christ so we might be free from self's slavery to follow and become the slave of Christ. If we're going to make our relationship with Jesus the first relationship, then the priority of our relationships to other people and things may have to be repented of and the new priority of Christ take their place. In repentance our first obedience will be to make God our priority and the love of our lives. Many Christians who have married know something of making a person the number-one love of their lives by turning from all other loves. Knowing God and living in relationship with Him will ultimately be no loss and all gain. When we come to Christ in salvation, it is to the supreme relationship, and in coming we learn of Him, and from Him what it means to love, and then we find in the mystery of salvation He has provided a love with which we might love Him. Turn then from your sin, your loves that would possess you. Turn to Jesus and cling to Him, the one who has died for you to demonstrate how much He loves you. This will be your first obedience every day.

John MacArthur, in speaking about one of his trips to Russia, said that the Russian Christians called themselves "Repenters." I thought at the time that this was a funny thing to call yourself, but the more I thought about it, the more I saw just how accurate it was. Every day when we obey God and come to His Son in our devotions, it will be the beginning of our repenting for that day. In order for two people to walk together, they must first agree to do so. My act of faith every morning says, "To whom shall we turn? You alone have the words of life" (John 6:68). God's will is that you come to Him before anything else. This will be a daily repentance, a daily step of turning from looking to yourself to looking unto Him and placing your trust in Him. Making that first obedience will make the second and third easier as we walk through the day. Like putting that furniture together, all other the steps of obedience will depend on this one.

"On the day the tabernacle, the tent of the covenant law, was set up, the cloud covered it. From evening till morning, the cloud above the tabernacle looked like fire. That is how it continued to be; the cloud covered it, and at night it looked like fire. Whenever the cloud lifted from above the tent, the Israelites set out; wherever the cloud settled, the Israelites encamped. At the Lord's command the Israelites set out, and at his command they encamped. As long as the cloud stayed over the tabernacle, they remained in camp. When the cloud remained over the tabernacle a long time, the Israelites obeyed the Lord's order and did not set out. Sometimes the cloud was over the tabernacle only a few days; at the Lord's command they would encamp, and then at his command they would set out. Sometimes the cloud stayed only from evening till morning, and when it lifted in the morning, they set out. Whether by day or by night, whenever the cloud lifted, they set out. Whether the cloud stayed over the tabernacle for two days or a month or a year, the Israelites would remain in camp and not set out; but when it lifted, they would set out. At the Lord's command they encamped, and at the Lord's command they set out" (Num. 9:15–22).

Devotions are our looking to the cloud over the Tabernacle. Is God moving or is God encamping? As with the Children of Israel, our question is, "What is God doing?" Your devotions will be your gazing on the clouds of glory and then responding to the movement of God. Whether we encamp or set out, we are doing it by looking unto God and will walk according to His pace. When the Israelites would set up camp, the Tabernacle would be placed in the middle of the camp so all could see God. As we look to Jesus every day to see if we are on the move or not, we have the added grace of being transformed into His image as we gaze upon Him.

Listen closely: Do you hear the knocking? Listen closely: Do you hear Him call your name? He said He would. Get quiet and listen closely, and He will say, "Here I am, come follow me, or walk according to my Spirit; this is the way walk ye in it." He is the "law of the Spirit of life." Every other law you have known is one of death, condemnation, and disappointment. This is because you can never keep it, and you always fall short. If you have made your devotions just another law for you to keep, then you are headed for disappointment. God's only remedy for our failure is to give us a new law, the law of the Spirit of life. He gives to us a living person who will carry out His commands through you. He gives us a living law, one with power enabling us to obey. God by the Holy Spirit breathes His life into us. He breathes into us the ability to draw near Him, to love Him and to obey Him.

Devotions are the starting point, and staying point, for every Christian, no matter what your gift, situation, circumstances, ethnicity, or socioeconomic situation. You were saved to first glorify Jesus. You have been called to come and fellowship with this living person. You have been called into a love relationship with Jesus. You have been called into sonship so you can use your position as a son to come into His presence and use your inheritance to help a lost and dying world.

We have all heard of the gauntlets that people have to run to get to see a president or CEO of a large company. God has seen to it that you can knock and let those great powers who surround this greatest of beings hear, "Just tell God it's his son." You will hear God reply, "Bring him to me now!" We come to Almighty God, who created this universe with a word, and He wants to be with us. He wants to gather His children in His arms. Ask the Father to increase your faith to help you believe that you have been invited to have the pleasure of God's company, that you might have alone time with Him. More than this, when you do answer the invitation, you can ask of God whatsoever you want, as a Son would. You can come and learn of Him through fellowship and communion. You can be declared the friend of God and encouraged to come to God's throne room to ask for grace and mercy in times of need. We have been taught that we can come with confidence and boldness to this throne. This is the fount of life for the Christian, and out of these times of union with Jesus will come everything you need for life and ministry.

This is just another way of saying, "Lord fill me with your Spirit." God is trying to turn your attention to the beauty of His Son so you might be changed by looking at Him. Isn't that what David asked the Lord for? "One thing I ask of the Lord, this is what I seek: that I may dwell in the house of the Lord all the days of my life, to gaze on the beauty of the Lord and to seek Him in His temple" (Ps. 27:4). Set a test for yourself and see if what I'm saying isn't true. Go to the scriptures for 10, 20, or 30 days and just look upon Jesus. Read the Gospel accounts and see how He lived and what He did as something He did for you. Look at the wonder of His life, and worship Him for being someone worthy of all praise honor and glory. See if this doesn't have a transforming effect on your life. See if God doesn't blow the mists of the morning away that you might see the glories of your God and King. We have that ability to come and look; we have the honor of coming into the throne room of God and speaking with Him, if we will but accept it. The highest price ever paid for anything on this earth was paid that you might come to the court of the King of kings without shame and gaze upon His glories, that you might come as a son and draw near to your Father and worship Him, honor Him, praise Him, adore Him, and ask Him to show you His glory. Test God and see if He will not open the windows of heaven and pour out a great blessing upon you.

Today we have a prodigal Church. We have taken our inheritance and wasted it on ourselfs . Now broke and powerless we wake up in a pigsty. We have been busy doing our will but called it God's will. I believe some of the Church is waking up from the fog of self-focus and seeing their poverty and remembering what their Father's house was like and how rich He is. I believe God is calling us back to Himself. Much of the Church is in the swine pen, filthy and stinking like the pigs. Think of your Heavenly Father, who scans the horizon looking for you. He longs that you will return and feast with Him. We are building kingdoms and are starving for God. We are walking around in our own filth; we have lost the Pearl of Great Price and have only the stinking clothes on our backs. When will you raise your head from the swine and remember our Father and return to Him? We have lived without the presence of our Father for some time. Our money is spent, and we are pretending to be rich while wearing our rags. We must come back to the Father with humility, hoping only to be servants in His house. Maybe the Father just wants to have a feast with you for many days, so come home and join the banquet prepared for you. The Father is looking out to the horizon to see if you are coming home. He is longing that you will return to the secret place, to the place of believing that He exists and that He rewards those who seek Him. Come home to the embrace of your Father. Come home and be dressed in the robes of wealth. Come home and have your feet shod with the Gospel. Come home and see Him put that family ring on your finger. Come home to the greatest feast you will ever have, one of reunion with your Father. Celebrate with Him the recovery of fellowship, the recovery of intimacy. Celebrate your homecoming with your Father. Come home and hear your Father toast you at the banquet: "'For this son of mine was dead and is alive again; he was lost and is found.' So they began to celebrate" (Luke 15:24).

Your devotions will keep you in His presence, and in His presence, you will be changed, empowered, and instructed as to what the Lord wants you to do. Coming to God in devotions is the act of faith in which we believe He exists and is the rewarder of those who diligently seek Him. This act of faith will be your means of transformation into a new image, one that looks like Jesus. This first obedience is one that must be mastered and repeated all the days of your life. Many in the Church aren't seeking God and don't believe that He will reward those who will. They don't believe He will speak to them or manifest Himself to them. Believe and look at Christ lifted up like the serpent in the wilderness and be healed of your lack of faith; look at Jesus and be filled with love you can love Him with. Buy from Christ eye salve that you might see Him again and live in the light of His love (Rev. 3:18). Your first obedience will be to obey His call to come and believe in the One He has sent and gaze upon Him daily.

Chapter 12

THE INVITATION

"Come to me, all you who are weary and burdened, and I will give you rest."
(Matt. 11:28)

A **DEAR FRIEND** of mine spent more than 25 years as an assistant coach in the NFL. He was one of the best defensive line coaches the game has ever produced. He told me, "If you were on a team, or if you're in their camp, somebody in that organization wanted you, somebody in that organization chose you. Scouts and coaches looked at a lot of players, looking at both strengths and weaknesses, and out of all the options before them they picked you." What was my friend's point? You weren't there by accident; you were a part of that team because somebody wanted you and chose you and then invited you to camp. Your devotions don't begin with you or with what you want, even something as good as desiring God. Your devotions began with God making a choice, and that choice was you. The Apostle Paul would say that this choice was made a long time ago: "Chosen before the foundation of the world" (Eph. 4:1). God chose you to be on His team, a part of His family, His desire in this choice is to have fellowship with those He chose.

If you are reading this, if you are on your way to seeking a deeper and fuller relationship with God, it is because God chose you to be on His team. Jesus said no one could come unto Him unless the Father enabled them (John 6:65). God is putting together a team to worship His Son, "For they are kind of worshipers the Father seeks" (John 4:23). God is enabling and assembling loving hearts to pour out love and devotion on His Son, who is worthy of all praise, honor, glory, and love. The team He has assembled here on earth is made up of men and women from every tribe and language and people and nation. Meditate on this for a minute: God is selecting people to worship His son from all over the earth, and one of His choices was you. God starts your devotions by selecting you in His draft. Of all the people on the planet He could have chosen, He chose you. The question we struggle with is, "Why did God choose me?" Once He selects you in His draft, He sends you an invitation to come to His camp.

Your devotions didn't begin with you deciding you were going to seek God and spend more time with Him. They began with God deciding He was going to select you and then seek you out and save you. Devotions begin with God choosing the team He wants to surround His Son with. Unlike football teams, God's choice is not based on talent or ability to play. One of the mysteries of Christianity is the strange and peculiar people He picks to be on His team. If we had to pick God's team, we wouldn't pick some of the people He picks. God doesn't pick the best of humankind. "Brothers, think of what you were when you were called. Not many of you were wise by human standards; not many were of noble birth. But God chose the foolish things of the world to shame the wise; God chose the weak things of the world to shame the strong. He chose the lowly things of this world and the despised things—and the things that are not—to nullify the things that are, so that no one may boast before Him" (I Cor. 1:26). God didn't pick you because you were the biggest, strongest, or fastest. He didn't pick you because you were the most righteous or faithful. He may have picked you because you were the weak thing, the despised thing, so His glory could be manifest in your weakness. You don't have to be good—righteous—to be on this team; you only have to believe in the One He has sent: His name is Jesus.

We may never understand why He picked us, and that isn't the important thing; He picked you because He wanted you. Meditate on that for a minute: God wanted you and chose you to come and worship Him. God picked you out of seven billion people, out of all the people on the planet. He picks out men and women to be with Him. Out of all the people on the planet He could have picked, He picked you. God picked you to come and love and worship His Son, the Lord Jesus Christ. So great is the work of Jesus Christ on our behalf that our voices can come into the very courts of Heaven into the presence of Christ and speak to

Him as a man, face-to-face. Our devotions are a place God created for us to come and be with Him and be to the glory of His praise. As the earth spins, new days are born every minute. At the beginning of each of those new days, God has people waking up to start the day praising His Son. The planet becomes a nonstop platform for the worship of Jesus Christ. God wants you to come into His presence and enjoy His love and gifts and with those gifts join the choirs that worship nonstop the worthy Lamb of God.

In 2017 my son and beautiful daughter-in-law were married. They put together a wedding that was as beautiful as any I had ever seen. The first thing they had to do was to choose who would be on the guest list. Once they had fought through all their choices and had a finalized their list, they needed to officially invite each person. The invitations were a work of art, so beautiful that we have framed ours and have it on display in our home. Along with the invitations came a self-addressed envelope so those who were invited could send back the RSVP card. I remember their frustration with some of their "friends" who would not respond to the beautiful invitation or were so late that they had to contact them again in order to get a count for the dinner they were preparing for their guests. As they were forced to recontact some of the people they had already spent time and money contacting, I heard my son say, "Why did we spend all this money for these invitations if people aren't going to respond to them?" God has done the same thing for us. He chooses those He wants to come to be with Him and then He sends them a formal invitation by the Holy Spirit. Every time the Gospel is spoken or written or preached, it is an invitation to come to God. By the way, God's invitation to you is ultimately a wedding invitation. Could this God say the same thing? "Why did I spend all this on these invitations if they won't respond and come?"

Like my son and daughter-in-law, after God has made His choice, He sends out an invitation to come and be with Him. God's invitation begins as a Word, and then it is made flesh and becomes a living invitation, one that speaks and calls to men to come and follow Him. God has sent to mankind the most beautiful invitation ever. This is the way that John describes God's invitation to us. "In the beginning was the Word, and the Word was with God, and the Word was God. He was with God in the beginning. Through Him all things were made; without Him nothing was made that has been made. In Him was life, and that life was the light of men.… To all who received Him, to those who believed in his name, He gave the right to become the children of God.… The Word became flesh and made his dwelling among us. We have seen his glory, the glory of the one and only Son, who came from the Father, full of grace and truth" (John 1:1–14). Notice how the Gospel of God begins as a Word. Then that Word becomes flesh and dwells among mankind . Now this Word made flesh opens His mouth and says, "Come, follow me." Here is God's personal invitation manifest in the flesh, crying out to us God's personal invitation of reconciliation. God makes His Son the invitation, His Son revealed to us by the Spirit and through the written Word of God. Think back to that day when you received your personal invitation to come to God, to enter His palace, His courts, and come to His throne of grace and mercy. Coming into the Kingdom of God is by invitation only. If you have received God's invitation, Jesus, know that in receiving this invitation you will receive the love and fellowship that comes with this living invitation. Coming into the Kingdom of God is first by His choice, and then through His formal invitation. Finally, we respond to that invitation by faith, believing the invitation and coming to the wedding.

Jesus Christ is God's invitation to come to His eternal feast, to come into His presence and live with Him, both now and forevermore. Jesus's life, death, and resurrection are the power of God unto salvation. Look at Jesus and believe, and you shall live, you shall enter the Kingdom of Heaven, and you shall become a child of God. The Gospel is God's invitation and enabling for restored fellowship and entry into His presence. Has there ever been a more precious or beautiful invitation to anything? To all who receive the invitation, to all who believe it, God grants the right to be the sons of God. We must remember that God's invitation is His enabling. When He invites someone to come, He enables them to come by paying all the expenses incurred. The cost of this invitation and enabling would be the highest price that was ever paid for anything. God chooses you, invites you, and then pays all the expenses of getting you into His presence and into fellowship with Himself. All our expenses are paid in Jesus Christ. Jesus Christ, God's Son, was and is the price God paid for our coming unto Him. God has paid the highest price that was ever paid for anything, that you might come and eat and drink without price, eat and drink freely of the love He has for you.

Several years ago, while working as an ironworker, my son fell 30 feet and landed on his head. He suffered a traumatic brain injury. That day on the job his partner was a Marine who also had been a paramedic. My son sustained multiple fractures of his face and head, and also a broken arm and broken ribs, which had punctured his lung, causing it to fill with blood. Russ, his partner, got to Bobby in seconds and rolled him over and cleared his airway, keeping him from drowning in his own blood. He worked on Bobby until the ambulance arrived. So effective was he that they had him get in the ambulance and stay with Bobby all the way to the hospital. They told us later that if Russ hadn't been there, Bobby may have drowned in his own blood. Years later, when Bobby got married, he invited Russ to the wedding out of gratitude for what he had done. He not only sent Russ an invitation but paid for the plane ticket and his room. He not only invited him, he paid his way, and this is what God has done for us: He invites us and then makes sure our travel to the destination and the room to stay in are paid in full. God wants you to be with Him. He wants you at the wedding. Your part is to believe the invitation and say yes to it.

When we answer this invitation, it is also an invitation for God to be our personal teacher. "A good tutor may teach more in a day than another in a month" (Isaac Ambrose, *Looking Unto Jesus*). Jesus was the greatest teacher who ever lived. Two thousand years after His departure from this earth, we are still amazed at His sermons and stories. We have studied these for 2,000 years and have found no bottom to them yet. This Teacher says, "I will put my law in their minds and write it on their hearts.… No longer will a man teach his neighbor, or a man his brother, saying, 'Know the Lord,' because they will all know me" (Jer. 31:33–34). How will they know Him? In this dispensation we have a special teacher who will come to our devotions and lead us into all truth. When you come to your secret place, you never have to come alone, and you don't have to depend on your own abilities or mental powers to discover the Lord. God sends to you in this secret place a teacher to lead you into all truth. The work of this teacher is to instruct you in who Jesus is; and in the seeing who He is, you will be changed into His image. We are not saying that there is now no need for teachers in the Church—we do need them—but you will have a private tutor who will come and reveal to you what no human teacher can, and that is Jesus in all His glory by the Spirit. What many don't realize is that God's invitation is an invitation to His individual instruction. "I will instruct you and teach you in the way you should go; I will counsel you with my loving eye on you" (Ps. 32:8).

Jesus is jealous for you, for your time, and wants to be with you. God's invitation comes with all you will need to lead you into all truth. This is the Spirt of wisdom and revelation that Paul prays for in Ephesians chapter one. The purpose of that Spirit of wisdom and revelation is to teach you to know Him better, to know God better. No longer will a man teach his neighbor, saying "Know the Lord," because His Spirit will be doing the teaching Himself, revealing Himself to men, causing them to know Him better. Paul asks again in Ephesians chapter three that God would strengthen them with power in their inner being that they might know the height and depth and width and breadth of the love of God.

If that were not enough, we have the picture of Jesus standing at the door of our lives in the book of Revelation. "Behold, I stand at the door and knock: if any man hear my voice, and open the door, I will come in to him, and will sup with him, and he with me" (Rev. 3:20). The picture here is one of Jesus seeking us. He has come to our house and is knocking on the door, asking permission to come in. Jesus is initiating the contact. The whole of salvation is God seeking and saving that which was lost. If you answer the knock and open the door, Jesus will come in and sup with you. Jesus wants to love you and be loved in return. How badly does Jesus want this? He paid the highest price that was ever paid for anything, to have this time with you.

Jesus is the invitation to come and sup with Him, to have a dinner with the King of kings. Jesus is knocking; Jesus is asking you to let Him come in. Jesus wants to have time with you; Jesus wants to be with you. All you have to do is believe in the One God has sent to open the door. Jesus's goal is that you and He might become one in this fellowship, one as He and the Father are one. Think of it: Jesus invites you to be with Him, to enjoy His company, and to break bread, dining together. To have fellowship, conversation, and a meal with King Jesus: What could be better than this? To have a chance to speak with Him, and not just once. To be able to come to Him with questions, thanks, and rejoicing. To cry out to Him in our despair, or to ask anything of Him, to thank Him, rejoice with Him, to share the deepest thoughts of our hearts, and to confess our deepest sins to Him.

For most people, an invitation to the White House is an honor. For the president of the United States to ask for your company at his table is considered a high honor. You would have to make travel plans to get there. You might have to purchase some new clothes for the occasion, for many of the events there require formal dress. What work obligations would you change or drop in order to go to the White House? Would this invitation be something you might brag about later to others? Would you save the invitation as one of the trophies of your life? Compare the president's invitation with an invitation from the real King of the universe knocking at your door. With the invitation from the president of United States there would be certain costs in travel and in dressing for the occasion, most of which we wouldn't think twice about paying. What does cost to be with the King of kings? None, He has paid all costs, that you might come and buy wine and milk without price (Isa. 55:1). God has spent His most precious jewel that He might purchase some of your time to be with you. All you need to do is answer the door. Having and maintaining your devotions is the way we open the door and let Him come in.

By knocking on our doors, Jesus is letting us know that He wants to be with us. The King of glory, the King of kings, the Lord of lords, the Lord of all realms requests the pleasure of your company for dinner, at the palace of His presence, today and every day hereafter. He desires your company, your fellowship, your conversation, your presence, so much so that He was willing to pay all expenses for you to get there. The cost for this time together was His own blood and His own life. Look at the Cross and see how much the Savior wants you to open the door of devotions. Look and see what He's done so that it might be so. We talk about our devotions as being time we spend with the Lord. You should also think of devotions as the place where the Lord spends His time with you. He desires your company, He desires you, He desires to be alone with you. He wants to be alone with the one He loves.

Our desire for His company will never be anything more than a reflection of His desire to be with us. If you have the desire to seek Jesus, it is only because He has revealed to you just how much He loves you and wants you to be with Him. Paul says in II Corinthians 4 that God made His light shine in our hearts to give us the light of the knowledge of the glory of God in the face of Christ. God gives us the revelation of His glory, of Himself, in the face of Jesus Christ. In seeing something of God's glory, we should know that part of that glory is His love for us. We will see that glory in face of Christ Jesus. The revelation of God's love and glory can be overwhelming. This love is so immense it can smash a human's heart, leading the individual to repentance. Part of the revelation of God's glory is the revelation of how much He loves you. As you look into the face of a person, into their eyes, you can see more clearly their love or hate for you. When God reveals the look of love for you on His Son's face, it may be more than you can bear. While I'm seeking Jesus, He at the same time is actively seeking me. He has written an invitation for us to come, if we will but answer it. "For He came to seek and to save that which was lost" (Luke 19:10).

When my children were small, we would play hide and seek. I would choose my hiding place on the basis of their ability to discover it. My ultimate goal was to let them find me and to rejoice with them in their ability to discover me. "Oh, you have found me, you are so good at finding my hiding places!" I think there is a sense in which God plays hide and seek with us. He hides in such a way that we will find Him and then makes us feel like the finding was all us. How hard is it to find someone knocking on the door?

How humble must the Lord be if He would come and knock on the doors of our lives, asking entry. He is the One who creates and sustains all things by the word of His mouth. He asks permission of us to open the door of our hearts to Him. Doesn't it seem a little humiliating for the King of kings to stand knocking at the door of a peasant, waiting for him to open the door and let Him in? Wouldn't you think it humiliating for the King of glory to send an invitation to someone to join Him, only to have it ignored? Or to have them tell Him, "I lost the invitation, please send a second," only to have that one ignored as well. How humble must the Lord be that He would condescend to come to us and knock at the door of our lives and wait for us to open to Him, the King of glory. How many times has God sent you an invitation to come to supper? What are you waiting for, Church? Why don't we except His invitation, open the door, and come into His presence? Why don't people want to be with the King of kings? Maybe they don't really believe that He exists and that He is the rewarder of those who diligently seek Him. Our devotions are the act of faith by which we open the door of our lives to Jesus, allowing Him to enter and sup with us.

Jesus prayed in John 17 that we would be one with Him as He and the Father are one. Think of what He prayed there, that we would be one: one heart, one mind, one purpose, and one in love. He prayed that we would have a full measure of His joy. He also wants us to know the height and depth and breadth of His love, to know that love and to know Him better. Jesus is telling us that His desire, dare we say His longing, is to come to have intimate fellowship with us. There are many people we know with whom we would never have dinner, for the friendship never gets deep enough to share a meal together. Jesus doesn't want some superficial relationship with us; He wants to be one with us. This is what He prayed for. We celebrate holidays and special occasions over a meal. We do this with those we know and love, those with whom we have a deep relationship. These meals are often times of great joy and laughter, as we celebrate being together. Shouldn't we have the same joy and a sense of celebration when we sit down and feast with our Lord? Jesus invites us to banquet with Him, What hinders you from feasting with the Lord of glory? He waits just outside the door of your heart.

The Laodiceans were familiar with the legend of an importunate salesman. This solicitor was so determined to vend his wares that he turned day to night, and long after people had retired he continued to knock at the doors of the cottagers. The curious thing about the whole circumstance was that the citizens tolerated him and even sought his wares, for certain very powerful reasons. The things he sold were vital to life; furthermore, these things were to be had from no other source in the world; and finally, the salesman was really the king of the nation in disguise, out on a quest of mercy, giving away his precious goods that couldn't be found anywhere else.

When it comes to devotions, we are those who only open the door to the King who longs to pour out His riches upon us. We think that we are bringing devotion or love to Him, but He ends up bringing His love and devotion to us. What do we have that we have not received? Is it true that the King of Heaven would come to our door and knock and ask entrance? What would you miss if you ignored His knocking and refused to open the door to Him? What are you missing? Who is this one who is just outside the door of our heart, knocking?

I want you to notice something about Jesus knocking here. He says, "Behold, I stand at the door and knock: if any man hear my voice, and open the door, I will come in to him, and will sup with him, and he with me." His words have a strange twist here. He says, "I stand at the door and knock, if any man hear my voice…" How do we get from knocking to hearing His voice? Have you ever knocked on someone's door, knowing they were home, and there was no answer? What would you do next if the knocking didn't bring an answer? You would cry out, "Hey, Steve, open the door! It's Dave; I'm here to see you. Let me in, man!" Would you whisper it or shout it? Most of us would shout it, getting louder and louder until someone answered the door. I'm not saying that Jesus is screaming at us, but I do believe He knocks and asks in a way that is clearly heard. We have to reject and ignore the clear knocking and the clear voice of Jesus asking to come in. Open your ears to hear, and open the door of your heart to fellowship with the greatest person you will ever meet, Christ the King.

The word for "knock" in this verse is the same one used by Jesus in Matthew 7, where he says, "Ask and it will be given to you, seek and you shall find, knock and the door shall be opened to you." Jesus saying that if you knock on his door he will answer. Now the picture is of Jesus knocking on our door. Will we answer, and if we answer, what will happen? If He is knocking on your door and you open to Him, what will He do? He will come in and sup with you. This is a promise for our devotions: Open, and He will come in. Open, and He will sup and fellowship with us. Open, and you and He will share life and all eternity together. Open this door, and open yourself to the love of God. On the other side of the door is the person of Christ by His Holy Spirit with all the fruit of His life, His love, His joy, and His peace. Here is the great adventure of life, the great business of life, to know and to grow in love and fellowship with Jesus Christ. Having our devotions daily will open the door of your heart to His life, His will, His glory, presence, and love, and the experience of His being. What does Jesus want? He wants you to open the door. Come to the door by your devotions, listen for the knocking, listen for His voice and with the heart and hand of faith take the door handle, turn it, and open it to see the wonder of the one who stands on the other side awaiting your company. Behold, He carries gifts with Him, gifts for you. What kind of an insult, what kind of sin, would it be to reject God's knocking at your heart's door? What kind of insult would it be just to leave Him standing there with the door shut in His face? He knows you're home.

You may think to yourself, I have never received an invitation from God. "For God so loved the world that He gave his one and only Son, that whoever believes in Him shall not perish but have eternal life" (John 3:16). Here is your invitation. To answer the invitation, you have only to believe in Jesus. Repent and believe the Gospel, and you will be saved. Turn from your sin of not believing that Jesus lived and died for you, that He rose from the grave and ascended into Heaven and lives there now, being your righteousness before the Father. Repent of your doubt that He wants to be with you to fellowship and sup with you today. Turn from your sin of self-righteousness, thinking you don't need Jesus and that you can do anything you want and be anything you want without Him. Believe in the One God has sent as an invitation to oneness with Himself and to abundant life. The invitation is not just for the sinner but for the saint as well. If you have been a Christian for many years but your heart has grown cold, He is knocking. If you have lost your first love, come back to where you found it and find it again by looking unto Jesus. Repent and again believe God's invitation to come to Him and do what you did when you first believed. Now you have been invited. What will you do with the invitation?

Chapter 13

PILGRIMAGE TO GOD

 "Blessed are those whose strength is in you, whose hearts are set on pilgrimage."
(Ps. 84:12)

A GROUP OF four people crawl along a lonely highway making their way to the city of Lhasa, the capital of the Tibetan Buddhist world. They have traveled thousands of miles, and their journey has taken over two months to bring them to the most sacred place in Tibetan Buddhism. All four of the pilgrims are in their 60s. One of the four, a woman, said her elderly parents tried to talk her out of going, but she wouldn't be swayed. She said that while she journeys, she prays for her parents as well as herself. These four pilgrims are not alone, as every year thousands make the same pilgrimage to Lhasa. Some quit, some die on the way, but most arrive at what is to them a holy city.

There are no fancy amenities along the way, no restaurants, hotels, no bathrooms with running water for most of these pilgrims. They carry with them small tents for shelter from the elements and a place to sleep at night. Their food for this journey is barley flour mixed with water to form a paste they eat with their hands. They have little else to sustain them. The hardship, deprivation, and suffering they experience along the way are part of what they are seeking, knowing that the harder it is for them, the more merit they will earn with the Buddha and the more purification for their souls.

What most interests me is the way they travel along the road. There is no vehicle to carry them; all is done on foot, but it is not just walking or hiking. They travel not one step at a time but one prostration at a time. They lie prostrate on the ground with their arms stretched out overhead, then they stand, taking a few small steps to the point their hands had reached, and then they repeat it. This is how they travel, one prostration at a time, moving one body length at a time. They literally inchworm their way for thousands of miles. Some cover their hands with blocks of wood or heavy cloth to avoid blisters and other injuries to them. Heavy cloth is worn on the body and legs, as the road would quickly wear out all clothing. It is said that a journey of a thousand miles begins with one step, but here the journey of thousands of miles begins with one prostration ("Buddhists crawl from China to Tibet temple for pilgrimage," BBC News, August 6, 2013).

The journey of prostrations is done to be seen by the Buddha, to honor him, to earn his blessing and protection in this life and the next. It is said that 100,000 of these prostrations earn the supplicant's purity in Tibetan Buddhism. These people are devotees, and their prayers, prostrations, and pilgrimage are their devotions to Buddha. A devotee's business is to pour devotion on the one to whom he is devoted. Christian, are you devoted to God, and how to you show it? Do you have devotions? How many prostrations have you poured out before your God? Our God is real and not dead, yet people who have a dead god live as if their god were alive, and we with a living God act at times as if He were dead.

In the above example of the Buddhists, there is an integration of their devotion into their daily lives as each act of devotion is the means of travel to Lhasa. Our devotions will be our means of travel through this strange land on our way home. Each prostration each morning of worship will be another step toward Christ and one step closer to our goal of being with Him in glory. Our pilgrimage of devotion will be integrated into all areas of our lives and not just a few moments in the morning before we run to work or start our day. The Buddhists' devotions of prayer and prostrations were how they traveled. They didn't leave their devotions behind in a closet in the morning but walked out into the day using that devotion every step of the way. Each step is a prostration before their god and a step closer to Lhasa. That devotion keeps the goal ever before them and saturates their day with acts of love for the god they seek. How sad to think that for these pilgrims on their way to Lhasa it will be like the prophets of Baal, who battled with Elijah to call down fire. "There was no response, no one answered, no one paid attention." (I Kings 18:26). But for the follower of the living God, the end of devotion poured out on God will be a deep revelation of God and the outpouring of His love into our hearts. With that heart filled with the love for God, we walk through our day and pour the same love on those we work with and those we serve as we do the duties of the day. As with the pilgrims above, each day for the Christian starts out on the same road, heading in the same direction looking to the same goal, God Himself. Each day becomes a step of drawing closer to God and a step closer to our final goal of life with Him in Heaven. Like many whom Christian met on his pilgrimage to God in *The Pilgrim's Progress*, some have left the pilgrimage's path and taken roads that don't lead to God. They have turned from the path of devotions and no longer tread this road to the Celestial City.

Christian, do you demonstrate through your actions that God is your business? Do you spend on your God what the pagan spends on his dead god? We have the promise of discovering our God if we seek Him with all our hearts. What efforts, what energies, what monies are you spending to seek and find your God? Compare the level of your commitment and devotion to your God with that of the Buddhists above. Are you expending any measurable devotion toward your God? Are you on a journey, or pilgrimage, to discover God? Does your life reflect a burning ambition to know the God of the Bible and fellowship with Him? Do you carry that devotion and love for God with you as you move, one prostration after another, through your day?

What would happen if Christians spent a month or two like the Buddhists above in just seeking our God? What would happen if you were willing to suffer any hardship and deprivation, to fast and pray, if only you could see Jesus? Revival might happen, in the individual and then in the Church. What price are you now paying to seek and find your God? What price would you pay to find Him and know Him? Your pilgrimage will be one of seeking God first all the days of your life.

I want you to see your great business as a pilgrimage, a journey into God, into discovering who He is. If God is eternal, then our journey will be eternal into the life of God. One inch into the depths of God is far greater than a million miles into the knowledge of this fallen world. Paul prayed that we might know something of the height and depth and width and breadth of the love of God. He was speaking about the enormousness and eternity of God and His love. Our business is to journey into the love of God, and we are commanded to remain there. Our pilgrimage is to sail into the vastness of the sea of God's love, to know God and know His love.

Our devotions are where we pick our bundles and backpacks for our lifelong pilgrimage into God. Devotions are our first step daily on our pilgrim path and road to God. Once on that road God will place opportunities for service and ministry to others. These opportunities will not turn us aside from the great site of God but will happen as we keep the goal in site and journey into God. Devotions are our safari into the great country of God, where we bring back the trophies of his grace, mercy, and love. Conversion brings with it a new trade, a new business, a new living, "For me to live is Christ" (Phil. 1:21). With our new life in Christ, we become surveyors of God, taking expeditions to measure the height, depth, width, and breadth of the love of God. You will have a new guide One who will lead you into all truth, One who will guide us as trek the boundless limits of God's love and help us navigate the great sea of God as we sail into eternity.

Every day will not be the same as we pilgrims travel to the city of our God. Some days will be easy travel with fair breezes and sunshine, of seeing the glory of God. There will be days of storm when wind and rain pelt and soak us and resist every step we take. There will be days when the sun is eclipsed, and we walk in the dark and wonder if we will ever see the sunshine of God again. There will be days we feel as if we are climbing over a mountain, and each step comes with the pain of burning muscles and the panting for air. Other days we will feel like we are pushing through thick forest with heavy underbrush of thorn and brier, where we are raked and sawn by their branches. There will also be days on the downhill side of the mountain where miles are covered with ease, and the gravity and wind push you along, and you seem to be flying.

Remember, it is a pilgrimage; it will take not a single day but rather all the days of your life to arrive on that golden shore, that Celestial City, when we will journey no more. As the pilgrim cannot carry with him all his worldly possessions, you too must set aside many things and carry only what will help you grow in the grace and knowledge of Christ on this journey. On this pilgrimage only one thing matters, and that is to see the glory of God in the face of Christ Jesus. There will be days when you don't think you can take another step. Don't give up, but take one more step and then another. Don't rest until you have seen the glory you traveled so far to see, the glory of God Himself. From the first day of your spiritual life to your last here on earth, you are just a pilgrim traveling through. Every day you will pick up your backpack of devotions and travel with the help and love of God through one more day. You will see that you are not alone on your pilgrimage but that you share the road with Jesus, just as His disciples did that day on the road to Emmaus. You will see that there are some days when you are weary; on those days

He will pick up your pack and carry it for you. You will see that your devotions and your pilgrimage are one and the same.

Devotions are not just a little Bible reading and prayer. Many different elements will overlap in our devotions. Seeking God, loving God, having a personal relationship with God, worshipping God, hearing and seeing God, serving God, faith, trust, and obedience all find their intersection in devotions. There should be a living quality to our devotions, for they involve two living persons and the interaction and communion between those two persons. Devotions should be alive and vibrant, yet they are often dead and boring. Are you seeking and finding God? Do you know something of the Spirit of wisdom and revelation? Do you know the speaking God, or is all quiet on the devotional front? Godless devotions are epidemic in the Church and the root of many of our problems. "The world is perishing for the lack of the knowledge of God, and the Church is famishing for want of His presence" (A.W. Tozer, *The Pursuit of God*).

The goal of this writing is not that of focusing on your techniques for your devotions. We are not looking at the form and practice of these times but at the goal. The goal is God Himself, not blessings, gifts or peace that He may or may not give.

Devotions can be mistakenly seen as a starting point on the way to something else, as if they were something you graduated from. Along with neglect and self-focus can come the thought that there is something more important to do than just have devotions. You may think devotions are good but winning souls is better, and if I must choose between the two, I'll choose winning souls. I've heard pastors say, "We don't want to get stuck on devotions, we want to move on to ministry, to get plugged in, and work for Christ. You don't want to be so heavenly minded that you're no earthly good." The importance of devotions seems to fade in the light of reaching souls or growing the Church. Like Martha, we can see serving as more important than the one to be served. The time demands of ministry can quickly swallow up all our devotion time and leave none for Christ. The demands of life and ministry can swallow up your whole life if you let them. In *The Pilgrim's Progress* there were many things on the road that were a temptation for Christian to quit his pilgrimage, and so it will be with you. Setting priorities that demand alone time with God are a must for the Christian. Being busy with ministry can never be a justification for ignoring God, for God is your great business.

The devotional life—pilgrimage—is a necessary part of ministry. Without that intimacy with Christ, you are on you own, and you can't build the Kingdom of God on your own. Your ministry can become more important than your love relationship with God. When this happens, there is an imbalance in the life. Christians justify their absence from the presence of God with the Kingdom business they are doing. David Wilkerson, pastor of Times Square Church in New York City and founder of Teen Challenge, said in a sermon that he realized that ministry had at times robbed him of his worship. Worship, devotion, and intimacy overlap and are parts of the same thing. Wilkerson said, "All true ministry comes out of intimacy with Christ." When the minister or Christian leaves his pilgrim path to God, his ministry will suffer.

The devotional life and ministry are like parts of the same clock: Take out one little gear, and the clock comes to a stop, for the power that drives it is interrupted. The devotional life is the act by which the branch drinks of the vine and has life-giving sap that will produce fruit, and if there is no drinking, there will be no true fruit. Men are very good at building ministries without God; they have learned how to continue in ministry when the power of God is no longer thereBuilding a spiritual kingdom and building a man-made kingdom can look similar, while the end is completely different. Without the devotional life, the ministry of man will suffer but with it, ministry should prosper. How much ministry done here on earth will we see burned like wood hay and stubble? Could this be why we are seeing so much failure in the pulpit today? Proud men believing they could do ministry for God without God only to discover they can't even conquer their own flesh. Apart from God we can do nothing.

The object of a person's love has a powerful pull on them, a gravity if you will. When a body in space come nears a planet, the gravity of that planet pulls it in until it is said to be trapped by the gravitational pull. Once it is trapped, it can't get away. What we love has a powerful gravity that will pull us closer and closer until we are united. That object can be God or it can be something else. That object can be something like ministry, good works, things that while good in themselves can pull us out of our orbit around God. Setting our focus on God daily is the best way to keep our goal in site and to keep the proper balance in our spiritual lives and power in our ministries. The devotional life is the pilgrimage we take until by His gravity we crash into God.

A bucket list item for motorcycle riders in America is the Pacific Coast Highway in California. The scenery is spectacular: Big Sur, sea lions, mountains diving right into the ocean. We decided to make this ride with some dear friends of ours who lived in Arizona and started our trip from their house. Picking up our rental, we rode to their house to begin our adventure. Arriving there, I had to do a U-turn in the street to get the bike headed in the right direction. That day happened to be garbage day on my friend's street, and all the garbage cans were out in the street. Where I made my U-turn there were two garbage cans in the street, and I began to look at them so I wouldn't hit them. The more I looked at them, the more I went toward them. I couldn't take my eyes off them, and of course I ran right into them. When I hit the garbage cans, the bike fell over, breaking off the clutch lever and scratching up the paint job. Of course my friend had to be standing in his driveway watching the whole embarrassing debacle. My wife was on the back and went over with me, and she was giving me what-for, while my partner was giving me that "I can't believe you just did that" look. We had to take the bike back to the dealer with half a clutch lever to get the bike fixed, which prompted more looks and more questions about how this happened. Our friends were patient, but it did cost us a delay and $2,000 to get it fixed. The $2,000 was nothing compared to the embarrassment I felt at having done it under the watchful eye of my friend.

After that ride, I was determined never to embarrass myself like that again, so I took another motorcycle safety course. One of the things this course taught you was how to handle your bike in tight turns and at slow speeds, exactly what I needed. My instructor said that when you are turning a motorcycle in tight quarters, your motorcycle will go where you're looking. At first, I had trouble believing what he was saying. When I had my little accident, I was looking right at the garbage cans I was trying to miss, and I plowed right into them. I should have been looking where I wanted to go, not where I didn't want to go. I had to commit myself to his teaching: Look where you want to go, and the bike will follow. When I applied what my instructor taught, I discovered it worked; it was simple but true. I believe this principle also applies to our spiritual lives: Where we look is where we will go. What are you looking at today, Christian? Are you looking at Jesus or at something else?

What we are looking at, we will be drawn toward. Many Christians fill their devotional lives with ministry, the problems they are having or with their needs and shortages. Prayer lists can look like a hospital register, or a wish list, or a list of failures one is trying to avoid. By constantly looking at the things we are trying to avoid, we keep running into them. Looking at a wish list of needs and wants can lead to frustration, for we never seem to get all we want or need. The more we look at these things, the less we will look at Christ. Fix your eyes on Jesus, and watch the gravitational pull begin. Look to Jesus, and the direction of your life will change, and you will find you are moving closer to Christ.

Just a note here for clarity: We have said in many places in this writing that you should have faith in God, believe in God, trust in God, and look unto God. In all these cases it would be clearer to say you should have faith in Jesus Christ. Pilgrim keep your goal the same every day and keep it ever before you. Our looking, trusting, and believing are in the person of Jesus Christ, who is God in the flesh. Our worship or looking is to be focused on Jesus. "Know that a person is not justified by the works of the law, but by faith in Jesus Christ. So we, too, have put our faith in Christ Jesus that we may be justified by faith in Christ and not by the works of the law, because by the works of the law no one will be justified" (Gal. 2:19). Jesus is God in the flesh, having taken on our human nature. Jesus is the One we are to be beholding and worshipping. "Remember this: let our faith, in the more direct and immediate exercise of it, be pitched upon Christ, as God in the flesh" (Isaac Ambrose, *Looking Unto Jesus*). "The Son is the image of the invisible God, the first-born over all creation" (Col. 1:15). Jesus is the image of the invisible God we can understand, the definition of God we are more able to comprehend.

Just like the motorcycle training, I had to take my eyes off everything that wasn't Jesus. I had to take my eyes off my need, my sin and failures, my ministry and focus on where I really wanted to go—into the presence of Christ. Your pilgrimage must make Christ the goal of your devotional life. You will find that traveling on your pilgrimage to Christ is the only safe place for the Christian. Where you look is where you will go. If you are looking to Christ, you will move in that direction. If you are looking at something else, that is where you'll find your life heading. It was as if the body automatically aimed the bike to what I looked at, without my even thinking about it. The instructor said, "You will go where you are looking." The Christian life is like that motorcycle training. What you are looking at will determine the course of your life. If you fix your eyes on Jesus, you will be drawn toward Him. If you fix your eyes on ministry, on the needs in your life, or on pleasure, you will move in those directions. So the question for us is what are we really looking at and in what direction are our lives moving. Remember, if you fix your eyes on Jesus, you will not only move in that direction but you will find power to be transformed into His image.

Pilgrim, what is your goal, and what are you looking at now? Are you looking at the garbage cans of your life—the failures, the sin, the lusts, the hatreds? If you are, you will only plow right back into them. Much of our counseling starts with looking at the very problems we are having, and many find the gravity of these problems and sins too much to escape. Then we find verses that are supposed to help us overcome that sin, memorizing them, thinking there is power in the law to deliver us. "If righteousness could be gained through the law, Christ died for nothing!" (Gal. 2:21). Giving someone the law has no power to free them from that sin. Subjective truth doesn't deliver; objective truth delivers. Giving someone verses about their sin may not help; having someone look at Jesus will transform and deliver the individual.

The goal of much Bible study, or many devotions, is to know "How then shall we live?" Knowing the law is not the enabling, for there is no power in the law to save. "For if a law had been given that could impart life, then righteousness would certainly come by the law" (Gal. 3:21). If life doesn't come by the law, then how does it come? It comes by looking unto Jesus. "The life I now live in the body, I live by faith in the Son of God, who loved me and gave himself for me" (Gal. 2:20). Sounds too easy, doesn't it? If we don't study the Bible to know the rules to live by, then why do we study it? We study the Word of God to know the God of the Word. We study the Word to see Jesus on every page, and in seeing Him there, we will be transformed. Knowing the God of the Word and living by faith in Him, looking unto Him, is what changes us. A person can end up with a knowledge of Scripture that puffs up and is empty of any power, and separates one from Christ. The power of the Word is in the revelation of Jesus, the Gospel. He is the Law of the Spirit of life, a law we can finally obey by faith and a law that transforms us into His likeness.

The most beautiful thing a human being can see is Jesus. Jesus is not just another beautiful thing among many. He is the most beautiful vision a human being can see. The vision that God gave to John in the book of Revelation was first the revelation of Christ and then of His judgments upon the earth. "In his right hand he held seven stars, and coming out of his mouth was a sharp, double-edged sword. His face was like the sun shining in all its brilliance. When I saw him, I fell at his feet as though dead. Then he placed his right hand on me and said: 'Do not be afraid. I am the First and the Last'" (Rev. 1:16–17). Can you imagine what it would be like to feel the hand of the Savior placed on you and hear His words, "Do not be afraid"? When we have this revelation of the Christ of the Gospel we will fall dead at His feet, only to feel the love of His hand on us to bear us up and tell us not to be afraid.

One day we'll see an unobstructed view of God in Heaven, and not only will it be glorious, it will also be completely transformative. "Dear friends, now we are the children of God, and what we will be has not yet been made known. But we know that when Christ appears, we shall be like Him, for we shall see Him as He is" (I John 3:2). There is a principle here that many teachers overlook. Why will we be like Him? Because we will be better at obedience, because we'll know the law perfectly? No, we will be like Him because we will see Him. The vision, beauty, glory of God is so great, so glorious, and powerful that it changes those who see it. It turns the viewer into the vision.

This principle of being changed by beholding God is woven throughout the Bible, yet many in the Church have missed it. Too many of our pulpits have hidden this precious principle, the vision of God, under the debris of ministry, rules, and 12-step programs. Looking at rules and steps, we go from defeat to defeat. With the vision of Christ buried, many Christians suffer from spiritual depression and powerlessness. Spiritual life for many has become the law, church, small groups, ministries, or foreign missions. Because there is no vision of God preached or taught, there is no vision of Jesus and no relationship with the living Christ. This lack of vision of Christ has caused many to think they won't be able to see Jesus until they die and get to Heaven. Our Christianity becomes a wait-and-see faith, not a look-and-live faith. "Without a vision the people perish" (Prov. 29:18). We must return to preaching the Gospel so our people will have a vision of Jesus, God in the flesh, and seeing Him we will fall down as if dead, then to feel His hand upon us telling us to get up and follow Him.

God told Moses that Moses could not see His face or he would die, so God gave him an alternative: He let Moses see what he could of God without dying. As an ironworker, I used to do a lot of welding. Welding produces a very bright light, so bright it can cause injury to the eyes and even blindness. The welder must look at this light if he is to weld anything together. So how can he look at the light and not be injured? Safety equipment must be provided that will dim the light enough to protect the welder's eyes while still allowing him to see well enough to do his job. The welder uses a welding hood that has a very dark glass he looks through. This glass filters out the dangerous rays, allowing him to look at the bright light for hours without damaging his eyes. He may not be able to see the full glory of the welding light, but what he does see is enough to do his work. "For now we see through a glass, darkly, but then face to face. Now I know in part; but then shall I know, even as also I am known" (I Cor. 13:12). We may not see the full glory of our God now, but there is much glory we can see, and what we can see will transform us into Jesus's image and allow us to do our work for God. Like the welder, we do our work as we look at the bright light of His glory. Our pilgrimage is to come daily and look upon the glory of God in the face of Christ Jesus, and as we look at this light, we will build the Kingdom of God.

As the Buddhist pilgrims looked to Lhasa and the Buddha, we look to Christ as our goal. We will see something of Christ's glory now on earth through a glass darkly, but one day we will see His full glory in Heaven face-to-face when we are finished with our pilgrimage on earth. God wants us to look at His Son, to fill our vision with Him, a vision that will transform. Our pilgrimage is our daily journey into the very presence and vision of Christ. He will be the great North Star of our travels, and looking unto Him we will journey safely home.

> *Be Thou my vision, O Lord of my heart.*
> *Naught be all else to me, save that Thou art.*
> *Thou my best thought, by day or by night.*
> *Waking or sleeping, Thy presence my light …*
> *Heart of my own heart, whatever befall,*
> *Still be my vision, O ruler of all.*
> (Ancient Irish, translated by Eleanor Hull)

Our hope and prayer for this book is that you to might ask God to show you His glory, trusting Him to put you in the cleft of the rock and cover you with His hand that is to be removed when we can tolerate the view of the glory of God. Having seen the glory, we would come down from the mountain with radiant faces, telling the story of what we have seen and heard, the story of a meeting with God. Our devotions are the place we come to meet with God and to behold Him. The incidental action of this beholding is our transformation into the image of Christ. In your devotional time you will discover that the seemingly passive activity of beholding Christ will transform you into His image. Your pilgrimage is a journey to God Himself, one that will take you through this life and land you on the shores of Heaven, where you will see the face of God, and then it will not kill you but thrill you for all of eternity.

Chapter 14

REBUILD THE ALTAR

"Then Elijah said to all the people, 'Come here to me.' They came to him, and he repaired the altar of the Lord, which had been torn down." (I Kings 18:30)

IT WAS ON Thursday, November 19, 1863, that Abraham Lincoln, after waiting through a two-hour oration by Edward Everett, stepped forward to dedicate the Soldiers' National Cemetery at Gettysburg. Lincoln said in his two-minute speech, "The world will little note, nor long remember what we say here." Lincoln was almost right, for most of the world forgot that Everett was even there. (By the way, *The New York Times*, with its inimitable sense of what matters, printed Everett's full speech and noted that "Mr. Lincoln also spoke.") Lincoln's words were remembered and memorialized in the life of the nation. One of the lines from that great speech was, "We are met on a great battlefield of that war." Gettysburg was one of the bloodiest battles of the war, where some 50,000 men from both sides "gave the last full measure of devotion." Today we too are "engaged in a great civil war," a contest pitting light against the darkness, truth against lies and deception, freedom against the great slaver Satan and his minions. The secular culture and its thoughts on all aspects of life battle for the minds of our children as the schools and universities come under the enemy's smoke screens of deception. The destruction and redefinition of the nuclear family and home, exaltation of illicit sex, and the hatred and censorship of Christianity are evidence of the spiritual battlefield we stand on today. Many in the Church are oblivious of the war that is going on around them as they struggle with their own selfishness. If you quiet your mind and soul, I believe you will hear the war drum beating out the call to assemble and prepare for the battle. The Captain of the Lord's host is striding into the battlefield to lead His armies from the front. He has stopped the retreating army of the Church and is organizing a counter-attack, but we must look and listen to the Commander who will teach us how to fight.

This captain doesn't need great numbers. Remember Gideon? He needs only those who will yield to His training and tactics. What is needed is the ability to project power onto the battlefield, power that will overcome the enemy and defeat him, power that will be manifest in our own lives to overcome the enemy within and then to project that power onto the battlefield. Let's look at an Old Testament example of how this captain conquered His enemies and took back the culture in days long ago.

"We wrestle not against flesh and blood but against spiritual powers in high places" (Eph. 6:12). The contest today is not one of political, financial, or corporate power. It is not even philosophical. The contest is spiritual power against spiritual power. Our problem is we think we can overcome spiritual powers with human political power, but we can't. "Listen, King Jehoshaphat and all who live in Judah and Jerusalem! This is what the Lord says to you: Do not be afraid or discouraged because of this vast army. For the battle is not yours, but God's" (II Chron. 20:15). What we need today is the power of God to challenge and overcome the power of darkness, to tear down the altars of Baal and with a mighty revelation of God, to cause the people to cry, "The Lord, He is God, the Lord, He is God!" But our own altars are torn down They lie in ruin, and few if any are calling on God.

When the Children of Israel went into the Promised Land, God demanded the total annihilation of the inhabitants and their false gods. Like so many things with God's people, the conquest of the land was almost all, but not quite. Pockets of peoples and their false gods were left to fester in their own rebellion that would grow until one day it would rise up and overthrow Jehovah's rule over the hearts of Israel. Here lay the yeast of idolatry that would eventually work its way through the whole lump of dough. Idolatry, like cancer, will eat up everything around it until there is nothing left of the host. By the time Elijah was on the scene, Israel's idolatry had eaten almost all the host, leaving only 7,000 who had not bowed the knee to Baal. Idolatry, like cancer, must be completely cut out, or it will come back with a vengeance. Have you ever known someone with cancer to tell the doctor not to cut it out even if that surgery would heal them? No, when it comes to something that is going to kill you, you want it all out; all must be removed. God understood that idolatry, like cancer, if not dealt with radically, would grow back and kill the spiritual life of His people. It is the same for us today: The idolaters of the world are pressing their religion upon us, and whether we know it or not we are succumbing to its pressures. I watched in horror recently as a "Christian" school had a transvestite waltzing down the aisle of its chapel to speak to the children. The pressure to conform to the world and to compromise with sin is greater than ever in the Church in America. The yeast of the devil has gotten into the lump of the Church and is leavening it as we speak.

Another problem we face in the Church of Jesus Christ in America is the yeast of the Pharisees, the yeast of self-righteousness that makes us think we can be righteous, or that we can build the Kingdom of God with our human gifts and strengths. Some of this yeast was picked up in our public education that trains us to learn a principle and then act upon that principle without God's help. We suffer from the growing yeast of cultural pressures, and the yeast of pragmatism taking precedence over the power and control the Holy Spirit. We have let this yeast work through the whole lump until we have perverted the worship of God like Israel did with the golden calf. We call it Jehovah worship, but it has all the form and trimmings of idolatry and is powerless to save. We, like Israel, think we are worshipping God, but we have developed a synthetic religion that is all form and no power. We have traded the glory of God for the glory of men and have settled for self-trust in lieu of trust in the Son of God. We are committing idolatry while practicing a religion that may still have sound doctrine. "Son of man, have you seen what the elders of the house of Israel are doing in the darkness, each at the shrine of his own idol?" (Ezek. 8:12). We have traded the worship of God for the worship of our own secret gods and idols hidden away in the darkness of our hearts. We have traded the fire of God from Heaven for strange fire, the power and gifts of men, and don't realize God has written "Ichabod" over many of our houses of worship. Like Elijah's time, the need today is for a man or woman who knows God to step forward and call down the fire of heaven, and in this single act challenge the prophets of Baal in our day.

Our day is much like Elijah's, with pagan rulers like Ahab and Jezebel on the throne and their prophets ruling over and killing the prophets of God. Today God's prophets are losing the battle of culture in the world in which they live. Like God's prophets back then, they are being persecuted and driven out of the public square. They are made to look irrelevant and stupid by the "prophets of science." It is as if God's prophets today are in hiding, driven from mainstream culture. I would say the false prophets of this day are winning.

They have conquered the schools and the minds of many of our children. Thank God there are Christian educators who are still fighting to train young people in the ways of God, yet in the public square I believe we are losing ground if not the battle. The prophets of Baal today are dressed in the garb of academics, politicians, and psychologists, and with camouflaged robes, as preachers who climb into our pulpits to teach their people a false religion by preaching a woke gospel. We are losing our church, and we are losing our country. When God was about to lose His nation, He sent one man to stand against the power of that day. This man was a "man of like passions." He was a man just like us, who knew God and prayed to Him, and God stopped the rain for three and half years. This same God would lead this prophet to challenge the rulers of his day to a test of power and fire.

Jehovah worship was just about dead in Israel: Only 7,000 had not bowed the knee to Baal. Odds were that most of these would not openly worship their God if their prophets and priests were being killed. Those prophets and priests who escaped the sword were in hiding, running for their lives. Jezebel wanted to extinguish the worship of Jehovah and was killing the prophets and tearing down the altars of the Lord. Obadiah, Ahab's servant, was hiding and feeding 100 of the prophets of God in two caves. Jezebel wouldn't be satisfied until she had totally extinguished Jehovah worship. It sounds much like today, as the atheists, ACLU, and others will not be satisfied until every vestige of Christianity is eliminated from society. In a manner similar to Elijah's time, the rulers of our day in academia, government, and the media are seeking to censor, stifle, and extinguish any vestige of Christianity in our country. A president of the United States recently went so far as to say that this was not a Christian nation. The sad thing about his statement, and the reason I think it hurt so many of us Christians, is that he was right. Even though 70 to 75 percent of Americans would claim some affiliation with Christianity, affiliation with the term "Christianity" and being a born-again Christian filled with the demonstration and power of the Holy Spirit are not the same thing. The contest we are involved in is one of power, and if there is no power in the individual Christian's experience to change the individual and overcome the power of sin in his or her life, there will be no power to change the culture. When our culture was changed and transformed, it was because the fire of God had fallen on individuals and our churches, not from trust in our political power to change things around us. Today we may have the cart before the horse. Are we going to politicians seeking power to change America, or are we going to God? The rulers of our day are trying to control thought and speech, extinguishing any that is unlike their own. It was no accident that our churches were closed by the powers that be during Covid. Who's winning?

Jezebel and her prophets were not tolerant of the old religion and had killed the prophets of God, tearing down His altars. As the prophets of Jehovah were being pushed out and killed, the prophets of Baal and Asherah had rushed in to take their place. "Believe what I believe or die" was the message of that ancient day, and it is the same message we are hearing in America today. They are not killing us yet, but they are trying to cancel anyone who opposes their religion. Hatred for anything that isn't PC or woke is the rule of the day. What is the answer to this determined persecution and pressure to extinguish Christianity from the public square? It is the same answer God had back then—a man or woman who will call on God until He answers with fire from heaven.

The odds for Elijah were 850 to 1. The odds might be even greater for us today. If God is on the side of the one, then the odds are in the favor of the one. With God, one is the majority. God is looking for a man or woman to stand in the gap and pray down fire from heaven. His man in Ahab's day was Elijah. James writes in his epistle that Elijah was a man "just like us." God is not calling great men and women of power; God is calling weak men and women through whom He might manifest His great power. If you are a weak person, then you are just the type God is looking for to call down fire from heaven that will destroy the powers that rage against the Church in America today. God is looking for men and women just like you to face the prophets of Baal and call down the fire of God. Will you be one to accept God's call and go up on the mountain to face the agents of evil with nothing but an altar and prayer? Will you be one to see what Elijah saw, the fire of heaven falling and causing the people to see who the real God in Israel was?

In 1949, revival came to the Isle of Lewis in the Hebrides. Two women had a burden for their island church and began to pray that God would rend the heavens and come down. Many who reported on that revival attributed the start of the revival to these two praying women. In a small cottage by the roadside in the village of Barvas lived two elderly women, Peggy and Christine Smith. They were 84 and 82 years old, respectively. Peggy was blind, and her sister was bent almost double with arthritis. They were unable to attend public worship, but their humble cottage became a sanctuary where they met with God. To them came the promise: "I will pour water upon him that is thirsty and floods upon the dry ground" (Isa. 44:3), and they pleaded for this day and night in prayer. By our standards they would be considered poor, insignificant, crippled women. Instead of being worried about what they didn't have or about their infirmities, they were worried about the spiritual condition of their church. These women took it upon themselves to pray until revival came. They spent hours in prayer, sometimes praying through the night from 10 p.m. to 3 or 4 a.m. in their little cottage. They were old and infirm and could not even attend some of the meetings when revival broke out, but they prayed down fire from heaven. Are you old, are you infirm, are you in wheelchair, is your health broken, are you weak and despised by all but Christ, are you a woman, a minority-group member, uneducated, poor, weak by the standards of the world? You are just the one Jesus is looking for to rebuild the altar and call down fire. Many of our pastors and leaders are too busy with ministry to pray, so maybe God can use you to call down fire by going to Christ and not letting go of Him until you see fire from heaven. If you pray, perhaps the elders of your church will be encouraged to come and pray with you as some elders did with Peggy and Christine.

There was nothing special or superhuman about Elijah. He was a normal human being with a great God who acted on his behalf. Elijah asked his God to shut off the rain and in this way laid siege to the land, starving the people until they were ready to listen to God's message. The famine attacked and removed the very things the false gods were supposed to supply. Three years of famine brought forth a final confrontation between God and Baal. It was winner take all, and though they may not have known it at the time, the prophets of Baal were putting their lives on the line as well. God set up this contest to demonstrate His power to the children of Israel. "Summon the people from all over Israel to meet me on Mount Carmel" (I Kings 18:19). God wanted to show the people Baal's power, of lack thereof, as contrasted and compared to His. Elijah asked the people, "How long will you waver between two opinions?… If the Lord is God follow Him, if Baal is God follow him" (I Kings 18:21). The question easily follows: How do we know which god is the real God? That was exactly what God wanted to demonstrate by this contest on Mount Carmel.

I believe God has brought us to a place similar to Elijah's. The power of true religion is waning. The prophets of Baal mock us and push us out of the public square. We are here like Elijah to depend completely on the Lord with no reserve, no safety net, to set up again the altar of Jehovah and call down fire. I believe the Church is at the end of our human strength of what man can do without God and are failing for the lack of power, for the lack of fire. The Salvation Army was born from revival fire from heaven, and fire became one the two words on its shield: "Blood and Fire": God's blood through His Son and God's fire through His Spirit. Our need today is fire from heaven, and it doesn't come through organization and programs. These are but the aftermath of the fire falling. The fire comes when the altar is rebuilt and men and woman call on God as Elijah did. Every major revival was preceded by God pouring out a spirit of supplication upon His people, and people crying out to God for that which He alone could provide. Do you have an altar and are you crying out to God for fire from heaven as the answer for your needs and the needs of your church and nation?

The contest rules in Elijah's situation were very simple: Set a sacrifice on your altar, and pray to your god, and the god who answers by sending fire from heaven is the winner. Elijah even let the prophets of Baal go first. All they had to do was call down fire from heaven. When the spectators saw fire fall on the sacrifice, they'd know who the true God was.

The view from a top of Mt. Carmel would have been spectacular. Elijah would have seen thousands of people like ants climbing to the top of the mount. As he stood on the summit, he would have seen scattered about him altars to the false gods Baal and Asherah and perhaps others. There was the altar to Jehovah in ruin. The summit of Mount Carmel may have looked like many of our minds and souls, with altars to false gods that we look to for position, possessions, and pleasure. What shrines and altars have we set up in our lives that have kept us from using Jehovah's altar to worship him and cry out to him? If we are honest, many of us will find the altar of the Lord lies in ruin in our hearts. We have been offering sacrifice on other altars, and His altar lies in ruin. What idolatries are we practicing? What wicked and detestable things are we doing in secret? What creepy crawling things have we drawn on the walls of our hearts? What evil worship are we practicing in the house of God? Elijah found the altar of the Lord in ruin and waited and watched as the prophets of Baal shouted their abracadabras, but he did nothing until they exhausted themselves with human worship.

What rage must have burned in Elijah's heart as he saw this sacred place violated with the altars and props of idol worship. Perhaps these altars of false worship dotted the top of Mt. Carmel, and the nation that had worshipped at some of these false gods' altars was called to return to the scene of its crime. Here would have been the altars where many of them had bowed and offered sacrifice. God was giving the revelation of grace and mercy as He was reminding them of their crimes against Him, yet He was ready to receive their repentance. Now an offering would be made that the people would not forget for the rest of the lives.

There is a great analogy of Elijah's day with ours today. I believe that if we, like Elijah, look around carefully, we would find that the altar of the Lord lies in ruins in America. It lies in ruins in most of our hearts. Our prayerlessness is epidemic. Walk among the altars on your Mt. Carmel, and see where you have been spending your life and who you are worshipping and praying to for salvation. Look at the altars that you have bowed your knee to and ask yourself the question: "Have I ever seen fire fall on my altar?" Trust God to give you a tour of your religious life, a walk on the top of your Mt. Carmel, to see the places where you may have mixed your worship of God with the idols of the world. The altars and idols of our day are not as clearly formed as they were when Elijah walked the people up the mountain. Today our altars are more of modern thought, philosophy, and groupthink, altars of position, possessions, and pleasure. We are mixing the truth of God's Word with the strange ideas of the world. We are forming our own Golden Calves and bowing before them.

A friend of mine who was doing ministry in Japan was staying at the home of a Japanese pastor. He tells how he got lost going through a maze of rooms in the home, only to come upon a god shelf hidden in one of these inner, unseen rooms of the house. He was shocked and told me how many of the Japanese who come to Christ go home and smash the god shelf. The god shelf is where the pictures and tokens of family members who have died are placed and are venerated. Here was the real altar of his heart, and he was still worshipping a false god.

"How long will you waver between two opinions?" How long will you let other things, gods, interfere with your worship of God? How long will you waver, thinking that you are OK because you're just as good as people around you? How long will you live with an evolving, flexible doctrine or one that changes with your whims? How long will you practice a false religion that has no fire in it? What God did with Elijah, I believe He wants to do with us today. Watch and listen, wavering Church.

God loves contests of power with His enemies. He never loses. Today we are surrounded by the prophets of Baal, who have taken over the universities, media, and halls of Congress, the positions of power and influence. We are being chased out of the public square and running to hide in caves, hoping Obadiah will come and feed us. What do we need? We don't need more organization, more education, more money or political influence; what we need is God. We need God's holy power and consuming fire to fall on us. When this power and fire falls on the Church, it is called revival. What if we would have the courage of Elijah, crying to God and calling down fire in the great contest against the prophets of Baal of our day, a fire that turns the hearts of the people back to God and kills the prophets of Baal and drives their devotees from the public square, a fire that will light a passion for God and His glory in our hearts and become the treasure of our lives, a fire that will call a nation back to God?

The contest that God sets up through His servant Elijah is to have two altars, two sacrifices, and then let the two gods fight it out. The God who answers with fire is the winner. It would appear that the altar of Baal was in good shape and needed no repair. These prophets of Baal had to be arrogant even to accept Elijah's challenge. Was there anything in their past worship that would have led them to think that Baal would answer from heaven with fire? The prophets of Baal got the contest rules from Elijah, and they began. After some time when Baal had not answered with fire, Elijah offered some sarcastic instructions to the dancing prophets to help them in calling down fire. Their intercession went on all day with increasing intensity. Finally, in a frenzy of prayer and worship to Baal, they ended up offering their own blood on the altar as they cut themselves, thinking this would awaken Baal and cause him to send fire. "But there was no response, no one answered, no one paid attention." This must have been some scene: hours of dancing, praying, and prophesying, even cutting themselves—but still nothing, not a spark, not an ember, not even a warm spot on the altar. "No one answered, no one paid attention."

One of the reasons we don't have our prayers answered, and it is one we don't want to talk about in the Church today, is that we are worshipping a false god, one we have made up, one like the Golden Calf Aaron made for the people in the desert at Sinai. The Golden Calf was Jehovah-worship mixed with other religions, making it nothing but idolatry. Many Christians today are mixing true Christianity with the thoughts and ideas of the world, making nothing of their great heritage and powerful religion. Some have thought of God as some strong bull or Golden Calf, the creation of their own imaginations that they worship so it will give them what they want. We practice our Christianity to get what we want from our god, who is seen as some kind of genie. We rub the lamp of this false religion and hope our genie appears and grants three wishes. Because many Christians are worshipping false gods, those of their own creation, "There is no response, no one answers and no one pays attention to their prayers." Dead gods and those created by the imaginations of men don't answer with fire from heaven. If your god is not answering your prayers, maybe you're calling on a dead god like the prophets of Baal, one of your own imagination instead of the God revealed in the Bible.

Elijah bade the people come to him, and he "repaired the altar of the Lord, which was in ruins ... The Israelites have rejected your covenant, broken down your altars, and put your prophets to death." I have watched in my lifetime as the prophets of Baal in our day have torn down the altars of God in America. When man turns against the religion of God, his rejection often turns to hatred and anger until it can't even tolerate the presence of that religion. They not only reject it but often must tear down those things that symbolize that thought or truth. Today we see this with the removal of any symbol of Christianity, from crosses and nativity scenes to the Ten Commandments on public grounds. Today in America we are pulling down statues, and soon we may be burning Bibles and tearing down churches. What is the answer for the loss of our Christian religion and values? The same as it was for Elijah: rebuild the altar of the Lord.

Here we have the altar of the Lord, which was in ruins—by the hand of Israelites, by the hand of those who should have kept it in good repair and used it to call on Jehovah. The yeast of false religions had gotten into the nation of Israel and had worked its way through the lump. Israel was not calling on the true God; they were calling on false gods for help. God called Elijah to rebuild the altar of the Lord, using the prophet to act out a drama that would communicate to the people what He wanted them to do: renew the Covenant, rebuild the altar, and then call on the Lord until you see Him answer from heaven with holy fire that consumes everything. Elijah took 12 stones and rebuilt the altar of the Lord.

Like Elijah, I believe God is calling the Church of Jesus Christ to rebuild the altar of the Lord, the altar of private worship, the altar of family worship, and the altar of corporate prayer and worship in the Church. Once these altars are rebuilt and we begin to call on God instead of men, I believe we will see fire fall from heaven again, and the people will shout, "The Lord, He is God, the Lord, He is God!" The early apostles when confronted with the division of food and waiting on tables turned that work over to deacons so they could give themselves to prayer and the ministry of the Word. The truth is that we are all called to prayer and the Word. Abraham, called out of Ur, went to a land that he didn't know, following the lead of God. In that new land he built altars to God and worshipped. He communicated, fellowshipped, with His God. Abraham was called the friend of God. We are also called to come and build an altar to God, to worship Him and cry out to Him.

Our first call is to fellowship with God, God who has called you into fellowship with His Son, Jesus Christ, our Lord. Prayer and the Word are the avenue of fellowship with Christ. When we rebuild the altar of worship and fellowship with God in our lives, He becomes real to us. It is at the rebuilding of this altar that we come into His presence, know His will, and are empowered to do it. So come and answer the call, like Elijah's, to rebuild God's altar in your life, and cry out to God until you see fire fall. Rebuild the altar to Jehovah in your life and call down fire on yourself and then your church and then your country. See what happens when you rebuild the altar of Jehovah and what happens when you worship there.

The brook where Elijah is staying runs dry, and God moves him to Zarephath to meet a widow who is about to cook her last meal and then die. Elijah prays, and the widow's flour barrel and cruse of oil will not run out until the rains start again. While Elijah is living with the widow, her son dies. Elijah prays and stretches himself out upon the son three times, and the son comes back to life. Elijah comes from spending time with God to this house where miracles are performed. This man is about to face the prophets of Baal and pray down fire from heaven and turn the people's hearts back to God. God chooses a man who will believe Him and do what He asks. Elijah had believed for oil and flour that wouldn't run out, and he believed God to raise the dead, and he goes on to defeat the prophets of Baal with a prayer. Will you believe God and do what He asks and go where He leads? Will you trust God to release power in you and in your church and then in your country with nothing but a prayer? Elijah was a man who knew God, a man who walked and talked with God, a man just like you.

What does God do in evil and dark times? God raises up a man, a man of like passions, a man or a woman just like you. I doubt many of us would say we see ourselves to be an Elijah. Do you think Elijah saw himself as something great before God got ahold of him? God tells us He uses the weak thing to confound the strong, the foolish thing to confound the wise. Elijah was that weak and foolish thing whom God chose to deliver His people. Can you bring your weakness to Jesus and let Him use it? God isn't looking for great and powerful men and women; He's looking for weakness, that His glory might be manifest. Bring the little you have and watch what God can do with it. Come rebuild the altar like Elijah and meet with God. From these secret meetings He will send you out to deliver others. In this secret meeting He may rain down fire to kindle a flame in the Church and in the hearts of those around you. Come to Jesus because He is worthy and see what He makes out of you. Some pots are for common use and some for noble.

Before we go any farther, let me ask you a question: What is the condition of your altar to God? Is it in ruins? Has it been a while since you have prayed there? The observatory we have talked about building is an altar to this living God. The worship we have talked about is offered on this altar; the devotions we have talked about are placed on this altar. The altar of our lives will be the place where we meet with God daily and pour out our sacrifices of love and praise. The secret place we meet with him is an altar where we commune with the living God. If your altar is in ruin, what will you do about it? Will you, like Elijah, rebuild the altar of the Lord in your life? Do you have a dedicated place, a room, a closet, where you go to meet with God and offer to Him your heart and soul and mind as a living sacrifice? Is there that place in your life where you gaze upon Christ in all His glory, where that glory enters your heart and you are filled with the fire of God, the Holy Spirit? Many Christians do not believe that their great need is God and what He can pour out on their altars. Many are ignorant that the life they have been called to is one of fellowship with the living God.

What we need today is the same fire from God that Elijah called down and that turned the people back to God. This is the manifest presence of God by His Spirit in our lives. What is the condition of your altar? What is the condition of your avenue to God? No longer do we offer the sacrifice of animals, for the once-and-for-all sacrifice of the Lord Jesus Christ has been laid upon our altars by which we can individually approach God. We come and cry out to our God that He might once again pour out fire on our altars and then upon the Church in the name of Jesus our great sacrifice.

If your altar lies in ruins, repair it by coming again to the place where you used to meet with God. Come again by the blood of the Lamb of God and pour out your praise and worship of this one. When you have heaped worship on Him, listen and see if God doesn't ask you to call down fire from heaven. Call down revival fire where the glory of God will fill the land. See if He won't baptize your altar with fire and consume all that is offered there. See if you might not be consumed, and all that is left are the flames of the glory of God for men to see and, seeing those flames, be changed as well. Rebuild your altar, and let God change you until you look like Jesus. Here is where revival starts. It begins with one individual and spreads to churches and then spreads to communities. Won't you rebuild the altar of the Lord and cry out to Him for fire from heaven? Give your God no rest until He answers from heaven with holy fire.

Would you pray with me as Elijah did? "Lord, the God of Abraham, Isaac and Israel, let it be known today that you are God in Israel and that I am your servant and have done all these things at your command. Answer me, Lord, answer me, so these people will know that you, Lord, are God, and that you are turning their hearts back again." Then the fire of the Lord fell and burned up the sacrifice, the wood, the stones and the soil, and also licked up the water in the trench. When all the people saw this, they fell prostrate and cried, "The Lord—he is God! The Lord—he is God!" (I Kings 18:36–39). As God provided a ram to take the place of Isaac on Abraham's altar, He has provided a perfect sacrifice as the means of our approach to Him. This sacrifice is the means of our coming, the means by which we cry to God for fire from heaven. Will God not see us and hear us when we cry to Him by the sacrifice of His Son? Will He not give us what we ask in the name of one who was slain for us? Remember, when God saw the blood on the doorposts of the dwellings of the Israelites, the angel of death passed by. When God sees the blood of His son on the doorposts of the hearts and altars of those who cry out to Him night and day, will he not answer with fire from heaven? Rebuild the altar of the Lord, and see if He won't pour out fire in our day. Cry out to Him until fire falls and the people around you fall prostrate and cry "The Lord—he is God, the Lord—He is God." Here are the stones, here is the great God, here is the perfect sacrifice, living yet. What hinders you from becoming an

Elijah in this day? What hinders you from rebuilding the altar of the Lord, and what might you see if you do? "Then the fire of the Lord fell and burned up the sacrifice, the wood, the stones and the soil, and also licked up the water in the trench. When all the people saw this, they fell prostrate and cried, "The Lord—he is God! The Lord—he is God!" (I Kings 18:36–39).

CLOSING

> *"Therefore, since we are surrounded by such a great cloud of witnesses, let us throw off everything that hinders and the sin that so easily entangles. And let us run with perseverance the race marked out for us, fixing our eyes on Jesus, the pioneer and perfecter of faith."*
> *(Hebrews 12:1–2)*

LILIAS TROTTER was born in 1853 in England, the daughter of a wealthy stockbroker. Lilias later went to Algeria as a missionary in 1889 and there poured out the rest of her life. When she was young, she and her mother were greatly influenced by the Higher Life movement, also known as the Keswick Movement. She was active in Christian ministry before becoming a missionary, serving as secretary of Welbeck Street YWCA in London. She did a considerable amount of teaching, and she fearlessly canvassed the streets around Victoria Station for prostitutes, to train them with employable skills or just give them a night in a hostel. She joined the volunteers who counseled inquirers during one of the D.L. Moody campaigns in London. Before going to Africa as a missionary, Trotter suffered from physical and emotional exhaustion and had surgery that left her ill, her heart damaged by the procedure. Her health was so poor that when she applied to the North Africa mission, she failed the health examination. Because she had the means to be self-supporting, the mission said she might work in harmony with it without being an official member. With her ill health, she had to return to England or the continent for regular convalescence during her time in North Africa. Here was one who gave her weakness and ill health to the Savior to use, and use her He did.

Lilias Trotter was a gifted and nearly self-taught artist. During a stay in Venice, her mother sent some of Lilias's drawings to the famous art critic and social philosopher John Ruskin. He saw great potential in her work and praised Trotter's artistic skill. She became an informal student of his and a good friend. Ruskin told Lilias if she would devote herself to her art, "she would be the greatest living painter and do things that would be immortal" (Miriam Huffman Rockness, *A Passion for the Impossible: The life of Lilias Trotter*). She had a love for art and a love for Christ and wrestled with the question of the one to which she should give her life. In May of 1879 she decided she could not be focused on her painting and the Kingdom of God at the same time and chose to focus her life on Christ and His Kingdom. There are several biographies and even some films made about her life that are worth looking at. She and Ruskin remained friends, but he never stopped hoping she might return to art. Like Lilias Trotter, you and I must choose what we will focus our lives on. Will you make your goal and vision Christ, or will some talent or other love or goal fill your vision and rob you of a life with Christ? Lilias wrote a pamphlet titled "Focussed" in which we can see why she made the choice she did and why we should choose similarly. I have included her pamphlet here for you to read because it is the perfect summation of what we have been saying in this book.

"Focussed: A Story and a Song," by Lilias Trotter

> *It was in a little wood in early morning. The sun was climbing behind a steep cliff in the east, and its light was flooding nearer and nearer and then making pools among the trees. Suddenly, from a dark corner of purple brown stems and tawny moss there shone out a great golden star. It was just a dandelion, and half withered—but it was full-face to the sun, and had caught into its heart all the glory it could hold, and was shining so radiantly that the dew that lay on it still made a perfect aureole round its head. And it seemed to talk, standing there—to talk about the possibility of making the very best of these lives of ours.*

For if the Sun of Righteousness has risen upon our hearts, there is an ocean of grace and love and power lying all around us, an ocean to which all earthly light is but a drop, and it is ready to transfigure us, as the sunshine transfigured the dandelion, and on the same condition—that we stand full face to God.

Gathered up, focused lives, intent on one aim—Christ—these are the lives on which God can concentrate blessedness. It is "all for all" by a law as unvarying as any law that governs the material universe. We see the principle shadowed in the trend of science; the telephone and the wireless in the realm of sound, the use of radium and the ultraviolet rays in the realm of light.

All these work by gathering into focus currents and waves that, dispersed, cannot serve us. In every branch of learning and workmanship the tendency of these days is to specialize—to take up one point and follow it to the uttermost.

And Satan knows well the power of concentration; if a soul is likely to get under the sway of the inspiration, "this one thing I do," he will turn all his energies to bring in side-interests that will shatter the gathering intensity.

And they lie all around, these interests. Never has it been so easy to live in half a dozen good harmless worlds at once—art, music, social science, games, motoring, the following of some profession, and so on. And between them we run the risk of drifting about, the "good" hiding the "best" even more effectually than it could be hidden by downright frivolity with its smothered heartache at its own emptiness.

It is easy to find out whether our lives are focused, and if so, where the focus lies. Where do our thoughts settle when consciousness comes back in the morning? Where do they swing back when the pressure is off during the day? Does this test not give the clue? Then dare to have it out with God—and after all, that is the shortest way. Dare to lay bare your whole life and being before Him, and ask Him to show you whether or not all is focused on Christ and His glory. Dare to face the fact that unfocussed, good and useful as it may seem, it will prove to have failed of its purpose.

What does this focusing mean? Study the matter and you will see that it means two things—gathering in all that can be gathered, and letting the rest drop. The working of any lens—microscope, telescope, camera—will show you this. The lens of your own eye, in the room where you are sitting, as clearly as any other. Look at the window bars, and the beyond is only a shadow; look through at the distance, and it is the bars that turn into ghosts. You have to choose which you will fix your gaze upon and let the other go.

Are we ready for a cleavage to be wrought through the whole range of our lives, like the division long ago at the taking of Jericho, the division between things that could be passed through the fire of consecration into "the treasury of the Lord," and the things that, unable to "bide the fire" must be destroyed? All aims, all ambitions, all desires, all pursuits—shall we dare to drop them if they cannot be gathered sharply and clearly into the focus of "this one thing I do"?

Will it not make life narrow, this focusing? In a sense, it will—just as the mountain path grows narrower, for it matters more and more, the higher we go, where we set our feet—but there is always, as it narrows, a wider and wider outlook, and purer, clearer air. Narrow as Christ's life was narrow, this is our aim; narrow as regards self-seeking, broad as the love of God to all around. Is there anything to fear in that?

And in the narrowing and focusing, the channel will be prepared for God's power—like the stream hemmed between the rock-beds, that wells up in a spring—like the burning glass that gathers the rays into an intensity that will kindle fire. It is worthwhile to let God see what He can do with these lives of ours, when "to live is Christ."

How do we bring things to a focus in the world of optics? Not by looking at the things to be dropped, but by looking at the one point that is to be brought out.

Turn full your soul's vision to Jesus, and look and look at Him, and a strange dimness will come over all that is apart from Him, and the Divine "attrait" by which God's saints are made, even in this 20th century, will lay hold of you. For "He is worthy" to have all there is to be had in the heart that He has died to win.

Helen Lemmel was also born in England, about 10 years after Lillias Trotter, and emigrated to the United States in 1875 with her family when she was 12. She was a gifted musician, songwriter, and singer. In 1907 Helen traveled to Germany for four years of intensive vocal training, and while there she met and married her husband. They returned to the United States in 1911, where she continued singing in the gospel music circuits and became the vocal music teacher at Moody Bible Institute in Chicago. Helen had an affliction that left her blind. Not being able to cope with her blindness, her husband abandoned her. She later retired from Moody and moved to Seattle where she continued to write hymns. She wrote some 500 hymns in her lifetime but ended up living on government assistance in sparse surroundings, dying at age 97 in 1961.

Lillias's pamphlet, "Focussed," was read to Helen Lemmel. One line in the story especially affected her: "Turn full your soul's vision to Jesus, and look and look at Him, and a strange dimness will come over all that is apart from Him." The words haunted her and were repeated over and over again in her mind. Inspired by those words in the pamphlet she wrote both the music and lyrics to the hymn "Turn Your Eyes upon Jesus." After hearing Helen Lemmel's hymn, Lillias Trotter revised her original pamphlet, combined it with Helen's song, and gave it the full title "Focused: A Story and A Song."

We will never be anything more than little dandelions that the glory of God shines on, giving us a glow of righteousness and power to transform us into the image of Jesus. The focused life is one focused on Jesus. Many Christians are focused on things other than Christ. They might even be focused on good things, only to discover that those things weren't the best. They might be focused on Christian ministry, or being better Christians by keeping the law, only to find the work impossible. The truth is that we are changed by beholding the glorious Lamb of God, by keeping our focus on Him. If you just start by simply looking unto Jesus, I believe you will find, as Paul did, that "we all, with open face beholding as in a glass the glory of the Lord, are changed into the same image from glory to glory, even as by the Spirit of the Lord" (II Cor. 3:18, KJV).

If, as Helen Lemmel wrote, you turn your eyes upon Jesus, not only will the things of earth grow dim, you will also grow brighter, reflecting the glory of God being shone into your heart in the face of Christ Jesus. You will find that in the focus on Christ you will begin to look like Him by looking at Him. Sing the refrain; you know it, don't you? Sing it and look at Jesus; sing it and look until you look like Jesus. Looking unto Jesus is the great business; won't you make it yours?